Political Ideologies

An Introduction

sixth edition

SIXTH EDITION
POLITICAL IDEOLOGIES
An Introduction

ANDREW HEYWOOD

macmillan education   palgrave

First edition 1992
Second edition 1998
Third edition 2003
Fourth edition 2007
Fifth edition 2012
Sixth edition 2017

Published by PALGRAVE

Palgrave in the UK is an imprint of Macmillan Publishers Limited, registered in England, company number 785998, of 4 Crinan Street, London, N1 9XW.

Palgrave® and Macmillan® are registered trademarks in the United States, the United Kingdom, Europe and other countries.

ISBN 978–1–137–60602–0 hardback
ISBN 978–1–137–60601–3 paperback

This book is printed on paper suitable for recycling and made from fully managed and sustained forest sources. Logging, pulping and manufacturing processes are expected to conform to the environmental regulations of the country of origin.

A catalogue record for this book is available from the British Library.

A catalog record for this book is available from the Library of Congress.

For Jean

Summary of Contents

Contents

Figures

Boxes

PERSPECTIVES ON . . .

TENSIONS WITHIN . . .

POLITICAL IDEOLOGIES IN ACTION . . .

Preface to the sixth edition

The first edition of *Political Ideologies* was written against the back-drop of the Eastern European Revolutions of 1989–91. In retrospect, the 'collapse of communism' was both a manifestation of and a catalyst for a series of profoundly significant, and in many ways intercon-nected, politico-historical developments. Among the most important of these were the growth of the global capitalist economy, the rise of ethnic nationalism and religious fundamentalism, the advent of post-modern or 'information' societies, the emergence of a US-dominated unipolar world order, and the birth of global terrorism. In dizzying ways, history appeared to have speeded up. The certainties and simi-larities of old came to be doubted or, in some cases, were discarded altogether. These processes had major implications for political ideolo-gies. Socialism was commonly declared to be dead; some proclaimed the final triumph of western liberalism while others pointed out that it was in crisis; nationalism was adapted in the light of the challenges posed by globalization and multiculturalism; and so forth.

This sixth edition has been thoroughly revised and updated in the light of key ideological developments in recent years. The most substan-tial change from the previous edition is the inclusion of a new chapter, on Islamism (Chapter 11). This reflects the fact that the intersection between politics and Islam has developed into a major and enduring theme in world affairs. Islamism is indisputably the most politically significant manifestation of 'religious fundamentalism' (the theme that this chapter replaces). Religious fundamentalism, nevertheless, continues to be addressed, although this is more as a *style* of politics that (like populism) may have a variety of ideological manifestations, rather than as an ideology in its own right. For example, the extent to which Islamism can be seen as a form of Islamic fundamentalism is discussed in Chapter 11, while other forms of fundamentalism are understood as expressions of religious nationalism in Chapter 6.

Other changes in this edition include the following. The upsurge in populism in Europe and the USA, especially in the period since the Crash of 2007–09, is examined in terms of its impact on conservatism, socialism and nationalism. The relationship between transgender politics and feminism is explored in Chapter 8, and the coverage of topics such as the left/right divide and Christian democracy has been expanded. The discussion of neoliberalism has been shifted from Chapter 2 to Chapter 3, both to reduce repetition and because neoliberalism is (arguably) more appropriately addressed in the context of conservatism. In Chapter 9, the term 'green ideology' is now used in preference to 'ecologism'. This is because green ideology is a broader (and probably more familiar) term, and that ecologism is perhaps better treated as part of a collection of themes that define the ideology, instead of as its very essence. Finally, new, full-page and illustrated 'Political ideologies in action' features have been added to examine the relationship between aspects of ideological theory and political practice.

I would like to thank all those at Palgrave who contributed to the production of this book, particularly Stephen Wenham, my publisher, Chloe Osborne and Amy Wheeler, as well as the anonymous reviewers who commented at various points in its development. Discussions with friends and colleagues, notably Karen and Doug Woodward, Angela and David Maddison, Barbara and Chris Clarkson, and Christina Dacey, also helped to sharpen the ideas and arguments advanced here. The book is dedicated to my wife, Jean, without whose advice, encouragement and support none of the editions of this book would have seen the light of day.

Acknowledgements

The author and publishers would like to thank the following, who have kindly given permission for the use of pictorial copyright material (names in brackets indicate the subjects of photographs):

Press Association, pp. 38 (The US Constitution), 52 (Immanuel Kant, Thomas Jefferson), 53 (James Madison, John Stuart Mill), 78 (Thomas Hobbes, Edmund Burke, Friedrich von Hayek), 79 (Irving Kristol), 80 (Margaret Thatcher and Ronald Reagan), 125 (Karl Marx, Vladimir Ilich Lenin, Eduard Bernstein), 125 (Herbert Marcuse, Leon Trotsky), 149 (Spain during the Civil War), 152 (William Godwin, Pierre-Joseph Proudhon), 153 (Henry David Thoreau), 184 (Jean-Jacques Rousseau, Johann Gottfried Herder), 185 (Mohandas Gandhi), 186 (Independence for India and Pakistan), 206 (The March on Rome),197 (Benito Mussolini, Adolf Hitler, Alfred Rosenberg), 226 (Legalizing Abortion), 236 (Simone de Beauvoir, Betty Friedan, Kate Millett, Mary Wollstonecraft), 237 (Germaine Greer, Andrea Dworkin), 265(Arne Naess, James Lovelock, Rudolf Bahro), 288 (The Canadian Multiculturalism Act), 292 (Isaiah Berlin, Edward Said), 303 (Iran's Islamic Revolution), 317 (Ayatollah Khomeini, Abul Ala Maududi); Getty Images, pp. 52 (Jeremy Bentham), 85 (Robert Nozick), 104 (China's Cultural Revolution), 124 (Robert Owen), 185 (Charles Maurras, Frantz Fanon), 212 (H.S. Chamberlain), 237 (bell hooks), 317 (Yusuf al-Qaradawi, Abdullah Azzam), 262 (The Rio 'Earth' Summit); Alamy, 52 (John Locke), 152 (Max Stirner), 153 (Mikhail Bakunin, Peter Kropotkin), 184 (Guiseppe Mazzini, Woodrow Wilson), 212 (Joseph Arthur Gobineau, Friedrich Nietzsche, Giovanni Gentile), 265 (Ernst Friedrich Schumacher), 292 (Charles Taylor); Library of Congress, pp. 52 (Adam Smith), 185 (Marcus Garvey); The Library of the London School of Economics and Political Science, pp. 85 (Michael Oakeshott), 125 (Richard Henry Tawney); 329 Nigel Stead (Anthony Giddens); The People's History Museum, p. 125 (Antonio Gramsci);

Ludwig von Mises Institute, p. 152 (Josiah Warren), 153 (Murray Rothbard), 317 (Sayyid Qutb); Janet Biehl, p. 265 (Murray Bookchin); Peg Scorpinski, p. 265 (Carolyn Merchant); Bhikhu Parekh, p. 292; James Tully, p. 293; Jeremy Waldron, p. 293; Jon Trowbridge, p. 237 (Jean Bethke Elshtain); Will Kymlicka, p293; Harvard University, p. 53 (John Rawls); Jane Reed/Harvard University, p. 329 (Daniel Bell); Jon Chase/Harvard Staff Photographer, p. 329 (Samuel P. Huntington); Francis Fukuyama, p. 329.

Every effort has been made to contact all copyright holders, but if any have inadvertently been omitted the publishers will be pleased to make the necessary arrangement at the earliest opportunity.

Political Ideologies and Why They Matter

Preview

All people are political thinkers. Whether they know it or not, people use political ideas and concepts whenever they express their opinion or speak their mind. Everyday language is littered with terms such as 'freedom', 'fairness', 'equality', 'justice' and 'rights'. In the same way, words such as 'conservative', 'liberal', 'socialist', 'communist' and 'fascist' are regularly employed by people either to describe their own views, or those of others. However, even though such terms are familiar, even commonplace, they are seldom used with any precision or a clear grasp of their meaning. What, for instance, is 'equality'? What does it mean to say that all people are equal? Are people born equal; should they be treated by society as if they are equal? Should people have equal rights, equal opportunities, equal political influence, equal wages? Similarly, words such as 'socialist' or 'fascist' are commonly misused. What does it mean to call someone a 'fascist'? What values or beliefs do fascists hold, and why do they hold them? How do socialist views differ from those of, say, liberals, conservatives or anarchists? This book examines the substantive ideas and beliefs of the major political ideologies.

This introductory chapter reflects on the nature of political ideology. It does so by examining the role of ideas in politics, the life and (sometimes convoluted) times of the concept of ideology, the structure of ideological thought, the extent to which ideologies conform to a left/right divide, and the changing landscape of political ideologies. In the process, it discusses issues such as why and when a body of political thought should be classified as an ideology (as well as what this implies) and whether there is evidence that so-called 'new' ideologies are in the process of displacing the 'classical' ideologies of old. The notion of the end of ideology is examined in Chapter 12.

The role of ideas

Not all political thinkers have accepted that ideas and ideologies are of much importance. Politics has sometimes been thought to be little more than a naked struggle for power. If this is true, political ideas are mere propaganda, a form of words or collection of slogans designed to win votes or attract popular support. Ideas and ideologies are therefore simply 'window dressing', used to conceal the deeper realities of political life. The opposite argument has also been put, however. The UK economist John Maynard Keynes (1883–1946), for example, argued that the world is ruled by little other than the ideas of economic theorists and political philosophers. As he put it in the closing pages of his *General Theory*:

> Practical men, who believe themselves to be quite exempt from any intellectual influences, are usually the slaves of some defunct economist. Madmen in authority, who hear voices in the air, are distilling their frenzy from some academic scribbler of a few years back.   (Keynes [1936] 1963)

This position highlights the degree to which beliefs and theories provide the wellspring of human action. The world is ultimately ruled by 'academic scribblers'. Such a view suggests, for instance, that modern capitalism (see p. 97) developed, in important respects, out of the classical economics of Adam Smith (see p. 52) and David Ricardo (1772–1823), that Soviet communism was shaped significantly by the writing of Karl Marx (see p. 124) and V. I. Lenin (see p. 124), and that the history of Nazi Germany can only be understood by reference to the doctrines advanced in Adolf Hitler's *Mein Kampf*.

In reality, both of these accounts of political life are one-sided and inadequate. Political ideas are not merely a passive reflection of vested interests or personal ambition, but have the capacity to inspire and guide political action itself and so to shape material life. At the same time, political ideas do not emerge in a vacuum: they do not drop from the sky like rain. All political ideas are moulded by the social and historical circumstances in which they develop and by the political ambitions they serve. Quite simply, political thought and political practice are inseparably linked. Any balanced and persuasive account of political life must therefore acknowledge the constant interplay between ideas and ideologies on the one hand, and historical and social forces on the other.

Ideas and ideologies influence political life in a number of ways. They:

- structure political understanding and so set goals and inspire activism
- shape the nature of political systems
- act as a form of social cement.

In the first place, ideologies provide a perspective, or 'lens', through which the world is understood and explained. People do not see the world as it is, but only as they expect it to be: in other words, they see it through a veil of ingrained beliefs, opinions and assumptions. Whether consciously or subconsciously, everyone subscribes to a set of political beliefs and values that guide their behaviour and influence their conduct. Political ideas and ideologies thus set goals that inspire political activism. In this respect, politicians are subject to two very different influences. Without doubt, all politicians want power. This forces them to be pragmatic, to adopt those policies and ideas that are electorally popular or win favour with powerful groups, such as business or the military. However, politicians seldom seek power simply for its own sake. They also possess beliefs, values and convictions (if to different degrees) about what to do with power when it is achieved.

Second, political ideologies help to shape the nature of political systems. Systems of government vary considerably throughout the world and are always associated with particular values or principles. Absolute monarchies were based on deeply established religious ideas, notably the divine right of kings. The political systems in most contemporary western countries are founded on a set of liberal-democratic principles. Western states are typically founded on a commitment to limited and constitutional government, as well as the belief that government should be representative, in the sense that it is based on regular and competitive elections. In the same way, traditional communist political systems conformed to the principles of Marxism–Leninism. Even the fact that the world is divided into a collection of nation-states and that government power is usually located at the national level reflects the impact of political ideas, in this case of nationalism and, more specifically, the principle of national self-determination.

Finally, political ideas and ideologies can act as a form of social cement, providing social groups, and indeed whole societies, with a set of unifying beliefs and values. Political ideologies have commonly been associated with particular social classes – for example, liberalism with the middle classes, conservatism with the landed aristocracy, socialism with the working class, and so on. These ideas reflect the life experiences, interests and aspirations of a social class, and therefore help to foster a sense of belonging and solidarity. However, ideas and ideologies can also succeed in binding together divergent groups and classes within a society. For instance, there is a unifying bedrock of liberal-democratic values in most western states, while in Muslim countries Islam has established a common set of moral principles and beliefs. In providing society with a unified political culture, political ideas help to promote order and social stability. Nevertheless, a unifying set of political ideas and values can develop naturally within a society, or it can be enforced from above in an attempt to manufacture obedience and exercise control. The clearest examples of such 'official' ideologies have been found in fascist, communist and religious fundamentalist regimes.

Views of ideology

This book is primarily a study of political ideologies, rather than an analysis of the nature of ideology. Much confusion stems from the fact that, though obviously related, 'ideology' and 'ideologies' are quite different things to study. To examine 'ideology' is to consider a particular *type* of political thought, distinct from, say, political science or political philosophy. The study of political ideology thus involves reflection on questions about the nature, role and significance of this category of thought, and about which sets of political ideas and arguments should be classified as ideologies. For instance, is ideology true or false, liberating or oppressive, or inevitable or merely transitory? Similarly, are nationalism and multiculturalism ideologies in the same sense as liberalism and socialism?

On the other hand, to study 'ideologies' is to be concerned with analysing the *content* of political thought, to be interested in the ideas, doctrines and theories that have been advanced by and within the various ideological traditions. For example, what can liberalism tell us about freedom? Why have socialists traditionally supported equality? How do anarchists defend the idea of a stateless society? Why have fascists regarded struggle and war as healthy? In order to examine such 'content' issues, however, it is necessary to consider the 'type' of political thought we are dealing with. Before discussing the characteristic ideas and doctrines of the so-called ideologies, we need to reflect on why these sets of ideas have been categorized as ideologies. More importantly, what does the categorization tell us? What can we learn about, for instance, liberalism, socialism, feminism and fascism from the fact that they are classified as ideologies?

The first problem confronting any discussion of the nature of ideology is that there is no settled or agreed definition of the term, only a collection of rival definitions. As David McLellan (1995) commented, 'Ideology is the most elusive concept in the whole of the social sciences.' Few political terms have been the subject of such deep and impassioned controversy. This has occurred for two reasons. In the first place, as all concepts of ideology acknowledge a link between theory and practice, the term uncovers highly contentious debates about the role of ideas in politics and the relationship between beliefs and theories on the one hand, and material life or political conduct on the other. Second, the concept of ideology has not been able to stand apart from the ongoing struggle between and among political ideologies. For much of its history, the term 'ideology' has been used as a political weapon, a device with which to condemn or criticize rival sets of ideas or belief systems. Not until the second half of the twentieth century was a neutral and apparently objective concept of ideology widely employed, and even then disagreements persisted over the social role and political significance of ideology. Among the meanings that have been attached to ideology are the following:

- a political belief system
- an action-orientated set of political ideas
- the ideas of the ruling class
- the world-view of a particular social class or social group
- political ideas that embody or articulate class or social interests
- ideas that propagate false consciousness among the exploited or oppressed
- ideas that situate the individual within a social context and generate a sense of collective belonging

- an officially sanctioned set of ideas used to legitimize a political system or regime
- an all-embracing political doctrine that claims a monopoly of truth
- an abstract and highly systematic set of political ideas.

The origins of the term are nevertheless clear. The word ideology was coined during the French Revolution by Antoine Destutt de Tracy (1754–1836), and was first used in public in 1796. For de Tracy, *idéologie* referred to a new 'science of ideas', literally an *idea*-ology. With a rationalist zeal typical of the **Enlightenment**, he believed that it was possible to uncover the origins of ideas objectively, and proclaimed that this new science would come to enjoy the same status as established sciences such as biology and zoology. More boldly, since all forms of enquiry are based on ideas, de Tracy suggested that ideology would eventually come to be recognized as the queen of the sciences. However, despite these high expectations, this original meaning of the term has had little impact on later usage, which has been influenced by both Marxist and non-Marxist thinking.

> **ENLIGHTENMENT**
> An intellectual movement that reached its height in the eighteenth century and challenged traditional beliefs in religion, politics and learning in general in the name of reason and progress.

Marxist views

The career of ideology as a key political term stems from the use made of it in the writings of Karl Marx. Marx's use of the term, and the interest shown in it by later generations of Marxist thinkers, largely explains the prominence ideology enjoys in modern social and political thought. Yet the meaning Marx ascribed to the concept is very different from the one usually accorded it in mainstream political analysis. Marx used the term in the title of his early work *The German Ideology* ([1846] 1970), written with his lifelong collaborator Friedrich Engels (1820–95). This also contains Marx's clearest description of his view of ideology:

> The ideas of the ruling class are in every epoch the ruling ideas, i.e. the class which is the ruling material force of society, is at the same time the ruling intellectual force. The class which has the means of material production at its disposal, has control at the same time over the means of mental production, so that thereby, generally speaking, the ideas of those who lack the means of mental production are subject to it.   (Marx and Engels, [1846] 1970)

> **FALSE CONSCIOUSNESS**
> A Marxist term denoting the delusion and mystification that prevents subordinate classes from recognizing the fact of their own exploitation.

Marx's concept of ideology has a number of crucial features. First, ideology is about *delusion* and mystification: it perpetrates a false or mistaken view of the world, what Engels later referred to as '**false consciousness**'. Marx used ideology as a critical concept, the purpose of which is to unmask a process of systematic mystification. His own ideas he classified as scientific, because they were designed accurately to uncover the workings of history and society. The contrast between ideology and science, between falsehood and truth, was thus vital to Marx's use of the term. Second, ideology is linked to the *class system*. Marx believed that the distortion implicit in ideology stems from the fact that it reflects the interests and perspective on society of the ruling class. The ruling class is unwilling to recognize itself as an oppressor and, equally, is anxious to reconcile the oppressed to their oppression. The class system is thus presented upside down, a notion Marx conveyed through the image of the camera obscura, the inverted picture that is produced by a camera lens or the human eye. Liberalism, which portrays rights that can only be exercised by the propertied and privileged as universal entitlements, is therefore the classic example of ideology.

Third, ideology is a manifestation of *power*. In concealing the contradictions on which capitalism, in common with all class societies, is based, ideology serves to hide from the exploited proletariat the fact of its own exploitation, and thereby upholds a system of unequal class power. Ideology literally constitutes the 'ruling' ideas of the age. Finally, Marx treated ideology as a *temporary* phenomenon. Ideology will only continue so long as the class system that generates it survives. The proletariat – in Marx's view, the 'grave digger' of capitalism – is destined not to establish another form of class society, but rather to abolish class inequality altogether by bringing about the collective ownership of wealth. The interests of the proletariat thus coincide with those of society as a whole. The proletariat, in short, does not need ideology because it is the only class that needs no illusions.

Later generations of Marxists, if anything, showed a greater interest in ideology than did Marx himself. This largely stems from the fact that Marx's confident prediction of capitalism's doom proved to be highly optimistic, encouraging later Marxists to focus on ideology as one of the factors explaining the unexpected resilience of the capitalist mode of production. However, important shifts in the meaning of the term also took place. In particular, all classes came to be seen to possess ideologies. In *What Is to Be Done?* ([1902] 1988), Lenin thus described the ideas of the proletariat as 'socialist ideology' or 'Marxist ideology', phrases that would have been absurd for Marx. For Lenin and most later Marxists, ideology referred to the distinctive ideas of a particular social class, ideas that advance its interests regardless of its class position. However, as all classes, the proletariat as well as the bourgeoisie, have an ideology, the term was robbed of its negative or pejorative connotations. Ideology no longer implied necessary falsehood and mystification, and no longer stood in contrast to science; indeed, 'scientific socialism' (Marxism) was recognized as a form of proletarian ideology.

The Marxist theory of ideology was perhaps developed furthest by Antonio Gramsci (see p. 125). Gramsci ([1935] 1971) argued that the capitalist class system is upheld not simply by unequal economic and political power, but by what he termed the '**hegemony**'

> **HEGEMONY**
> The ascendency or domination of one element of a system over others; for Marxists, hegemony implies ideological domination.

of bourgeois ideas and theories. Hegemony means leadership or domination and, in the sense of ideological hegemony, it refers to the capacity of bourgeois ideas to displace rival views and become, in effect, the common sense of the age. Gramsci highlighted the degree to which ideology is embedded at every level in society: in its art and literature; in its education system and mass media; in everyday language; and in popular culture. This bourgeois hegemony, Gramsci insisted, could only be challenged at the political and intellectual level, which means through the establishment of a rival 'proletarian hegemony', based on socialist principles, values and theories.

The capacity of capitalism to achieve stability by manufacturing legitimacy was also a particular concern of the Frankfurt School, a group of mainly German neo-Marxists who fled the Nazis and later settled in the USA. Its most widely known member, Herbert Marcuse (see p. 125), argued in *One-Dimensional Man* (1964) that advanced industrial society has developed a 'totalitarian' character through the capacity of its ideology to manipulate thought and deny expression to oppositional views. By manufacturing false needs and turning humans into voracious consumers, modern societies are able to paralyse criticism through the spread of widespread and stultifying affluence. According to Marcuse, even the tolerance that appears to characterize liberal capitalism serves a repressive purpose, in that it creates the impression of free debate and argument, thereby concealing the extent to which indoctrination and ideological control take place.

Non-Marxist views

One of the earliest attempts to construct a non-Marxist concept of ideology was undertaken by the German sociologist Karl Mannheim (1893–1947). Like Marx, he acknowledged that people's ideas are shaped by their social circumstances, but, in contrast to Marx, he strove to rid ideology of its negative implications. In *Ideology and Utopia* ([1929] 1960), Mannheim portrayed ideologies as thought systems that serve to defend a particular social order, and that broadly express the interests of its dominant or ruling group. Utopias, on the other hand, are idealized representations of the future that imply the need for radical social change, invariably serving the interests of oppressed or subordinate groups. He further distinguished between 'particular' and 'total' conceptions of ideology. 'Particular' ideologies are the ideas and beliefs of specific individuals, groups or parties, while 'total' ideologies encompass the entire *Weltanschauung*, or 'world-view', of a social class, society or even historical period. In this sense, Marxism, liberal capitalism and Islamism can each be regarded as 'total' ideologies. Mannheim nevertheless held that all ideological systems, including utopias, are distorted, because each offers a partial, and necessarily self-interested, view of social reality. However, he argued that the attempt to uncover objective truth need not be abandoned altogether. According to Mannheim, objectivity is strictly the preserve of the 'socially unattached

PERSPECTIVES ON... IDEOLOGY

LIBERALS, particularly during the Cold War period, have viewed ideology as an officially sanctioned belief system that claims a monopoly of truth, often through a spurious claim to be scientific. Ideology is therefore inherently repressive, even totalitarian; its prime examples are communism and fascism.

CONSERVATIVES have traditionally regarded ideology as a manifestation of the arrogance of rationalism. Ideologies are elaborate systems of thought that are dangerous or unreliable because, being abstracted from reality, they establish principles and goals that lead to repression, or are simply unachievable. In this light, socialism and liberalism are clearly ideological.

SOCIALISTS, following Marx, have seen ideology as a body of ideas that conceal the contradictions of class society, thereby promoting false consciousness and political passivity among subordinate classes. Liberalism is the classic ruling-class ideology. Later Marxists adopted a neutral concept of ideology, regarding it as the distinctive ideas of any social class, including the working class.

FASCISTS are often dismissive of ideology as an over-systematic, dry and intellectualized form of political understanding based on mere reason rather than passion and the will. The Nazis preferred to portray their own ideas as a Weltanschauung or 'world-view', and not as a systematic philosophy.

GREENS have tended to regard all conventional political doctrines as part of a super-ideology of industrialism. Ideology is thus tainted by its association with arrogant humanism and growth-orientated economics – liberalism and socialism being its most obvious examples.

ISLAMISTS have treated key religious texts as ideology, on the grounds that, by expressing the revealed word of God, they provide a programme for comprehensive social reconstruction. Secular ideologies, by contrast, are rejected because they are not founded on religious principles and so lack moral substance.

intelligentsia', a class of intellectuals who alone can engage in disciplined and dispassionate enquiry because they have no economic interests of their own.

The subsequent career of the concept was marked deeply by the emergence of totalitarian dictatorships in the inter-war period, and by the heightened ideological tensions of the Cold War of the 1950s and 1960s. Liberal theorists in particular portrayed the regimes that developed in Fascist Italy, Nazi Germany and Stalinist Russia as historically new and uniquely oppressive systems of rule, and highlighted the role played by 'official' ideologies in suppressing debate and criticism, and promoting regimented obedience. Writers as different as Karl Popper (1945), Hannah Arendt (1951), J. L. Talmon (1952) and Bernard Crick (1962) and the 'end

Key concept

Pragmatism

Pragmatism, broadly defined, refers to behaviour that is shaped in accordance with practical circumstances and goals, rather than principles or ideological objectives. As a philosophical tradition, associated with 'classical pragmatists' such as William James (1842–1910) and John Dewey (1859–1952), pragmatism is a method for settling metaphysical disputes that seeks to clarify the meaning of concepts and hypotheses by identifying their practical consequences. The benefits of pragmatism in politics are that it allows policies and political assertions to be judged 'on their merits' (on the basis of 'what works'), and that it prevents ideology from becoming divorced from reality and turning into mere wishful thinking. Critics, however, equate pragmatism with a lack of principle or a tendency to follow public opinion rather than lead it.

of ideology' theorists examined in Chapter 12, came to use the term 'ideology' in a highly restrictive manner, seeing fascism and communism as its prime examples. According to this usage, ideologies are 'closed' systems of thought, which, by claiming a monopoly of truth, refuse to tolerate opposing ideas and rival beliefs. Ideologies are thus 'secular religions'; they possess a 'totalizing' character and serve as instruments of social control, ensuring compliance and subordination. However, not all political creeds are ideologies by this standard. For instance, liberalism, based as it is on a fundamental commitment to freedom, tolerance and diversity, is the clearest example of an 'open' system of thought (Popper, 1945).

A distinctively conservative concept of ideology can also be identified. This is based on a long-standing conservative distrust of abstract principles and philosophies, born out of a sceptical attitude towards rationalism (see p. 31) and progress. The world is viewed as infinitely complex and largely beyond the capacity of the human mind to fathom. The foremost modern exponent of this view was Michael Oakeshott (see p. 85). 'In political activity', Oakeshott argued in *Rationalism in Politics* (1962), 'men sail a boundless and bottomless sea'. From this perspective, ideologies are seen as abstract systems of thought, sets of ideas that are destined to simplify and distort social reality because they claim to explain what is, frankly, incomprehensible. Ideology is thus equated with dogmatism: fixed or doctrinaire beliefs that are divorced from the complexities of the real world. Conservatives have therefore rejected the 'ideological' style of politics, based on attempts to reshape the world in accordance with a set of abstract principles or pre-established theories. Until infected by the highly ideological politics of the New Right, conservatives had preferred to adopt what Oakeshott called a 'traditionalist stance', which spurns ideology in favour of pragmatism (see p. 9), and looks to experience and history as the surest guides to human conduct.

Since the 1960s, however, the term 'ideology' has gained a wider currency through being refashioned according to the needs of conventional social and political analysis. This has established ideology as a neutral and objective concept, the political baggage once attached to it having been removed. Martin Seliger (1976), for example, defined an ideology as 'a set of ideas by which men posit, explain and justify the ends and means of organized social action, irrespective of whether such action aims to preserve, amend, uproot or rebuild a given social order'. An ideology is therefore an action-orientated system of thought. So defined, ideologies are neither good nor bad, true nor false, open nor closed, liberating nor oppressive – they can be all these things.

The clear merit of this social-scientific concept is that it is inclusive, in the sense that it can be applied to all 'isms', to liberalism as well as Marxism, to conservatism as well as fascism, and so on. The drawback of any negative concept of ideology is that it is highly restrictive. Marx saw liberal and conservative ideas as ideological but regarded his own as scientific; liberals classify communism and fascism as ideologies but refuse to accept that liberalism is also one; traditional conservatives condemn liberalism, Marxism and fascism as ideological but portray conservatism as merely a 'disposition'. However, any neutral concept of ideology also has its dangers. In particular, in offloading its political baggage the term may be rendered so bland and generalized that it loses its critical edge completely. If ideology is interchangeable with terms such as 'belief system', 'world-view', 'doctrine' or 'political philosophy', what is the point of continuing to pretend that it has a separate and distinctive meaning?

Contours of ideology

Any short or single-sentence definition of ideology is likely to provoke more questions than it answers. Nevertheless, it provides a useful and necessary starting point. In this book, ideology is understood as the following:

> An ideology is a more or less coherent set of ideas that provides the basis for organized political action, whether this is intended to preserve, modify or overthrow the existing system of power. All ideologies therefore have the following features. They:
>
> (a) offer an account of the existing order, usually in the form of a 'world-view'
> (b) advance a model of a desired future, a vision of the 'good society'
> (c) explain how political change can and should be brought about – how to get from (a) to (b). (See Figure 1.1.)

This definition is neither original nor novel, and is entirely in line with the social-scientific usage of the term. It nevertheless draws attention to some of the important and distinctive features of the phenomenon of ideology. In particular, it emphasizes that the complexity of ideology derives from the fact that it straddles the conventional boundaries between descriptive and **normative** thought, and between political theory and

NORMATIVE
The prescription of values and standards of conduct; what 'should be' rather than what 'is'.

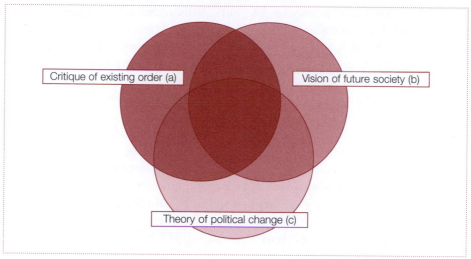

Figure 1.1   Features of ideology

political practice. Ideology, in short, brings about two kinds of synthesis: between understanding and commitment, and between thought and action.

Fusing understanding and commitment

In relation to the first synthesis, ideology blurs the distinction between what 'is' and what 'should be'. Ideologies are descriptive in that, in effect, they provide individuals and groups with an intellectual map of how their society works and, more broadly, with a general view of the world. This, for instance, helps to explain the important integrative capacity of ideology, its ability to 'situate' people within a particular social environment. However, such descriptive understanding is deeply embedded within a set of normative or prescriptive beliefs, both about the adequacy of present social arrangements and about the nature of any alternative or future society. Ideology therefore has a powerful emotional or affective character: it is a means of expressing hopes and fears, sympathies and hatreds, as well as of articulating beliefs and understanding.

As (a) and (b) listed above are linked, 'facts' in ideologies inevitably tend to merge into and become confused with 'values'. One of the implications of this is that no clear distinction can be made between ideology and science. In this light, it is helpful to treat ideologies as **paradigms**, in the sense employed by Thomas Kuhn in *The Structure of Scientific Revolutions* (1962). Kuhn defined a paradigm as 'the entire constellation of beliefs, values, techniques and so on shared by members of a given community'. In effect, it constitutes a framework within which the search for political

> **PARADIGM**
> A set of related principles, doctrines and theories that help to structure the process of intellectual enquiry.

knowledge takes place, a language of political discourse. For instance, much of academic political science and, still more clearly, mainstream economics, draws on individualist and rationalist assumptions that have an unmistakable liberal heritage. The notion of ideology as an intellectual framework, or political language, is also important because it highlights the depth at which ideology structures human understanding. The tendency to deny that one's own beliefs are ideological (often while condemning other people for committing precisely the same sin) can be explained by the fact that, in providing the very concepts through which the world becomes intelligible, our own ideology is effectively invisible. We fail, or refuse, to recognize that we look at the world through a veil of theories, presuppositions and assumptions that shape what we see and thereby impose meaning on the world. As Gramsci pointed out, ideology comes to assume the status of 'common sense'.

Fusing thought and action

The second synthesis, the fusion of thought and action, reflected in the linkage between (b) and (c) in the list above, is no less significant. Seliger (1976) drew attention to this when referring to what he called the 'fundamental' and 'operative' levels of ideology. At a fundamental level, ideologies resemble political philosophies in that they deal with abstract ideas and theories, and their proponents may at times seem to be engaged in dispassionate enquiry. Although the term 'ideologue' is often reserved for crude or self-conscious supporters of particular ideologies, respected political philosophers such as John Locke (see p. 52), John Stuart Mill (see p. 53) and Friedrich Hayek (see p. 84) each worked within and contributed to ideological traditions. At an operative level, however, ideologies take the form of broad political movements, engaged in popular mobilization and the struggle for power. Ideology in this guise may be expressed in 'sloganizing', political rhetoric, party manifestos and government policies. While ideologies must, strictly speaking, be both idea-orientated and action-orientated, certain ideologies are undoubtedly stronger on one level than the other. For instance, fascism has always emphasized operative goals and, if you like, the politics of the deed. Anarchism, on the other hand, especially since the mid-twentieth century, has largely survived at a fundamental or philosophical level.

Nevertheless, ideologies invariably lack the clear shape and internal consistency of political philosophies: they are only *more* or *less* coherent. This apparent shapelessness stems in part from the fact that ideologies are not hermetically sealed systems of thought; rather, they are, typically, fluid sets of ideas that overlap with other ideologies and shade into one another. This not only fosters ideological development but also leads to the emergence of hybrid ideological forms, such as liberal conservatism, socialist feminism and conservative nationalism. Moreover, each ideology contains a range of divergent, even rival, traditions and viewpoints. Not uncommonly, disputes between supporters of the same ideology are more passionate and bitter than arguments between supporters of rival ideologies, because what is at stake is the true nature of the ideology in question – what is 'true' socialism, 'true' liberalism or 'true' anarchism?

Such conflicts, both between and within ideological traditions, are made more confusing by the fact that they are often played out with the use of the same political vocabulary, each side investing terms such as 'freedom', 'democracy', 'justice' and 'equality' with their own meanings. This highlights the problem of what W. B. Gallie (1955–6) termed 'essentially contested concepts'. These are concepts about which there is such deep controversy that no settled or agreed definition can ever be developed. In this sense, the concept of ideology is certainly 'essentially contested', as indeed are the other terms examined in the 'Perspectives on …' boxes found in this book.

Clearly, however, there must be a limit to the incoherence or shapelessness of ideologies. There must be a point at which, by abandoning a particularly cherished principle or embracing a previously derided theory, an ideology loses its identity or, perhaps, is absorbed into a rival ideology. Could liberalism remain liberalism if it abandoned its commitment to liberty? Would socialism any longer be socialism if it developed an appetite for violence and war? One way of dealing with this problem, following Michael Freeden (1996), is to highlight the morphology, the form and structure, of an ideology in terms of its key concepts, in the same way that the arrangement of furniture in a room helps us to distinguish between a kitchen, a bedroom, a lounge, and so on. Each ideology is therefore characterized by a cluster of core, adjacent and peripheral concepts, not all of which need be present for a theory or a doctrine to be recognized as belonging to that ideology. A kitchen, for instance, does not cease to be a kitchen simply because the sink or the cooker is removed. Similarly, a kitchen remains a kitchen over time despite the arrival of new inventions such as dishwashers and microwave ovens.

However, ideologies may be either 'thick' or 'thin', in terms of the configuration of their conceptual furniture. Whereas liberalism, conservatism and socialism are based on a broad and distinctive set of values, doctrines and beliefs, others, such as anarchism and feminism, are more thin-centred, often having a 'cross-cutting' character, in that they incorporate elements from 'thicker' ideological traditions (see Figure 1.2). This also explains why there is (perhaps unresolvable) debate and

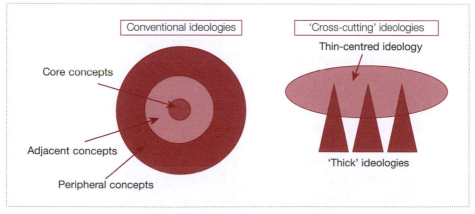

Figure 1.2   Contrasting ideological structures

confusion about whether nationalism and multiculturalism in particular are ideologies in their own right or merely embellishments to other, 'host', ideologies. But what does this tell us about the relationship between ideology, truth and power?

Ideology, truth and power

For Marx, as we have seen, ideology was the implacable enemy of truth. Falsehood is implicit in ideology because, being the creation of the ruling class, its purpose is to disguise exploitation and oppression. Nevertheless, as Mannheim recognized, to follow Marx in believing that the proletariat needs no illusion or ideology is to accept a highly romanticized view of the working masses as the emancipators of humankind. However, Mannheim's own solution to this problem, a faith in free-floating intellectuals, does not get us much further. All people's views are shaped, consciously or subconsciously, by broader social and cultural factors, and while education may enable them to defend these views more fluently and persuasively, there is little evidence that it makes those views any less subjective or any more dispassionate.

This implies that there exists no objective standard of truth against which ideologies can be judged. Indeed, to suggest that ideologies can be deemed to be either true or false is to miss the vital point that they embody values, dreams and aspirations that are, by their very nature, not susceptible to scientific analysis. No one can 'prove' that one theory of justice is preferable to any other, any more than rival conceptions of human nature can be tested by surgical intervention to demonstrate once and for all that human beings possess rights, are entitled to freedom, or are naturally selfish or naturally sociable. Ideologies are embraced less because they stand up to scrutiny and logical analysis, and more because they help individuals, groups and societies to make sense of the world in which they live. As Andrew Vincent (2009) put it, 'We examine ideology as fellow travellers, not as neutral observers'.

Nevertheless, ideologies undoubtedly embody a claim to uncover truth; in this sense, they can be seen, in Michel Foucault's (1991) words, as 'regimes of truth'. By providing us with a language of political discourse, a set of assumptions and presuppositions about how society does and should work, ideology structures both what we think and how we act. As a 'regime of truth', ideology is always linked to power. In a world of competing truths, values and theories, ideologies seek to prioritize certain values over others, and to invest legitimacy in particular theories or sets of meanings. Furthermore, as ideologies provide intellectual maps of the social world, they help to establish the relationship between individuals and groups on the one hand, and the larger structure of power on the other. Ideologies therefore play a crucial role in either upholding the prevailing power structure (by portraying it as fair, natural, rightful or whatever) or in weakening or challenging it, by highlighting its iniquities or injustices and by drawing attention to the attractions of alternative power structures.

Left and right

The origins of the terms 'left' and 'right' in politics date back to the French Revolution and the seating arrangements of radicals and aristocrats at the first meeting of the Estates General in 1789. The left/right divide therefore originally reflected the stark choice between revolution and reaction. The terms have subsequently been used to highlight a divide that supposedly runs throughout the world of political thought and action, helping both to provide insight into the nature of particular ideologies and to uncover relationships between political ideologies more generally. Left and right are usually understood as the poles of a political spectrum, enabling people to talk about the 'centre-left', the 'far right' and so on. This is in line with a linear political spectrum that travels from left wing to right wing, as shown in Figure 1.3. However, the terms left and right have been used to draw attention to a variety of distinctions.

Stemming from their original meanings, left and right have been used to sum up contrasting attitudes to political change in general, left-wing thinking welcoming change, usually based on a belief in **progress**, while right-wing thinking resists change and seeks to defend the **status quo**. Inspired by works such as Adorno et al.'s *The Authoritarian Personality* (1950), attempts have been made to explain ideological differences, and especially rival attitudes to change, in terms of people's psychological needs, motives and desires (Jost et al., 2003). In this light, conservative ideology, to take one example, is shaped by a deep psychological aversion to uncertainty and instability (an idea examined in Chapter 3). An alternative construction of the left/right divide focuses on different attitudes to economic organization and the role of the state. Left-wing views thus support intervention and collectivism (see p. 99), while right-wing views favour the market and individualism (see p. 28). Bobbio (1996), by contrast, argued that the fundamental basis for the distinction between left and right lies in differing attitudes to equality, left-wingers advocating greater equality while right-wingers treat equality as either impossible or undesirable. This may also help to explain the continuing relevance of the left/right divide, as the 'great problem of inequality' remains unresolved at both national and global levels.

PROGRESS
Moving forward; the belief that history is characterized by human advancement underpinned by the accumulation of knowledge and wisdom.

STATUS QUO
The existing state of affairs.

Figure 1.3   Linear spectrum

As a means of providing insight into the character of political ideologies and how they relate to one another, the traditional linear political spectrum nevertheless has a range of drawbacks. These include the following:

- As all ideologies contain rival, or even contradictory, elements, locating them clearly on a linear political spectrum against a single criterion can be notoriously difficult. Anarchism, for instance, can be seen as either ultra-left-wing or ultra-right-wing, since it encompasses both anarcho-communist and anarcho-capitalist tendencies. Similarly, although fascism is usually portrayed as a 'far right' ideology, it contains elements that have a 'leftist' character, not least an anti-capitalist strain that articulates hostility towards big business.
- The ideologies that are traditionally placed at the extreme wings of the linear spectrum may have more in common with one another than they do with their 'centrist' neighbours. During the Cold War period in particular, it was widely claimed that communism and fascism resembled one another by virtue of a shared tendency towards totalitarianism (see p. 207). Such a view led to the idea that the political spectrum should be horseshoe-shaped, not linear (see Figure 1.4).
- As political ideologies manifest themselves differently in different geographical contexts, it may be impossible to assign them an agreed left/right identity. Thus, while in the USA liberalism is viewed as more left-wing than conservatism (the former being linked to 'big' government and the latter to 'minimal' government), the opposite is often the case in continental Europe, where it is common for liberalism to be associated with free-market thinking, and conservatism to be associated with social intervention, especially when it is influenced by Christian democracy.
- As political ideologies are fluid entities, capable, some would argue, of almost constant re-invention, our notions of left and right must be regularly updated. This fluidity can be seen in the case of reformist socialist parties in many parts of the world, which, since the 1980s, have tended to distance themselves from a belief in nationalization and welfare and, instead, embrace market economics. The implication of this for the left/right divide

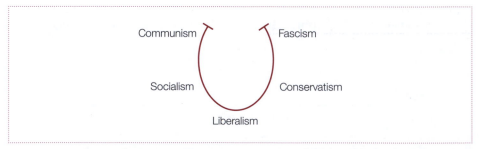

Figure 1.4 **Horseshoe spectrum**

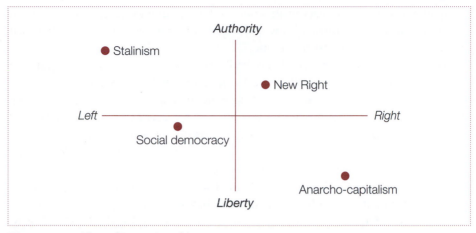

Figure 1.5   **Two-dimensional spectrum**

is either that reformist socialism has shifted to the right, moving from the centre-left to the centre-right, or that the spectrum itself has shifted to the right, redefining reformist socialism, and therefore leftism, in the process.

- A final drawback is that as ideological debate has developed and broadened over the years, the linear spectrum has seemed increasingly simplistic and generalized, the left/right divide only capturing one dimension of a more complex series of political interactions. This has given rise to the idea of the two-dimensional spectrum, with, as pioneered by Eysenck (1964), a liberty/ authority vertical axis being added to the established left/right horizontal axis (see Figure 1.5). Others, however, have gone further and argued that the left/right divide has effectively been rendered redundant as a result of the advent of so-called 'new' ideological traditions. This notion is discussed in Chapter 12 (see pp. 327–8).

New ideologies for old?

Ideology may have been an inseparable feature of politics since the late eighteenth century (it is often traced back to the 1789 French Revolution), but its content has changed significantly over time, with the rate of ideological transformation having accelerated since the 1960s. New ideologies have emerged, some once-potent ideologies have faded in significance, and all ideologies have gone through a process of sometimes radical redefinition and renewal. Political ideology arose out of a transition from feudalism to industrial capitalism. In simple terms, the earliest, or 'classical', ideological traditions – liberalism, conservatism and socialism – developed as contrasting attempts to shape emergent industrial society. While liberalism championed the cause of individualism, the market and, initially at least, minimal government, conservatism stood in defence of an increasingly embattled *ancien régime*, and socialism advanced the quite different vision of a society based on community, equality and cooperation.

As the nineteenth century progressed, each of these ideologies acquired a clearer doctrinal character, and came to be associated with a particular social class or stratum of society. Simply put, liberalism was the ideology of the rising middle class, conservatism was the ideology of the aristocracy or nobility, and socialism was the ideology of the growing working class. In turn, political parties developed to articulate the interests of these classes and to give 'operative' expression to the various ideologies. These parties therefore typically had a programmatic character. The central theme that emerged from ideological argument and debate during this period was the battle between two rival economic philosophies: capitalism and socialism. Political ideology thus had a strong economic focus. The battle lines between capitalism and socialism were significantly sharpened by the 1917 Russian Revolution, which created the world's first socialist state. Indeed, throughout what is sometimes called the 'short' twentieth century (from the outbreak of the First World War in 1914 to the collapse of communism in 1989–91), and particularly during the Cold War period (1945–90), international politics was structured along ideological lines, as the capitalist West confronted the communist East.

However, since around the 1960s, the ideological landscape has been transformed. Not only have major changes occurred within established or 'classical' ideologies (for instance, in the rise of the New Left, the New Right and, most dramatically, with the collapse of orthodox communism), but a series of 'new' ideological traditions have also emerged. The most significant of these are set out in Figure 1.6. The designation of these ideologies as 'new' can nevertheless be misleading, as each of them has roots that stretch back to the nineteenth century, if not beyond. Moreover, they have also tended to draw heavily on existing, mainstream ideologies, giving them, typically, a hybrid or cross-cutting character. These ideologies are 'new', though, in the sense that they have given particular areas of ideological debate a prominence they never previously enjoyed. In the process, they have fostered the emergence of fresh and challenging ideological perspectives. But why

'Classical' ideologies	'New' ideologies
Liberalism	Feminism
Conservatism	Green ideology
Socialism	Multiculturalism
Nationalism	Islamism
Anarchism	
Fascism (?)	

Figure 1.6 'Classical' and 'new' ideologies

has this process of ideological transformation occurred? The three main reasons are the following:

- the emergence of postindustrial societies and 'new' social movements
- the collapse of communism and the changing world order
- the rise of globalization and of cosmopolitan sensibilities.

The structure and nature of modern societies have undergone a profound process of change since about the 1950s. Social thinkers have heralded this change in a variety of ways. For example, Beck (1992) proclaimed the transition from the 'first' to the 'second' modernity, Giddens (1994) analysed the shift from 'simple' to 'reflexive' modernity, while Baumann (2000) discussed the change from 'solid' to 'liquid' modernity. At the heart of these changes, however, is the transition from industrial societies to postindustrial ones. Industrial societies tended to be solidaristic, in that they were based on relatively clear class divisions (crudely, those between capital and labour), which, in turn, helped to structure the political process, including the party system, interest-group competition and ideological debate. Postindustrial societies are different in a number of ways. They tend, in the first place, to be more affluent societies, in which the struggle for material subsistence has become less pressing for a growing proportion of people. In conditions of wider prosperity, individuals express more interest in 'quality of life' or 'postmaterial' issues. These are typically concerned with morality, political justice and personal fulfilment, and include issues such as gender equality, world peace, cultural recognition, environmental protection and animal rights. Second, the structure of society and the nature of social connectedness have altered. Whereas industrial societies tended to generate 'thick' social bonds, based on social class and nationality in particular, postindustrial societies tend to be characterized by growing **individualization** and 'thinner' and more fluid social bonds. This has been reflected in the growth of so-called 'new' **social movements**, such as the women's movement, the environmental or green movement and the peace movement, which have played a key role in reshaping political identities and articulating new ideological agendas.

The ideological ramifications of the collapse of communism have been profound and wide-ranging, and, in many ways, continue to unfold. The ideology most clearly affected has been socialism. Revolutionary socialism, especially in its Soviet-style, Marxist–Leninist guise, was revealed as a spent force, both because of the economic failings of central planning and because of the system's association with state authoritarianism (see p. 74). However, democratic socialism has also been affected; some argue that it has been fatally compromised. In particular, democratic socialists have lost faith in 'top-down' state control, and have come to accept the market as the only reliable means of generating wealth. The collapse of communism, and the general retreat from socialism, has provided opportunities for new

INDIVIDUALIZATION
The process through which people are encouraged to see themselves as individuals, possibly at the expense of their sense of social/moral responsibility.

SOCIAL MOVEMENT
A collective body distinguished by a high level of commitment and political activism, but often lacking clear organization.

Key concept

Globalization

Globalization is the emergence of a web of interconnectedness which means that our lives are shaped increasingly by events that occur, and decisions that are made, at a great distance from us, thus giving rise to 'supraterritorial' connections between people. However, globalization is a complex process that has a range of manifestations. *Economic* globalization

is the process through which national economies have, to a greater or lesser extent, been absorbed into a single global economy. *Cultural* globalization is the process whereby information, commodities and images produced in one part of the world have entered into a global flow that tends to 'flatten out' cultural differences worldwide. *Political* globalization is the process through which policy-making responsibilities have been passed from national governments to international organizations.

ideological forces. Chief among these have been nationalism, particularly ethnic nationalism, which has displaced Marxism–Leninism as the leading ideology in many postcommunist states, and religious fundamentalism (see p. 188), which, in its various forms, has had profound significance in the developing world. The advent of global terrorism, through the attacks on New York and Washington on 11 September 2001, and the initiation of the so-called 'war on terror' had further consequences for political ideologies. The 'war on terror' highlighted the emergence of new ideological battle lines that, some believe, may define global politics in the twenty-first century. In the widely discussed if highly controversial thesis of Samuel Huntington (see p. 329), the ideological battle between capitalism and communism has been displaced by a 'clash of civilizations' (see p. 310), in which the most significant division is between Islam and the West.

Globalization (see p. 20) is not a single process but a complex of processes, sometimes overlapping and interlocking but also, at times, contradictory and oppositional ones. In its economic, cultural and political forms, globalization forges connections between previously unconnected people, communities, institutions and societies. This interconnectedness, however, has had sharply contrasting implications. On the one hand, it has stimulated homogenizing trends that have seen a 'flattening out' of economic, cultural and other differences between the countries and regions of the world. In ideological terms, this homogenizing trend has been closely associated with the advance of liberalism, whether in the form of a liberal economic order (based

COSMOPOLITANISM
The belief that the world constitutes a single moral, and possibly political, community, in that people have obligations towards all other people in the world (see p. 191).

on free trade and free markets), the spread of liberal democracy (see p. 40), or the growth of **cosmopolitan** sensibilities, often linked to the idea of human rights (see p. 58). However, on the other hand, globalization has been a distinctively asymmetrical process that has spawned new forms of inequality and generated a range of oppositional forces. These include a strengthening of religious fundamentalism in the developing world, leading, as Benjamin Barber (1995) put it, to a confrontation between 'Jihad' and 'MacWorld', and the emergence of an anti-globalization or anti-capitalist movement in the developed world that has recast, and sometimes bolstered, the ideas of anarchism, feminism and green ideology.

The 'new' ideologies are not only new, but also differ from 'classical' ideologies in a range of other ways. This has altered the focus and sometimes the terms of ideological debate. Three broad differences can be identified. In the first place, there has been a shift away from economics and towards culture. Liberalism, conservatism and socialism were primarily concerned with issues of economic organization, or at least their moral vision was grounded in a particular economic model. By contrast, and in their various ways, the 'new' ideologies are more interested in culture than in economics: their primary concerns tend to be orientated around people's values, beliefs and ways of life, rather than economic well-being or even social justice.

Second, there has been a shift from social politics to identity politics (see p. 282). Identity links the personal to the social, in seeing the individual as 'embedded' in a particular cultural, social, institutional and ideological context, but it also highlights the scope for personal choice and self-definition, reflecting a general social trend towards individualization. In this sense, the 'new' ideologies offer individuals not worked-out sets of political solutions that 'fit' their social position, but, rather, provide them with a range of ideological options. This means that political activism has become, in effect, a lifestyle choice. Finally, there has been a shift from **universalism** to **particularism**. Whereas, most clearly, liberalism and socialism shared an Enlightenment faith in reason and progress, reflecting the belief that there is a common core to human identity shared by people everywhere, 'new' ideologies, such as feminism, ethnic nationalism, multiculturalism and the various forms of religious fundamentalism, stress the importance of factors such as gender, locality, culture and ethnicity. In that sense, they practise the 'politics of difference' rather than the politics of universal emancipation.

UNIVERSALISM
The belief that it is possible to uncover certain values and principles that are applicable to all people and all societies, regardless of historical, cultural and other differences.

PARTICULARISM
The belief that historical, cultural and other differences between people and societies are more significant than what they have in common.

Using this book

This book examines each ideology or ideological tradition in turn. They are organized, roughly, in chronological terms, so that the larger process of ideological development, whereby one ideology influences others and so on, can be mapped out. Each chapter has the same general structure:

- Following a Preview, which highlights the broad nature of the ideology, the origins and historical development of the ideology in question are examined.

- The next main section explains and analyses the core themes of the ideology, the values, doctrines and theories that, taken together, define the shape or morphology of the ideology. This section highlights what is distinctive about each ideological tradition, but also notes overlaps with other ideologies, where relevant.
- The following sections deal with the sub-traditions that characterize each and every political ideology. The focus here is not only on the distinctive features of each sub-tradition, many of which are, in any case, hybrid ideological constructs (conservative nationalism, socialist feminism, liberal multiculturalism and so on), but also on the internal coherence, or lack of coherence, of the ideology as a whole. This section therefore focuses on areas of disagreement between supporters of the same ideology.
- The final main section examines contemporary developments within the ideological tradition in question and reflects, in particular, on how, and to what extent, it has been reshaped in the light of globalizing tendencies.
- Definitions of key terms, highlighted in the text, appear on the page where they are used, instead of in a separate glossary.
- Boxed material can be found in each chapter, providing more information about:
  - major thinkers in each tradition
  - key concepts
  - major events in the history of the ideology
  - rival perspectives on important political themes
  - points of tension within each ideology
  - how the ideology is configured internally.
- Each chapter concludes with a list of questions for discussion, and suggestions for further reading. A full bibliography appears at the end of the book.
- As a navigational aid, the index entries for material in boxes are in **bold**, and the on-page definitions are in *italics*.
- The companion website features, among other things, a searchable glossary of key terms, advice about websites to support further study, and articles and other material relevant to political ideologies.

(?) QUESTIONS FOR DISCUSSION

- Are 'practical men' really the slaves of 'academic scribblers' (Keynes)?
- How does the Marxist concept of ideology differ from the mainstream concept?
- Is ideology necessarily false? If so, why?
- Can 'socially unattached' intellectuals rise above ideology?
- Are all political ideas ideological, or only some of them?
- To what extent do ideologies differ in terms of their conceptual structure?
- How does an ideology differ from a philosophy?
- To what extent does the left/right divide aid our understanding of political ideologies?
- How should the political spectrum be presented, and why?
- What is new about the 'new' ideologies?
- To what extent has ideological commitment become a life-style choice?
- Does the rise of 'new' ideologies mean that the old ones are now defunct?

(📖) FURTHER READING

Festenstein, M. and M. Kenny, *Political Ideologies: A Reader and Guide* (2005). A very useful collection of extracts from key texts on ideology and ideologies, supported by lucid commentaries.

Freeden, M., *Ideology: A Very Short Introduction* (2004). An accessible and lively introduction to the concept: an excellent starting place.

Freeden, M. et al., *The Oxford Handbook of Political Ideologies* (2015). A wide-ranging, up-to-date and authoritative account of debates about the nature of ideology and the shape of the various ideological traditions.

McLellan, D., *Ideology* (1995). A clear and short yet comprehensive introduction to the elusive concept of ideology.

CHAPTER

2 Liberalism

Preview

The term 'liberal' has been in use since the fourteenth century but has had a wide variety of meanings. The Latin *liber* referred to a class of free men; in other words, men who were neither serfs nor slaves. It has meant generous, as in 'liberal' helpings of food and drink; or, in reference to social attitudes, it has implied openness or open-mindedness. It also came to be associated increasingly with the ideas of freedom and choice. The term 'liberalism', to denote a political allegiance, made its appearance much later: it was not used until the early part of the nineteenth century, being first employed in Spain in 1812. By the 1840s, the term was widely recognized throughout Europe as a reference to a distinctive set of political ideas. However, it was taken up more slowly in the UK: though the Whigs started to call themselves Liberals during the 1830s, the first distinctly Liberal government was not formed until Gladstone took office in 1868.

The central theme of liberal ideology is a commitment to the individual and the desire to construct a society in which people can satisfy their interests and achieve fulfilment. Liberals believe that human beings are, first and foremost, individuals, endowed with reason. This implies that each individual should enjoy the maximum possible freedom consistent with a like freedom for all. However, although individuals are entitled to equal legal and political rights, they should be rewarded in line with their talents and their willingness to work. Liberal societies are organized politically around the twin principles of constitutionalism and consent, designed to protect citizens from the danger of government tyranny. Nevertheless, there are significant differences between classical liberalism and modern liberalism. Classical liberalism is characterized by a belief in a 'minimal' state, whose function is limited to the maintenance of domestic order and personal security. Modern liberalism, in contrast, accepts that the state should help people to help themselves.

Origins and development

As a systematic political creed, liberalism may not have existed before the nineteenth century, but it was based on ideas and theories that had developed during the previous 300 years. Indeed, as Paul Seabright (2004) argued, the origins of liberalism can perhaps be traced back as far as to early agricultural societies, when people started living in settled communities and were forced, for the first time, to find ways of trading and living with strangers. Nevertheless, liberalism as a developed ideology was a product of the breakdown of **feudalism** in Europe, and the growth, in its place, of a market or capitalist society. In many respects, liberalism reflected the aspirations of the rising middle classes, whose interests conflicted with the established power of absolute monarchs and the landed aristocracy. Liberal ideas were radical: they sought fundamental reform and even, at times, revolutionary change. The English Revolution of the seventeenth century, and the American Revolution of 1776 and French Revolution of 1789 each embodied elements that were distinctively liberal, even though the word 'liberal' was not at the time used in a political sense. Liberals challenged the absolute power of the monarchy, supposedly based on the doctrine of the '**divine right** of kings'. In place of **absolutism**, they advocated constitutional and, later, representative government. Liberals criticized the political and economic privileges of the landed aristocracy and the unfairness of a feudal system in which social position was determined by the 'accident of birth'. They also supported the movement towards freedom of conscience in religion and questioned the authority of the established church.

The nineteenth century was in many ways the liberal century. As industrialization spread throughout western countries, liberal ideas triumphed. Liberals advocated an industrialized and market economic order 'free' from government interference, in which businesses would be allowed to pursue profit and states encouraged to trade freely with one another. Such a system of industrial capitalism developed first in the UK, from the mid-eighteenth century onwards, and subsequently spread to North America and throughout Europe, initially into western Europe and then, more gradually, into eastern Europe. From the twentieth century onwards industrial capitalism exerted a powerful appeal for developing states in Africa, Asia and Latin America, especially when social and political development was defined in essentially western terms. However, developing-world states have sometimes been resistant to the attractions of liberal capitalism because their political cultures have emphasized community rather than the individual. In such cases, they have provided more fertile ground for the growth of socialism, nationalism or religious fundamentalism (see p. 188), rather than western liberalism.

FEUDALISM
A system of agrarian-based production that is characterized by fixed social hierarchies and a rigid pattern of obligations.

DIVINE RIGHT
The doctrine that earthly rulers are chosen by God and thus wield unchallengeable authority; divine right is a defence for monarchical absolutism.

ABSOLUTISM
A form of government in which political power is concentrated in the hands of a single individual or small group, in particular, an absolute monarchy.

Liberalism has undoubtedly been the most powerful ideological force shaping the western political tradition. Nevertheless, historical developments since the nineteenth century have clearly influenced the nature and substance of liberal ideology. The character of liberalism changed as the 'rising middle classes' succeeded in establishing their economic and political dominance. The radical, even revolutionary, edge of liberalism faded with each liberal success. Liberalism thus became increasingly conservative, standing less for change and reform, and more for the maintenance of existing – largely liberal – institutions. Liberal ideas, too, could not stand still. From the late nineteenth century onwards, the progress of industrialization led liberals to question, and in some ways to revise, the ideas of early liberalism. Whereas early or **classical liberalism** had been defined by the desire to minimize government interference in the lives of its citizens, **modern liberalism** came to be associated with welfare provision and economic management. As a result, some commentators have argued that liberalism is an incoherent ideology, embracing contradictory beliefs, notably about the desirable role of the state.

> **CLASSICAL LIBERALISM**
> A tradition within liberalism that seeks to maximize the realm of unconstrained individual action, typically by establishing a minimal state and a reliance on market economics.
>
> **MODERN LIBERALISM**
> A tradition within liberalism that provides (in contrast to classical liberalism) a qualified endorsement for social and economic intervention as a means of promoting personal development.

Core themes: the primacy of the individual

Liberalism is, in a sense, the ideology of the industrialized West. So deeply have liberal ideas permeated political, economic and cultural life that their influence can become hard to discern, liberalism appearing to be indistinguishable from 'western civilization' in general. Liberal thinkers in the eighteenth and nineteenth centuries, influenced by an Enlightenment belief in universal reason, tended to subscribe to an explicitly foundationist form of liberalism, which sought to establish fundamental values and championed a particular vision of human flourishing or excellence, usually linked to personal autonomy. This form of liberalism was boldly universalist, in that it implied that human history would be marked by the gradual but inevitable triumph of liberal principles and institutions. Progress, in short, was understood in strictly liberal terms.

During the twentieth century, however, it became fashionable to portray liberalism as morally neutral. This was reflected in the belief that liberalism gives priority to 'the right' over 'the good'. In other words, liberalism strives to establish the conditions in which people and groups can pursue the good life as each defines it, but it does not prescribe or try to promote any particular notion of what is good. From this perspective, liberalism is not simply an ideology but a 'meta-ideology'; that is, a body of rules that lays down the grounds on which political and ideological debate can take place. However, this does not mean that liberalism is simply a philosophy of 'do your own thing'. While liberalism undoubtedly favours openness, debate and self-determination, it is also characterized by a powerful moral thrust. The moral and ideological stance of liberalism is embodied in a commitment to a distinctive set of values and beliefs. The most important of these are:

- individualism
- freedom
- reason
- justice
- toleration.

Individualism

In the modern world, the concept of the individual is so familiar that its political significance is often overlooked. In the feudal period, there was little idea of individuals having their own interests or possessing personal and unique identities. Rather, people were seen as members of the social groups to which they belonged: their family, village, local community or social class. Their lives and identities were largely determined by the character of these groups in a process that changed little from one generation to the next. However, as feudalism was displaced by increasingly market-orientated societies, individuals were confronted by a broader range of choices and social possibilities. They were encouraged, perhaps for the first time, to think *for* themselves, and to think *of* themselves in personal terms. A serf, for example, whose family might always have lived and worked on the same piece of land, became a 'free man' and acquired some ability to choose for whom to work, or perhaps the opportunity to leave the land altogether and look for work in the growing towns or cities.

As the certainties of feudal life broke down, a new intellectual climate emerged. Rational and scientific explanations gradually displaced traditional religious theories, and society was increasingly understood from the viewpoint of the human individual. Individuals were thought to possess personal and distinctive qualities: each was of special value. This was evident in the growth of natural rights theories in the seventeenth and eighteenth centuries, which are discussed later, in relation to classical liberalism. Immanuel Kant (see p. 52) expressed a similar belief in the dignity and equal worth of human beings in his conception of individuals as 'ends in themselves' and not merely as means for the achievement of the ends of others. However, emphasizing the importance of the individual has two contrasting implications. First, it draws attention to the uniqueness of each human being: individuals are defined primarily by inner qualities and attributes specific to themselves. Second, they nevertheless each share the same status in that they are all, first and foremost, individuals. Many of the tensions within liberal ideology can, indeed, be traced back to these rival ideas of uniqueness and equality.

Key concept

Individualism

Individualism is the belief in the supreme importance of the individual over any social group or collective body. In the form of methodological individualism, this suggests that the individual is central to any political theory or social explanation – all statements about society should be made in terms of the individuals who compose it. Ethical individualism, on the other hand, implies that society should be constructed so as to benefit the individual, giving moral priority to individual rights, needs or interests. Classical liberals and the New Right subscribe to *egoistical* individualism, which places emphasis on self-interestedness and self-reliance. Modern liberals, in contrast, have advanced a *developmental* form of individualism that prioritizes human flourishing over the quest for interest satisfaction.

A belief in the primacy of the individual is the characteristic theme of liberal ideology, but it has influenced liberal thought in different ways. It has led some liberals to view society as simply a collection of individuals, each seeking to satisfy his or her own needs and interests. Such a view has been equated with **atomism**; indeed, it can lead to the belief that 'society' itself does not exist, but is merely a collection of self-sufficient individuals. Such extreme individualism is based on the assumption that the individual is egoistical, essentially self-seeking, and largely self-reliant. C. B. Macpherson (1973) characterized early liberalism as 'possessive individualism', in that it regarded the individual as 'the proprietor of his own person or capacities, owing nothing to society for them'. In contrast, later liberals have held a more optimistic view of **human nature**, and have been more prepared to believe that egoism is tempered by a sense of social responsibility, especially a responsibility for those who are unable to look after themselves. Whether **egoism** is unrestrained or is qualified by a sense of social responsibility, liberals are united in their desire to create a society in which each person is capable of developing and flourishing to the fullness of his or her potential.

ATOMISM
A belief that society is made up of a collection of self-interested and largely self-sufficient individuals, or atoms, rather than social groups.

HUMAN NATURE
The essential and innate character of all human beings: what they owe to nature rather than to society (see p. 68).

EGOISM
A concern for one's own welfare or interests, or the theory that the pursuit of self-interest is an ethical priority.

Freedom

A belief in the supreme importance of the individual leads naturally to a commitment to individual **freedom**. Individual liberty (liberty and freedom being interchangeable) is for liberals the supreme political value and, in many ways, the unifying principle within liberal ideology. For early liberals, liberty was a natural right, an essential requirement for leading a truly human existence. It also gave individuals the opportunity to pursue their own interests by exercising

FREEDOM (OR LIBERTY)
The ability to think or act as one wishes, a capacity that can be associated with the individual, a social group or a nation (see p. 29).

PERSPECTIVES ON... FREEDOM

LIBERALS give priority to freedom as the supreme individualist value. While classical liberals support negative freedom, understood as the absence of constraints – or freedom of choice – modern liberals advocate positive freedom in the sense of personal development and human flourishing.

CONSERVATIVES have traditionally endorsed a weak view of freedom as the willing recognition of duties and responsibilities, negative freedom posing a threat to the fabric of society. The New Right, however, endorses negative freedom in the economic sphere, freedom of choice in the marketplace.

SOCIALISTS have generally understood freedom in positive terms to refer to self-fulfilment achieved through either free creative labour or cooperative social interaction. Social democrats have drawn close to modern liberalism in treating freedom as the realization of individual potential.

ANARCHISTS regard freedom as an absolute value, believing it to be irreconcilable with any form of political authority. Freedom is understood to mean the achievement of personal autonomy, not merely being 'left alone' but being rationally self-willed and self-directed.

FASCISTS reject any form of individual liberty as a nonsense. 'True' freedom, in contrast, means unquestioning submission to the will of the leader and the absorption of the individual into the national community.

GREENS, particularly deep ecologists, treat freedom as the achievement of oneness, self-realization through the absorption of the personal ego into the ecosphere or universe. In contrast with political freedom, this is sometimes seen as 'inner' freedom, freedom as self-actualization.

ISLAMISTS see freedom as essentially an inner or spiritual quality. Freedom means conformity to the revealed will of God, spiritual fulfilment being associated with submission to religious authority.

choice: the choice of where to live, for whom to work, what to buy and so on. Later liberals have seen liberty as the only condition in which people are able to develop their skills and talents and fulfil their potential.

Nevertheless, liberals do not accept that individuals have an absolute entitlement to freedom. If liberty is unlimited it can become 'licence', the right to abuse others. In *On Liberty* ([1859] 1972) John Stuart Mill argued that 'the only purpose for which power can be rightfully exercised over any member of a civilized community, against his will, is to prevent harm to others'. Mill's position is libertarian (see p. 78) in that it accepts only the most minimal restrictions on individual freedom, and then only in order to prevent 'harm to others'. He distinguished clearly between actions that are 'self-regarding', over which individuals should exercise absolute freedom, and those that are 'other-regarding', which can restrict the freedom of others or do them damage. Mill did not accept any restrictions on the individual that are designed to prevent a person from damaging himself or herself, either physically or morally. Such a view suggests, for example, that laws forcing car drivers to put on seat belts or motorcyclists to wear crash helmets are as unacceptable as any form of censorship that limits what an individual may read or listen to. Radical libertarians may defend the right of people to use addictive drugs, such as heroin and cocaine, on the same grounds. Although the individual may be sovereign over his or her body and mind, each must respect the fact that every other individual enjoys an equal right to liberty. This has been expressed by John Rawls (see p. 53) in the principle that everyone is entitled to the widest possible liberty consistent with a like liberty for all.

While liberals agree about the value of liberty, they have not always agreed about what it means for an individual to be 'free'. In his 'Two Concepts of Liberty' ([1958] 1969), Isaiah Berlin (see p. 292) distinguished between a 'negative' theory of liberty and a 'positive' one. Early or classical liberals have believed in **negative freedom**, in that freedom consists in each person being left alone, free from interference and able to act in whatever way he or she may choose. This conception of freedom is 'negative' in that it is based on the absence of external restrictions or constraints on the individual. Modern liberals, on the other hand, have been attracted to a more 'positive' conception of liberty – **positive freedom** – defined by Berlin as the ability to be one's own master; to be autonomous. Self-mastery requires that the individual is able to develop skills and talents, broaden his or her understanding, and gain fulfilment. This led to an emphasis on the capacity of human beings to develop and ultimately achieve self-realization. These rival conceptions of liberty have not merely stimulated academic debate within liberalism, but have also encouraged liberals to hold very different views about the desirable relation-ship between the individual and the state.

NEGATIVE FREEDOM
The absence of external restrictions or constraints on the individual, allowing freedom of choice.

POSITIVE FREEDOM
Self-mastery or self-realization; the achievement of autonomy or the development of human capacities.

Reason

The liberal case for freedom is closely linked to a faith in reason. Liberalism is, and remains, very much part of the Enlightenment project. The central theme of the Enlightenment was the desire to release humankind from its bondage to superstition and ignorance, and unleash an 'age of reason'. Key Enlightenment thinkers included Jean-Jacques Rousseau (see p. 184), Immanuel Kant, Adam Smith (see p. 52) and Jeremy Bentham (see p. 52). Enlightenment rationalism (see p. 31) influenced liberalism in a number of ways. In the first place, it strengthened its faith in both the individual and freedom. To the extent that human beings are rational,

Key concept
Rationalism

Rationalism is the belief that the world has a rational structure, and that this can be disclosed through the exercise of human reason and critical enquiry. As a philosophical theory, rationalism is the belief that knowledge flows from reason rather than experience, and thus contrasts with empiricism. As a general principle, however, rationalism places a heavy emphasis on the capacity of human beings to understand and explain their world, and to find solutions to problems. While rationalism does not dictate the ends of human conduct, it certainly suggests how these ends should be pursued. It is associated with an emphasis on principle and reason-governed behaviour, as opposed to a reliance on custom or tradition, or on non-rational drives and impulses.

thinking creatures, they are capable of defining and pursuing their own best interests. By no means do liberals believe that individuals are infallible in this respect, but the belief in reason builds into liberalism a strong bias against **paternalism**. Not only does paternalism prevent individuals from making their own moral choices and, if necessary, from learning from their own mistakes, but it also creates the prospect that those invested with responsibility for others will abuse their position for their own ends.

A further legacy of rationalism is that liberals are inclined to view human history in terms of progress. Progress literally means advance, a movement forward. In the liberal view, the expansion of knowledge, particularly through the scientific revolution, enabled people not only to understand and explain their world but also to help shape it for the better. In short, the power of reason gives human beings the capacity to take charge of their own lives and fashion their own destinies. Reason emancipates humankind from the grip of the past and from the weight of custom and tradition. Each generation is thus able to advance beyond the last as the stock of human knowledge and understanding increases progressively. This also explains the characteristic liberal emphasis on education. People can better or improve themselves through the acquisition of knowledge and the abandonment of prejudice and superstition. Education, particularly in the modern liberal view, is therefore a good in itself. It is a vital means of promoting personal self-development and, if extended widely, of bringing about social advancement.

Reason, moreover, is significant in highlighting the importance of discussion, debate and argument. While liberals are generally optimistic about human nature, seeing people as reason-guided creatures, they have seldom subscribed to the utopian creed of human perfectibility because they recognize the power of self-interest and egoism. The inevitable result of this is rivalry and conflict. Individuals battle for scarce resources, businesses compete to increase profits, states struggle for security or strategic advantage, and

PATERNALISM
Authority exercised from above for the guidance and support of those below, modelled on the relationship between fathers and children (see p. 76).

so on. The liberal preference is clearly that such conflicts be settled through debate and negotiation. The great advantage of reason is that it provides a basis on which rival claims and demands can be evaluated – do they 'stand up' to analysis; are they 'reasonable'? Furthermore, it highlights the cost of not resolving disputes peacefully: namely, violence, bloodshed and death. Liberals therefore typically deplore the use of force and aggression; for example, war is invariably seen as an option of the very last resort. From the liberal perspective, the use of force is justified either on the grounds of self-defence or as a means of countering oppression, but always and only after reason and argument have been exhausted.

Justice

Justice denotes a particular kind of moral judgement, in particular one about the distribution of rewards and punishment. In short, justice is about giving each person what he or she is 'due'. The narrower idea of social justice refers to the distribution of material rewards and benefits in society, such as wages, profits, housing, medical care, welfare benefits and so on. The liberal theory of justice is based on a belief in equality of various kinds. In the first place, individualism implies a commitment to foundational equality. Human beings are seen to be 'born' equal in the sense that each individual is of equal moral worth, an idea embodied in the notion of natural rights or human rights (see p. 58).

Second, foundational equality implies a belief in formal equality or equal citizenship, the idea that individuals should enjoy the same formal status within society, particularly in terms of the distribution of rights and entitlements. Consequently, liberals fiercely disapprove of any social privileges or advantages that are enjoyed by some but denied to others on the basis of 'irrational' factors such as gender, race, colour, creed, religion or social background. Rights should not be reserved for any particular class of person, such as men, whites, Christians or the wealthy. This is the sense in which liberalism is 'difference blind'. The most important forms of formal equality are legal equality and political equality. The former emphasizes 'equality before the law' and insists that all non-legal factors be strictly irrelevant to the process of legal decision-making. The latter is embodied in the idea of 'one person, one vote; one vote, one value', and underpins the liberal commitment to democracy.

Third, liberals subscribe to a belief in equality of opportunity. Each and every individual should have the same chance to rise or fall in society. The game of life, in that sense, must be played on a level playing field. This is not to say that there should be equality of outcome or reward, or that living conditions and social circumstances should be the same for all. Liberals believe social equality to be undesirable because people are not born the same. They possess different talents and skills, and some are prepared to work

JUSTICE
A moral standard of fairness and impartiality; social justice is the notion of a fair or justifiable distribution of wealth and rewards in society.

EQUALITY
The principle that human beings are of identical worth or are entitled to be treated in the same way; equality can have widely differing applications.

much harder than others. Liberals believe that it is right to reward merit (ability and the willingness to work); indeed, they think it is essential to do so if people are to have an incentive to realize their potential and develop the talents with which they were born. Equality, for a liberal, means that individuals should have an equal opportunity to develop their unequal skills and abilities.

This leads to a belief in 'meritocracy'. A meritocratic society is one in which inequalities of wealth and social position solely reflect the unequal distribution of talent and application among human beings, or are based on factors beyond human control; for example, luck or chance (though some liberals believe that all aspects of luck, including natural ability, should be irrelevant to distributive justice, a position called 'luck egalitarianism' (Dworkin 2000)). Such a society is socially just because individuals are judged not by their gender, the colour of their skin or their religion, but according to their talents and willingness to work, or what Martin Luther King called 'the content of their character'. By extension, social equality is unjust because it treats unlike individuals alike. However, liberal thinkers have disagreed about how these broad principles of justice should be applied in practice. Classical liberals have endorsed strict meritocracy on both economic and moral grounds. Economically, they place heavy stress on the need for incentives. Morally, justice requires that unequal individuals are not treated equally. Modern liberals, on the other hand, have taken social justice to imply a belief in some measure of social equality. For example, in *A Theory of Justice* (1970), John Rawls argued that economic inequality is only justifiable if it works to the benefit of the poorest in society.

MERITOCRACY
Literally, rule by those with merit, merit being intelligence plus effort; a society in which social position is determined exclusively by ability and hard work.

Toleration

PLURALISM
A belief in diversity or choice, or the theory that political power is or should be widely and evenly dispersed (see p. 290).

TOLERATION
Forbearance; a willingness to accept views or actions with which one is in disagreement.

AUTONOMY
Literally, self-government; the ability to control one's own destiny by virtue of enjoying independence from external influences.

The liberal social ethic is characterized very much by a willingness to accept and, in some cases, celebrate moral, cultural and political diversity. Indeed, an acceptance of **pluralism** can be said to be rooted in the principle of individualism, and the assumption that human beings are separate and unique creatures. However, the liberal preference for diversity has been associated more commonly with **toleration**. This commitment to toleration, attributed to the French writer Voltaire (1694–1778), is memorably expressed in the declaration that, 'I detest what you say but will defend to the death your right to say it.' Toleration is both an ethical ideal and a social principle. On the one hand, it represents the goal of personal **autonomy**; on the other, it establishes a set of rules about how human beings should behave towards one another. The liberal case for toleration first emerged in the seventeenth century in the attempt by writers such as John Milton (1608–74) and John Locke (see p. 52) to defend religious freedom. Locke argued that, since the proper function of government is to protect life, liberty and property, it has no right to meddle in 'the care of men's souls'. Toleration should be extended to all matters regarded as 'private', on the grounds that, like religion, they concern moral questions that should be left to the individual.

In *On Liberty* ([1859] 1972), J. S. Mill developed a wider justification for toleration that highlighted its importance to society as well as the individual. From the individual's point of view, toleration is primarily a guarantee of personal autonomy and is thus a condition for moral self-development. Nevertheless, toleration is also necessary to ensure the vigour and health of society as a whole. Only within a free market of ideas will 'truth' emerge, as good ideas displace bad ones and ignorance is progressively banished. Contest, debate and argument, the fruit of diversity or multiplicity, are therefore the motor of social progress. For Mill, this was particularly threatened by democracy and the spread of 'dull conformism', linked to the belief that the majority must always be right. Mill ([1859] 1972) was thus able to argue as follows:

> If all mankind minus one, were of one opinion, and only one person were of the contrary opinion, mankind would be no more justified in silencing that one person, than he, if he had the power, would be justified in silencing mankind.

Sympathy for toleration and diversity is also linked to the liberal belief in a balanced society, one not riven by fundamental conflict. Although individuals and social groups pursue very different interests, liberals hold that there is a deeper harmony or balance among these competing interests. For example, the interests of workers and employers differ: workers want better pay, shorter hours and improved working conditions; while employers wish to increase their profits by keeping their production costs – including wages – as low as possible. Nevertheless, these competing interests also complement one another: workers need jobs, and employers need labour. In other words, each group is essential to the achievement of the other group's goals. Individuals and groups may pursue self-interest, but a natural equilibrium will tend to assert itself. The relationship between liberalism, pluralism and diversity is examined further in Chapter 11, in connection with multiculturalism.

Liberalism, government and democracy

The liberal state

LAW
Established and public rules of social conduct, backed up by the machinery of the state, the police, courts and prisons.

Liberals do not believe that a balanced and tolerant society will simply develop naturally out of the free actions of individuals and voluntary associations. This is where liberals disagree with anarchists, who believe that both **law** and

government are unnecessary. Liberals fear that free individuals may wish to exploit others, steal their property or even turn them into slaves if it is in their interests to do so. They may also break or ignore contracts when doing so is to their advantage. The liberty of one person is always, therefore, in danger of becoming a licence to abuse another; each person can be said to be both a threat to, and under threat from, every other member of society. Our liberty requires that they are restrained from encroaching on our freedom and, in turn, their liberty requires that they are safeguarded from us. Liberals have traditionally believed that such protection can only be provided by a sovereign **state**, capable of restraining all individuals and groups within society. Freedom can therefore only exist 'under the law'; as John Locke put it, 'where there is no law there is no freedom'.

This argument is the basis of the **social contract** theories, developed by seventeenth-century writers such as Thomas Hobbes (see p. 84) and John Locke, which, for liberals, explains the individual's political obligations towards the state. Hobbes and Locke constructed a picture of what life had been like before government was formed, in a stateless society or what they called a **'state of nature'**. As individuals are selfish, greedy and power-seeking, the state of nature would be characterized by an unending civil war of each against all, in which, in Hobbes' words, human life would be 'solitary, poor, nasty, brutish and short'. As a result, they argued, rational individuals would enter into an agreement, or 'social contract', to establish a sovereign government, without which orderly and stable life would be impossible. All individuals would recognize that it is in their interests to sacrifice a portion of their liberty in order to set up a system of law; otherwise their rights, and indeed their lives, would constantly be under threat. Hobbes and Locke were aware that this 'contract' is a historical fiction. The purpose of the social contract argument, however, is to highlight the value of the sovereign state to the individual. In other words, Hobbes and Locke wished individuals to behave as if the historical fiction were true, by respecting and obeying government and law, in gratitude for the safety and security that only a sovereign state can provide.

The social contract argument embodies two important liberal attitudes towards the state in particular, and political authority in general:

- political authority comes, in a sense, 'from below'
- the state acts as an umpire or neutral referee in society.

In the first place, social contract theory suggest that the state is created *by* individuals and *for* individuals; it exists in order to serve their needs and interests.

GOVERNMENT
The machinery through which collective decisions are made on behalf of the state, usually comprising a legislature, executive and judiciary.

STATE
An association that establishes sovereign power within a defined territorial area, usually possessing a monopoly of coercive power.

SOCIAL CONTRACT
A (hypothetical) agreement among individuals through which they form a state in order to escape from the disorder and chaos of the 'state of nature'.

STATE OF NATURE
A pre-political society characterized by unrestrained freedom and the absence of established authority.

Government arises out of the agreement, or consent, of the governed. This implies that citizens do not have an absolute obligation to obey all laws or accept any form of government. If government is based on a contract, made by the governed, government itself may break the terms of this contract. When the legitimacy of government evaporates, the people have the right of rebellion.

Second, in social contract theory, the state is not created by a privileged elite, wishing to exploit the masses, but by an agreement among all the people. The state therefore embodies the interests of all its citizens and acts as a neutral referee when individuals or groups come into conflict with one another. For instance, if individuals break contracts made with others, the state applies the 'rules of the game' and enforces the terms of the contract, provided, of course, that each party had entered into the contract voluntarily and in full knowledge. The essential characteristic of any such referee is that its actions are, and are seen to be, impartial. Liberals thus regard the state as a neutral arbiter among the competing individuals and groups within society.

Constitutionalism

Though liberals are convinced of the need for government, they are also acutely aware of the dangers that government embodies. In their view, all governments are potential tyrannies against the individual. On the one hand, this is based on the fact that government exercises sovereign power and so poses a constant threat to individual liberty. On the other hand, it reflects a distinctively liberal fear of power. As human beings are self-seeking creatures, if they have power – the ability to influence the behaviour of others – they will naturally use it for their own benefit and at the expense of others. Simply put, the liberal position is that egoism plus power equals corruption. This was expressed in Lord Acton's famous warning: 'Power tends to corrupt, and absolute power corrupts absolutely', and in his conclusion: 'Great men are almost always bad men' (1956). Liberals therefore fear arbitrary government and uphold the principle of limited government. Government can be limited, or 'tamed', through the establishment of constitutional constraints and, as discussed in the next section, by democracy.

A constitution is a set of rules that seeks to allocate duties, powers and functions among the various institutions of government. It therefore constitutes the rules that govern the government itself. As such, it both defines the extent of government power and limits its exercise. Support for constitutionalism can take two forms. In the first place, the powers of government bodies and politicians can be limited by the introduction of external and, usually, legal constraints. The most important of these is a so-called written constitution, which codifies the major powers and responsibilities of government institutions within a single document. The first such document was the US Constitution (see p. 38), but during the

DEMOCRACY
Rule by the people; democracy implies both popular participation and government in the public interest, and can take a wide variety of forms (see p. 41).

WRITTEN CONSTITUTION
A single authoritative document that defines the duties, powers and functions of government institutions and so constitutes 'higher' law.

Key concept

Constitutionalism

Constitutionalism, in a narrow sense, is the practice of limited government brought about by the existence of a constitution. Constitutionalism in this sense can be said to exist when government institutions and political processes are effectively constrained by constitutional rules. More broadly, constitutionalism refers to a set of political values and aspirations that reflect the desire to protect liberty through the establishment of internal and external checks on government power. It is typically expressed in support for constitutional provisions that establish this goal; notably, a codified constitution, a bill of rights, separation of powers, bicameralism and federalism (see p. 39) or decentralization. Constitutionalism is thus a species of political liberalism.

nineteenth and twentieth centuries written constitutions were adopted in all liberal democracies, with the exception of the UK, Israel and New Zealand. In many cases, **bills of rights** also exist, which entrench individual rights by providing a legal definition of the relationship between the individual and the state. The earliest example was the 'Declaration of the Rights of Man and the Citizen', which was passed by France's National Constituent Assembly in 1789. Where neither written constitutions nor bills of rights exist, as in the UK, liberals have stressed the importance of statute law in checking government power through the principle of the **rule of law**. This was expressed most clearly in nineteenth-century Germany, in the concept of the *Rechtsstaat*, a state ruled by law.

Second, constitutionalism can be established by the introduction of internal constraints which disperse political power among a number of institutions and create a network of 'checks and balances'. As the French political philosopher Montesquieu (1689–1775) put it, 'power should be a check to power' (Montesquieu [1748] 1969). All liberal political systems exhibit some measure of internal fragmentation. This can be achieved by applying the doctrine of the **separation of powers**, proposed by Montesquieu himself. This seeks to prevent any individual or small group from gaining dictatorial power by controlling the legislative, executive and judicial functions of government. A particular emphasis is placed on the judiciary. As the judiciary interprets the meaning of law, both constitutional and statutory, and therefore reviews the powers of government itself, it must enjoy formal independence and political neutrality if it is to protect the individual from the state. Other devices for fragmenting government power include cabinet government (which checks the power of the prime minister), parliamentary government (which checks the power of the executive), bicameralism (which

BILL OF RIGHTS
A constitutional document that specifies the rights and freedoms of the individual and so defines the relationship between the state and its citizens.

RULE OF LAW
The principle that all conduct and behaviour, of private citizens and government officials, should conform to a framework of law.

SEPARATION OF POWERS
The principle that legislative, executive and judicial power should be separated through the construction of three independent branches of government.

POLITICAL IDEOLOGIES IN ACTION . . .
Making the US Constitution

EVENTS: Between May and September 1787, delegates from 12 of the original 13 states (Rhode Island did not send a delegate) met in Philadelphia to draft the US Constitution. The task confronting what became known as the Constitutional Conference was, some 11 years after rebelling against British colonial rule by issuing the Declaration of Independence, to establish a system of national government that would be more effective than the Articles of Confederation, adopted in 1781. The ratification of the Constitution in 1797 marked the founding of the United States of America.

SIGNIFICANCE: The 'Founding Fathers' were influenced by concerns and sympathies that had an unmistakable liberal character, meaning that the US Constitution became perhaps the classic example of liberal constitutionalism in practice. The opening words of the 'Preamble to the Constitution', 'We the people of the United States of America', reflect the influence of social-contract thinking. Although the Founding Fathers recognized the need for an effective national government, they were acutely aware that this government – like all governments – could become a tyranny against the people. The Constitution was therefore constructed on the basis of an elaborate network of checks and balances, at the heart of which was a separation of powers between the legislature, the executive and the judiciary, which ensured both the independence and interdependence of Congress, the presidency and the Supreme Court. For example, although only Congress could make laws, these laws could be vetoed by the president, but the president's veto could be overturned by a two-thirds vote in both houses of Congress, the House of Representatives and the Senate.

However, the US Constitution may have been shaped as much by practical concerns as by principled ones. In particular, the emphasis on limited government may have had less to do with the desire to protect individual freedom and more to do with the fact that the newly-independent states were desperate not to replace the despotism of the British Crown with the despotism of US national government, or the despotism of an over-powerful president. Similarly, the economic interpretation of the Constitution suggests that its framers may have been significantly affected by their own backgrounds and interests, desiring above all to protect property by placing constraints on government democratic power (Beard, [1913] 1952). In this view, the underlying purpose of the Constitution may have been to prevent a political revolution from developing into a social revolution.

checks the power of each legislative chamber) and territorial divisions such as federalism (see p. 39), devolution and local government (which check the power of central government).

Liberal democracy

Liberal democracy is the dominant political force in the developed world, and increasingly in the developing world. Indeed, the collapse of communism and the advance of 'democratization' (usually understood to imply the introduction of liberal-democratic reforms; that is, electoral democracy and economic liberalization) in Asia, Latin America and Africa, especially since the 1980s, led 'end of history' theorists to proclaim the worldwide triumph of western liberal democracy. However, liberal democracy is a very particular form of democracy. Its 'liberal' features are reflected in a network of internal and external checks on government that are designed to guarantee **civil liberty** and ensure a healthy **civil society**. The 'democratic' character of liberal democracy is based on a system of regular and competitive elections, conforming to the principles of universal suffrage and political equality.

The hybrid nature of liberal democracy reflects a basic ambivalence within liberalism towards democracy. In many ways, this is rooted in the competing implications of individualism, which both embodies a fear of collective power and leads to a belief in political equality. In the nineteenth century, liberals often saw democracy as threatening or dangerous. In this respect, they echoed the ideas of earlier political theorists, such as Plato and Aristotle, who viewed democracy as a system of rule by the masses at the expense of wisdom and property. The central liberal concern has been that democracy can become the enemy of individual liberty. This arises from the fact that 'the people' are not a single entity but rather a collection of individuals and

CIVIL LIBERTY
The private sphere of existence, belonging to the citizen, not to the state; freedom from government.

CIVIL SOCIETY
A realm of autonomous associations and groups, formed by private citizens and enjoying independence from the government; civil society includes businesses, clubs, families and so on.

Key concept
Federalism

Federalism (from the Latin *foedus*, meaning 'pact' or 'covenant') usually refers to legal and political structures that distribute power between two distinct levels of government, neither of which is subordinate to the other. Its central feature is therefore the principle of shared sovereignty. 'Classical' federations are few in number: for example, the USA, Switzerland, Belgium, Canada and Australia. However, many more states have federal–type features. Most federal, or federal–type, states were formed by the coming together of a number of established political communities; they are often geographically large and may have culturally diverse populations. Federalism may nevertheless also have an international dimension, providing the basis, in particular, for regional integration, as in the case of 'European federalism'.

Key concept

Liberal Democracy

A liberal democracy is a political regime in which a 'liberal' commitment to limited government is blended with a 'democratic' belief in popular rule. Its key features are: (1) the right to rule is gained through success in regular and competitive elections based on universal adult suffrage; (2) constraints on government imposed by a constitution, institutional checks and balances, and protections for individual rights; and (3) a vigorous civil society including a private enterprise economy, independent trade unions and a free press. While liberals view liberal democracy as being universally applicable, on the grounds that it allows for the expression of the widest possible range of views and beliefs, critics regard it as the political expression of either western values or capitalist economic structures.

groups, possessing different opinions and opposing interests. The 'democratic solution' to conflict is a recourse to numbers and the application of majority rule: the principle that the will of the majority or the greatest number should prevail over that of the minority. Democracy thus comes down to the rule of the 51 per cent, a prospect that the French politician and social commentator Alexis de Tocqueville (1805–59) famously described as 'the tyranny of the majority'. Individual liberty and minority rights can thus be crushed in the name of the people. James Madison articulated similar views at the Philadelphia Convention in 1787. Madison argued that the best defence against majoritarianism is a network of checks and balances that would make government responsive to competing minorities and safeguard the propertied few from the propertyless masses.

Liberals have expressed particular reservations about democracy, not merely because of the danger of majority rule, but also because of the make-up of the majority in modern, industrial societies. As far as J. S. Mill was concerned, for instance, political wisdom is unequally distributed and is largely related to education. The uneducated are more likely to act according to narrow class interests, whereas the educated are able to use their wisdom and experience for the good of others. He therefore insisted that elected politicians should speak for themselves rather than reflect the views of their electors, and he proposed a system of plural voting that would disenfranchise the illiterate and allocate one, two, three or four votes to people depending on their level of education or social position. Ortega y Gasset (1883–1955), the Spanish social thinker, expressed such fears more dramatically in *The Revolt of the Masses* ([1930] 1972). Gasset warned that the arrival of mass democracy had led to the overthrow of civilized society and the moral order, paving the way for authoritarian rulers to come to power by appealing to the basest instincts of the masses.

> **MAJORITARIANISM**
> A belief in majority rule; majoritarianism implies either that the majority dominates the minority, or that the minority should defer to the judgement of the majority.

PERSPECTIVES ON... DEMOCRACY

LIBERALS understand democracy in individualist terms as consent expressed through the ballot box, democracy being equated with regular and competitive elections. While democracy constrains abuses of power, it must always be conducted within a constitutional framework to prevent majoritarian tyranny.

CONSERVATIVES endorse liberal-democratic rule but with qualifications about the need to protect property and traditional institutions from the untutored will of 'the many'. The New Right, however, has linked electoral democracy to the problems of over-government and economic stagnation.

SOCIALISTS traditionally endorsed a form of radical democracy based on popular participation and the desire to bring economic life under public control, dismissing liberal democracy as simply capitalist democracy. Nevertheless, modern social democrats are now firmly committed to liberal-democratic structures.

ANARCHISTS endorse direct democracy and call for continuous popular participation and radical decentralization. Electoral or representative democracy is merely a façade that attempts to conceal elite domination and reconcile the masses to their oppression.

FASCISTS embrace the ideas of totalitarian democracy, holding that a genuine democracy is an absolute dictatorship, as the leader monopolizes ideological wisdom and is alone able to articulate the 'true' interests of the people. Party and electoral competition are thus corrupt and degenerate.

GREENS have often supported radical or participatory democracy. 'Dark' greens have developed a particular critique of electoral democracy that portrays it as a means of imposing the interests of the present generation of humans on (unenfranchised) later generations, other species and nature as a whole.

By the twentieth century, however, a large proportion of liberals had come to see democracy as a virtue, though this was based on a number of arguments and doctrines. The earliest liberal justification for democracy was founded on **consent**, and the idea that citizens must have a means of protecting themselves from the encroachment of government. In the seventeenth century, John Locke developed a limited theory of *protective* democracy by arguing that voting rights should be extended to the propertied, who could then defend their natural rights against government. If government, through taxation, possesses the power to expropriate property, citizens are entitled to protect themselves by controlling the composition of the tax-making body – the legislature. During the American Revolution, this idea was taken up in the slogan: 'No taxation without

CONSENT
Assent or permission; in politics, usually an agreement to be governed or ruled.

representation'. Utilitarian theorists such as Jeremy Bentham (see p. 52) and James Mill (1773–1836) developed the notion of democracy as a form of protection for the individual into a case for universal suffrage. Utilitarianism (see p. 46) implies that individuals will vote to advance or defend their interests as they define them. Bentham came to believe that universal suffrage (conceived in his day as manhood suffrage) is the only way of promoting 'the greatest happiness for the greatest number'.

A more radical endorsement of democracy is linked to the virtues of political participation. This has been associated with the ideas of J.-J. Rousseau, but received a liberal interpretation in the writings of J. S. Mill. In a sense, Mill encapsulates the ambivalence of the liberal attitude towards democracy. In its unrestrained form, democracy leads to tyranny, but, in the absence of democracy, ignorance and brutality will prevail. For Mill, the central virtue of democracy is that it promotes the 'highest and most harmonious' development of human capacities. By participating in political life, citizens enhance their understanding, strengthen their sensibilities and achieve a higher level of personal development. This form of *developmental* democracy holds democracy to be, primarily, an educational experience. As a result, while he rejected political equality, Mill believed that the franchise should be extended to all but those who are illiterate and, in the process, suggested (radically for his time) that suffrage should also be extended to women.

However, since the mid-twentieth century, liberal theories about democracy have tended to focus less on consent and participation and more on the need for **consensus** in society. This can be seen in the writings of pluralist theorists, who have argued that organized groups, not individuals, have become the primary political actors, and portrayed modern industrial societies as increasingly complex, characterized by competition between and among rival interests. From this point of view, the attraction of democracy is that it is the only system of rule capable of maintaining balance or equilibrium within complex and fluid modern societies. As *equilibrium* democracy gives competing groups a political voice, it binds them to the political system and so maintains political stability.

CONSENSUS
A broad agreement on fundamental principles that allows for disagreement on matters of emphasis or detail.

Classical liberalism

Classical liberalism was the earliest liberal tradition. Classical liberal ideas developed during the transition from feudalism to capitalism, and reached their high point during the early industrialization of the nineteenth century. As a result, classical liberalism has sometimes been called 'nineteenth-century liberalism'. The cradle of classical liberalism was the UK, where the capitalist and industrial revolutions were the most advanced. Its ideas have always been more deeply rooted in Anglo-Saxon countries, particularly the UK and the USA, than in other parts of the world. However, classical liberalism is not merely a nineteenth-century form of liberalism, whose ideas are now only of historical interest. Its principles and theories, in fact, have had growing appeal from the second half of the twentieth century onwards. Though what is called neoclassical liberalism, or neoliberalism (see p. 83), initially had the greatest impact in the UK and the USA, its influence has spread much more broadly, in large part fuelled by the advance of globalization (see p. 20), as discussed in the final section of this chapter.

Classical liberal ideas have taken a variety of forms, but they have a number of common characteristics. Classical liberals:

- subscribe to egoistical individualism. They view human beings as rationally self-interested creatures, with a pronounced capacity for self-reliance. Society is therefore seen as atomistic, composed of a collection of largely self-sufficient individuals, meaning that the characteristics of society can be traced back to the more fundamental features of human nature.
- believe in negative freedom. The individual is free in so far as he or she is left alone, not interfered with or coerced by others. As stated earlier, freedom in this sense is the absence of external constraints on the individual.
- regard the state as, in Thomas Paine's words, a 'necessary evil'. It is necessary in that, at the very least, it lays down the conditions for orderly existence; and it is evil in that it imposes a collective will on society, thereby limiting the freedom and responsibilities of the individual. Classical liberals thus believe in a minimal state, which acts, using Locke's metaphor, as a 'nightwatchman'. In this view, the state's proper role is restricted to the maintenance of domestic order, the enforcement of contracts, and the protection of society against external attack.
- have a broadly positive view of civil society. Civil society is not only deemed to be a 'realm of freedom' – in comparison to the state, which is a 'realm of coercion' – but it is also seen to reflect the principle of balance or equilibrium. This is expressed most clearly in the classical liberal belief in a self-regulating market economy.

Classical liberalism nevertheless draws on a variety of doctrines and theories. The most important of these are:

- natural rights
- utilitarianism
- economic liberalism
- social Darwinism.

NATURAL RIGHTS
God-given rights that are fundamental to human beings and are therefore inalienable (they cannot be taken away).

Natural rights

The **natural rights** theorists of the seventeenth and eighteenth centuries, such as John Locke in England and Thomas Jefferson in America, had a considerable influence on the development of liberal ideology. Modern political debate is littered with references to 'rights' and claims to possess 'rights'. A right, most simply, is an entitlement to act or be treated in a particular way. Such entitlements may be either moral or legal in character. For Locke and Jefferson, rights are 'natural' in that they are invested in human beings by nature or God. Natural rights are now more commonly called human rights. They are, in Jefferson's words, 'inalienable' because human beings are entitled to them by virtue of being human: they cannot, in that sense, be taken away. Natural rights are thus thought to establish the essential conditions for leading a truly human existence. For Locke, there were three such rights: 'life, liberty and property'. Jefferson did not accept that property was a natural or God-given right, but rather one that had developed for human convenience. In the American Declaration of Independence he therefore described inalienable rights as those of 'life, liberty and the pursuit of happiness'.

The idea of natural or human rights has affected liberal thought in a number of ways. For example, the weight given to such rights distinguishes authoritarian thinkers such as Thomas Hobbes from early liberals such as John Locke. As explained earlier, both Hobbes and Locke believed that government was formed through a 'social contract'. However, Hobbes ([1651] 1968) argued that only a strong government, preferably a monarchy, would be able to establish order and security in society. He was prepared to invest the king with sovereign or absolute power, rather than risk a descent into a 'state of nature'. The citizen should therefore accept *any* form of government because even repressive government is better than no government at all. Locke, on the other hand, argued against arbitrary or unlimited government. Government is established in order to protect natural rights. When these are protected by the state, citizens should respect government and obey the law. However, if government violates the rights of its citizens, they in turn have the right of rebellion. Locke thus approved of the English Revolution of the seventeenth century, and applauded the establishment of a constitutional monarchy in 1688.

For Locke, moreover, the contract between state and citizen is a specific and limited one: its purpose is to protect a set of defined natural rights. As a result, Locke believed in limited government. The legitimate role of government is limited to the protection of 'life, liberty and property'. Therefore, the realm of government should not extend beyond its three 'minimal' functions:

- maintaining public order and protecting property
- providing defence against external attack
- ensuring that contracts are enforced.

Other issues and responsibilities are properly the concern of private individuals. Thomas Jefferson expressed a similar sentiment a century later when he declared: 'That government is best which governs least.'

Utilitarianism

Natural rights theories were not the only basis of early liberalism. An alternative and highly influential theory of human nature was put forward in the early nineteenth century by the utilitarians, notably Jeremy Bentham and James Mill. Bentham regarded the idea of rights as 'nonsense' and called natural rights 'nonsense on stilts'. In their place, he proposed what he believed to be the more scientific and objective idea that individuals are motivated by self-interest, and that these interests can be defined as the desire for pleasure, or happiness, and the wish to avoid pain, both calculated in terms of utility. The principle of utility is, furthermore, a moral principle in that it suggests that the 'rightness' of an action, policy or institution can be established by its tendency to promote happiness. Just as each individual can calculate what is morally good by the quantity of pleasure an action will produce, so the principle of 'the greatest happiness for the greatest number' can be used to establish which policies or institutions will benefit society at large.

Utilitarian ideas have had a considerable impact on classical liberalism. In particular, they have provided a moral philosophy that explains how and why individuals act as they do. The utilitarian conception of human beings as rationally self-interested creatures was adopted by later generations of liberal thinkers. Moreover, each individual is thought to be able to perceive his or her own best interests. This cannot be done on their behalf by some paternal authority, such as the state. Bentham argued that individuals act so as to gain pleasure or happiness in whatever way they choose. No one else can judge the quality or degree of their happiness. If each individual is the sole judge of what will give him or her pleasure, then the individual alone can determine what is morally right. On the other hand, utilitarian ideas can also have illiberal implications. Bentham held that the principle of utility could be applied to society at large and not merely to individual human behaviour. Institutions and legislation can be judged by the yardstick of 'the greatest happiness'. However, this formula has majoritarian implications, because it uses the happiness of 'the greatest number' as a standard of what is morally correct, and therefore allows that the interests of the majority outweigh those of the minority or the rights of the individual.

> **UTILITY**
> Use-value; in economics, utility describes the satisfaction that is gained from the consumption of material goods and services.

Economic liberalism

The late eighteenth and early nineteenth centuries witnessed the development of classical economic theory in the work of political economists such as Adam Smith and David Ricardo (1770–1823). Smith's *The Wealth of Nations* ([1776] 1976) was in many respects the first economics textbook. His ideas drew heavily on liberal and rationalist assumptions about human nature and made a powerful contribution to the debate about the desirable role of government within civil society. Smith

Key concept

Utilitarianism

Utilitarianism is a moral philosophy that was developed by Jeremy Bentham and James Mill. It equates 'good' with pleasure or happiness, and 'evil' with pain or unhappiness. Individuals are therefore assumed to act so as to maximize pleasure and minimize pain, these being calculated in terms of utility or use-value, usually seen as satisfaction derived from material consumption. The 'greatest happiness' principle can be used to evaluate laws, institutions and even political systems. *Act* utilitarianism judges an act to be right if it produces at least as much pleasure-over-pain as any other act. *Rule* utilitarianism judges an act to be right if it conforms to a rule which, if generally followed, produces good consequences.

wrote at a time of wide-ranging government restrictions on economic activity. Mercantilism, the dominant economic idea of the sixteenth and seventeenth centuries, had encouraged governments to intervene in economic life in an attempt to encourage the export of goods and restrict imports. Smith's economic writings were designed to attack mercantilism, arguing instead for the principle that the economy works best when it is left alone by government.

Smith thought of the economy as a market, indeed as a series of interrelated markets. He believed that the market operates according to the wishes and decisions of free individuals. Freedom within the market means freedom of choice: the ability of the businesses to choose what goods to make, the ability of workers to choose an employer, and the ability of consumers to choose what goods or services to buy. Relationships within such a market – between employers and employees, and between buyers and sellers – are therefore voluntary and contractual, made by self-interested individuals for whom pleasure is equated with the acquisition and consumption of wealth. Economic theory therefore drew on utilitarianism, in constructing the idea of 'economic man', the notion that human beings are essentially egoistical and bent on material acquisition.

The attraction of classical economics was that, while each individual is materially self-interested, the economy itself is thought to operate according to a set of impersonal pressures – market forces – that tend naturally to promote economic

MERCANTILISM
A school of economic thought that emphasizes the state's role in managing international trade and delivering prosperity.

MARKET
A system of commercial exchange between buyers and sellers, controlled by impersonal economic forces: 'market forces'.

prosperity and well-being. For instance, no single producer can set the price of a commodity – prices are set by the market, by the number of goods offered for sale and the number of consumers who are willing to buy. These are the forces of supply and demand. The market is a self-regulating mechanism; it needs no guidance from outside. The market should be 'free' from government interference because it is managed by what Smith referred to as an 'invisible hand'. This idea of a self-regulating market reflects the liberal belief in a naturally existing harmony among the conflicting interests within society. Smith ([1776] 1976) expressed the economic version of this idea as:

> It is not from the benevolence of the butcher, the brewer or the baker that we expect our dinner, but from their regard to their own interests.

Free-market ideas became economic orthodoxy in the UK and the USA during the nineteenth century. The high point of free-market beliefs was reached with the doctrine of laissez-faire. This suggests that the state should have no economic role, but should simply leave the economy alone and allow businesspeople to act however they please. *Laissez-faire* ideas opposed all forms of factory legislation, including restrictions on the employment of children, limits to the number of hours worked, and any regulation of working conditions. Such economic individualism is usually based on a belief that the unrestrained pursuit of profit will ultimately lead to general benefit. *Laissez-faire* theories remained strong in the UK throughout much of the nineteenth century, and in the USA they were not seriously challenged until the 1930s.

However, since the late twentieth century, faith in the free market has been revived through the rise of neoliberalism. Neoliberalism was counter-revolutionary: it aimed to halt, and if possible reverse, the trend towards 'big' government that had dominated most western countries, especially since 1945. Although it had its greatest initial impact in the two countries in which free-market economic principles had been most firmly established in the nineteenth century, the USA and the UK, from the 1980s onwards neoliberalism exerted a wider influence. At the heart of neoliberalism's assault on the 'dead hand' of government lies a belief in market fundamentalism. In that light, neoliberalism can be seen to go beyond classical economic theory. For instance, while Adam Smith is rightfully viewed as the father of market economics, he also recognized the limitations of the market and certainly did not subscribe to a crude utility-maximizing model of human nature. Thus, although some treat neoliberalism as a form of revived classical liberalism, others see it is a form of economic libertarianism (see p. 78), which perhaps has more in common with the anarchist tradition, and in particular anarcho-capitalism (discussed in Chapter 5), than it does with the liberal tradition. The matter is further complicated by the fact that in the case of both 'Reaganism' in the USA and 'Thatcherism' in the UK, neoliberalism formed part of a larger, New Right ideological project that sought to foster *laissez-faire* economics with an essentially conservative social philosophy. This project is examined in more detail in Chapter 3.

FREE MARKET
The principle or policy of unfettered market competition, free from government interference.

LAISSEZ-FAIRE
Literally, 'leave to do'; the doctrine that economic activity should be entirely free from government interference.

MARKET FUNDAMENTALISM An absolute faith in the market, reflecting the belief that the market mechanism offers solutions to all economic and social problems.

Social Darwinism

One of the distinctive features of classical liberalism is its attitude to poverty and social equality. An individualistic political creed will tend to explain social circumstances in terms of the talents and hard work of each individual human being. Individuals make what they want, and what they can, of their own lives. Those with ability and a willingness to work will prosper, while the incompetent or the lazy will not. This idea was memorably expressed in the title of Samuel Smiles' book *Self-Help* ([1859] 1986) which begins by reiterating the well-tried maxim that 'Heaven helps those who help themselves'. Such ideas of individual responsibility were widely employed by supporters of *laissez-faire* in the nineteenth century. For instance, Richard Cobden (1804–65), the UK economist and politician, advocated an improvement of the conditions of the working classes, but argued that it should come about through 'their own efforts and self-reliance, rather than from law'. He advised them to 'look not to Parliament, look only to yourselves'.

Ideas of individual self-reliance reached their boldest expression in Herbert Spencer's *The Man versus the State* ([1884] 1940). Spencer (1820–1904), the UK philosopher and social theorist, developed a vigorous defence of the doctrine of *laissez-faire*, drawing on ideas that the UK scientist Charles Darwin (1809–82) had developed in *The Origin of Species* ([1859] 1972). Darwin developed a theory of evolution that set out to explain the diversity of species found on Earth. He proposed that each species undergoes a series of random physical and mental changes, or mutations. Some of these changes enable a species to survive and prosper: they are pro-survival. Other mutations are less favourable and make survival more difficult or even impossible. A process of 'natural selection' therefore decides which species are fitted by nature to survive, and which are not. By the end of the nineteenth century, these ideas had extended beyond biology and were increasingly affecting social and political theory.

Spencer, for example, used the theory of natural selection to develop the social principle of 'the survival of the fittest'. People who are best suited by nature to survive, rise to the top, while the less fit fall to the bottom. Inequalities of wealth, social position and political power are therefore natural and inevitable, and no attempt should be made by government to interfere with them. Spencer's US disciple William Sumner (1840–1910) stated this principle boldly in 1884, when he asserted that 'the drunkard in the gutter is just where he ought to be'.

Modern liberalism

Modern liberalism is sometimes described as 'twentieth-century liberalism'. Just as the development of classical liberalism was closely linked to the emergence of industrial capitalism in the nineteenth century, so modern liberal ideas were related to the further development of industrialization. Industrialization had brought about a massive expansion of wealth for some, but was also accompanied by the spread of slums, poverty, ignorance and disease. Moreover, social inequality became more difficult to ignore as a growing industrial working class was seen to be disadvantaged by low pay, unemployment and degrading living and working conditions. These developments had an impact on UK liberalism from the late nineteenth century onwards, but in other countries they did not take effect until much later; for example, US liberalism was not affected until the depression of the 1930s. In these changing historical circumstances, liberals found it progressively more difficult to maintain the belief that the arrival of industrial capitalism had brought with it general prosperity and liberty for all. Consequently, many came to revise the early liberal expectation that the unrestrained pursuit of self-interest produced a socially just society. As the idea of economic individualism came increasingly under attack, liberals rethought their attitude towards the state. The minimal state of classical theory was quite incapable of rectifying the injustices and inequalities of civil society. Modern liberals were therefore prepared to advocate the development of an interventionist or enabling state.

However, modern liberalism has been viewed in two, quite different, ways:

- Classical liberals have argued that modern liberalism effectively broke with the principles and doctrines that had previously defined liberalism, in particular that it had abandoned individualism and embraced collectivism (see p. 99).
- Modern liberals, however, have been at pains to point out that they built on, rather than betrayed, classical liberalism. In this view, whereas classical liberalism is characterized by clear theoretical consistency, modern liberalism represents a marriage between new and old liberalism, and thus embodies ideological and theoretical tensions, notably over the proper role of the state.

The distinctive ideas of modern liberalism include:

- individuality
- positive freedom
- social liberalism
- economic management.

Individuality

John Stuart Mill's ideas have been described as the 'heart of liberalism'. This is because he provided a 'bridge' between classical and modern liberalism: his ideas look both back to the early nineteenth century and forward to the twentieth century and beyond. Mill's interests ranged from political economy to the campaign for female suffrage, but it was the ideas developed in *On Liberty* ([1859] 1972) that show Mill most clearly as a contributor to modern liberal thought. This work contains some of the boldest liberal statements in favour of individual freedom. Mill suggested that, 'Over himself, over his own body and mind, the individual is sovereign', a conception of liberty that is essentially negative as it portrays freedom in terms of the absence of restrictions on an individual's 'self-regarding' actions. Mill believed this to be a necessary condition for liberty, but not in itself a sufficient one. He thought that liberty was a positive and constructive force. It gave individuals the ability to take control of their own lives, to gain autonomy or achieve self-realization.

Mill was influenced strongly by European romanticism and found the notion of human beings as utility maximizers both shallow and unconvincing. He believed passionately in **individuality**. The value of liberty is that it enables individuals to develop, to gain talents, skills and knowledge and to refine their sensibilities. Mill disagreed with Bentham's utilitarianism in so far as Bentham believed that actions could only be distinguished by the quantity of pleasure or pain they generated. For Mill, there were 'higher' and 'lower' pleasures. Mill was concerned to promote those pleasures that develop an individual's intellectual, moral or aesthetic sensibilities. He was clearly not concerned with simple pleasure-seeking, but with personal self-development, declaring that he would rather be 'Socrates dissatisfied than a fool satisfied'. As such, he laid the foundations for a developmental model of individualism that placed emphasis on human flourishing rather than the crude satisfaction of interests.

> **INDIVIDUALITY**
> Self-fulfilment achieved through the realization of an individual's distinctive or unique identity or qualities; what distinguishes one person from all others.

Positive freedom

The clearest break with early liberal thought came in the late nineteenth century with the work of T. H. Green (see p. 53), whose writing influenced a generation of so-called 'new liberals' such as L. T. Hobhouse (1864–1929) and J. A. Hobson (1854–1940). Green believed that the unrestrained pursuit of profit, as advocated by classical liberalism, had given rise to new forms of poverty and injustice. The economic liberty of the few had blighted the life chances of the many. Following J. S. Mill, he rejected the early liberal conception of human beings as essentially self-seeking utility maximizers, and suggested a more optimistic view of human nature. Individuals, according to Green, have sympathy for one another; their egoism is therefore constrained by some degree of **altruism**. The individual possesses social responsibilities and not merely individual responsibilities, and is therefore linked to other individuals by ties of caring and empathy. Such a conception of human nature was clearly influenced by socialist ideas that emphasized the sociable and cooperative nature of humankind. As a result, Green's ideas have been described as 'socialist liberalism'.

Green also challenged the classical liberal notion of freedom. Negative freedom merely removes external

> **ALTRUISM**
> Concern for the interests and welfare of others, based either on enlightened self-interest or a belief in a common humanity.

constraints on the individual, giving the individual freedom of choice. In the case of the businesses that wish to maximize profits, negative freedom justifies their ability to hire the cheapest labour possible; for example, to employ children rather than adults, or women rather than men. Economic freedom can therefore lead to exploitation, even becoming the 'freedom to starve'. Freedom of choice in the marketplace is therefore an inadequate conception of individual freedom.

In the place of a simple belief in negative freedom, Green proposed that freedom should also be understood in positive terms. In this light, freedom is the ability of the individual to develop and attain individuality; it involves people's ability to realize their individual potential, attain skills and knowledge, and achieve fulfilment. Thus, whereas negative freedom acknowledges only legal and physical constraints on liberty, positive freedom recognizes that liberty may also be threatened by social disadvantage and inequality. This, in turn, implied a revised view of the state. By protecting individuals from the social evils that cripple their lives, the state can expand freedom, and not merely diminish it. In place of the minimal state of old, modern liberals therefore endorsed an enabling state, exercising an increasingly wide range of social and economic responsibilities.

While such ideas undoubtedly involved a revision of classical liberal theories, they did not amount to the abandonment of core liberal beliefs. Modern liberalism drew closer to socialism, but it did not place society before the individual. For T. H. Green, for example, freedom ultimately consisted in individuals acting morally. The state could not force people to be good; it could only provide the conditions in which they were able to make more responsible moral decisions. The balance between the state and the individual had altered, but the underlying commitment to the needs and interests of the individual remained. Modern liberals share the classical liberal preference for self-reliant individuals who take responsibility for their own lives; the essential difference is the recognition that this can only occur if social conditions allow it to happen. The central thrust of modern liberalism is therefore the desire to help individuals to help themselves.

Social liberalism

The twentieth century witnessed the growth of state intervention in most western states and in many developing ones. Much of this intervention took the form of social welfare: attempts by government to provide welfare support for its citizens by overcoming poverty, disease and ignorance. If the minimal state was typical of the nineteenth century, during the twentieth century modern states became **welfare states**. This occurred as a consequence of a variety of historical and ideological factors. Governments, for example, sought to achieve national efficiency, healthier work forces and stronger armies. They also came under electoral pressure for social reform from newly enfranchised

WELFARE STATE
A state that takes primary responsibility for the social welfare of its citizens, discharged through a range of social-security, health, education and other services.

KEY FIGURES IN... LIBERALISM

John Locke (1632–1704) An English philosopher and politician, Locke was a consistent opponent of absolutism and is often portrayed as the philosopher of the 1688 'Glorious Revolution' (which established a constitutional monarchy in England). Using social contract theory and accepting that, by nature, humans are free and equal, Locke upheld constitutionalism, limited government and the right of revolution, but the stress he placed on property rights prevented him from endorsing political equality or democracy in the modern sense. Locke's foremost political work is *Two Treatises of Government* (1690).

Adam Smith (1723–90) A Scottish economist and philosopher, Smith is usually seen as the founder of the 'dismal science'. In *The Theory of Moral Sentiments* (1759), he developed a theory of motivation that tried to reconcile human self-interestedness with unregulated social order. Smith's most famous work, *The Wealth of Nations* (1776), was the first systematic attempt to explain the workings of the economy in market terms. Although he is sometimes portrayed as a free-market theorist, Smith was nevertheless aware of the limitations of *laissez-faire*.

Immanuel Kant (1724–1804) A German philosopher, Kant's 'critical' philosophy holds that knowledge is not merely an aggregate of sense impressions; it depends on the conceptual apparatus of human understanding. Kant's political thought was shaped by the central importance of morality. He believed that the law of reason dictates categorical imperatives, the most important of which is the obligation to treat others as 'ends', and never only as 'means'. Kant's most important works include *Critique of Pure Reason* (1781) and *Metaphysics of Morals* (1785).

Thomas Jefferson (1743–1826) A US political philosopher and statesman, Jefferson was the principal author of the Declaration of Independence (1776) and later served as the third president of the USA (1801–09). Jefferson advocated a democratic form of agrarianism that sought to blend a belief in rule by a natural aristocracy with a commitment to limited government and *laissez-faire*, though he also exhibited sympathy for social reform. In the USA, 'Jeffersonianism' stands for resistance to strong central government and a stress on individual freedom and responsibility, and states' rights.

Jeremy Bentham (1748–1832) A British philosopher, legal reformer and founder of utilitarianism, Bentham developed a moral and philosophical system based on the belief that human beings are rationally self-interested creatures, or utility maximizers. Using the principle of general utility – 'the greatest happiness for the greatest number' – he advanced a justification for *laissez-faire* economics, constitutional reform and, in later life, political democracy. Bentham's key works include *A Fragment on Government* (1776) and *An Introduction to the Principles of Morals and Legislation* (1789).

James Madison (1751–1836) A US statesman and political theorist, Madison played a major role in writing the US Constitution and served as the fourth president of the USA (1809–17). Madison was a leading proponent of pluralism and divided government, urging the adoption of federalism, bicameralism and the separation of powers as the basis of US government. Madisonianism thus implies a strong emphasis on checks and balances as the principal means of resisting tyranny. His best-known political writings are his contributions to *The Federalist* (1787–8).

John Stuart Mill (1806–73) A British philosopher, economist and politician, Mill's varied and complex work straddles the divide between classical and modern forms of liberalism. His opposition to collectivist tendencies and traditions was firmly rooted in nineteenth-century principles, but his emphasis on the quality of individual life, reflected in a commitment to individuality, as well as his sympathy for causes such as female suffrage and workers' cooperatives, looked forward to later developments. Mill's major writings include *On Liberty* (1859), *Utilitarianism* (1861) and *Considerations on Representative Government* (1861).

T. H. (Thomas Hill) Green (1836–82) A British philosopher and social theorist, Green highlighted the limitations of early liberal doctrines and in particular *laissez-faire*. Influenced by Aristotle and Hegel, Green argued that humans are by nature social creatures, a position that helped liberalism to reach an accommodation with welfarism and social justice. His idea of 'positive' freedom had a major influence on the emergence of so-called 'new liberalism' in the UK. His chief works include *Lectures on the Principles of Political Obligation* (1879–80) and *Prolegomena to Ethics* (1883).

John Rawls (1921–2002) A US political philosopher, Rawls used a form of social contract theory to reconcile liberal individualism with the principles of redistribution and social justice. In his major work, *A Theory of Justice* (1970), he developed the notion of 'justice as fairness', based on the belief that behind a 'veil of ignorance' most people would accept that the liberty of each should be compatible with a like liberty for all, and that social inequality is only justified if it works to the benefit of the poorest in society.

See also **Isaiah Berlin** (p. 292) and **Robert Nozick** (p. 85).

industrial workers and, in some cases, the peasantry. However, the political argument for welfarism has never been the prerogative of any single ideology. It has
been put, in different ways, by socialists, liberals, conservatives, feminists and
even at times by fascists. Within liberalism, the case for social welfare has been
made by modern liberals, in marked contrast to classical liberals, who extol the
virtues of self-help and individual responsibility.

Modern liberals defend welfarism on the basis of equality of opportunity. If
particular individuals or groups are disadvantaged by their social circumstances,
then the state possesses a social responsibility to reduce or remove these disadvantages to create equal, or at least more equal, life chances. Citizens have thus
acquired a range of welfare or social rights, such as the right to work, the right
to education and the right to decent housing. Welfare rights are positive rights
because they can only be satisfied by the positive actions of government, through
the provision of state pensions, benefits and, perhaps, publicly funded health and
education services. During the twentieth century, liberal parties and liberal governments were therefore converted to the cause of social welfare. For example, the
expanded welfare state in the UK was based on the Beveridge Report (1942), which
set out to attack the so-called 'five giants' – want, disease, ignorance, squalor and
idleness. It memorably promised to protect citizens 'from the cradle to the grave'.
In the USA, liberal welfarism developed in the 1930s during the administration of
F. D. Roosevelt, but reached its height in the 1960s with the 'New Frontier' policies
of John F. Kennedy, and Lyndon Johnson's 'Great Society' programme.

Social liberalism was further developed in the second half of the twentieth century with the emergence of so-called social-democratic liberalism, especially in the
writings of John Rawls (see p. 53). Social-democratic liberalism is distinguished by its
support for relative social equality, usually seen as the defining value of socialism. In
A Theory of Justice (1970), Rawls developed a defence of redistribution and welfare
based on the idea of 'equality as fairness'. He argued that, if people were unaware of their
social position and circumstances, they would view an egalitarian society as 'fairer'
than an inegalitarian one, on the grounds that the desire to avoid poverty is greater
than the attraction of riches. He therefore proposed the 'difference principle': that
social and economic inequalities should be arranged so as to benefit the least well-
off, recognizing the need for some measure of inequality to provide an incentive to
work. Nevertheless, such a theory of justice remains liberal rather than socialist, as
it is rooted in assumptions about egoism and self-interest, rather than a belief in
social solidarity.

Economic management

In addition to providing social welfare, twentieth-century western governments
also sought to deliver prosperity by 'managing' their economies. This once again
involved rejecting classical liberal thinking, in particular its belief in a self-regulating
free market and the doctrine *of laissez-faire*. The abandonment of *laissez-faire* came
about because of the increasing complexity of industrial capitalist economies and

Key concept
Keynesianism

Keynesianism refers, narrowly, to the economic theories of J. M. Keynes (1883–1946) and, more broadly, to a range of economic policies that have been influenced by these theories. Keynesianism provides an alternative to neoclassical economics and, in particular, advances a critique of the 'economic anarchy' of *laissez-faire* capitalism. Keynes argued that growth and employment levels are largely determined by the level of 'aggregate demand' in the economy, and that government can regulate demand, primarily through adjustments to fiscal policy, so as to deliver full employment. Keynesianism came to be associated with a narrow obsession with 'tax and spend' policies, but this ignores the complexity and sophistication of Keynes' economic writings. Influenced by economic globalization, a form of *neo-Keynesianism* has emerged that rejects 'top-down' economic management but still acknowledges that markets are hampered by uncertainty, inequality and differential levels of knowledge.

their apparent inability to guarantee general prosperity if left to their own devices. The Great Depression of the 1930s, sparked off by the Wall Street Crash of 1929, led to high levels of unemployment throughout the industrialized world and in much of the developing world. This was the most dramatic demonstration of the failure of the free market. After World War II, virtually all western states adopted policies of economic intervention in an attempt to prevent a return to the pre-war levels of unemployment. To a large extent these interventionist policies were guided by the work of the UK economist John Maynard Keynes (1883–1946).

In *The General Theory of Employment, Interest and Money* ([1936] 1963), Keynes challenged classical economic thinking and rejected its belief in a self-regulating market. Classical economists had argued that there was a 'market solution' to the problem of unemployment and, indeed, all other economic problems. Keynes argued, however, that the level of economic activity, and therefore of employment, is determined by the total amount of demand – aggregate demand – in the economy. He suggested that governments could 'manage' their economies by influencing the level of aggregate demand. Government spending is, in this sense, an 'injection' of demand into the economy. Taxation, on the other hand, is a 'withdrawal' from the economy: it reduces aggregate demand and dampens down economic activity. At times of high unemployment, Keynes recommended that governments should 'reflate' their economies by either increasing public spending or cutting taxes. Unemployment could therefore be solved, not by the invisible hand of capitalism, but by government intervention, in this case by running a budget deficit, meaning that the government literally 'overspends'.

Keynesian demand management thus promised to give governments the ability to manipulate employment and growth levels, and hence to secure general prosperity. As with the provision of social welfare, modern liberals have seen economic management as being constructive in promoting prosperity and harmony in civil society. Keynes was not opposed to capitalism; indeed, in many ways, he was its saviour. He simply argued that unrestrained private enterprise is unworkable within complex industrial societies. The first, if limited, attempt to apply Keynes' ideas was undertaken in the USA during Roosevelt's 'New Deal'. By the end of World War II, Keynesianism was widely established as an economic orthodoxy in the West, displacing the older belief in *laissez-faire*. Keynesian policies were credited with being the key to the 'long boom', the historically unprecedented economic growth of the 1950s and 1960s, which witnessed the achievement of widespread affluence, at least in western countries. However, the re-emergence of economic difficulties in the 1970s generated renewed sympathy for the theories of classical political economy, and led to a shift away from Keynesian priorities. Nevertheless, the failure of the free-market revolution of the 1980s and 1990s to ensure sustained economic growth resulted in the emergence of the 'new' political economy, or neo-Keynesianism. Although this recognized the limitations of the 'crude' Keynesianism of the 1950s–1970s period, it nevertheless marked a renewed awareness of the link between unregulated capitalism and low investment, short-termism and social fragmentation.

Liberalism in a global age

How has liberalism been affected by the forces of globalization? Has western liberalism been transformed into global liberalism? So-called 'accelerated' globalization from the 1980s onwards, together with associated developments, can be seen to have supported the worldwide ascendancy of liberalism in a number of ways. However, 'hegemonic liberalism' wears not one face but many, reflecting not only the multifarious nature of liberalism but also, at times, its internal tensions. The first 'face' of global liberalism is neoliberalism, which is so closely linked to economic globalization that many commentators treat neoliberalism and globalization as if they are part of the same phenomenon: 'neoliberal globalization'. The link occurs for a variety of reasons. In particular, intensified international competition encourages governments to deregulate their economies and reduce tax levels in the hope of attracting inward investment and preventing **transnational corporations** (TNCs) from relocating elsewhere. Strong downward pressure is also exerted on public spending, and especially on welfare budgets, by the fact that, in the context of heightened global competition, the control of inflation has displaced the maintenance of full employment as the principal goal of economic policy. Such pressures, together with the revived growth and productivity rates of the US economy during the 1990s and the relatively sluggish performance of other models of national capitalism, in Japan and Germany in particular, meant that neoliberalism appeared to stand unchallenged as the dominant ideology of the 'new' world economy. Only a few states, such as China, were able to deal with neoliberal globalization on their own terms, limiting their exposure to competition by, for example, holding down their exchange rate.

TRANSNATIONAL CORPORATION
A company that controls economic activity in two or more countries, developing corporate strategies and processes that transcend national borders.

One of the commonly alleged implications of neoliberal globalization has been a tendency towards peace

TENSIONS WITHIN... LIBERALISM

Classical liberalism	VS	Modern liberalism
economic liberalism	⟷	social liberalism
egoistical individualism	⟷	developmental individualism
maximize utility	⟷	personal growth
negative freedom	⟷	positive freedom
minimal state	⟷	enabling state
free-market economy	⟷	managed economy
rights-based justice	⟷	justice as fairness
strict meritocracy	⟷	concern for the poor
individual responsibility	⟷	social responsibility
safety-net welfare	⟷	cradle-to-grave welfare

and international law and order, brought about by growing economic interdependence. Such thinking can be traced back to the birth of **commercial liberalism** in the nineteenth century, based on the classical economics of David Ricardo and the ideas of the so-called 'Manchester liberals', Richard Cobden (1804–65) and John Bright (1811–89). The key theme within commercial liberalism is a belief in the virtues of **free trade**. Free trade has economic benefits, as it allows each country to specialize in the production of goods and services that it is best suited to produce, the ones in which they have 'comparative advantage'. However, free trade is no less important in drawing states into a web of interdependence which means that the material costs of international conflict are so great that warfare becomes virtually unthinkable. Cobden and Bright argued that free trade would draw people of different races, creeds and languages together into what Cobden described as 'the bonds of eternal peace'. Evidence to support such thinking can be found in the decline in the post-World War II period of traditional inter-state wars, modern wars being much more frequently civil wars fought either between non-state actors (armies of insurgents, terrorist groups, ethnic or religious movements and the like) or between states and non-state actors.

COMMERCIAL LIBERALISM
A form of liberalism that emphasizes the economic and international benefits of free trade, leading to mutual benefit and general prosperity, as well as peace among states.

FREE TRADE
A system of trade between states not restricted by tariffs or other forms of protectionism.

The second 'face' of global liberalism is liberal democracy, which has now developed beyond its western heartland and become a worldwide force. In

Key concept
Human rights

Human rights are rights to which people are entitled by virtue of being human; they are a modern and secular version of 'natural' rights. Human rights are *universal* (in the sense that they belong to human beings everywhere, regardless of race, religion, gender and other differences), *fundamental* (in that a human being's entitlement to them cannot be removed), *indivisible* (in that civic and political rights, and economic, social and cultural rights are interrelated and co-equal in importance) and *absolute* (in that, as the basic grounds for living a genuinely human life, they cannot be qualified). 'International' human rights are set out in a collection of UN and other treaties and conventions.

many ways, the high point of liberal optimism came in the aftermath of the collapse of communism, when 'end of history' theorists, such as Francis Fukuyama (see p. 329), proclaimed that western liberal democracy had established itself as the final form of human government. This was demonstrated, moreover, by the process of 'democratization' that was under way in Africa, Asia and Latin America, which involved the spread of competitive party systems and a growing enthusiasm for market reforms. By 2000, about two-thirds of the states in the world had political systems that exhibited significant liberal-democratic features, with democratic movements seemingly springing up in more and more parts of the world. For liberals, this provided further optimism about the prospects for international peace. In a tradition of **republican liberalism** that can be traced back to Woodrow Wilson (see p. 184), if not to Kant, liberals have argued that autocratic or authoritarian states are inherently militaristic and aggressive, while democratic states are naturally peaceful, especially in their dealings with other democratic states. In this view, not only do democratic pressures restrain a state's tendency towards conflict and war (because it is the public themselves who will be doing the killing and dying), but cultural bonds also develop among democratic states that incline them to find non-violent ways of resolving disputes or disagreements. Liberal optimism about advancing peace has nevertheless been dented since the early 2000s by indications of the reversal of democratization, not least associated with the failure of the Arab Spring.

The third 'face' of global liberalism arises from the fact that the advance of globalization has had an important ethical dimension. This reflects the fact that widening global interconnectedness, especially as facilitated by the 'new' media and the information and communications revolution, has strengthened that idea

REPUBLICAN LIBERALISM
A form of liberalism that highlights the benefits of republican government and, in particular, emphasizes the link between democracy and peace.

that justice now extends 'beyond borders'. As people know more about events that occur and circumstances that exist in other parts of the world, it becomes more difficult to confine their moral sensibilities merely to members of their own state; potentially, these extend to the whole of humanity. Such 'cosmopolitan' (see p. 191) thinking, often linked to the idea of global

Key concept

Postmodernism

Postmodernism is a controversial and confusing term that was first used to describe experimental movements in western arts, architecture and cultural development in general. As a tool of social and political analysis, postmodernism highlights the shift away from societies structured by industrialization and class solidarity to increasingly fragmented and pluralistic 'information societies', in which individuals are transformed from producers to consumers, and individualism replaces class, and religious and ethnic loyalties. Postmodernists argue that there is no such thing as certainty; the idea of absolute and universal truth must be discarded as an arrogant pretence. Emphasis is placed instead on discourse, debate and democracy.

justice, has typically drawn on liberal principles and assumptions, the most important being the doctrine of human rights. This is the idea that certain rights and freedoms are so fundamental to human existence that all people, regardless of nationality, race, religion, gender and so on, should be entitled to them. Indeed, it is sometimes argued that the norm of state sovereignty in world affairs has been replaced by the rival norm of human rights. Although this process began in 1948 with adoption of the UN Universal Declaration of Human Rights, it was boosted significantly by the end of the Cold War, which led some to argue that the doctrine of human rights had transcended rivalry between capitalism and communism. Evidence of this came in the 1990s with the rise of **humanitarian intervention** in northern Iraq, Haiti, Kosovo and elsewhere. Human rights and humanitarianism generally have also had an impact on strategies for promoting development and tackling global poverty. For example, Amartya Sen's (1999) highly influential notion of 'development as freedom' draws explicitly on modern liberal thinking about positive freedom and empowerment, and is expressed in the emphasis that the UN and other bodies place on measuring social progress in terms of '**human development**'.

HUMANITARIAN INTERVENTION
Military intervention in the affairs of another state that is carried out in pursuit of humanitarian rather than strategic objectives.

HUMAN DEVELOPMENT
A standard of human well-being that reflects people's ability to lead fulfilled and creative lives, taking into account factors such as life expectancy, education, ecological sustainability and gender equality.

However, liberal triumphalism needs to be tempered by the recognition of new challenges and threats to liberalism. One of these comes from the nature of capitalism and the implications of a global capitalist system. While the socialist challenge appears to have been defeated, is this defeat, or the defeat of other forms of anti-capitalism (see p. 161), permanent? The tendency within capitalism towards inequality, an inevitable feature of private enterprise and market economics, suggests that oppositional forces to liberal capitalism might always arise. A second challenge to liberalism comes from a recognition of the growing importance of difference or diversity. The earliest such attack on liberalism was launched by communitarian thinkers, who rejected individualism as facile, on the grounds that it suggests that the self is 'unencumbered'. Such a view has also been taken up by multiculturalists, who advance a collective notion of identity based on culture, ethnicity, language or religion. At best, such ideas may only be accommodated within a 'post-liberal' framework (Gray, 1995b), and many believe that liberalism and multiculturalism are opposing forces (discussed in Chapter 11). A further attack on liberalism has been mounted by postmodern thinkers, who have proclaimed the effective collapse of the Enlightenment project, on which liberalism and other rationalist ideologies are based.

Challenges to liberalism also come from beyond its western homeland. There is as much evidence that the end of the Cold War has unleashed non-liberal, even anti-liberal, political forces, as there is evidence of the 'triumph' of liberal democracy. In eastern Europe and parts of the developing world, resurgent nationalism, whose popular appeal is based on strength, certainty and security, has often proved more potent than equivocal liberalism. Moreover, this nationalism is associated more commonly with ethnic purity and authoritarianism than with liberal ideals such as self-determination and civic pride. Various forms of fundamentalism (see p. 305), quite at odds with liberal culture, have also arisen in the Middle East and parts of Africa and Asia (as discussed in Chapter 10). Furthermore, where successful market economies have been established they have not always been founded on the basis of liberal values and institutions. For instance, the political regimes of East Asia may owe more to Confucianism's ability to maintain social stability than to the influence of liberal ideas such as competition and self-striving. Far from moving towards a unified, liberal world, political development in the twenty-first century may thus be characterized by growing ideological diversity. Islamism, Confucianism and even authoritarian nationalism may yet prove to be enduring rivals to western liberalism.

(?) QUESTIONS FOR DISCUSSION

- In what sense is liberalism linked to the Enlightenment project?
- Why do liberals reject unlimited freedom?
- How convincing is the liberal notion that human beings are reason-guided creatures?
- Which forms of equality do liberals support, and which do they reject?
- Why do liberals believe that power tends to corrupt, and how do they think it can be 'tamed'?
- Is liberal democracy a contradiction in terms?
- How do classical liberals defend unregulated capitalism?
- How far are modern liberals willing to go in endorsing social and economic intervention?
- Do modern liberals have a coherent view of the state?
- Is liberal democracy the final solution to the problem of political organization?
- To what extent is cosmopolitanism based on liberal assumptions?
- Are liberal principles universally valid?

(📖) FURTHER READING

Bellamy, R., *Liberalism and Modern Society: An Historical Argument* (1992). An analysis of the development of liberalism that focuses on the adaptations necessary to apply liberal values to new social realities.

Fawcett, E., *Liberalism: The Life of an Idea* (2015). A fluent and stimulating history of liberal thinking from the early nineteenth century to the present day.

Gray, J., *Liberalism*, 2nd edn (1995). A short and not uncritical introduction to liberalism as the political theory of modernity; contains a discussion of postliberalism.

Kelly, P., *Liberalism* (2005). An engagingly written defence of liberalism as a normative political theory, which particularly examines its link to equality.

Conservatism

Preview

In everyday language, the term 'conservative' has a variety of meanings. It can refer to moderate or cautious behaviour, a lifestyle that is conventional, even conformist, or a fear of or refusal to change, particularly denoted by the verb 'to conserve'. 'Conservatism' was first used in the early nineteenth century to describe a distinctive political position or ideology. In the USA, it implied a pessimistic view of public affairs. By the 1820s, the term was being used to denote opposition to the principles and spirit of the 1789 French Revolution. In the UK, 'Conservative' gradually replaced 'Tory' as a title of the principal opposition party to the Whigs, becoming the party's official name in 1835.

As a political ideology, conservatism is defined by the desire to conserve, reflected in a resistance to, or at least a suspicion of, change. However, while the desire to resist change may be the recurrent theme within conservatism, what distinguishes conservatism from rival political creeds is the distinctive way in which this position is upheld, in particular through support for tradition, a belief in human imperfection, and the attempt to uphold the organic structure of society. Conservatism nevertheless encompasses a range of tendencies and inclinations. The chief distinction within conservatism is between what is called traditional conservatism and the New Right. Traditional conservatism defends established institutions and values on the ground that they safeguard the fragile 'fabric of society', giving security-seeking human beings a sense of stability and rootedness. The New Right is characterized by a belief in a strong but minimal state, combining economic libertarianism with social authoritarianism, as represented by neoliberalism and neoconservatism.

Origins and development

Conservative ideas arose in reaction to the growing pace of political, social and economic change, which, in many ways, was symbolized by the French Revolution. One of the earliest, and perhaps the classic, statement of conservative principles is contained in Edmund Burke's (see p. 84) *Reflections on the Revolution in France* ([1790] 1968), which deeply regretted the revolutionary challenge to the *ancien régime* that had occurred the previous year. During the nineteenth century, western states were transformed by the pressures unleashed by industrialization and reflected in the growth of liberalism, socialism and nationalism. While these ideologies preached reform, and at times supported revolution, conservatism stood in defence of an increasingly embattled traditional social order.

Conservative thought varied considerably as it adapted itself to existing traditions and national cultures. UK conservatism, for instance, has drawn heavily on the ideas of Burke, who advocated not blind resistance to change, but rather a prudent willingness to 'change in order to conserve'. In the nineteenth century, UK conservatives defended a political and social order that had already undergone profound change, in particular the overthrow of the absolute monarchy, as a result of the English Revolution of the seventeenth century. Such pragmatic principles have also influenced the conservative parties established in other Commonwealth countries. The Canadian Conservative Party adopted the title Progressive Conservative precisely to distance itself from reactionary ideas. In continental Europe, where some autocratic monarchies persisted throughout much of the nineteenth century, a very different and more authoritarian form of conservatism developed, which defended monarchy and rigid autocratic values against the rising tide of reform. Only with the formation of Christian democratic parties after World War II did continental conservatives, notably in Germany and Italy, fully accept political democracy and social reform. The USA, on the other hand, has been influenced relatively little by conservative ideas. The US system of government and its political culture reflect deeply established liberal and progressive values, and politicians of both major parties – the Republicans and the Democrats – have traditionally resented being labelled 'conservative'. It is only since the 1960s that overtly conservative views have been expressed by elements within both parties, notably by southern Democrats and the wing of the Republican Party that was associated in the 1960s with Barry Goldwater, and which supported Ronald Reagan in the 1980s and later George W. Bush.

As conservative ideology arose in reaction to the French Revolution and the process of modernization in the West, it is less easy to identify political conservatism outside Europe and North America. In Africa, Asia and Latin America, political movements have developed that sought to resist change and preserve traditional ways of life, but they have seldom employed specifically conservative arguments and values. An exception to this is perhaps the Japanese Liberal Democratic Party (LDP), which has dominated politics in Japan since 1955. The LDP has close links with business interests and is committed to promoting a healthy private sector. At the same time, it has attempted to preserve traditional Japanese values and customs, and has therefore supported distinctively conservative principles such as loyalty, duty and **hierarchy**. In other countries, conservatism has exhibited a populist-authoritarian character. Perón in Argentina and Khomeini (see p. 317) in Iran, for instance, both established regimes based on strong central authority, but also mobilized mass popular support on issues such as nationalism, economic progress and the defence of traditional values.

While conservatism is the most intellectually modest of political ideologies, it has also been remarkably resilient, perhaps because of this fact. In many ways, conservatism has prospered because it has been unwilling to be tied down to a fixed system of ideas. Nevertheless, it has undergone major changes since the 1970s, shaped by growing concerns about the welfare state and economic management. Particularly prominent in this respect were the Thatcher governments in the UK (1979–90) and the Reagan administration in the USA (1981–9), both of which practised an unusually radical and ideological brand of conservatism, commonly termed the **New Right**. New Right ideas have drawn heavily on free-market economics and, in so doing, have exposed deep divisions within conservatism. Indeed, commentators argue that 'Thatcherism' and 'Reaganism', and the New Right project in general, do not properly belong within conservative ideology at all, so deeply are they influenced by classical liberal economics. The New Right has challenged traditional conservative economic views, but it nevertheless remains part of conservative ideology. In the first place, it has not abandoned traditional conservative social principles such as a belief in order, authority and discipline,

HIERARCHY
A pyramidically ranked system of command and obedience, in which social position is unconnected with individual ability.

NEW RIGHT
An ideological trend within conservatism that embraces a blend of neoliberalism (see p. 83) and neoconservatism (see p. 88).

and in some respects it has strengthened them. Furthermore, the New Right's enthusiasm for the free market has exposed the extent to which conservatism had already been influenced by liberal ideas. From the late nineteenth century onwards, conservatism has been divided between paternalistic support for state intervention and a libertarian commitment to the free market. The significance of the New Right is that it sought to revive the electoral fortunes of conservatism by readjusting the balance between these traditions in favour of libertarianism (see p. 78).

Core themes: the desire to conserve

The character of conservative ideology has been the source of particular argument and debate. For example, it is often suggested that conservatives have a clearer understanding of what they oppose than of what they favour. In that sense, conservatism has been portrayed as a negative philosophy, its purpose being simply to preach resistance to, or at least suspicion of, change. However, if conservatism were to consist of no more than a knee-jerk defence of the *status quo*, it would be merely a political attitude rather than an ideology. In fact, many people or groups can be considered 'conservative', in the sense that they resist change, without in any way subscribing to a conservative political creed. For instance, socialists who campaign in defence of the welfare state or nationalized industries could be classified as conservative in terms of their actions, but certainly not in terms of their political principles. The desire to resist change may be the recurrent theme within conservatism, but what distinguishes conservatives from supporters of rival political creeds is the distinctive way they uphold this position.

A second problem is that to describe conservatism as an ideology is to risk irritating conservatives themselves. They have often preferred to describe their beliefs as an 'attitude of mind' or 'common sense', as opposed to an 'ism' or ideology. Others have argued that what is distinctive about conservatism is its emphasis on history and experience, and its distaste for rational thought. Conservatives have thus typically eschewed the 'politics of principle' and adopted instead a traditionalist political stance (see p. 9, for a discussion of the conservative view of ideology). Their opponents have also lighted upon this feature of conservatism, sometimes portraying it as little more than an unprincipled apology for the interests of a ruling class or elite. However, both conservatives and their critics ignore the weight and range of theories that underpin conservative 'common sense'. Conservatism is neither simple pragmatism (see p. 9) nor mere opportunism. It is founded on a particular set of political beliefs about human beings, the societies they live in, and the importance of a distinctive set of political values. As such, like liberalism and socialism, it should rightfully be described as an ideology. The most significant of its central beliefs are:

- tradition
- human imperfection
- society
- hierarchy and authority
- property.

Tradition

Conservatives have argued against change on a number of grounds. A central and recurrent theme of conservatism is its defence of **tradition**. For some conservatives, this emphasis on tradition reflects their religious faith. If the world is thought to have been fashioned by God the Creator, traditional customs and practices in society will be regarded as 'God given'. Burke thus believed that society was shaped by 'the law of our Creator', or what he also called 'natural law'. If human beings tamper with the world, they are challenging the will of God, and as a result they are likely to make human affairs worse

TRADITION
Values, practices or institutions that have endured through time and, in particular, been passed down from one generation to the next.

rather than better. Since the eighteenth century, however, it has become increasingly difficult to maintain that tradition reflects the will of God. As the pace of historical change accelerated, old traditions were replaced by new ones, and these new ones – for example, free elections and universal suffrage – were clearly seen to be man-made rather than in any sense 'God given'. Nevertheless, the religious objection to change has been kept alive by modern fundamentalists, particularly those who believe that God's wishes have been revealed to humankind through the literal truth of religious texts. Such ideas are discussed in Chapter 11.

Most conservatives, however, support tradition without needing to argue that it has divine origins. Burke, for example, described society as a partnership between 'those who are living, those who are dead and those who are to be born'. G. K. Chesterton (1874–1936), the UK novelist and essayist, expressed this idea as follows:

> Tradition means giving votes to the most obscure of all classes: our ancestors. It is a democracy of the dead. Tradition refuses to submit to the arrogant oligarchy of those who merely happen to be walking around.   (Chesterton, 1908)

Tradition, in this sense, reflects the accumulated wisdom of the past. The institutions and practices of the past have been 'tested by time', and should therefore be preserved for the benefit of the living and for generations to come. This is the sense in which we should respect the actions, or 'votes', of the dead, who will always outnumber the living. Such a notion of tradition reflects an almost Darwinian belief that those institutions and customs that have survived have only done so because they have worked and been found to be of value. They have been endorsed by a process of 'natural selection' and demonstrated their fitness to survive. Conservatives in the UK, for instance, argue that the institution of monarchy should be preserved because it embodies historical wisdom and experience. In particular, the crown has provided the UK with a focus of national loyalty and respect 'above' party politics; quite simply, it has worked.

Conservatives also venerate tradition because it generates, for both society and the individual, a sense of identity. Established customs and practices are ones that individuals can recognize; they are familiar and reassuring. Tradition thus provides people with a feeling of 'rootedness' and belonging, which is all the stronger because it is historically based. It generates social cohesion by linking people to the past and providing them with a collective sense of who they are. Change, on the other hand, is a journey into the unknown: it creates uncertainty and insecurity, and so endangers our happiness. Tradition therefore consists of rather more than political institutions that have stood the test of time. It encompasses all those customs and social practices that are familiar and generate security and belonging, ranging from the judiciary's insistence on wearing traditional robes and wigs, to campaigns to preserve, for example, the traditional colour of letterboxes or telephone boxes.

Human imperfection

In many ways, conservatism is a 'philosophy of human imperfection' (O'Sullivan, 1976). Other ideologies assume that human beings are naturally 'good', or that they can be made 'good' if their social circumstances are improved. In their most extreme form, such beliefs are utopian and envisage the perfectibility of human-kind in an ideal society. Conservatives dismiss these ideas as, at best, idealistic dreams, and argue instead that human beings are both imperfect and unperfectible.

Human imperfection is understood in several ways. In the first place, human beings are thought to be *psychologically* limited and dependent creatures. In the view of conservatives, people fear isolation and instability. They are drawn psychologically to the safe and the familiar, and, above all, seek the security of knowing 'their place'. Such a portrait of human nature is very different from the image of individuals as self-reliant, enterprising 'utility maximizers' proposed by early liberals. The belief that people desire security and belonging has led conservatives to emphasize the importance of social order, and to be suspicious of the attractions of liberty. Order ensures that human life is stable and predictable; it provides security in an uncertain world. Liberty, on the other hand, presents individuals with choices and can generate change and uncertainty. Conservatives have often echoed the views of Thomas Hobbes (see p. 84) in being prepared to sacrifice liberty in the cause of social order.

Whereas other political philosophies trace the origins of immoral or criminal behaviour to society, conservatives believe it is rooted in the individual. Human beings are thought to be *morally* imperfect. Conservatives hold a pessimistic, even Hobbesian, view of human nature. Humankind is innately selfish and greedy, anything but perfectible; as Hobbes put it, the desire for 'power after power' is the primary human urge. Some conservatives explain this by reference to the Old Testament doctrine of 'original sin'. Crime is therefore not a product of inequality or social disadvantage, as socialists and modern liberals tend to believe; rather, it is a consequence of base human instincts and appetites. People can only be persuaded to behave in a civilized fashion if they are deterred from expressing their violent and anti-social impulses. And the only effective deterrent is law, backed up by the knowledge that it will be strictly enforced. This explains the conservative preference for strong government and for 'tough' criminal justice regimes, based, often, on long prison sentences and the use of corporal or even capital punishment. For conservatives, the role of law is not to uphold liberty, but to preserve order. The concepts of 'law' and 'order' are so closely related in the conservative mind that they have almost become a single, fused concept.

Humankind's *intellectual* powers are also thought to be limited. Conservatives have traditionally believed that the world is simply too complicated for human reason to grasp fully. The political world, as Michael Oakeshott (see p. 85) put it, is 'boundless and bottomless'. Conservatives are therefore suspicious of abstract ideas and systems of thought that claim to understand what is, they argue, simply

PERSPECTIVES ON... HUMAN NATURE

LIBERALS view human nature as a set of innate qualities intrinsic to the individual, placing little or no emphasis on social or historical conditioning. Humans are self-seeking and largely self-reliant creatures; but they are also governed by reason and are capable of personal development, particularly through education.

CONSERVATIVES believe that human beings are essentially limited and security-seeking creatures, drawn to the known, the familiar, the tried and tested. Human rationality is unreliable, and moral corruption is implicit in each human individual. The New Right nevertheless embraces a form of self-seeking individualism (see p. 27).

SOCIALISTS regard humans as essentially social creatures, their capacities and behaviour being shaped more by nurture than by nature, and particularly by creative labour. Their propensity for cooperation, sociability and rationality means that the prospects for personal growth and social development are considerable.

ANARCHISTS advance a complex theory of human nature in which rival potentialities reside in the human soul. While the human 'core' may be morally and intellectually enlightened, a capacity for corruption lurks within each and every individual.

FASCISTS believe that humans are ruled by the will and other non-rational drives, most particularly by a deep sense of social belonging focused on the nation or race. Although the masses are fitted only to serve and obey, elite members of the national community are capable of personal regeneration as 'new men' through dedication to the national or racial cause.

FEMINISTS usually hold that men and women share a common human nature, gender differences being culturally or socially imposed. Separatist feminists nevertheless argue that men are genetically disposed to domination and cruelty, while women are naturally sympathetic, creative and peaceful.

GREENS, particularly deep ecologists, see human nature as part of the broader ecosystem, even as part of nature itself. Materialism, greed and egoism therefore reflect the extent to which humans have become alienated from the oneness of life and thus from their own true nature. Human fulfilment requires a return to nature.

incomprehensible. They prefer to ground their ideas in tradition, experience and history, adopting a cautious, moderate and above all pragmatic approach to the world, and avoiding, if at all possible, doctrinaire or dogmatic beliefs. High-sounding political principles such as the 'rights of man', 'equality' and 'social justice' are fraught with danger because they provide a blueprint for the reform or remodelling of the world. Reform and revolution, conservatives warn, often lead to greater suffering rather than less. For a conservative, to do nothing may be preferable to doing something, and a conservative will always wish to ensure, in Oakeshott's words, that 'the cure is not worse than the disease'. Nevertheless, conservative support for both traditionalism and pragmatism has weakened as a result of the rise of the New Right. In the first place, the New Right is radical, in that it has sought to advance free-market reforms by dismantling inherited welfarist and interventionist structures. Second, the New Right's radicalism is based on rationalism (see p. 31) and a commitment to abstract theories and principles, notably those of economic liberalism.

Organic society

Conservatives believe, as explained earlier, that human beings are dependent and security-seeking creatures. This implies that they do not, and cannot, exist outside society, but desperately need to belong, to have 'roots' in society. The individual cannot be separated from society, but is part of the social groups that nurture him or her: family, friends or peer group, workmates or colleagues, local community and even the nation. These groups provide individual life with security and meaning, a stance often called **social conservatism**. As a result, traditional conservatives are reluctant to understand freedom in 'negative' terms, in which the individual is 'left alone' and suffers, as the French sociologist Émile Durkheim (1856–1917) put it, from **anomie**. Freedom is, rather, a willing acceptance of social obligations and ties by individuals who recognize their value. Freedom involves 'doing one's duty'. When, for example, parents instruct children how to behave, they are not constraining their liberty, but providing guidance for their children's benefit. To act as a dutiful son or daughter and conform to parental wishes is to act freely, out of a recognition of one's obligations. Conservatives believe that a society in which individuals know only their rights, and do not acknowledge their duties, would be rootless and atomistic. Indeed, it is the bonds of duty and obligation that hold society together.

Such ideas are based on a very particular view of society, sometimes called **organicism**. Conservatives have traditionally thought of society as a living thing, an organism, whose parts work together just as the brain, heart, lungs and liver do within a human organism. Organisms differ from artefacts or machines in two important respects. First, unlike machines, organisms are not simply a collection of individual parts that can be arranged or rearranged at will. Within an organism, the whole is more than a collection of its

SOCIAL CONSERVATISM
The belief that society is fashioned out of a fragile network of relationships which need to be upheld through duty, traditional values and established institutions.

ANOMIE
A weakening of values and normative rules, associated with feelings of isolation, loneliness and meaninglessness.

ORGANICISM
A belief that society operates like an organism or living entity, the whole being more than a collection of its individual parts.

individual parts; the whole is sustained by a fragile set of relationships between and among its parts, which, once damaged, can result in the organism's death. Thus, a human body cannot be stripped down and reassembled in the same way as, say, a bicycle. Second, organisms are shaped by 'natural' factors rather than human ingenuity. An organic society is fashioned, ultimately, by natural necessity. For example, the family has not been 'invented' by any social thinker or political theorist, but is a product of natural social impulses such as love, caring and responsibility. In no sense do children in a family agree to a 'contract' on joining the family – they simply grow up within it and are nurtured and guided by it.

The use of the 'organic metaphor' for understanding society has some profoundly conservative implications. A mechanical view of society, as adopted by liberals and most socialists, in which society is constructed by rational individuals for their own purposes, suggests that society can be tampered with and improved. This leads to a belief in progress, either in the shape of reform or revolution. If society is organic, its structures and institutions have been shaped by forces beyond human control and, possibly, human understanding. This implies that its delicate 'fabric' should be preserved and respected by the individuals who live within it. Organicism also shapes our attitude to particular institutions, society's 'parts'. These are viewed from a **functionalist** perspective: institutions develop and survive for a reason, and this reason is that they contribute to maintaining the larger social whole. In other words, by virtue of existing, institutions demonstrate they are worthwhile and desirable. Any attempt to reform or, worse, abolish an institution is thus fraught with dangers.

However, the rise of the New Right has weakened support within conservatism for organic ideas and theories. In line with the robust individualism (see p. 27) of classical liberalism, libertarian conservatives, including neoliberals, have held that society is a product of the actions of self-seeking and largely self-reliant individuals. This position was memorably expressed in Margaret Thatcher's assertion, paraphrasing Jeremy Bentham (see p. 52) that, 'There is no such thing as society, only individuals and their families'.

> **FUNCTIONALISM**
> The theory that social institutions and practices should be understood in terms of the functions they carry out in sustaining the larger social system.

Hierarchy and authority

Conservatives have traditionally believed that society is naturally hierarchical, characterized by fixed or established social gradations. Social equality is therefore rejected as undesirable and unachievable; power, status and property are always unequally distributed. Conservatives agree with liberals in accepting natural inequality among individuals: some are born with talents and skills that are denied to others. For liberals, however, this leads to a belief in meritocracy, in which individuals rise or fall according to their abilities and willingness to work. Traditionally, conservatives have believed that inequality is more deep-rooted. Inequality is an inevitable feature of an organic society, not merely a consequence of individual differences. Pre-democratic conservatives such as Burke were, in this way, able to embrace the idea

PERSPECTIVES ON... SOCIETY

LIBERALS regard society not as an entity in its own right but as a collection of individuals. To the extent that society exists, it is fashioned out of voluntary and contractual agreements made by self-interested human beings. Nevertheless, there is a general balance of interests in society that tends to promote harmony and equilibrium.

CONSERVATIVES believe that society should be viewed as an organism, a living entity. Society thus has an existence outside the individual, and in a sense is prior to the individual; it is held together by the bonds of tradition, authority and a common morality. Neoliberals nevertheless subscribe to a form of liberal atomism.

SOCIALISTS have traditionally understood society in terms of unequal class power, economic and property divisions being deeper and more genuine than any broader social bonds. Marxists believe that society is characterized by class struggle, and argue that the only stable and cohesive society is a classless one.

ANARCHISTS believe that society is characterized by unregulated and natural harmony, based on the natural human disposition towards cooperation and sociability. Social conflict and disharmony are thus clearly unnatural, a product of political rule and economic inequality.

NATIONALISTS view society in terms of cultural or ethnic distinctiveness. Society is thus characterized by shared values and beliefs, ultimately rooted in a common national identity. This implies that multinational or multicultural societies are inherently unstable.

FASCISTS regard society as a unified organic whole, implying that individual existence is meaningless unless it is dedicated to the common good rather than the private good. Nevertheless, membership of society is strictly restricted on national or racial grounds.

FEMINISTS have understood society in terms of patriarchy and an artificial division between the 'public' and 'private' spheres of life. Society may therefore be seen as an organized hypocrisy designed to routinize and uphold a system of male power.

MULTICULTURALISTS view society as a mosaic of cultural groups, defined by their distinctive ethnic, religious or historical identities. The basis for wider social bonds, cutting across cultural distinctiveness, is thus restricted, perhaps, to civic allegiance.

NATURAL ARISTOCRACY
The idea that talent and leadership are innate or inbred qualities that cannot be acquired through effort or self-advancement.

of a 'natural aristocracy'. Just as the brain, the heart and the liver all perform very different functions within the body, the various classes and groups that make up society also have their own specific roles. There must be leaders and there must be followers; there must be managers and there must be workers; for that matter, there must be those who go out to work and those who stay at home and bring up children. Genuine social equality is therefore a myth; in reality, there is a natural inequality of wealth and social position, justified by a corresponding inequality of social responsibilities. The working class might not enjoy the same living standards and life chances as their employers, but, at the same time, they do not have the livelihoods and security of many other people resting on their shoulders. Hierarchy and organicism have thus invested in traditional conservatism a pronounced tendency towards paternalism (see p. 76).

The belief in hierarchy is strengthened by the emphasis conservatives place on **authority**. Conservatives do not accept the liberal belief that authority arises out of contracts made by free individuals. In liberal theory, authority is thought to be established by individuals for their own benefit. In contrast, conservatives believe that authority, like society, develops naturally. In this case, it arises from the need to ensure that children are cared for, kept away from danger, have a healthy

> **AUTHORITY**
> The right to exert influence over others by virtue of an acknowledged obligation to obey.

diet, go to bed at sensible times and so on. Such authority can only be imposed 'from above', quite simply because children do not know what is good for them. It does not and cannot arise 'from below': in no sense can children be said to have agreed to be governed. Authority is therefore rooted in the nature of society and all social institutions. In schools, authority should be exercised by the teacher; in the workplace, by the employer; and in society at large, by government. Conservatives believe that authority is necessary and beneficial as people need the guidance, support and security that comes from knowing 'where they stand' and what is expected of them. Authority thus counters rootlessness and anomie.

This has led conservatives to place special emphasis on leadership and discipline. Leadership is a vital ingredient in any society because it is the capacity to give direction and provide inspiration for others. Discipline is not just mindless obedience but a willing and healthy respect for authority. Authoritarian conservatives go further and portray authority as absolute and unquestionable. Most conservatives, however, believe that authority should be exercised within limits and that these limits are imposed not by an artificial contract but by the natural responsibilities that authority entails. Parents should have authority over their children, but this does not imply the right to treat them in any way they choose. The authority of a parent is intrinsically linked to the obligation to nurture, guide and, if necessary, punish their children. Thus it does not empower a parent to abuse a child or, for instance, sell the child into slavery.

Property

> **PROPERTY**
> The ownership of physical goods or wealth, whether by private individuals, groups of people or the state.

Property is an asset that possesses a deep and, at times, almost mystical significance for conservatives. Liberals believe that property reflects merit: those who work hard and possess talent will, and should, acquire wealth. Property, therefore, is 'earned'. This doctrine has an attraction for those conservatives who regard the ability to accumulate wealth as an important economic incentive. Nevertheless, conservatives also hold that property has a range of psychological and social advantages. For example, it provides security. In an uncertain and unpredictable world, property ownership gives people a sense of confidence and assurance, something to 'fall back on'. Property, whether the ownership of a house or savings in the bank, provides individuals with a source of protection. Conservatives therefore believe that thrift – caution in the management of money – is a virtue in itself and have sought to encourage private savings and investment in property. Property ownership also promotes a range of important social values. Those who possess and enjoy their own property are more likely to respect the property of others. They will also be aware that property must be safeguarded from disorder and lawlessness. Property owners therefore have a 'stake' in society; they have an interest, in particular, in maintaining law and order. In this sense, property ownership can promote what can be thought of as the 'conservative' values of respect for law, authority and social order.

However, a deeper and more personal reason why conservatives support property ownership is that it can be regarded as an extension of an individual's personality. People 'realize' themselves, even see themselves, in what they own. Possessions are not merely external objects, valued because they are useful – a house to keep us warm and dry, a car to provide transport and so on – but also reflect something of the owner's personality and character. This is why, conservatives point out, burglary is a particularly unpleasant crime: its victims suffer not only the loss of, or damage to, their possessions, but also the sense that they have been personally violated. A home is the most personal and intimate of possessions, it is decorated and organized according to the tastes and needs of its owner and therefore reflects his or her personality. The proposal of traditional socialists that property should be 'socialized', owned in common rather than by private individuals, thus strikes conservatives as particularly appalling because it threatens to create a soulless and depersonalized society.

Conservatives, however, have seldom been prepared to go as far as classical liberals in believing that individuals have an *absolute* right to use their property however they may choose. While libertarian conservatives, and therefore the neoliberals, support an essentially liberal view of property, conservatives have traditionally argued that all rights, including property rights, entail obligations. Property is not an issue for the individual alone, but is also of importance to society. This can be seen, for example, in the social bonds that cut across generations. Property is not merely the creation of the present generation. Much of it – land, houses, works of art – has been passed down from earlier generations. The present generation is, in that sense, the custodian of the wealth of the nation and has a duty to preserve and protect it for the benefit of future generations. Harold Macmillan, the UK Conservative prime minister 1957–63, expressed just such a position in the 1980s when he objected to the Thatcher government's policy of **privatization**, describing it as 'selling off the family silver'.

PRIVATIZATION
The transfer of state assets from the public to the private sector, reflecting a contraction of the state's responsibilities.

Authoritarian conservatism

Whereas all conservatives would claim to respect the concept of authority, few modern conservatives would accept that their views are authoritarian. Nevertheless, while contemporary conservatives are keen to demonstrate their commitment to democratic, particularly liberal-democratic, principles, there is a tradition within conservatism that has favoured authoritarian rule, especially in continental Europe. At the time of the French Revolution, the principal defender of autocratic rule was the French political thinker Joseph de Maistre (1753–1821). De Maistre was a fierce critic of the French Revolution, but, in contrast to Burke, he wished to restore absolute power to the hereditary monarchy. He was a reactionary and was quite unprepared to accept any reform of the *ancien régime*, which had been overthrown in 1789. His political philosophy was based on willing and complete subordination to 'the master'. In *Du Pape* ([1817] 1971) de Maistre went further and argued that above the earthly monarchies a supreme spiritual power should rule in the person of the pope. His central concern was the preservation of order, which alone, he believed, could provide people with safety and security. Revolution, and even reform, would weaken the chains that bind people together and lead to a descent into chaos and oppression.

Throughout the nineteenth century, conservatives in continental Europe remained faithful to the rigid and hierarchical values of autocratic rule, and stood unbending in the face of rising liberal, nationalist and socialist protest. Nowhere was authoritarianism more entrenched than in Russia, where Tsar Nicholas I (1825–55), proclaimed the principles of 'orthodoxy, autocracy and nationality', in contrast to the values that had inspired the French Revolution: 'liberty, equality and fraternity'. Nicholas's successors stubbornly refused to allow their power to be constrained by constitutions or the development of parliamentary institutions. In Germany, constitutional government did develop, but Otto von Bismarck, the imperial chancellor, 1871–90, ensured that it remained a sham. Elsewhere, authoritarianism remained particularly strong in Catholic countries. The papacy suffered not only the loss of its

Key concept

Authoritarianism

Authoritarianism is belief in or the practice of government 'from above', in which authority is exercised over a population with or without its consent. Authoritarianism thus differs from authority. The latter rests on legitimacy, and in that sense arises 'from below'. Authoritarian thinkers typically base their views on either a belief in the wisdom of established leaders or the idea that social order can only be maintained by unquestioning obedience. However, authoritarianism is usually distinguished from totalitarianism (see p. 207). The practice of government 'from above', which is associated with monarchical absolutism, traditional dictatorships and most forms of military rule, is concerned with the repression of opposition and political liberty, rather than the more radical goal of obliterating the distinction between the state and civil society.

temporal authority with the achievement of Italian unification, which led Pope Pius IX to declare himself a 'prisoner of the Vatican', but also an assault on its doctrines with the rise of secular political ideologies. In 1864, Pius IX condemned all radical or progressive ideas, including those of nationalism, liberalism and socialism, as 'false doctrines of our most unhappy age', and when confronted with the loss of the papal states and Rome, he proclaimed in 1870 the edict of papal infallibility. The unwillingness of continental conservatives to come to terms with reform and democratic government extended well into the twentieth century. For example, conservative elites in Italy and Germany helped to overthrow parliamentary democracy and bring Benito Mussolini (see p. 213) and Adolf Hitler (see p. 213) to power by providing support for, and giving respectability to, rising fascist movements.

In other cases, conservative-authoritarian regimes have looked to the newly enfranchised masses for political support. This happened in nineteenth-century France, where Louis Napoleon succeeded in being elected president, and later in establishing himself as Emperor Napoleon III, by appealing to the smallholding peasantry, the largest element of the French electorate. The Napoleonic regime fused authoritarianism with the promise of economic prosperity and social reform in the kind of plebiscitary dictatorship more commonly found in the twentieth century. Bonapartism has parallels with twentieth-century Perónism. Juan Perón was dictator of Argentina 1946–55, and proclaimed the familiar authoritarian themes of obedience, order and national unity. However, he based his political support not on the interests of traditional elites, but on an appeal to the impoverished masses, the 'shirtless ones', as Perón called them. The Perónist regime was **populist** in that it moulded its policies according to the instincts and wishes of the common people, in this case popular resentment against 'Yankee imperialism', and a widespread desire for economic and social progress. Similar regimes have developed in parts of Africa, Asia and the Middle East. However, although such regimes have tended to consolidate the position of conservative elites, and often embrace a distinctively conservative form of nationalism, authoritarian-populist regimes such as Perón's perhaps exhibit features that are associated more closely with fascism than conservatism.

> **POPULISM**
> A belief that popular instincts and wishes are the principal legitimate guide to political action, often reflecting distrust of or hostility towards political elites (see p. 291).

Paternalistic conservatism

While continental conservatives adopted an attitude of uncompromising resistance to change, a more flexible and ultimately more successful Anglo-American tradition can be traced back to Edmund Burke. The lesson that Burke drew from the French Revolution was that change can be natural or inevitable, in which case it should not be resisted. 'A state without the means of some change', he suggested, 'is without the means of its conservation' (Burke [1790] 1968). The characteristic style of Burkean conservatism is cautious, modest and pragmatic; it reflects a suspicion of fixed principles, whether revolutionary or reactionary. As Ian Gilmour (1978) put it, 'the wise Conservative travels light'. The values that conservatives hold most dear – tradition, order, authority, property and so on – will be safe only if policy is developed in the light of practical circumstances and experience. Such a position will rarely justify dramatic or radical change, but accepts a prudent willingness to 'change in order to conserve'. Pragmatic conservatives support neither the individual nor the state in principle, but are prepared to support either, or, more frequently, recommend a balance between the two, depending on 'what works'. In practice, the reforming impulse in conservatism has also been associated closely with the survival into the modern period of neo-feudal paternalistic values, as represented in particular by One Nation conservatism.

One Nation conservatism

The Anglo-American paternalistic tradition is often traced back to Benjamin Disraeli (1804–81), UK prime minister in 1868 and again 1874–80. Disraeli developed his political philosophy in two novels, *Sybil* (1845) and *Coningsby* (1844), written before he assumed ministerial responsibilities. These novels emphasized the principle of social obligation, in stark contrast to the extreme individualism then dominant within the political establishment. Disraeli wrote against a background of growing industrialization, economic inequality and, in continental Europe at least, revolutionary upheaval. He tried to draw attention to the danger of Britain being divided into 'two nations: the Rich and the Poor'. In the best conservative tradition, Disraeli's argument was based on a combination of prudence and principle.

On the one hand, growing social inequality contains the seeds of revolution. A poor and oppressed working class, Disraeli feared, would not simply accept its misery. The revolutions that had broken out in Europe in 1830 and 1848 seemed to bear out this belief. Reform would therefore be sensible, because, in stemming the tide of revolution, it would ultimately be in the interests of the rich. On the other hand, Disraeli appealed to moral values. He suggested that wealth and privilege brought with them social obligations, in particular a responsibility for the poor

Key concept

Paternalism

Paternalism literally means to act in a fatherly fashion. As a political principle, it refers to power or authority being exercised over others with the intention of conferring benefit or preventing harm. Social welfare and laws such as the compulsory wearing of seat belts in cars are examples of paternalism.

'Soft' paternalism is characterized by broad consent on the part of those subject to paternalism. 'Hard' paternalism operates regardless of consent, and thus overlaps with authoritarianism. The basis for paternalism is that wisdom and experience are unequally distributed in society; and those in authority 'know best'. Opponents argue that authority is not to be trusted and that paternalism restricts liberty and contributes to the 'infantilization' of society.

or less well-off. In so doing, Disraeli drew on the organic conservative belief that society is held together by an acceptance of duty and obligations. He believed that society is naturally hierarchical, but also held that inequalities of wealth or social privilege give rise to an inequality of responsibilities. The wealthy and powerful must shoulder the burden of social responsibility, which, in effect, is the price of privilege. These ideas were based on the feudal principle of *noblesse oblige*, the obligation of the aristocracy to be honourable and generous. For example, the landed nobility claimed to exercise a paternal responsibility for their peasants, as the king did in relation to the nation. Disraeli recommended that these obligations should not be abandoned, but should be expressed, in an increasingly industrialized world, in social reform. Such ideas came to be represented by the slogan 'One Nation'. In office, Disraeli was responsible both for the Second Reform Act of 1867, which for the first time extended the right to vote to the working class, and for the social reforms that improved housing conditions and hygiene.

Disraeli's ideas had a considerable impact on conservatism and contributed to a radical and reforming tradition that appeals both to the pragmatic instincts of conservatives and to their sense of social duty. In the UK, these ideas provide the basis of so-called 'One Nation conservatism', whose supporters sometimes style themselves as 'Tories' to denote their commitment to pre-industrial, hierarchic and paternal values. Disraeli's ideas were subsequently taken up in the late nineteenth century by Randolph Churchill in the form of 'Tory democracy'. In an age of widening political democracy, Churchill stressed the need for traditional institutions – for example, the monarchy, the House of Lords and the church – to enjoy a wider base of social support. This could be achieved by winning working-class votes for the Conservative Party by continuing Disraeli's policy of social reform. One Nation conservatism can thus be seen as a form of Tory welfarism.

The high point of the One Nation tradition was reached in the 1950s and 1960s, when conservative governments in the UK and elsewhere came to practise a version of Keynesian social democracy, managing the economy in line with the goal of full employment and supporting enlarged welfare provision. This stance was based

Key concept

Toryism

'Tory' was used in eighteenth-century Britain to refer to a parliamentary faction that (as opposed to the Whigs) supported monarchical power and the Church of England, and represented the landed gentry; in the USA, it implied loyalty to the British crown. Although in the mid-nineteenth century the British Conservative Party emerged out of the Tories, and in the UK 'Tory' is still widely (but unhelpfully) used as a synonym for Conservative, Toryism is best understood as a distinctive ideological stance within broader conservatism. Its characteristic features are a belief in hierarchy, tradition, duty and organicism. While 'high' Toryism articulates a neo-feudal belief in a ruling class and a pre-democratic faith in established institutions, the Tory tradition is also hospitable to welfarist and reformist ideas, provided these serve the cause of social continuity.

on the need for a non-ideological, 'middle way' between the extremes of *laissez-faire* liberalism and socialist state planning. Conservatism was therefore the way of moderation, and sought to draw a balance between rampant individualism and overbearing collectivism (see p. 99). In the UK, this idea was most clearly expressed in Harold Macmillan's *The Middle Way* ([1938] 1966). Macmillan, who was to be prime minister from 1957 to 1963, advocated what he called 'planned capitalism', which he described as 'a mixed system which combines state ownership, regulation or control of certain aspects of economic activity with the drive and initiative of private enterprise'. Such ideas later resurfaced, in the USA and the UK, in the notions of 'compassionate conservatism'. However, paternalist conservatism only provides a qualified basis for social and economic intervention. The purpose of One Nationism, for instance, is to consolidate hierarchy rather than to remove it, and its wish to improve the conditions of the less well-off is limited to the desire to ensure that the poor no longer pose a threat to the established order.

Libertarian conservatism

Although conservatism draws heavily on pre-industrial ideas such as organicism, hierarchy and obligation, the ideology has also been much influenced by liberal ideas, especially classical liberal ideas. This is sometimes seen as a late-twentieth-century development, neoliberals having in some way 'hijacked' conservatism in the interests of classical liberalism. Nevertheless, liberal doctrines, especially those concerning the free market, have been advanced by conservatives since the late eighteenth century, and can be said to constitute a rival tradition to conservative paternalism. These ideas are libertarian in that they advocate the greatest possible economic liberty and the least possible government regulation of social life. Libertarian conservatives have not simply converted to liberalism, but believe that liberal economics is compatible with a more traditional, conservative social philosophy, based on values such as authority and duty. This is evident in the work

Key concept

Libertarianism

Libertarianism refers to a range of theories that give strict priority to liberty (understood in negative terms) over other values, such as authority, tradition and equality. Libertarians thus seek to maximize the realm of individual freedom and minimize the scope of public authority, typically seeing the state as the principal threat to liberty. The two best-known libertarian traditions are rooted in the idea of individual rights (as with Robert Nozick, see p. 85) and in *laissez-faire* economic doctrines (as with Friedrich von Hayek, see p. 84), although socialists have also embraced libertarianism. Libertarianism is sometimes distinguished from liberalism on the grounds that the latter, even in its classical form, refuses to give priority to liberty over order. However, it differs from anarchism in that libertarians generally recognize the need for a minimal state, sometimes styling themselves as 'minarchists'.

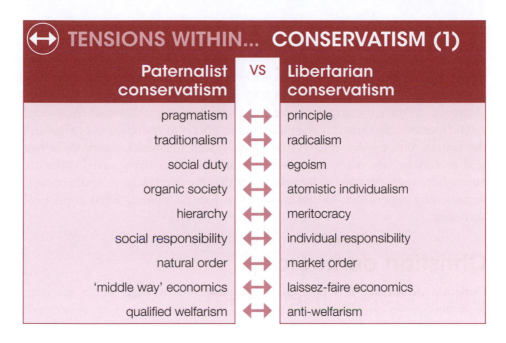

↔ TENSIONS WITHIN... CONSERVATISM (1)

Paternalist conservatism	VS	Libertarian conservatism
pragmatism	↔	principle
traditionalism	↔	radicalism
social duty	↔	egoism
organic society	↔	atomistic individualism
hierarchy	↔	meritocracy
social responsibility	↔	individual responsibility
natural order	↔	market order
'middle way' economics	↔	laissez-faire economics
qualified welfarism	↔	anti-welfarism

of Edmund Burke, in many ways the founder of traditional conservatism, but also a keen supporter of the **economic liberalism** of Adam Smith.

The libertarian tradition has been strongest in those countries where classical liberal ideas have had the greatest impact, once again the UK and the USA. As early as the late eighteenth century, Burke expressed a strong preference for free trade in commercial affairs and a competitive, self-regulating market economy in domestic affairs. The free market is efficient and fair, but it is also, Burke believed, natural and necessary. It is 'natural' in that it reflects a desire for wealth, a 'love of lucre', that is part of human nature. The laws of the market are therefore 'natural laws'. He accepted that working conditions dictated by the market are, for many, 'degrading, unseemly, unmanly and often most unwholesome', but insisted that they would suffer further if the 'natural course of things' were to be disturbed. The capitalist free market could thus be defended on the grounds of tradition, just like the monarchy and the church.

Libertarian conservatives are not, however, consistent liberals. They believe in economic individualism and 'getting government off the back of business', but are less prepared to extend this principle of individual liberty to other aspects of social life. Conservatives, even libertarian conservatives, have a more pessimistic view of human nature. A strong state is required to maintain public order and ensure that authority is respected. Indeed, in some respects libertarian conservatives are attracted to free-market theories precisely because they

ECONOMIC LIBERALISM
A belief in the market as a self-regulating mechanism that tends naturally to deliver general prosperity and opportunities for all (see p. 42).

promise to secure social order. Whereas liberals have believed that the market economy preserves individual liberty and freedom of choice, conservatives have at times been attracted to the market as an instrument of social discipline. Market forces regulate and control economic and social activity. For example, they may deter workers from pushing for wage increases by threatening them with unemployment. As such, the market can be seen as an instrument that maintains social stability and works alongside the more evident forces of coercion: the police and the courts. While some conservatives have feared that market capitalism will lead to endless innovation and restless competition, upsetting social cohesion, others have been attracted to it in the belief that it can establish a 'market order', sustained by impersonal 'natural laws' rather than the guiding hand of political authority.

Christian democracy

Christian democracy is a political and ideological movement which has been prominent in western and central Europe and, to a lesser extent, Latin America. It has usually been classified as a moderate or progressive form of conservatism, albeit one that typically resists precise doctrinal expression. In the aftermath of World War II, Christian democratic parties emerged in Belgium, the Netherlands, Austria, Germany and Italy, the most significant ones being the Christian Democratic Union (CDU)/Christian Social Union in then-West Germany and, until its collapse in 1993, the Christian Democratic Party (DC) in Italy. Christian democratic thinking has nevertheless had a wider impact, affecting centre-right parties in France, the Benelux countries, much of Scandinavia and parts of post-communist Europe which are not 'confessional' parties or formally aligned to the Christian democratic movement. This certainly applies in the case of the European People's Party (EPP), the major centre-right group in the European Parliament and the Parliament's largest political group since 1999. In Latin America, significant Christian democratic parties have developed in countries such as Chile, Venezuela, Ecuador, Guatemala and El Salvador.

However, the ideological origins of Christian democracy can be traced back to well before 1945 and the break between continental European conservatism and authoritarianism in the early post-fascist period. Christian democratic thinking gradually took shape during the nineteenth century as the Catholic Church attempted to come to terms with the ramifications of industrialization and, in particular, the emergence of liberal capitalism. Indeed, in some respects, this process originated with the French Revolution and the explicit challenge that it posed to Church authority. The Catholic Church came, over time, to accept democratic political forms and to evince growing concern about the threats posed by unrestrained capitalism. The Centre party (*Zentrum*) in Germany, founded in 1870, was thus set up to defend the interests of the Catholic Church but also campaigned for a strengthening welfare provision.

> **CHRISTIAN DEMOCRACY**
> An ideological movement within European conservatism that is characterized by a commitment to the social market and qualified state intervention.

Pope Leo XIII's encyclical *Rerum Novarum* (1891) underlined the Vatican's open-ness to new thinking, in that it lamented the material suffering of the working class and emphasized the reciprocal duties of labour and capital.

Such developments are often seen to have been based on a distinctively Catholic social theory. In this view, as Protestantism is associated with the idea of spiritual salvation through individual effort, its social theory typically endorses individual-ism and extols the value of hard work, competition and personal responsibility. The 'Protestant ethic' has thus sometimes been treated as a form of capitalist ideology (Weber, [1904–5] 2011). Catholic social theory, by contrast, focuses on the social group rather than the individual, and has stressed balance or organic harmony rather than competition. In the writings of the French philosopher and political thinker Jacques Maritain (1884–1973), the leading figure in the attempt to develop an ideology of Christian democracy, this was expressed through the notion of 'integral humanism' (Maritain, [1936] 1996). Integral humanism underlines the role of cooperation in the achievement of shared practical goals, and thereby implies that unrestrained capitalism fails to serve the 'common good'.

Social market economy

Although Christian democracy is typically critical of *laissez-faire* capitalism, it certainly does not reject capitalism altogether. Rather, it advocates a 'third way' between market capitalism and socialism, often termed social capitalism. As such, clear parallels exist between Christian democracy and the neo-revisionist tradition within social democracy, examined in Chapter 4. The idea of social capitalism draws more heavily on the flexible and pragmatic ideas of economists such as Friedrich List (1789–1846) than on the strict market principles of classical political economy, as formulated by Adam Smith (see p. 52) and David Ricardo (1772–1823). A leading advocate of the *Zollverein* (the German customs union), List emphasized the economic importance of politics and political power, arguing, for instance, that state intervention should be used to protect infant industries from the rigours of foreign competition. The central theme in this model is the idea of a **social market**; that is, an attempt to marry the disciplines of market competition with the need for social cohesion and solidarity. The market is thus viewed not as an end in itself but rather as a means of generating wealth in order to achieve broader social ends.

In Germany, often seen as the natural home of social-market capitalism, this system is founded on a link between industrial and financial capital, in the form of a close relationship between business corpora-tions and regionally–based banks, which are often also major shareholders in the corporations. This has been the pivot around which Germany's economy has revolved since World War II, and it has orientated the economy towards long-term investment, rather than short–term profitability. Business organization in what has been called Rhine–Alpine capitalism also differs

SOCIAL MARKET
An economy that is structured by market principles and is relatively free from state interference, but which operates alongside comprehensive welfare provision and effective social services.

from Anglo–American capitalism in that it is based on 'social partnership', creating a form of democratic corporatism (see p. 208). Trade unions enjoy representation through works councils, and participate in annual rounds of wage negotiation that are usually industry–wide. This relationship is underpinned by comprehensive and well–funded welfare provisions that provide workers and other vulnerable groups with social guarantees. In this way, a form of 'stakeholder capitalism' has developed that takes into account the interests of workers and those of the wider community. This contrasts with the 'shareholder capitalism' found in the USA and the UK (Hutton, 1995).

Federalism

Finally, Christian democracy is characterized by a distrust of conventional forms of nationalism and an emphasis instead on the principles of federalism (see p. 39) and subsidiarity. This can be explained both ideologically and historically. Ideologically, federalism can be seen to apply ideas such as cooperation and partnership to the internal organization of the state, so bringing Christian democratic thinking on constitutional matters into line with its thinking on the economy and society. However, powerful historical forces also encouraged Christian democracy to move in this direction, not least the widespread destruction wreaked across continental Europe by World War II, allied to the belief that rampant nationalism and over-strong central government had been major causes of the war. Christian democratic parties have therefore often favoured the establishment of federalism at the state level, as has occurred in Austria, Belgium and Germany, but have also advocated political union,

SUBSIDIARITY
The principle that decisions should be made at the lowest appropriate level.

and not merely economic union, within the European Union. Influenced by Christian democratic thinking, the European People's Party has therefore been one of the keenest supporters of 'pooled' sovereignty and European federalism.

New Right

During the early post-1945 period, pragmatic and paternalistic ideas dominated conservatism through much of the western world. The remnants of authoritarian conservatism collapsed with the overthrow of the Portuguese and Spanish dictatorships in the 1970s. Just as conservatives had come to accept political democracy during the nineteenth century, after 1945 they came to accept a qualified form of social democracy. This tendency was confirmed by the rapid and sustained economic growth of the post-war years, the 'long boom', which appeared to bear out the success of 'managed capitalism'. During the 1970s, however, a set of more radical ideas developed within conservatism, challenging directly the Keynesian-welfarist orthodoxy. These 'New Right' ideas had their greatest initial impact in the USA and the UK, but they also came to be influential in parts of continental Europe, Australia and New Zealand, and had some kind of effect on western states across the globe.

The New Right is a broad term and has been used to describe ideas that range from the demand for tax cuts to calls for greater censorship of television and films, and even campaigns against immigration or in favour of repatriation. In essence, the New Right is a marriage between two apparently contrasting ideological traditions:

- The first of these is classical liberal economics, particularly the free-market theories of Adam Smith, which were revived in the second half of the twentieth century as a critique of 'big' government and economic and social intervention. This is called the liberal New Right, or neoliberalism (see p. 83).
- The second element in the New Right is traditional conservative – and notably pre-Disraelian – social theory, especially its defence of order, authority and discipline. This is called the conservative New Right, or neoconservatism (see p. 88).

The New Right thus attempts to fuse economic libertarianism with state and social authoritarianism. As such, it is a blend of radical, reactionary and traditional features. Its radicalism is evident in its robust efforts to dismantle or 'roll back' interventionist government and liberal or permissive social values. This radicalism is clearest in relation to neoliberalism, which draws on rational theories and abstract principles, and so dismisses tradition. New Right radicalism is nevertheless reactionary, in that both neoliberalism and neoconservatism usually hark back to a nineteenth-century 'golden age' of supposed economic vigour and moral fortitude. However, the New Right also makes an appeal to tradition, particularly through the emphasis neoconservatives place on so-called 'traditional values'.

Neoliberalism

Neoliberalism was a product of the end of the 'long boom' of the post-1945 period, which shifted economic thinking away from Keynesianism (see p. 55) and reawakened interest in earlier, free-market thinking. In this, it has operated at a national

Key concept
Neoliberalism

Neoliberalism (sometimes called 'neoclassical liberalism') is widely seen as an updated version of classical liberalism, particularly classical political economy. Its central theme is that the economy works best when left alone by government, reflecting a belief in free market economics and atomistic individualism. While unregulated market capitalism delivers efficiency, growth and widespread prosperity, the 'dead hand' of the state saps initiative and discourages enterprise. In short, the neoliberal philosophy is: 'market: good; state: bad'. Key neoliberal policies include privatization, spending cuts (especially in social welfare), tax cuts (particularly corporate and direct taxes) and deregulation. Neoliberalism is often equated with a belief in market fundamentalism; that is, an absolute faith in the capacity of the market mechanism to solve all economic and social problems.

KEY FIGURES IN... CONSERVATISM

Thomas Hobbes (1588–1679) An English political philosopher, Hobbes, in his classic work *Leviathan* (1651), used social contact theory to defend absolute government as the only alternative to anarchy and disorder, and proposed that citizens have an unqualified obligation towards their state. Though his view of human nature and his defence of authoritarian order have a conservative character, Hobbes' rationalist and individualist methodology prefigured early liberalism. His emphasis on power-seeking as the primary human urge has also been used to explain the behaviour of states in the international system.

Edmund Burke (1729–97) A Dublin-born British statesman and political theorist, Burke was the father of the Anglo-American conservative political tradition. In his major work, *Reflections on the Revolution in France* (1790), Burke deeply opposed the attempt to recast French politics in accordance with abstract principles such as 'the universal rights of man', arguing that wisdom resides largely in experience, tradition and history. Burke is associated with a pragmatic willingness to 'change in order to conserve', reflected, in his view, in the 'Glorious Revolution' of 1688.

Friedrich von Hayek (1899–1992) An Austrian economist and political philosopher, Hayek was a firm believer in individualism and market order, and an implacable critic of socialism. His pioneering work, *The Road to Serfdom* (1944) developed a then deeply unfashionable defence of *laissez-faire* and attacked economic intervention as implicitly totalitarian. In later works, such as *The Constitution of Liberty* (1960) and *Law, Legislation and Liberty* (1979), Hayek supported a modified form of traditionalism and upheld an Anglo-American version of constitutionalism that emphasized limited government.

level but also at an international level, through what is called neoliberal globalization (see p. 86). Neoliberal thinking is most definitely drawn from classical rather than modern liberalism. It amounts to a restatement of the case for a minimal state. This has been summed up as 'private, good; public, bad'. Neoliberalism is anti-statist. The state is regarded as a realm of coercion and unfreedom: collectivism restricts individual initiative and saps self-respect. Government, however benignly disposed, invariably has a damaging effect on human affairs. Instead, faith is placed in the individual and the market. Individuals should be encouraged to be self-reliant and to make rational choices in their own interests. The market is respected as a mechanism through which the sum of individual choices will lead to progress and general benefit. As such, neoliberalism has attempted to establish the dominance of libertarian ideas over paternalistic ones within conservative ideology.

The dominant theme within this anti-statist doctrine is an ideological commitment to the free market, particularly as revived in the work of economists such as Friedrich von Hayek and Milton Friedman (1912–2006). Free-market ideas gained

Michael Oakeshott (1901–90) A British political philosopher, Oakeshott advanced a powerful defence of a non-ideological style of politics that supported a cautious and piecemeal approach to change. Distrusting rationalism, he argued in favour of traditional values and established customs on the grounds that the conservative disposition is 'to prefer the familiar to the unknown, to prefer the tried to the untried, fact to mystery, the actual to the possible'. Oakeshott's best-known works include *Rationalism in Politics* (1962) and *On Human Conduct* (1975).

Irving Kristol (1920–2009) A US journalist and social critic, Kristol was one of the leading exponents of American neoconservatism. He abandoned liberalism in the 1970s and became increasingly critical of the spread of welfarism and the 'counterculture'. While accepting the need for a predominantly market-based economy and fiercely rejecting socialism, Kristol criticized libertarianism in the marketplace as well as in morality. His best-known writings include *Two Cheers for Capitalism* (1978) and *Reflections of a Neo-Conservative* (1983).

Robert Nozick (1938–2002) A US political philosopher, Nozick developed a form of rights-based libertarianism in response to the ideas of John Rawls (see p. 53). Drawing on Locke (see p. 52) and nineteenth-century US individualists, he argued that property rights should be strictly upheld, provided that property was justly purchased or justly transferred from one person to another. His major work, *Anarchy, State and Utopia* (1974), rejects welfare and redistribution, and advances the case for minimal government and minimal taxation. In later life, Nozick modified his extreme libertarianism.

renewed credibility during the 1970s as governments experienced increasing difficulty in delivering economic stability and sustained growth. Doubts consequently developed about whether it was in the power of government at all to solve economic problems. Hayek and Friedman, for example, challenged the very idea of a 'managed' or 'planned' economy. They argued that the task of allocating resources in a complex, industrialized economy was simply too difficult for any set of state bureaucrats to achieve successfully. The virtue of the market, on the other hand, is that it acts as the central nervous system of the economy, reconciling the supply of goods and services with the demand for them. It allocates resources to their most profitable use and thereby ensures that consumer needs are satisfied. In the light of the re-emergence of unemployment and inflation in the 1970s, Hayek and Friedman argued that government was invariably the cause of economic problems, rather than the cure.

The ideas of Keynesianism were one of the chief targets of neoliberal criticism. Keynes had argued that capitalist economies were not self-regulating. He placed particular emphasis on the 'demand side' of the economy, believing that the level of

POLITICAL IDEOLOGIES IN ACTION . . .
Rise of neoliberal globalization

EVENTS: Since the 1980s, economic development has, to a greater or lesser extent in different parts of the world, taken on a neoliberal guise. The wider, and seemingly irresistible, advance of neoliberalism has occurred, in part, through the influence of the institutions of global economic governance and the growing impact of globalization (see p. 20). In a process that began in the early 1970s, the World Bank and the International Monetary Fund (IMF) were converted to the ideas of what later became known as the 'Washington consensus', which was aligned to the economic agenda of Reagan and Thatcher and focused on policies such as free trade, the liberalization of capital markets, flexible exchange rates, balanced budgets and so on. Neoliberalism and globalization thus became a single, fused process, widely dubbed 'neoliberal globalization'.

SIGNIFICANCE: From an economic liberal perspective, the emergence of neoliberal globalization was both an inevitable and a welcome development. It was inevitable because economic development is intrinsically linked to the advance of market principles, the market being the only reliable means of generating wealth, and the surest guarantee of prosperity and economic opportunity. Market competition and the profit motive provide incentives for work and enterprise, and also allocate resources to their most profitable use. Just as national economies have been restructured on market lines, and often on free-market lines, so the world economy was sure to follow suit. This was especially the case because neoliberal globalization reflects the interests of all countries in all parts of the world. Although it makes the rich richer, it also makes the poor less poor, implying that the only countries that do not benefit from neoliberal globalization are the ones that – foolishly – do not participate in it.

Neo-Marxists and radical theorists nevertheless cast neoliberal globalization in a very different light, arguing that it has resulted in new and deeply entrenched patterns of poverty and inequality. In this view, neoliberal globalization is driven not by the magic of the market and the universal desire for material progress, but by the interests of transnational corporations and industrially advanced states generally, and particularly by the USA's determination to maintain its global economic hegemony. The losers in this global struggle are invariably in the developing world, where wages are low, regulation is weak or non-existent, and where production is increasingly orientated around global markets rather than local needs. Neoliberal globalization has thus been portrayed as a form of neo-imperialism.

economic activity and employment were dictated by the level of 'aggregate demand' in the economy. Milton Friedman, on the other hand, argued that there is a 'natural rate of unemployment', which is beyond the ability of government to influence. He also argued that attempts to eradicate unemployment by applying Keynesian techniques merely cause other, more damaging, economic problems, notably **inflation**. Inflation, neoliberals believe, threatens the entire basis of a market economy because, in reducing faith in money, the means of exchange, it discourages people from undertaking commercial or economic activity. However, Keynesianism had, in effect, encouraged governments to 'print money', albeit in a well-meaning attempt to create jobs. The free-market solution to inflation is to control the supply of money by cutting public spending, a policy practised by both the Reagan and the Thatcher administrations during the 1980s. Both administrations also allowed unemployment to rise sharply, in the belief that only the market could solve the problem.

Neoliberalism is also opposed to the mixed economy and public ownership, and practised so-called supply-side economics. Starting under Thatcher in the UK in the 1980s but later extending to many other western states, and most aggressively pursued in postcommunist states in the 1990s, a policy of privatization has effectively dismantled both mixed and collectivized economies by transferring industries from public to private ownership. Nationalized industries were criticized for being inherently inefficient, because, unlike private firms and industries, they are not disciplined by the profit motive. Neoliberalism's emphasis on the 'supply-side' of the economy was reflected in the belief that governments should foster growth by providing conditions that encourage producers to produce, rather than consumers to consume. The main block to the creation of an entrepreneurial, supply-side culture is high taxes. Taxes, in this view, discourage enterprise and infringe property rights, a stance sometimes called '**fiscal conservatism**'.

Neoliberalism is not only anti-statist on the grounds of economic efficiency and responsiveness, but also because of its political principles, notably its commitment to individual liberty. Neoliberals claim to be defending freedom against 'creeping collectivism'. At the extreme, these ideas lead in the direction of anarcho-capitalism (discussed in Chapter 5) and the belief that all goods and services, including the courts and public order, should be delivered by the market. The freedom defended by neoliberals is negative freedom: the removal of external restrictions on the individual. As the collective power of government is seen as the principal threat to the individual, freedom can only be ensured by 'rolling back' the state. This, in particular, means rolling back social welfare. In addition to economic arguments against welfare – for example, that increased social expenditure pushes up taxes, and that public services are inherently inefficient – neoliberals object to welfare on moral grounds. In the first place, the welfare state is criticized for having created a 'culture of dependency': it saps initiative and enterprise, and robs people of dignity and self-

INFLATION
A rise in the general price level, leading to a decline in the value of money.

FISCAL CONSERVATISM
A political-economic stance that prioritizes the lowering of taxes, cuts in public spending and reduced government debt.

respect. Welfare is thus the *cause* of disadvantage, not its cure. Such a theory resurrects the notion of the 'undeserving poor'. Charles Murray (1984) also argued that, as welfare relieves women of dependency on 'breadwinning' men, it is a major cause of family breakdown, creating an underclass largely composed of single mothers and fatherless children. A further neoliberal argument against welfare is based on a commitment to individual rights. Robert Nozick (1974) advanced this most forcefully in condemning all policies of welfare and redistribution as a violation of property rights. In this view, so long as property has been acquired justly, to transfer it, without consent, from one person to another amounts to 'legalized theft'. Underpinning this view is egoistical individualism, the idea that people owe nothing to society and are, in turn, owed nothing by society, a stance that calls the very notion of society into question.

Neoconservatism

Neoconservatism emerged in the USA in the 1970s as a backlash against the ideas and values of the 1960s. It was defined by a fear of social fragmentation or breakdown, which was seen as a product of liberal reform and the spread of '**permissiveness**'. In sharp contrast to neoliberalism, neoconservatives stress the primacy of politics and seek to strengthen leadership and authority in society. This emphasis on authority, allied to a heightened sensitivity to the fragility of society, demonstrates that neoconservatism has its roots in traditional or organic conservatism. However, it differs markedly from paternalistic conservatism, which also draws heavily on organic ideas. Whereas paternalistic conservatives believe, for instance, that community is best maintained by social reform and the reduction of poverty, neoconservatives look to strengthen community by restoring authority and imposing social discipline. Neoconservative authoritarianism is, to this extent, consistent with neoliberal libertarianism. Both of them accept the rolling back of the state's economic responsibilities.

> **PERMISSIVENESS**
> The willingness to allow people to make their own moral choices; permissiveness suggests that there are no authoritative values.

Key concept

Neoconservatism

Neoconservatism refers to developments within conservative ideology that relate to both domestic policy and foreign policy. In domestic policy, neoconservatism is defined by support for a minimal but strong state, fusing themes associated with traditional or organic conservatism with an acceptance of economic individualism and qualified support for the free market. Neoconservatives have typically sought to restore public order, strengthen 'family' or 'religious' values, and bolster national identity. In foreign policy, neoconservatism was closely associated with the Bush administration in the USA in the years following 9/11. Its central aim was to preserve and reinforce what was seen as the USA's 'benevolent global hegemony' by building up US military power and pursuing a policy of worldwide 'democracy promotion'.

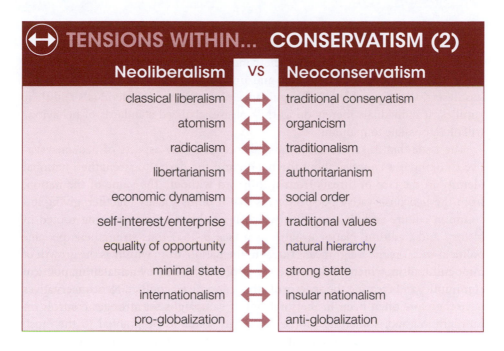

TENSIONS WITHIN... CONSERVATISM (2)		
Neoliberalism	**VS**	**Neoconservatism**
classical liberalism	⟷	traditional conservatism
atomism	⟷	organicism
radicalism	⟷	traditionalism
libertarianism	⟷	authoritarianism
economic dynamism	⟷	social order
self-interest/enterprise	⟷	traditional values
equality of opportunity	⟷	natural hierarchy
minimal state	⟷	strong state
internationalism	⟷	insular nationalism
pro-globalization	⟷	anti-globalization

Neoconservatives have developed distinctive views about both domestic policy and foreign policy. The two principal domestic concerns of neoconservatism have been with social order and public morality. Neoconservatives believe that rising crime, delinquency and anti-social behaviour are generally a consequence of a larger decline of authority that has affected most western societies since the 1960s. They have therefore called for a strengthening of social disciplines and authority at every level. This can be seen in relation to the family. For neoconservatives, the family is an authority system: it is both naturally hierarchical – children should listen to, respect and obey their parents – and naturally patriarchal. The husband is the provider and the wife the home-maker. This social authoritarianism is matched by state authoritarianism, the desire for a strong state reflected in a 'tough' stance on law and order. This led, in the USA and the UK in particular, to a greater emphasis on custodial sentences and to longer prison sentences, reflecting the belief that 'prison works'.

Neoconservatism's concern about public morality is based on a desire to reassert the moral foundations of politics. A particular target of neoconservative criticism has been the 'permissive 1960s' and the growing culture of 'doing your own thing'. In the face of this, Thatcher in the UK proclaimed her support for 'Victorian values', and in the USA organizations such as Moral Majority campaigned for a return to 'traditional' or 'family' values. Neoconservatives see two dangers in a permissive society. In the first place, the freedom to choose one's own morals or life-style could lead to the choice of immoral or 'evil' views. There is, for instance, a significant religious element in neoconservatism, especially in the USA. The second danger is not so much that people may adopt the *wrong* morals or lifestyles, but may simply choose *different* moral positions. In the neoconservative view, moral pluralism is threatening because it undermines the cohesion of society. A permissive society is a society that lacks ethical norms and unifying moral standards. It is a 'pathless desert', which provides neither guidance nor support for individuals and their families. If individuals merely do as they please, civilized standards of behaviour will be impossible to maintain.

The issue that links the domestic and foreign policy aspects of neoconservative thinking is a concern about the nation and the desire to strengthen national identity in the face of threats from within and without. The value of the nation, from the neoconservative perspective, is that it binds society together, giving it a common culture and civic identity, which is all the stronger for being rooted in history and tradition. National patriotism (see p. 164) thus strengthens people's political will. The most significant threat to the nation 'from within' is the growth of multiculturalism, which weakens the bonds of nationhood by threatening political community and creating the spectre of ethnic and racial conflict. Neoconservatives have therefore often been in the forefront of campaigns for stronger controls on immigration and, sometimes, for a privileged status to be granted to the 'host' community's culture (as discussed in Chapter 10). Such concerns have widened and deepened as a result of the advance of globalization, as discussed in the next section. The threats to the nation 'from without' are many and various. In the UK, the main perceived threat has come from the process of European integration; indeed, since the 1990s, UK conservatism has at times appeared to be defined by 'Euroscepticism'.

However, the nationalist dimension of neoconservative thinking also gave rise to a distinctive stance on foreign policy, particularly in the USA. Neoconservatism, in this form, was an approach to foreign policy-making that sought to enable the USA to take advantage of its unprecedented position of power and influence in the post-Cold War era. It consisted of a fusion of neo-Reaganism and 'hard' Wilsonianism (after Woodrow Wilson, see p. 184). Neo-Reaganism took the form of a Manichaean world-view, in which 'good' (represented by the USA) confronted 'evil' (represented by 'rogue' states and terrorist groups that possess or seek to possess, weapons of mass destruction). This implied that the USA should deter rivals and extend its global reach by achieving a position of 'strength beyond challenge' in military terms. 'Hard' Wilsonianism was expressed through the desire to spread US-style democracy throughout the world by a process of 'regime change', achieved by military means if necessary. Such 'neocon' thinking dominated US strategic thinking in the aftermath of the September 11 terrorist attacks on New York and Washington, particularly through the establishment of the 'war on terror' and the attacks on Afghanistan in 2001 and Iraq in 2003. Neoconservative foreign-policy thinking nevertheless declined in significance from about 2005 onwards, as

EUROSCEPTICISM
Hostility to European integration based on the belief that it is a threat to national sovereignty and/or national identity.

the USA recognized the limitations of achieving strategic objectives through military means alone, as well as the drawbacks of adopting a unilateral foreign-policy stance.

Conservatism in a global age

The changing character and political fortunes of conservatism since the 1980s can, to a large extent, be understood in terms of the impact of 'accelerated' globalization. For example, the rise of the New Right, particularly in its liberal, pro-market incarnation, occurred in the context of the collapse in the early 1970s of the Bretton Woods system of fixed exchange rates, which contributed to a remodelling of the world economy on neoliberal lines. Conservative parties and movements were often able to respond more quickly and more successfully to globalizing tendencies than their socialist and liberal counterparts, both because of their traditional pragmatism and because they were less deeply wedded to Keynesian-welfarist orthodoxies. Libertarian tendencies within conservatism therefore flourished at the expense of paternalist tendencies, although, as discussed earlier, this process occurred more rapidly, and was pursued with greater enthusiasm, in some countries more than others, with, for instance, Christian democratic parties being particularly resistant to the lure of neoliberalism. Nevertheless, while the 'heroic' phase of New Right politics, associated with figures such as Thatcher and Reagan, and the battle against 'big government' may have passed and given way to a more 'managerial' phase, this should not disguise the fact that market values had come to be accepted across the spectrum of conservative beliefs.

However, these shifts also confronted conservative ideology with a number of challenges. One of these was that the seeming collapse of the 'pro-state' or 'socialist' tendency that had dominated much of the post-1945 period, brought problems in its wake. To the extent that conservatism had come to be defined by its antipathy towards state control and economic management, the 'death of socialism' threatened to rob it of its unifying focus and ideological resolve. A further problem stemmed from concerns about the long-term viability of the free-market philosophy. Faith in the free market has always been limited, historically and culturally. Enthusiasm for unregulated capitalism has been a largely Anglo-American phenomenon that peaked during the nineteenth century in association with classical liberalism, and was revived in the late twentieth century through the advent of neoliberalism. 'Rolling back' the state in economic life may sharpen incentives, intensify competition and promote entrepreneurialism, but sooner or later its disadvantages become apparent, notably short-termism, low investment, widening inequality and increased social exclusion.

Nevertheless, the global financial crisis, which peaked in the autumn of 2008 with the world economy seemingly hovering on the brink of systemic collapse, precipitated developments that have had major ideological ramifications. The most significant of these developments was the steepest decline in global output since

Key concept

Populism

Populism (from the Latin *populus*, meaning 'the people') has been used to describe both distinctive political movements and a particular tradition of political thought. Movements or parties described as populist have been characterized by their claim to support the common people in the face of 'corrupt' economic or political elites. As a political tradition, populism reflects the belief that the instincts and wishes of the people provide the principal legitimate guide to political action. Populist politicians therefore make a direct appeal to the people and claim to give expression to their deepest hopes and fears, all intermediary institutions being distrusted. Although populism may be linked to any cause or ideology, it is often seen as implicitly authoritarian, 'populist' democracy being the enemy of 'pluralist' democracy.

the 1930s, causing tax revenues to plummet and government debt to soar, and even bringing the creditworthiness of some countries into question. Although the initial response to the financial crisis was a return to Keynesianism, in the form of a US-led coordinated policy of '**fiscal stimulus**', the crisis also provided new opportunities from neoliberalism. From a neoliberal perspective, soaring government debt is essentially a consequence of a failure to control state spending, implying that the solution to indebtedness is 'fiscal retrenchment', or '**austerity**'. For example, in the UK the election of a Conservative-led coalition government in 2010 led to a swift break with Keynesianism and the introduction of a programme of spending cuts more severe than those put in place under Thatcher in the 1980s. Whereas the adoption of austerity was essentially a political choice in the UK, in the case of Greece, Ireland, Spain, Portugal and Cyprus, a reordering of the economy along neoliberal lines was a condition of bailouts imposed during 2010–13 by the EU, the IMF and the European Central Bank.

FISCAL STIMULUS
An economic strategy designed to promote growth by either, or both, lowering taxes or increasing government spending.

AUSTERITY
Sternness or severity; as an economic strategy, austerity refers to public spending cuts designed to eradicate a budget deficit, underpinned by faith in market forces.

NATIONAL CONSERVATISM
A form of conservatism that prioritises the defence of national, cultural and, sometimes, ethnic identity over other concerns, often based on parallels between the family and the nation.

Finally, conservatism has not only contributed to struggles over the nature and direction of globalization, favouring the construction of a market-based world economy as opposed to a regulated or 'managed' one, but it has also served as a counter-globalization force, a mechanism of resistance. This has been most apparent in the rise of far-right and anti-immigration parties, which have drawn on **national conservatism** in adopting a 'backward-looking' and culturally, and perhaps ethnically, 'pure' model of national identity. In many ways, this development has been part of the wider revival of populism, which has seen growing disenchantment with conventional politics and the emergence of anti-establishment leaders and movements in many mature democracies, a phenomenon often called 'anti-politics' (see p. 135). Right-wing, populist parties, articulating concerns about immigration and multiculturalism, have become a feature of politics in many European states, a trend fuelled by the combination of EU enlargement and freedom of movement within the Union and, since 2015, by the migrant crisis in Europe.

The *Front National* in France, led by Marine Le Pen, the daughter of the founder of the party, Jean-Marie Le Pen, has attracted growing electoral support since the 1980s for a platform largely based on resistance to immigration. In 2012, Le Pen gained 6.4 million votes (18 per cent) in the first round of the presidential election. Other anti-immigration and anti-multiculturalist parties include the Freedom Party in Austria, the UK Independence Party, the Northern League in Italy, the *Vlaams Blok* in Belgium, the two Progress Parties in Norway and Denmark, and the Danish People's Party, which broke away from the Progress Party in 1995. Such national conservative parties and movements tend to prosper in conditions of fear, insecurity and social dislocation, their strength being their capacity to represent unity and certainty, binding national identity to tradition and established values. The link between conservatism and nationalism is examined in greater depth in Chapter 6.

? QUESTIONS FOR DISCUSSION

- Why, and to what extent, have conservatives supported tradition?
- Is conservatism a 'disposition' rather than a political ideology?
- Why has conservatism been described as a philosophy of imperfection?
- What are the implications of the belief that society is an organic entity?
- How does the conservative view of property differ from the liberal view?
- How far do conservatives go in endorsing authority?
- Is conservatism merely ruling class ideology?
- To what extent do conservatives favour pragmatism over principle?
- What are the similarities and differences between traditional conservatism and Christian democracy?
- How and why have neoliberals criticized welfare?
- To what extent are neoliberalism and neoconservatism compatible?
- Why and how have conservatives sought to resist globalization?

📖 FURTHER READING

Aughey, A. et al., *The Conservative Political Tradition in Britain and the United States* (1992). A stimulating examination of similarities and difference between conservative thought in the USA and the UK.

Honderich, T., *Conservatism: Burke, Nozick, Bush, Blair?* (2005). A distinctive and rigorously unsympathetic account of conservative thought; closely argued and interesting.

O'Hara, K., *Conservatism* (2011). A defence of a small-c sceptical conservatism that draws heavily on the writings of Burke and Oakeshott.

Scruton, R., *The Meaning of Conservatism* (2001). A stylish and openly sympathetic study that develops a distinctive view of the conservative tradition.

CHAPTER

4 Socialism

Preview

The term 'socialist' derives from the Latin *sociare*, meaning to combine or to share. Its earliest known usage was in 1827 in the UK, in an issue of the *Co-operative Magazine*. By the early 1830s, the followers of Robert Owen in the UK and Henri de Saint-Simon in France had started to refer to their beliefs as 'socialism' and, by the 1840s, the term was familiar in a range of industrialized countries, notably France, Belgium and the German states.

Socialism, as an ideology, has traditionally been defined by its opposition to capitalism and the attempt to provide a more humane and socially worthwhile alternative. At the core of socialism is a vision of human beings as social creatures united by their common humanity. This highlights the degree to which individual identity is fashioned by social interaction and the membership of social groups and collective bodies. Socialists therefore prefer cooperation to competition. The central, and some would say defining, value of socialism is equality, especially social equality. Socialists believe that social equality is the essential guarantee of social stability and cohesion, and that it promotes freedom, in the sense that it satisfies material needs and provides the basis for personal development. Socialism, however, contains a bewildering variety of divisions and rival traditions. These divisions have been about both 'means' (how socialism should be achieved) and 'ends' (the nature of the future socialist society). For example, communists or Marxists have usually supported revolution and sought to abolish capitalism through the creation of a classless society based on the common ownership of wealth. In contrast, democratic socialists or social democrats have embraced gradualism and aimed to reform or 'humanize' the capitalist system through a narrowing of material inequalities and the abolition of poverty.

Origins and development

Although socialists have sometimes claimed an intellectual heritage that goes back to Plato's *Republic* or Thomas More's *Utopia* ([1516] 1965), as with liberalism and conservatism, the origins of socialism lie in the nineteenth century. Socialism arose as a reaction against the social and economic conditions generated in Europe by the growth of industrial capitalism (see p. 97). Socialist ideas were quickly linked to the development of a new but growing class of industrial workers, who suffered the poverty and degradation that are so often features of early industrialization. Although socialism and liberalism have common roots in the Enlightenment, and share a faith in principles such as reason and progress, socialism emerged as a critique of liberal market society and was defined by its attempt to offer an alternative to industrial capitalism.

The character of early socialism was influenced by the harsh and often inhuman conditions in which the industrial working class lived and worked. Wages were typically low, child and female labour were commonplace, the working day often lasted up to twelve hours and the threat of unemployment was ever-present. In addition, the new working class was disorientated, being largely composed of first-generation urban dwellers, unfamiliar with the conditions of industrial life and work, and possessing few of the social institutions that could give their lives stability or meaning. As a result, early socialists often sought a radical, even revolutionary alternative to industrial capitalism. For instance, Charles Fourier (1772–1837) in France and Robert Owen (see p. 124) in the UK subscribed to **utopianism** in founding experimental communities based on sharing and cooperation. The Germans Karl Marx (see p. 124) and Friedrich Engels (1820–95) developed more complex and systematic theories, which claimed to uncover the 'laws of history' and proclaimed that the revolutionary overthrow of capitalism was inevitable.

In the late nineteenth century, the character of socialism was transformed by a gradual improvement in working-class living conditions and the advance of political democracy. The growth of trade unions, working-class political parties and sports and social clubs served to provide greater economic security and to integrate the working class into industrial society. In the advanced industrial societies of western Europe, it became increasingly difficult to continue to see the working class as a revolutionary force. Socialist political parties progressively adopted legal and constitutional tactics, encouraged by the gradual extension of the vote to working-class men. By World War I, the socialist world was clearly divided between those socialist parties that had sought power through the ballot box and preached reform, and those that proclaimed a continuing need for revolution. The Russian Revolution of 1917 entrenched this split: revolutionary socialists, following the example of V. I. Lenin (see p. 124) and the Bolsheviks, usually adopted the term

UTOPIANISM
A belief in the unlimited possibilities of human development, typically embodied in the vision of a perfect or ideal society, a utopia (see p. 143).

Key concept

Capitalism

Capitalism is an economic system as well as a form of property ownership. It has a number of key features. First, it is based on generalized commodity production, a 'commodity' being a good or service produced for exchange – it has market value rather than use value. Second, productive wealth in a capitalist economy is predominantly held in private hands. Third, economic life is organized according to impersonal market forces, in particular the forces of demand (what consumers are willing and able to consume) and supply (what producers are willing and able to produce). Fourth, in a capitalist economy, material self-interest and maximization provide the main motivations for enterprise and hard work. Some degree of state regulation is nevertheless found in all capitalist systems.

'**communism**', while reformist socialists described their ideas as either 'socialism' or '**social democracy**'.

The twentieth century witnessed the spread of socialist ideas into African, Asian and Latin American countries with little or no experience of industrial capitalism. Socialism in these countries often developed out of the anticolonial struggle, rather than a class struggle. The idea of class exploitation was replaced by that of colonial oppression, creating a potent fusion of socialism and nationalism, which is examined more fully in Chapter 5. The Bolshevik model of communism was imposed on eastern Europe after 1945; it was adopted in China after the revolution of 1949 and subsequently spread to North Korea, Vietnam, Cambodia and elsewhere. More moderate forms of socialism were practised elsewhere in the developing world; for example, by the Congress Party in India. Distinctive forms of African and Arab socialism also developed, being influenced respectively by the communal values of traditional tribal life and the moral principles of Islam. In Latin America in the 1960s and 1970s, socialist revolutionaries waged war against military dictatorships, often seen to be operating in the interests of US imperialism. The Castro regime, which came to power after the Cuban revolution of 1959, developed close links with the Soviet Union, while the Sandinista guerrillas, who seized power in Nicaragua in 1979, remained non-aligned. In Chile in 1970, Salvador Allende became the world's first democratically elected Marxist head of state, but was overthrown and killed in a CIA-backed coup in 1973.

COMMUNISM
The principle of the common ownership of wealth, or a system of comprehensive collectivization; communism is often viewed as 'Marxism in practice' (see p. 114).

SOCIAL DEMOCRACY
A moderate or reformist brand of socialism that favours a balance between the market and the state, rather than the abolition of capitalism.

Since the late twentieth century, socialism has suffered a number of spectacular reverses, leading some to proclaim the 'death of socialism'. The most dramatic of these reverses was, of course, the collapse of communism in the eastern European revolutions of 1989–91. However, rather than socialists uniting around the principles of western social democracy, these principles were thrown into doubt as parliamentary socialist parties in many parts of the world embraced ideas and policies that are more commonly associated with liberalism or even conservatism. The final section of this chapter looks at the extent to which these events were linked to globalization (see p. 20) and considers the extent to which socialist ideology has been radicalized in response to the 2007–9 global financial crisis.

Core themes: no man is an island

One of the difficulties of analysing socialism is that the term has been understood in at least three distinctive ways. From one point of view, socialism is seen as an economic model, usually linked to some form of collectivization and planning. Socialism, in this sense, stands as an alternative to capitalism, the choice between these two qualitatively different productive systems traditionally being seen as the most crucial of all economic questions. However, the choice between 'pure' socialism and 'pure' capitalism was always an illusion, as all economic forms have, in different ways, blended features of both systems. Indeed, modern socialists tend to view socialism not so much as an alternative to capitalism, but as a means of harnessing capitalism to broader social ends. The second approach treats socialism as an instrument of the labour movement. Socialism, in this view, represents the interests of the working class and offers a programme through which the workers can acquire political or economic power. Socialism is thus really a form of '**labourism**', a vehicle for advancing the interest of organized labour. From this perspective, the significance of socialism fluctuates with the fortunes of the working-class movement worldwide. Nevertheless, though the historical link between socialism and organized labour cannot be doubted, socialist ideas have also been associated with skilled craftsmen, the peasantry and, for that matter, with political and bureaucratic elites. That is why, in this book, socialism is understood in a third and broader sense as a political creed or ideology, characterized by a particular cluster of ideas, values and theories. The most significant of these are:

LABOURISM
A tendency exhibited by socialist parties to serve the interests of the organized labour movement rather than pursue broader ideological goals.

- community
- cooperation
- equality
- class politics
- common ownership.

Community

At its heart, socialism offers a unifying vision of human beings as social creatures, capable of overcoming social and economic problems by drawing on the power of the community rather than simply individual effort. This is a collectivist vision because it stresses the capacity of human beings for collective action, their willingness and ability to pursue goals by working together, as opposed to striving for personal self-interest. Most socialists, for instance, would be prepared to echo the words of the English metaphysical poet, John Donne (1571–1631):

> No man is an Island entire of itself;
> every man is a piece of the Continent, a part of the main . . .
> any man's death diminishes me, because I am involved in Mankind; and therefore never send to know for whom the bell tolls;
> it tolls for thee.

Human beings are therefore 'comrades', 'brothers' or 'sisters', tied to one another by the bonds of a common humanity. This is expressed in the principle of fraternity.

Socialists are far less willing than either liberals or conservatives to assume that human nature is unchanging and fixed at birth. Rather, they believe that human nature is malleable or 'plastic', shaped by the experiences and circumstances of social life. In the long-standing philosophical debate about whether 'nurture' or 'nature' determines human behaviour, socialists side resolutely with nurture. From birth – perhaps even while in the womb – each individual is subjected to experiences that mould and condition his or her personality. All human skills and attributes are learnt from society, from the fact that we stand upright to the language we speak. Whereas liberals draw a clear distinction between the 'individual' and 'society', socialists believe that the individual is inseparable from society. Human beings are neither self-sufficient nor self-contained; to think of them as separate or atomized 'individuals' is absurd. Individuals can only be understood, and understand themselves, through the social groups to which they belong. The behaviour of human beings therefore tells us more about the society in which they live and have been brought up, than it does about any abiding or immutable human nature.

FRATERNITY
Literally, brotherhood; bonds of sympathy and comradeship between and among human beings.

The radical edge of socialism derives not from its concern with what people are like, but with what they

Key concept
Collectivism

Collectivism is, broadly, the belief that collective human endeavour is of greater practical and moral value than individual self-striving. It thus reflects the idea that human nature has a social core, and implies that social groups, whether 'classes', 'nations', 'races' or whatever, are meaningful political entities. However, the term is used with little consistency. Mikhail Bakunin (see p. 153) and other anarchists used collectivism to refer to self-governing associations of free individuals. Others have treated collectivism as strictly the opposite of individualism (see p. 27), holding that it implies that collective interests should prevail over individual ones. It is also sometimes linked to the state as the mechanism through which collective interests are upheld, suggesting that the growth of state responsibilities marks the advance of collectivism.

have the capacity to become. This has led socialists to develop utopian visions of a better society, in which human beings can achieve genuine emancipation and fulfilment as members of a community. African and Asian socialists have often stressed that their traditional, preindustrial societies already emphasize the importance of social life and the value of community. In these circumstances, socialism has sought to preserve traditional social values in the face of the challenge from western individualism (see p. 27). As Julius Nyerere, president of Tanzania 1964–85, pointed out, 'We, in Africa, have no more real need to be "converted" to socialism, than we have of being "taught" democracy.' He therefore described his own views as 'tribal socialism'.

In the West, however, the social dimension of life has had to be 'reclaimed' after generations of industrial capitalism. This was the goal of nineteenth-century utopian socialists such as Charles Fourier and Robert Owen, who organized experiments in communal living. Fourier encouraged the founding of model communities, each containing about 1,800 members, which he called 'phalansteries'. Owen also set up a number of experimental communities, the best known being New Harmony in Indiana, 1824–9. The most enduring communitarian experiment has been the *kibbutz* system in Israel, which consists of a system of cooperative, usually rural, settlements that are collectively owned and run by their members. However, the communitarian emphasis of the *kibbutz* system has been substantially diluted since the 1960s by, for instance, the abandonment of collective child rearing.

Cooperation

If human beings are social animals, socialists believe that the natural relationship among them is one of **cooperation** rather than competition. Socialists believe that competition pits one individual against another, encouraging each of them to deny or ignore their social nature rather than embrace it. As a result, competition fosters only a limited range of social attributes and, instead, promotes selfishness and aggression. Cooperation, on the other hand, makes moral and economic sense. Individuals who work together rather than against each other develop bonds of sympathy, caring and affection. Furthermore, the energies of the community rather than those of the single individual can be harnessed. The Russian anarchist Peter Kropotkin (see p. 153), for example, suggested that the principal reason why the human species had survived and prospered was because of its capacity for 'mutual aid'. Socialists believe that human beings can be motivated by moral incentives, and not merely by material incentives. In theory, capitalism rewards individuals for the work they do: the harder they work, or the more abundant their skills, the greater their rewards will be. The moral incentive to work hard, however, is the desire to contribute to the common good, which develops out of a sympathy, or sense of responsibility, for fellow human beings, especially those in need. While few modern social democrats would contemplate the outright abolition of material incentives,

COOPERATION
Working together; collective effort intended to achieve mutual benefit.

they nevertheless insist on the need for a balance of some kind between material and moral incentives. For instance, socialists would argue that an important incentive for achieving economic growth is that it helps to finance the provision of welfare support for the poorest and most vulnerable elements in society.

The socialist commitment to cooperation has stimulated the growth of cooperative enterprises, designed to replace the competitive and hierarchic businesses that have proliferated under capitalism. Both producers' and consumers' cooperatives have attempted to harness the energies of groups of people working for mutual benefit. In the UK, cooperative societies sprang up in the early nineteenth century. These societies bought goods in bulk and sold them cheaply to their working-class members. The 'Rochdale Pioneers' set up a grocery shop in 1844 and their example was soon taken up throughout industrial England and Scotland. Producer cooperatives, owned and run by their workforce, are common in parts of northern Spain and the former Yugoslavia, where industry is organized according to the principle of workers' self-management. Collective farms in the Soviet Union were also designed to be cooperative and self-managing, though in practice they operated within a rigid planning system and were usually controlled by local party bosses.

Equality

A commitment to equality is in many respects the defining feature of socialist ideology, equality being the political value that most clearly distinguishes socialism from its rivals, notably liberalism and conservatism. Socialist **egalitarianism** is characterized by a belief in social equality, or equality of outcome. Socialists have advanced at least three arguments in favour of this form of equality. First, social equality upholds *justice* or fairness. Socialists are reluctant to explain the inequality of wealth simply in terms of innate differences of ability among individuals. Socialists believe that just as capitalism has fostered competitive and selfish behaviour, human inequality very largely reflects the unequal structure of society. They do not hold the naïve belief that all people are born identical, possessing precisely the same capacities and skills. An egalitarian society would not, for instance, be one in which all students gained the same mark in their mathematics examinations. Nevertheless, socialists believe that the most significant forms of human inequality are a result of unequal treatment by society, rather than unequal endowment by nature. Justice, from a socialist perspective, therefore demands that people are treated equally (or at least more equally) by society in terms of their rewards and material circumstances. Formal equality, in its legal and political senses, is clearly inadequate in itself because it disregards the structural inequalities of the capitalist system. Equality of opportunity, for its part, legitimizes inequality by perpetuating the myth of innate inequality.

EGALITARIANISM
A theory or practice based on the desire to promote equality; egalitarianism is sometimes seen as the belief that equality is the primary political value.

PERSPECTIVES ON... EQUALITY

LIBERALS believe that people are 'born' equal in the sense that they are of equal moral worth. This implies formal equality, notably legal and political equality, as well as equality of opportunity; but social equality is likely to threaten freedom and penalize talent. Whereas classical liberals emphasize the need for strict meritocracy and economic incentives, modern liberals argue that genuine equal opportunities require relative social equality.

CONSERVATIVES have traditionally viewed society as naturally hierarchical and have thus dismissed equality as an abstract and unachievable goal. Nevertheless, the New Right evinces a strongly individualist belief in equality of opportunity while emphasizing the economic benefits of material inequality.

SOCIALISTS regard equality as a fundamental value and, in particular, endorse social equality. Despite shifts within social democracy towards a liberal belief in equality of opportunity, social equality, whether in its relative (social democratic) or absolute (communist) sense, has been seen as essential to ensuring social cohesion and fraternity, establishing justice or equity, and enlarging freedom in a positive sense.

ANARCHISTS place a particular stress on political equality, understood as an equal and absolute right to personal autonomy, implying that all forms of political inequality amount to oppression. Anarcho-communists believe in absolute social equality achieved through the collective ownership of productive wealth.

FASCISTS believe that humankind is marked by radical inequality, both between leaders and followers and between the various nations or races of the world. Nevertheless, the emphasis on the nation or race implies that all members are equal, at least in terms of their core social identity.

FEMINISTS take equality to mean sexual equality, in the sense of equal rights and equal opportunities (liberal feminism) or equal social or economic power (socialist feminism) irrespective of gender. However, some radical feminists have argued that the demand for equality may simply lead to women being 'male-identified'.

GREENS advance the notion of biocentric equality, which emphasizes that all life forms have an equal right to 'live and blossom'. Conventional notions of equality are therefore seen as anthropocentric, in that they exclude the interests of all organisms and entities other than humankind.

Second, social equality underpins *community* and cooperation. If people live in equal social circumstances, they will be more likely to identify with one another and work together for common benefit. Equal outcomes therefore strengthen social solidarity. Social inequality, by the same token, leads to conflict and instability. This also explains why socialists have criticized equality of opportunity for breeding a 'survival of the fittest' mentality. R. H. Tawney (see p. 125), for example, dismissed the idea of equal opportunities as a 'tadpole philosophy', emphasizing the tiny proportion of tadpoles that develop into frogs.

Third, socialists support social equality because they hold that *need-satisfaction* is the basis for human fulfilment and self-realization. A 'need' is a necessity: it *demands* satisfaction; it is not simply a frivolous wish or a passing fancy. Basic needs, such as the need for food, water, shelter, companionship and so on, are fundamental to the human condition, which means that, for socialists, their satisfaction is the very stuff of freedom. Marx expressed this in his communist theory of distribution: 'From each according to his ability, to each according to his needs.' Since all people have broadly similar needs, distributing wealth on the basis of need-satisfaction clearly has egalitarian implications. Nevertheless, need-satisfaction can also have inegalitarian implications, as in the case of so-called 'special' needs, arising, for instance, from physical or mental disability.

While socialists agree about the virtue of social and economic equality, they disagree about the extent to which this can and should be brought about. Marxists and communists believe in *absolute* social equality, brought about by the abolition of private property and **collectivization** of productive wealth. Perhaps the most famous experiment in such radical egalitarianism took place in China under the 'Cultural Revolution' (see p. 104). Social democrats, however, believe in *relative* social equality, achieved by the redistribution of wealth through the welfare state and a system of **progressive taxation**. The social-democratic desire to tame capitalism rather than abolish it, reflects an acceptance of a continuing role for material incentives, and the fact that the significance of need-satisfaction is largely confined to the eradication of poverty. This, in turn, blurs the distinction between social equality and equality of opportunity.

> **COLLECTIVIZATION**
> The abolition of private property and the establishment of a comprehensive system of common or public ownership, usually through the mechanisms of the state.

> **PROGRESSIVE TAXATION**
> A system of taxation in which the rich pay a higher proportion of their income in tax than the poor.

Class politics

Socialists have traditionally viewed **social class** as the deepest and most politically significant of social divisions. Socialist class politics have been expressed in two ways, however. In the first, social class is an analytical tool. In pre-socialist societies at least, socialists have believed that human beings tend to think and act together with others with whom they share a common economic position or interest. In other words, social classes, rather than individuals, are the principal actors in history and therefore provide the key to understanding social and political change. This is demonstrated most clearly in the Marxist belief that historical change is the product

> **SOCIAL CLASS**
> A social division based on economic or social factors; a social class is a group of people who share a similar socio-economic position.

POLITICAL IDEOLOGIES IN ACTION . . .
China's 'Cultural Revolution'

SIGNIFICANCE: Mao portrayed the Cultural Revolution as a stark clash between 'socialism' and 'revisionism'. Ostensibly aimed at reviving the revolutionary spirit that had brought the Communist Party to power in 1949, its primary targets were the bureaucratization of the party, ideological degeneration in society as a whole and widening socio-economic inequality. Aside from any other motivations, such thinking clearly had a profound impact on tens of thousands of radicalized young people. However, as an exercise in socialist egalitarianism, the Cultural Revolution was a dismal failure. For one thing, political power came to be concentrated in the hands of Mao himself, supported by an elaborate and inescapable cult of personality. For another, as Chinese society descended into chaos (constrained after 1968 only as the army displaced the Red Guards) and was left with a barely functioning economy, the Cultural Revolution brought little discernible benefit to either the urban proletariat or the rural poor.

EVENTS: In August 1966, China's Communist leader, Mao Zedong, officially launched the 'Cultural Revolution' (known in full as 'The Great Proletarian Cultural Revelation'), which continued until Mao's death in 1976. One of the most complicated events in the history of the People's Republic of China, the Cultural Revolution had a profound effect on every aspect of Chinese society and politics. The nation's schools were shut down and a massive youth mobilization was instigated. As the movement escalated, students formed paramilitary groups called the Red Guards, which attacked and harassed 'capitalist roaders' and members of China's elderly and intellectual populations. Not only were wage differentials and all forms of privilege and hierarchy denounced, but even competitive sports like football were banned. There was also a dramatic purge of the Chinese Communist Party (CCP) as well as of officeholders in the economy, education and cultural institutions.

Rather than being seen as either an explosion of youthful idealism or an attempt to re-energize the Chinese Revolution, avoiding, in particular, mistakes that had been made in the Soviet Union, the Cultural Revolution may be better interpreted as a consequence of a struggle for power within the higher echelons of the CCP. His authority badly damaged by the failure of the Great Leap Forward (1958–61), Mao treated the Cultural Revolution primarily as an opportunity to sideline or remove his opponents, most notably State Chairman Liu Shaoqi.

of class conflict. The second form of socialist class politics focuses specifically on the working class, and is concerned with political struggle and emancipation. Socialism has often been viewed as an expression of the interests of the working class, and the working class has been seen as the vehicle through which socialism will be achieved. Nevertheless, social class has not been accepted as a necessary or permanent feature of society: socialist societies have either been seen as classless or as societies in which class inequalities have been substantially reduced. In emancipating itself from capitalist exploitation, the working class thus also emancipates itself from its own class identity, becoming, in the process, fully developed human beings.

Socialists have nevertheless been divided about the nature and importance of social class. In the Marxist tradition, class is linked to economic power, as defined by the individual's relationship to the means of production. From this perspective, class divisions are divisions between 'capital' and 'labour'; that is, between the owners of productive wealth (the **bourgeoisie**) and those who live off the sale of their labour power (the **proletariat**). This Marxist two-class model is characterized by irreconcilable conflict between the bourgeoisie and the proletariat, leading, inevitably, to the overthrow of capitalism through a proletarian revolution. Social democrats, on the other hand, have tended to define social class in terms of income and status differences between 'white collar' or non-manual workers (the middle class) and 'blue collar' or manual workers (the working class). From this perspective, the advance of socialism is associated with the *narrowing* of divisions between the middle class and the working class brought about through economic and social intervention. Social democrats have therefore believed in social amelioration and class harmony rather than social polarization and class war.

However, the link between socialism and class politics has declined significantly since the mid-twentieth century. This has largely been a consequence of declining levels of class solidarity and, in particular, the shrinkage of the traditional working class or urban proletariat. The waning in class politics is a consequence of deindustrialization, reflected in the decline of traditional labour-intensive industries such as coal, steel, shipbuilding and so on. Not only has this forced traditional socialist parties to revise their policies in order to appeal to middle-class voters, but it has also encouraged them to define their radicalism less in terms of class emancipation and more in relation to issues such as gender equality, ecological sustainability, or peace and international development.

> **BOURGEOISIE**
> A Marxist term denoting the ruling class of a capitalist society, the owners of productive wealth.
>
> **PROLETARIAT**
> A Marxist term denoting a class that subsists through the sale of its labour power; strictly speaking, the proletariat is not equivalent to the manual working class.

Common ownership

Socialists have often traced the origins of competition and inequality to the institution of private property, by which they usually mean productive wealth or 'capital', rather than personal belongings such as clothes, furniture or houses. This attitude to

PERSPECTIVES ON... **THE ECONOMY**

LIBERALS see the economy as a vital part of civil society and have a strong preference for a market or capitalist economic order based on property, competition and material incentives. However, while classical liberals favour laissez-faire capitalism, modern liberals recognize the limitations of the market and accept limited economic management.

CONSERVATIVES show clear support for private enterprise but have traditionally favoured pragmatic, if limited, intervention, fearing the free-for-all of laissez-faire and the attendant risks of social instability. The New Right, however, endorses unregulated capitalism.

SOCIALISTS in the Marxist tradition have expressed a preference for common ownership and absolute social equality, which in orthodox communism was expressed in state collectivization and central planning. Social democrats, though, support welfare or regulated capitalism, believing that the market is a good servant but a bad master.

ANARCHISTS reject any form of economic control or management. However, while anarcho-communists endorse common ownership and small-scale self-management, anarcho-capitalists advocate an entirely unregulated market economy.

FASCISTS have sought a 'third way' between capitalism and communism, often expressed through the ideas of corporatism, supposedly drawing labour and capital together into an organic whole. Planning and nationalization are supported as attempts to subordinate profit to the (alleged) needs of the nation or race.

GREENS condemn both market capitalism and state collectivism for being growth-obsessed and environmentally unsustainable. Economics must therefore be subordinate to ecology, and the drive for profit at any cost must be replaced by a concern with long-term sustainability and harmony between humankind and nature.

property sets socialism apart from liberalism and conservatism, which both regard property ownership as natural and proper. Socialists criticize private property for a number of reasons:

- Property is *unjust*: wealth is produced by the collective effort of human labour and should therefore be owned by the community, not by private individuals.
- It breeds acquisitiveness and so is *morally corrupting*. Private property encourages people to be materialistic, to believe that human happiness or fulfilment can be gained through the pursuit of wealth. Those who own property wish to accumulate more, while those who have little or no wealth long to acquire it.

- It is *divisive*. It fosters conflict in society; for example, between owners and workers, employers and employees, or simply the rich and the poor.

Socialists have therefore proposed that the institution of private property either be abolished and replaced by the common ownership of productive wealth, or, more modestly, that the right to property be balanced against the interests of the community. **Fundamentalist socialists**, such as Marx and Engels, envisaged the abolition of private property, and hence the creation of a classless, communist society in place of capitalism. Their clear preference was that property be owned collectively and used for the benefit of humanity. However, they said little about how this goal could be achieved in practice. When Lenin and the Bolsheviks seized power in Russia in 1917, they believed that socialism could be built through **nationalization**. This process was not completed until the 1930s, when Stalin's 'second revolution' witnessed the construction of a centrally planned economy, a system of state collectivization. 'Common ownership' came to mean 'state ownership', or what the Soviet constitution described as 'socialist state property'. The Soviet Union thus developed a form of **state socialism**.

FUNDAMENTALIST SOCIALISM
A form of socialism that seeks to abolish capitalism and replace it with a qualitatively different kind of society.

NATIONALIZATION
The extension of state or public ownership over private assets or industries, either individual enterprises or the entire economy (often called collectivization).

STATE SOCIALISM
A form of socialism in which the state controls and directs economic life, acting, in theory, in the interests of the people.

MIXED ECONOMY
An economy in which there is a mixture of publicly owned and privately owned industries.

Social democrats have also been attracted to the state as an instrument through which wealth can be collectively owned and the economy rationally planned. However, in the West, nationalization has been applied more selectively, its objective being not full state collectivization but the construction of a **mixed economy**. In the UK, for example, the Attlee Labour government (1945–51) nationalized what it called the 'commanding heights' of the economy: major industries such as coal, steel, electricity and gas. Through these industries, the government hoped to regulate the entire economy without the need for comprehensive collectivization. However, since the 1950s, parliamentary socialist parties have gradually distanced themselves from the 'politics of ownership', preferring to define socialism in terms of the pursuit of equality and social justice rather than the advance of public ownership.

Roads to socialism

Two major issues have divided competing traditions and tendencies within socialism. The first is the goals, or 'ends', for which socialists should strive. Socialists have held very different conceptions of what a socialist society should look like; in effect, they have developed competing definitions of 'socialism'. The principal disagreement here is between fundamentalist socialism and **revisionist socialism**, represented, respectively, by the communist and social democratic traditions. These traditions are examined in the next two sections of this chapter. This section discusses the second issue that has divided socialists: the 'means' they should use to achieve socialist ends, sometimes seen as the 'roads to socialism'. This concern with means follows from the fact that socialism has always had an oppositional character: it is a force for change, for the transformation of the capitalist or colonial societies in which it emerged. The 'road' that socialists have adopted is not merely a matter of strategic significance; it both determines the character of the socialist movement and influences the form of socialism eventually achieved. In other words, means and ends within socialism are often interconnected.

> **REVISIONIST SOCIALISM**
> A form of socialism that has revised its critique of capitalism and seeks to reconcile greater social justice with surviving capitalist forms.

Revolutionary socialism

Many early socialists believed that socialism could only be introduced by the revolutionary overthrow of the existing political system, and accepted that violence would be an inevitable feature of such a **revolution**. One of the earliest advocates of revolution was the French socialist Auguste Blanqui (1805–81), who proposed the formation of a small band of dedicated conspirators to plan and carry out a revolutionary seizure of power. Marx and Engels, on the other hand, envisaged a 'proletarian revolution', in which the class-conscious working masses would rise up and overthrow capitalism. The first successful socialist revolution did not, however, take place until 1917, when a dedicated and disciplined group of revolutionaries, led by Lenin and the Bolsheviks, seized power in Russia in what was more a *coup d'état* than a popular insurrection. In many ways, the Bolshevik Revolution served as a model for subsequent generations of socialist revolutionaries.

During the nineteenth century, revolutionary tactics were attractive to socialists for two reasons. First, the early stages of industrialization produced stark injustice as the working masses were afflicted by grinding poverty and widespread unemployment. Capitalism was viewed as a system of naked oppression and exploitation, and the working class was thought to be on the brink of revolution. When Marx and Engels wrote in 1848 that 'A spectre is haunting Europe – the spectre of Communism', they were writing against a background of revolt and revolution in many parts of the continent. Second, the working classes had few alternative means of political influence; indeed, almost everywhere they were excluded from political life. Where autocratic monarchies persisted throughout the nineteenth century, as in Russia, these were dominated by the landed aristocracy. Where constitutional and representative government had developed, the right to vote was usually restricted by a property qualification to the middle classes.

> **REVOLUTION**
> A fundamental and irreversible change, often a brief but dramatic period of upheaval; systemic change.

Revolution has, however, not merely been a tactical consideration for socialists; it also reflects their analysis of the state and of the nature of state power.

Whereas liberals believe the state to be a neutral body, responding to the interests of all citizens and acting in the common good, revolutionary socialists have viewed the state as an agent of class oppression, acting in the interests of 'capital' and against those of 'labour'. Marxists, for example, believe that political power reflects class interests, and that the state is a **bourgeois state**, inevitably biased in favour of capital. Political reform and gradual change are clearly pointless. Universal suffrage and regular and competitive elections are at best a façade, their purpose being to conceal the reality of unequal class and to misdirect the political energies of the working class. A class-conscious proletariat thus has no alternative: in order to build socialism, it has first to overthrow the bourgeois state through political revolution.

In the second half of the twentieth century, faith in revolution was most evident among socialists in the developing world. In the post-1945 period, many national liberation movements embraced the 'armed struggle', in the belief that colonial rule could neither be negotiated nor voted out of existence. In Asia, the Chinese Revolution of 1949, led by Mao Zedong (1893–1976), was the culmination of a long military campaign against both Japan and the Chinese Nationalists, the Kuomintang. Vietnamese national unity was achieved in 1975 after a prolonged war fought first against France, and subsequently against the USA. Until his death in 1967, Che Guevara, the Argentinian revolutionary, led guerrilla forces in various parts of Latin America and commanded troops during the Cuban revolution of 1959, which brought Fidel Castro to power. Similar revolutionary struggles took place in Africa: for example, the bitter war through which Algeria eventually gained independence from France in 1962.

The choice of revolutionary or insurrectionary political means had profound consequences for socialism. For instance, the use of revolution usually led to the pursuit of fundamentalist ends. Revolution had the advantage that it allowed the remnants of the old order to be overthrown and an entirely new social system to be constructed. Thus when the Khmer Rouge, led by Pol Pot, seized power in Cambodia in 1975, they declared 'Year Zero'. Capitalism could be abolished and a qualitatively different socialist society established in its place. Socialism, in this context, usually took the form of state collectivization, modelled on the Soviet Union during the Stalinist period. The revolutionary 'road' was nevertheless also associated with a drift towards dictatorship and the use of political repression. This occurred for a number of reasons. First, the use of force accustomed the new rulers to regard violence as a legitimate instrument of policy; as Mao put it, 'power resides in the barrel of a gun'. Second, revolutionary parties typically adopted military-style structures, based on strong leadership and strict discipline, that were merely consolidated once power was achieved. Third, in rooting out the vestiges of the old order, all oppositional forces were also removed, effectively preparing the way for the construction of totalitarian dictatorships. The revolutionary socialist

BOURGEOIS STATE
A Marxist term denoting a state that is bound to the interests of the bourgeoisie, and so perpetuates a system of unequal class power.

tradition, nevertheless, was fatally undermined by the collapse of communism, in what were, effectively, the counter-revolutions of 1989–91. This finally ended the divide that had opened up in socialist politics in 1917, and completed the conversion of socialism to constitutional and democratic politics. Where revolutionary socialism survives, it is only in pockets such as continuing Maoist insurgency in Peru and Nepal.

Evolutionary socialism

Although early socialists often supported the idea of revolution, as the nineteenth century progressed enthusiasm for popular revolt waned, at least in the advanced capitalist states of western and central Europe. Capitalism itself had matured and, by the late nineteenth century, the urban working class had lost its revolutionary character and was being integrated into society. Wages and living standards had started to rise, and the working class had begun to develop a range of institutions (working men's clubs, trade unions, political parties and so on) that both protected their interests and nurtured a sense of belonging within industrial society. Furthermore, the gradual advance of political democracy led to the extension of the franchise (the right to vote) to the working classes. By the end of World War I, a large majority of western states had introduced universal manhood suffrage, with a growing number extending voting rights also to women. The combined effect of these factors was to shift the attention of socialists away from violent insurrection and to persuade them that there was an alternative evolutionary, democratic or parliamentary road to socialism.

The Fabian Society, formed in 1884, took up the cause of parliamentary socialism in the UK. The Fabians, led by Beatrice Webb (1858–1943) and Sidney Webb (1859–1947), and including noted intellectuals such as George Bernard Shaw and H. G. Wells, took their name from the Roman General Fabius Maximus, who was noted for the patient and defensive tactics he had employed in defeating Hannibal's invading armies. In their view, socialism would develop naturally and peacefully out of liberal capitalism via a very similar process. This would occur through a combination of political action and education. Political action required the formation of a socialist party, which would compete for power against established parliamentary parties rather than prepare for violent revolution. They therefore accepted the liberal theory of the state as a neutral arbiter, rather than the Marxist belief that it is an agent of class oppression. The Webbs were actively involved in the formation of the UK Labour Party, and helped to write its 1918 constitution. The Fabians also believed that elite groups, such as politicians of all parties, civil servants, scientists and academics, could be converted to socialism through education. These elite groups would be 'permeated' by socialist ideas as they recognized that socialism is morally superior to capitalism, being based, for example, on biblical principles, and is more rational and efficient.

Fabian ideas also had an impact on the German Social Democratic Party (SPD), formed in 1875. The SPD quickly became the largest socialist party in Europe and, in 1912, the largest party in the German Reichstag. While committed in theory to a Marxist strategy, in practice it adopted a reformist approach, influenced by the ideas of Ferdinand Lassalle (1825–64). Lassalle had argued that the extension of political democracy could enable the state to respond to working-class interests, and he envisaged socialism being established through a gradual process of social reform, introduced by a benign state. Such ideas were developed more thoroughly by Eduard Bernstein (see p. 124), whose *Evolutionary Socialism* ([1898] 1962) developed ideas that paralleled the Fabian belief in **gradualism**. Bernstein was particularly impressed by the development of the democratic state, which he believed made the Marxist call for revolution redundant. The working class could use the ballot box to introduce socialism, which would therefore develop as an evolutionary outgrowth of capitalism. Such principles dominated the working-class political parties that sprang up around the turn of the century: the Australian Labour Party was founded in 1891, the UK Labour Party in 1900, the Italian Socialist Party in 1892, its French counterpart in 1905, and so on. They came, in the 1970s, to be adopted also by western communist parties, led by the Spanish, Italian and French communist parties. The resulting **Eurocommunism** was committed to pursuing a democratic road to communism and maintaining an open, competitive political system.

GRADUALISM
Progress brought about by gradual, piecemeal improvements, rather than dramatic upheaval; change through legal and peaceful reform.

EUROCOMMUNISM
A form of deradicalized communism, most influential in the 1970s, which attempted to blend Marxism with liberal-democratic principles.

The inevitability of gradualism?

The advent of political democracy in the late nineteenth and early twentieth centuries caused a wave of optimism to spread throughout the socialist movement, reflected, for example, in the Fabian notion of 'the inevitability of gradualism'. The idea that the victory of socialism was inevitable was not new. For instance, Marx had predicted the inevitable overthrow of capitalist society in a proletarian revolution. However, whereas Marx believed that history was driven forward by the irresistible forces of class conflict, evolutionary socialists highlighted the logic of the democratic process itself.

Their optimism was founded on a number of assumptions:

- First, the progressive extension of the franchise would eventually lead to the establishment of universal adult suffrage, and therefore of political equality.
- Second, political equality would, in practice, work in the interests of the majority; that is, those who decide the outcome of elections. Political

democracy would thus invest power in the hands of the working class, easily the most numerous class in any industrial society.

- Third, socialism was thought to be the natural 'home' of the working class. As capitalism is a system of class exploitation, oppressed workers will naturally be drawn to socialist parties, which offer them the prospect of social justice and emancipation. The electoral success of socialist parties would therefore be guaranteed by the numerical strength of the working class.
- Fourth, once in power, socialist parties would be able to carry out a fundamental transformation of society through a process of social reform. In this way, political democracy not only opened up the possibility of achieving socialism peacefully, it made this process inevitable.

Such optimistic expectations have, however, not been borne out in reality. Some have even argued that democratic socialism is founded on a contradiction: in order to respond successfully to electoral pressures, socialists have been forced to revise or 'water down' their ideological beliefs. Socialist parties have enjoyed periods of power in virtually all liberal democracies, with the exception of North America. However, they have certainly not been guaranteed power. The Swedish Social Democratic Labour Party (SAP) has been the most successful in this respect, having been in power alone, or as the senior partner in a coalition, for most of the period since 1951. Nevertheless, even the SAP has only once achieved 50 per cent of the popular vote (in 1968). The UK Labour Party gained its greatest support (49 per cent) in 1951, equalled by the Spanish Socialist Workers' Party in 1982. The SPD in Germany got 46 per cent of the vote in 1972, and the combined socialist and communist vote in Italy in 1976 amounted to 44 per cent. Moreover, although these parties have undoubtedly introduced significant social reforms when in power (usually involving the expansion of welfare provision and economic management), they have certainly not presided over any fundamental social transformation. At best, capitalism has been reformed, not abolished.

Democratic socialism has, in fact, encountered a number of problems not envisaged by its founding figures. In the first place, does the working class any longer constitute the majority of the electorate in advanced industrial societies? Socialist parties have traditionally focused their electoral appeal on urban manual workers, the 'factory fodder' of capitalist societies. Modern capitalism, however, has become increasingly technological, demanding a skilled workforce often engaged in technical rather than manual tasks. The 'traditional' working class, composed of manual labourers working in established 'heavy' industries, has thus declined in size, giving rise to the idea of so-called 'two-thirds, one-third' societies, in which poverty and disadvantage are concentrated in the '**underclass**'. In *The Culture of Contentment* (1992), J. K. Galbraith drew attention

UNDERCLASS
A classification of people who suffer from multiple forms of deprivation, and so are socially, politically and culturally marginalized.

to the emergence in modern societies, or at least among the politically active, of a 'contented majority' whose material affluence and economic security encourage them to be politically conservative. If working-class support no longer offers socialist parties the prospect of an electoral majority, they are either forced to appeal more broadly for support to other social classes, or to share power as a coalition partner with middle-class parties. Both options require socialist parties to modify their ideological commitments, either in order to appeal to electors who have little or no interest in socialism, or to work with parties that seek to uphold capitalism.

Furthermore, is the working class socialist at heart? Is socialism genuinely in the interests of the working class? Socialist parties have been forced to acknowledge the ability of capitalism to 'deliver the goods', especially since the Second World War. During the 1950s, socialist parties, once committed to fundamental change, revised their policies in an attempt to appeal to an increasingly affluent working class. A similar process has taken place since the 1980s, as socialist parties have struggled to come to terms with the changing class structure of capitalism as well as the pressures generated by economic globalization. In effect, socialism has come to be associated with attempts to make the market economy work, rather than with an attempt to re-engineer the social structure of capitalism. Such shifts are examined in more detail later, in connection with social democracy.

However, left-wing socialists have a different explanation for the declining socialist character of the working class. Rather than highlighting the benefits of capitalism or its changing class structure, they have emphasized the role of ideological manipulation. Marxists thus argue that '**bourgeois ideology**' pervades society, preventing the working class from perceiving the reality of its own exploitation. For example, Lenin proclaimed that without the leadership of a revolutionary party, the working class would only be able to gain 'trade union consciousness', a desire for material improvement within the capitalist system, but not full revolutionary '**class consciousness**'. Antonio Gramsci (see p. 125) emphasized that capitalism survives not through its economic power alone, but also through a process of 'ideological hegemony'.

BOURGEOIS IDEOLOGY

A Marxist term denoting ideas and theories that serve the interests of the bourgeoisie by disguising the contradictions of capitalist society.

CLASS CONSCIOUSNESS

A Marxist term denoting an accurate awareness of class interests and a willingness to pursue them; a class-conscious class is a class-for-itself.

Finally, can socialist parties, even if elected to power, carry out socialist reforms? Socialist parties have formed single-party governments in a number of western countries, including France, Sweden, Spain, the UK, Australia and New Zealand. Once elected, however, they have been confronted with entrenched interests in both the state and society. As early as 1902, the SPD leader Karl Kautsky (1854–1938) pointed out that 'the capitalist class rules but it does not govern, it contents itself with ruling the government'. This is made easier by the fact that political elites in the administration, courts and the military share the same social background as business elites. Moreover, elected governments, of whatever ideological inclination, must respect the power of big business, which is the major employer and investor in the economy as well as the wealthiest contributor to party funds. In other words, while democratic socialist parties may succeed in forming elected governments, there is the danger that they will merely win office without necessarily acquiring power.

Communism

The communist tradition within socialism is defined by a rejection of private property and a clear preference for common or collective ownership. It is a tradition that has a variety of manifestations, even overlapping with anarchism, as in the case of anarcho-communism (discussed in Chapter 5). However, its historically most significant association has undoubtedly been with Marxism. Strictly speaking, 'Marxism' as a codified body of thought only came into existence after Marx's death in 1883. It was the product of the attempt, notably by Marx's lifelong collaborator, Engels, Kautsky and the Russian theoretician Georgi Plekhanov (1857–1918), to condense Marx's ideas and theories into a systematic and comprehensive worldview that suited the needs of the growing socialist movement. This 'orthodox' Marxism, which is often portrayed as '**dialectical materialism**' (a term coined by Plekhanov and not used by Marx), later formed the basis of Soviet communism. Some see Marx as an economic determinist, while others proclaim him to be a humanist socialist. Moreover, distinctions have also been drawn between his early and later writings, sometimes presented as the distinction between the 'young Marx' and the 'mature Marx'. It is nevertheless clear that Marx himself believed he had developed a new brand of socialism that was scientific, in the sense that it was primarily concerned with disclosing the nature of social and historical development, rather than with advancing an essentially ethical critique of capitalism.

DIALECTICAL MATERIALISM
The crude and deterministic form of Marxism that dominated intellectual life in orthodox communist states.

Key concept

Communism

Communism, in its simplest sense, refers to the communal organization of social existence, especially through the collective ownership of property. For Marxists, communism is a theoretical ideal. In this sense, communism is characterized by classlessness (wealth is owned in common), rational economic organization (production-for-use replaces production-for-exchange) and statelessness (in the absence of class conflict, the state 'withers away'). 'Orthodox' communism refers to the societies founded in the twentieth century supposedly on the basis of Marxist principles. In such societies: (1) Marxism-Leninism was used as an 'official' ideology; (2) the communist party had a monopoly of power, based on its 'leading and guiding' role in society; and (3) economic life was collectivized and organized through a system of central planning.

At least three forms of Marxism can be identified. These are:

- classical Marxism
- orthodox communism
- neo-Marxism.

Classical Marxism

Philosophy

The core of classical Marxism – the Marxism of Marx – is a philosophy of history that outlines why capitalism is doomed and why socialism is destined to replace it, based on supposedly scientific analysis. But in what sense did Marx believe his work to be scientific? Marx criticized earlier socialist thinkers such as the French social reformer Saint-Simon (1760–1825), Fourier and Owen as 'utopians' on the basis that their socialism was grounded in a desire for total social transformation unconnected with the necessity of class struggle and revolution. Marx, in contrast, undertook a laborious empirical analysis of history and society, hoping thereby to gain insight into the nature of future developments. However, whether with Marx's help or not, Marxism as the attempt to gain historical understanding through the application of scientific methods, later developed into Marxism as a body of scientific truths, gaining a status more akin to that of a religion. Engels' declaration that Marx had uncovered the 'laws' of historical and social development was a clear indication of this transition.

HISTORICAL MATERIALISM
A Marxist theory that holds that material or economic conditions ultimately structure law, politics, culture and other aspects of social existence.

What made Marx's approach different from that of other socialist thinkers was that he subscribed to what Engels called the 'materialist conception of history', or **historical materialism** (see Figure 4.1). Rejecting the idealism of the German philosopher G. W. F. Hegel (1770–1831), who believed that history amounted to the unfolding of the so-called 'world spirit', Marx held

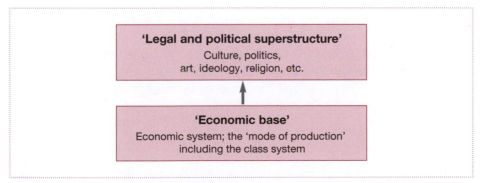

Figure 4.1 Historical materialism

material circumstances to be fundamental to all forms of social and historical development. This reflected the belief that the production of the means of subsistence is the most crucial of all human activities. Since humans cannot survive without food, water, shelter and so on, the way in which these are produced conditions all other aspects of life; in short, 'social being determines consciousness'. In the preface to *A Contribution to the Critique of Political Economy*, written in 1859, Marx gave this theory its most succinct expression, by suggesting that social consciousness and the 'legal and political superstructure' arise from the 'economic base', the real foundation of society. This 'base' consists essentially of the 'mode of production' or economic system – feudalism, capitalism, socialism and so on. This led Marx to conclude that political, legal, cultural, religious, artistic and other aspects of life could be explained primarily by reference to economic factors (see pp. 6–8 for an account of how this applies to Marx's theory of ideology).

While in other respects a critic of Hegel, Marx nevertheless embraced his belief that the driving force of historical change was the **dialectic**. In effect, progress is the consequence of internal conflict. For Hegel, this explained the movement of the 'world spirit' towards self-realization through conflict between a thesis and its opposing force, an antithesis, producing a higher level, a synthesis, which in turn constitutes a new thesis. Marx, as Engels put it, 'turned Hegel on his head', by investing this Hegelian dialectic with a materialistic interpretation. Marx thus explained historical change by reference to internal contradictions within each mode of production, arising from the existence of private property. Capitalism is thus doomed because it embodies its own antithesis, the proletariat, seen by Marx as the 'grave digger of capitalism'. Conflict between capitalism and the proletariat will therefore lead to a higher stage of development in the establishment of a socialist, and eventually a communist, society.

Marx's theory of history is therefore teleological, in the sense that it invests history with meaning or a purpose, reflected in its goal: classless communism. This goal would nevertheless only be achieved once history had developed through a series of stages or epochs, each characterized by its own economic structure and class system. In *The German Ideology* ([1846] 1970) Marx identified four such stages:

- primitive communism or tribal society, in which material scarcity provided the principal source of conflict
- slavery, covering classical or ancient societies and characterized by conflict between masters and slaves
- feudalism, marked by antagonism between land owners and serfs
- capitalism, dominated by the struggle between the bourgeoisie and the proletariat.

DIALECTIC
A process of development in which interaction between two opposing forces leads to a further or higher stage; historical change resulting from internal contradictions within a society.

Human history has therefore been a long struggle between the oppressed and the oppressor, the exploited and the exploiter. However, following Hegel, Marx envisaged an end of history, which would occur when a society was constructed that embodied no internal contradictions or antagonisms. This, for Marx, meant communism, a classless society based on the common ownership of productive wealth. With the establishment of communism, what Marx called the 'pre-history of mankind' would come to an end.

Economics

In Marx's early writings much of his critique of capitalism rests on the notion of **alienation**, which applies in four senses. Since capitalism is a system of production for exchange, it alienates humans from the *product* of their labour: they work to produce not what they need or what is useful, but 'commodities' to be sold for profit. They are also alienated from the *process* of labour, because most are forced to work under the supervision of foremen or managers. In addition, work is not social: individuals are encouraged to be self-interested and are therefore alienated from *fellow workers*. Finally, workers are alienated from *themselves*. Labour itself is reduced to a mere commodity and work becomes a depersonalized activity instead of a creative and fulfilling one.

However, in his later work, Marx analysed capitalism more in terms of class conflict and exploitation. Marx defined class in terms of economic power, specifically where people stand in relation to the ownership of the 'means of production', or productive wealth. He believed that capitalist society was being divided increasingly into 'two great classes facing one another: Bourgeoisie and Proletariat'. For Marx and later Marxists, the analysis of the class system provides the key to historical understanding and enables predictions to be made about the future development of capitalism: in the words of the *Communist Manifesto* ([1848] 1968), 'The history of all hitherto existing societies is the history of class struggle.' Classes, rather than individuals, parties or other movements, are the chief agents of historical change.

Crucially, Marx believed that the relationship between classes is one of irreconcilable antagonism, the subordinate class being necessarily and systematically exploited by the '**ruling class**'. This he explained by reference to the idea of '**surplus value**'. Capitalism's quest for profit can only be satisfied through the extraction of surplus value from its workers, by paying them less than the value their labour generates. Economic exploitation is therefore an essential feature of the capitalist mode of production, and it operates regardless of the meanness or generosity of particular employers. Marx was concerned not only to highlight the inherent instability of capitalism, based on irreconcilable class conflict, but also to analyse the

ALIENATION
To be separated from one's genuine or essential nature; used by Marxists to describe the process whereby, under capitalism, labour is reduced to being a mere commodity.

RULING CLASS
A Marxist term denoting the class that owns the means of production, and so wields economic and political power.

SURPLUS VALUE
A Marxist term denoting the value that is extracted from the labour of the proletariat by the mechanism of capitalist exploitation.

nature of capitalist development. In particular, he drew attention to its tendency to experience deepening economic crises. These stemmed, in the main, from cyclical crises of overproduction, plunging the economy into stagnation and bringing unemployment and immiseration to the working class. Each crisis would be more severe than the last, because, Marx calculated, in the long term the rate of profit would fall. This would eventually, and inevitably, produce conditions in which the proletariat, the vast majority of society, would rise up in revolution.

Politics

Marx's most important prediction was that capitalism was destined to be overthrown by a proletarian revolution. This would be not merely a political revolution that would remove the governing elite or overthrow the state machine, but a social revolution that would establish a new mode of production and culminate in the achievement of full communism. Such a revolution, he anticipated, would occur in the most mature capitalist countries – for example, Germany, Belgium, France or the UK – where the forces of production had expanded to their limit within the constraints of the capitalist system. Nevertheless, revolution would not simply be determined by objective conditions alone. The subjective element would be supplied by a 'class-conscious' proletariat, meaning that revolution would occur when both objective and subjective conditions were 'ripe'. As class antagonisms intensified, the proletariat would recognize the fact of its own exploitation and become a revolutionary force: a class for-itself and not merely a class in-itself. In this sense, revolution would be a spontaneous act, carried out by a proletarian class that would, in effect, lead or guide itself.

The initial target of this revolution was to be the bourgeois state. The state, in this view, is an instrument of oppression wielded by the economically dominant class. However, Marx recognized that there could be no immediate transition from capitalism to communism. A transitionary 'socialist' stage of development would last as long as class antagonisms persisted. This would be characterized by what Marx called the dictatorship of the proletariat. The purpose of this proletarian state was to safeguard the gains of the revolution by preventing counter-revolution carried out by the dispossessed bourgeoisie. However, as class antagonisms began to fade with the emergence of full communism, the state would 'wither away' – once the class system had been abolished, the state would lose its reason for existence. The resulting communist society would therefore be stateless as well as classless, and would allow a system of commodity production to give way to one geared to the satisfaction of human needs.

SOCIAL REVOLUTION
A qualitative change in the structure of society; for Marxists a social revolution involves a change in the mode of production and the system of ownership.

DICTATORSHIP OF THE PROLETARIAT
A Marxist term denoting the transitory phase between the collapse of capitalism and the establishment of full communism, characterized by the establishment of a proletarian state.

Orthodox communism

The Russian Revolution and its consequences dominated the image of communism in the twentieth century. The Bolshevik party, led by V. I. Lenin, seized power in a *coup d'état* in October 1917, and the following year adopted the name 'Communist Party'. As the first successful communist revolutionaries, the Bolshevik leaders enjoyed unquestionable authority within the communist world, at least until the 1950s. Communist parties set up elsewhere accepted the ideological leadership of Moscow and joined the Communist International, or 'Comintern', founded in 1919. The communist regimes established in eastern Europe after 1945, in China in 1949, in Cuba in 1959 and elsewhere, were consciously modelled on the structure of the Soviet Union. Thus, Soviet communism became the dominant model of communist rule, and the ideas of Marxism-Leninism became the ruling ideology of the communist world.

However, twentieth-century communism differed significantly from the ideas and expectations of Marx and Engels. In the first place, although the communist parties that developed in the twentieth century were founded on the theories of classical Marxism, they were forced to adapt these to the tasks of winning and retaining political power. Twentieth-century communist leaders had, in particular, to give greater attention to issues such as leadership, political organization and economic management than Marx had done. Second, the communist regimes were shaped by the historical circumstances in which they developed. Communist parties did not achieve power, as Marx had anticipated, in the developed capitalist states of western Europe, but in backward, largely rural countries such as Russia and China. In consequence, the urban proletariat was invariably small and unsophisticated, quite incapable of carrying out a genuine class revolution. Communist rule thus became the rule of a communist elite, and of communist leaders. Soviet communism, furthermore, was crucially shaped by the decisive personal contribution of the first two Bolshevik leaders, V.I. Lenin and Joseph Stalin (1879–1953).

Lenin was both a political leader and a major political thinker. His theories reflected his overriding concern with the problems of winning power and establishing communist rule. The central feature of **Leninism** was a belief in the need for a new kind of political party, a revolutionary party or vanguard party. Unlike Marx, Lenin did not believe that the proletariat would spontaneously develop revolutionary class consciousness, as the working class was deluded by bourgeois ideas and beliefs. He suggested that only a 'revolutionary party' could lead the working class from 'trade union consciousness' to revolutionary class consciousness. Such a party should be composed of professional and dedicated revolutionaries. Its claim to leadership would lie in its ideological wisdom, specifically its understanding of Marxist theory. This party could therefore act as the 'vanguard of the proletariat' because, armed with Marxism, it would perceive the genuine interests of the proletariat and would act to awaken the proletarian

LENINISM
Lenin's theoretical contributions to Marxism, notably his belief in the need for a revolutionary or 'vanguard' party to raise the proletariat to class consciousness.

class to its revolutionary potential. Lenin further proposed that the vanguard party should be organized according to the principles of **democratic centralism**.

When the Bolsheviks seized power in 1917 they did so as a vanguard party, and therefore in the name of the proletariat. If the Bolshevik Party was acting in the interests of the working class, it followed that opposition parties must represent the interests of classes hostile to the proletariat, in particular the bourgeoisie. The dictatorship of the proletariat required that the revolution be protected against its class enemies, which effectively meant the suppression of all parties other than the Communist Party. By 1920, Russia had become a one-party state. Leninist theory therefore implied the existence of a monopolistic party, which enjoys sole responsibility for articulating the interests of the proletariat and guiding the revolution toward its ultimate goal, that of 'building communism'.

Soviet communism was no less deeply influenced by the rule of Joseph Stalin, 1924–53, than that of Lenin. Indeed more so, as the Soviet Union was affected more profoundly by Stalin's 'second revolution' in the 1930s than it had been by the October Revolution. Stalin's most important ideological shift was to embrace the doctrine of 'Socialism in One Country', initially developed by Nikolai Bukharin. Announced in 1924, this proclaimed that the Soviet Union could succeed in 'building socialism' without the need for international revolution. After consolidating himself in power, however, Stalin oversaw a dramatic economic and political upheaval, beginning with the announcement of the first Five Year Plan in 1928. Stalin's Five Year Plans brought about rapid industrialization as well as the swift and total eradication of private enterprise. From 1929, agriculture was collectivized, and Soviet peasants were forced at the cost of literally millions of lives to give up their land and join state or collective farms. Economic **Stalinism** therefore took the form of state collectivization or 'state socialism'. The capitalist market was entirely removed and replaced by a system of central planning, dominated by the State Planning Committee, 'Gosplan', and administered by a collection of powerful economic ministries based in Moscow.

Major political changes accompanied this 'second revolution'. During the 1930s, Stalin used his power to brutal effect, removing anyone suspected of disloyalty or criticism in an increasingly violent series of purges carried out by the secret police, the NKVD. The membership of the Communist Party was almost halved, over a million people lost their lives, including all the surviving members of Lenin's Politburo, and many millions were imprisoned in labour camps, or gulags. Political Stalinism was therefore a form of totalitarian dictatorship, operating through a monolithic ruling party, in which all forms of debate or criticism were eradicated by terror in what amounted to a civil war conducted against the party itself.

DEMOCRATIC CENTRALISM

The Leninist principle of party organization, based on a supposed balance between freedom of discussion and strict unity of action.

STALINISM

A centrally planned economy supported by systematic and brutal political oppression, based on the structures of Stalin's Russia.

Neo-Marxism

While Marxism – or, more usually, Marxism-Leninism – was turned into a secular religion by the orthodox communist regimes of eastern Europe and elsewhere, a more subtle and complex form of Marxism developed in western Europe. Referred to as modern Marxism, western Marxism or neo-Marxism, this amounted to an attempt to revise or recast the classical ideas of Marx while remaining faithful to certain Marxist principles or aspects of Marxist methodology.

Two principal factors shaped the character of neo-Marxism. First, when Marx's prediction about the imminent collapse of capitalism failed to materialize, neo-Marxists were forced to re-examine conventional class analysis. In particular, they took a greater interest in Hegelian ideas and in the stress on 'Man the creator' found in Marx's early writings. Neo-Marxists were thus able to break free from the rigid 'base/superstructure' straitjacket. In short, the class struggle was no longer treated as the beginning and end of social analysis. Second, neo-Marxists were usually at odds with, and sometimes profoundly repelled by, the Bolshevik model of orthodox communism.

The Hungarian Marxist Georg Lukács (1885–1971) was one of the first to present Marxism as a humanistic philosophy, emphasizing the process of 'reification', through which capitalism dehumanizes workers by reducing them to passive objects or marketable commodities. Antonio Gramsci drew attention to the degree to which the class system is upheld not simply by unequal economic and political power, but also by bourgeois 'hegemony', the spiritual and cultural supremacy of the ruling class, brought about through the spread of bourgeois values and beliefs via civil society – the media, churches, youth movements, trade unions and so on. A more overtly Hegelian brand of Marxism was developed by the so-called Frankfurt School, whose leading early figures were Theodor Adorno (1903–69), Max Horkheimer

> **NEO-MARXISM**
> An updated and revised form of Marxism that rejects determinism, the primacy of economics and the privileged status of the proletariat.

Key concept

New Left

The New Left comprises thinkers and intellectual movements that emerged in the 1960s and early 1970s, seeking to revitalize socialist thought by developing a radical critique of advanced industrial society. The New Left rejected both 'old' left alternatives: Soviet-style state socialism and de-radicalized western social democracy. Influenced by the humanist writings of the 'young' Marx, and by anarchism and radical forms of phenomenology and existentialism, New Left theories are often diffuse. Common themes nevertheless include a fundamental rejection of conventional society ('the system') as oppressive, a commitment to personal autonomy and self-fulfilment in the form of 'liberation', disillusionment with the role of the working class as the revolutionary agent, sympathy for identity politics (see p. 282), and a preference for decentralization and participatory democracy.

(1895–1973) and Herbert Marcuse (see p. 125). Frankfurt theorists developed what was called 'critical theory', a blend of Marxist political economy, Hegelian philosophy and Freudian psychology, that came to have a considerable impact on the so-called 'New Left'. The leading exponent of the 'second generation' of the Frankfurt School is the German philosopher and social theorist Jürgen Habermas (born 1929). His wide-ranging work includes an analysis of 'crisis tendencies' in capitalist society that arise from tensions between capital accumulation and democracy.

The death of Marxism?

The year 1989 marked a dramatic watershed in the history of communism and in ideological history generally. Starting in April with student-led 'democracy movement' demonstrations in Tiananmen Square in Beijing and culminating in November in the fall of the Berlin Wall, the division of Europe into a capitalist West and a communist East was brought to an end. By 1991 the Soviet Union, the model of orthodox communism, had ceased to exist. Where communist regimes continue, as in China, Cuba, Vietnam, North Korea and elsewhere, they have either blended political Stalinism with market-orientated economic reform (most clearly in the case of China) or suffered increasing isolation (as in the case of North Korea). These developments were a result of a number of structural flaws from which orthodox communism suffered. Chief among these were that while central planning proved effective in bringing about early industrialization, it could not cope with the complexities of modern industrial societies and, in particular, failed to deliver the levels of prosperity enjoyed in the capitalist West from the 1950s onwards.

There is, nevertheless, considerable debate about the implications of the collapse of communism for Marxism. On the one hand, there are those who, like the 'end of history' theorist, Francis Fukuyama (1989, 1992), argue that the 'collapse of communism' is certain proof of the demise of Marxism as a world-historical force. On the other hand, there are those who argue that the Soviet-style communism that was rejected in the revolutions of 1989–91 differed markedly from the 'Marxism of Marx'. However, to point out that it was not Marxism but a Stalinist version of Marxism–Leninism that collapsed in 1989–91 is very far from demonstrating the continuing relevance of Marxism. A far more serious problem for Marxism is the failure of Marx's predictions (about the inevitable collapse of capitalism and its replacement by communism) to be realized. Quite simply, advanced industrial societies have not been haunted by the 'spectre of communism'. Even those who believe that Marx's views on matters such as alienation and exploitation continue to be relevant, have to accept that classical Marxism failed to recognize the remarkable resilience of capitalism and its capacity to recreate itself.

Some Marxists have responded to these problems by advancing 'post-Marxist' ideas and theories. Post-Marxism, nevertheless, has two implications. The first is that the Marxist project, and the historical materialism on which it is based, should be abandoned in favour of alternative ideas. This is evident in the writings of the one-time Marxist Jean-François Lyotard (1984), who suggested that Marxism as a totalizing theory of history, and for that matter all other 'grand narratives', had been made redundant by the emergence of postmodernity. In its alternative version, post-Marxism consists of an attempt to salvage certain key Marxist insights by attempting to reconcile Marxism with aspects of postmodernism (see p. 59) and poststructuralism. Ernesto Laclau and Chantal Mouffe (2014) accepted that the priority traditionally accorded to social class, and the central position of the working class in bringing about social change, were no longer sustainable. In so doing, they opened up space within Marxism for a wide range of other 'moments' of struggle, usually linked to so-called new social movements such as the women's movement, the ecological movement, the gay and lesbian movement, the peace movement, and so on.

Social democracy

As an ideological stance, social democracy took shape around the mid-twentieth century, resulting from the tendency among western socialist parties not only to adopt parliamentary strategies, but also to revise their socialist goals. In particular, they abandoned the goal of abolishing capitalism and sought instead to reform or 'humanize' it. Social democracy therefore came to stand for a broad balance between the market economy, on the one hand, and state intervention on the other.

Social democracy was most fully developed in the early post-1945 period, during which enthusiasm for social-democratic ideas and theories extended well beyond its socialist homeland, creating, in many western states, a social-democratic consensus. However, since the 1970s and 1980s, social democracy has struggled to retain its electoral and political relevance in the face of the advance of neoliberalism (see p. 83) and changed economic and social circumstances. The final decades of the twentieth century therefore witnessed a process of ideological retreat on the part of reformist socialist parties across the globe.

Key concept

Social Democracy

Social democracy is an ideological stance that supports a broad balance between market capitalism, on the one hand, and state intervention on the other. Being based on a compromise between the market and the state, social democracy lacks a systematic underlying theory and is, arguably, inherently vague. It is nevertheless associated with the following views: (1) capitalism is the only reliable means of generating wealth, but it is a morally defective means of distributing wealth because of its tendency towards poverty and inequality; (2) the defects of the capitalist system can be rectified through economic and social intervention, the state being the custodian of the public interest; (3) social change can and should be brought about peacefully and constitutionally.

KEY FIGURES IN... SOCIALISM

Robert Owen (1771–1858) A British socialist, industrialist and pioneer of the cooperative movement, Owen's *A New View of Society* (1816) envisaged a transformation in human nature consequent on a change in its environment, suggesting that progress requires the construction of a 'rational system of society'. Owen advanced a moral indictment of market capitalism, which he proposed should be replaced with a society based on small-scale cooperative communities in which property would be communally owned and essential goods freely distributed.

Karl Marx (1818–83) A German philosopher, economist and life-long revolutionary, Marx is usually portrayed as the father of twentieth-century communism. The centrepiece of Marx's thought is a 'scientific' critique of capitalism that highlights, in keeping with previous class society, systemic inequality and therefore fundamental instability. Marx's materialist theory of history holds that social development will inevitably culminate in the establishment of a classless communist society. His vast works include the *Communist Manifesto* (1848) (written with Friedrich Engels (1820–95)) and the three-volume *Capital* (1867, 1885 and 1894).

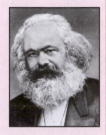

Eduard Bernstein (1850–1932) A German socialist politician and theorist, Bernstein attempted to revise and modernize orthodox Marxism in the light of changing circumstances. In *Evolutionary Socialism* (1898), Bernstein argued that economic crises were becoming less, not more, acute, and drew attention to the 'steady advance of the working class'. On this basis, he drew attention to the possibility of a gradual and peaceful transition to socialism, and questioned the distinction between liberalism and socialism, later abandoning all semblance of Marxism.

Vladimir Ilich Lenin (1870–1924) A Russian Marxist revolutionary and theorist, Lenin was the first leader of the Soviet state (1917–21). In *What Is to Be Done?* (1902), he emphasized the central importance of a tightly organized 'vanguard' party to lead and guide the proletarian class. In *Imperialism, the Highest Stage of Capitalism* (1916), he developed an economic analysis of colonialism, highlighting the possibility of turning world war into class war. *The State and Revolution* (1917) outlined Lenin's firm commitment to the 'insurrectionary road' and rejected 'bourgeois parliamentarianism'.

Ethical socialism

The theoretical basis for social democracy has been provided more by moral or religious beliefs than by scientific analysis. Social democrats have not accepted the materialist and highly systematic ideas of Marx and Engels, but rather advanced an essentially moral critique of capitalism. In short, socialism is portrayed as morally superior to capitalism because human beings are ethical creatures, bound to one another by the ties of love, sympathy and compassion. The moral vision that

Leon Trotsky (1879–1940) A Russian Marxist revolutionary and theorist, Trotsky joined forces with Lenin in 1917 but after Lenin's death was driven from power and eventually murdered by Stalin. Trotsky's chief theoretical contribution to Marxism was the theory of permanent revolution, which suggested that socialism could be established in Russia without the need for the bourgeois stage of development. Trotskyism is usually associated with an unwavering commitment to internationalism and an anti-Stalinism that highlights the dangers of bureaucratization, as outlined in *The Revolution Betrayed* (1937).

Richard Henry Tawney (1880–1962) A British social philosopher and historian, Tawney championed a form of socialism that emphasizes (moral) equality, a common humanity and service, firmly rooted in a Christian social moralism that is unconnected with Marx's class analysis. Stressing the basic value of fellowship and a sense of community, Tawney argued that the disorders of capitalism derived from the absence of a 'moral ideal', leading to unchecked acquisitiveness and widespread material inequality. Tawney's major works include *The Acquisitive Society* (1921) and *Equality* (1931).

Antonio Gramsci (1891–1937) An Italian Marxist and revolutionary, Gramsci tried to redress the emphasis within orthodox Marxism on economic and material factors. In his major work, *Prison Notebooks* (1929–35), Gramsci rejected any form of 'scientific' determinism by stressing, through the theory of 'hegemony' (the dominance of bourgeois ideas and beliefs), the importance of political and intellectual struggle. While he did not ignore the 'economic nucleus', he argued that bourgeois assumptions and values needed to be overthrown by the establishment of a rival 'proletarian hegemony'.

Herbert Marcuse (1898–1979) A German political philosopher and social theorist, Marcuse portrayed advanced industrial society as an all-encompassing system of repression that subdues argument and debate, and absorbs all forms of opposition. Drawing on Marxist, Hegelian and Freudian ideas, Marcuse held up the unashamedly utopian prospect of personal and sexual liberation, looking not to the conventional working class as a revolutionary force but to groups such as students, ethnic minorities, women and workers in the developing world. His key works include *Eros and Civilization* (1958) and *One-Dimensional Man* (1964).

underlies ethical socialism has been based on both humanistic and religious principles. Socialism in France, the UK and other Commonwealth countries has been influenced more strongly by the **humanist** ideas of Fourier, Owen and William Morris (1854–96) than by the 'scientific' creed of Karl Marx. However, ethical socialism has also drawn heavily on Christianity. For example, there is a long-established tradition of Christian socialism in the UK, reflected in the twentieth century in the works of R. H. Tawney. The Christian ethic that

> **HUMANISM**
> A philosophy that gives moral priority to the satisfaction of human needs and aspirations.

has inspired UK socialism is that of universal brotherhood, the respect that should be accorded to all individuals as creations of God, a principle embodied in the commandment 'Thou shalt love thy neighbour as thyself'. In *The Acquisitive Society* (1921), Tawney condemned unregulated capitalism because it is driven by the 'sin of avarice' rather than faith in a 'common humanity'.

Such religious inspiration has also been evident in the ideas of liberation theology, which has influenced many Catholic developing-world states, especially in Latin America. After years of providing support for repressive regimes in Latin America, Roman Catholic bishops meeting at Medellin, Colombia, in 1968 declared a 'preferential option for the poor'. The religious responsibilities of the clergy were seen to extend beyond the narrowly spiritual and to embrace the social and political struggles of ordinary people. Despite the condemnation of Pope John Paul II and the Vatican, radical priests in many parts of Latin America campaigned against poverty and political oppression and, at times, even backed socialist revolutionary movements. Similarly, socialist movements in the predominantly Muslim countries of North Africa, the Middle East and Asia have been inspired by religion. Islam is linked to socialism in that it exhorts the principles of social justice, charity and cooperation, and specifically prohibits usury or profiteering.

In abandoning scientific analysis in favour of moral or religious principles, however, social democracy weakened the theoretical basis of socialism. Social democracy has been concerned primarily with the notion of a just or fair distribution of wealth in society. This is embodied in the overriding principle of social democracy: **social justice**. Social democracy consequently came to stand for a broad range of views, extending from a left-wing commitment to extending equality and expanding the collective ownership of wealth, to a more right-wing acceptance of the need for market efficiency and individual self-reliance that may be difficult to distinguish from certain forms of liberalism or conservatism. Attempts have nevertheless been made to give social democracy a theoretical basis, usually involving re-examining capitalism itself and redefining the goal of socialism.

> **SOCIAL JUSTICE**
> A morally justifiable distribution of wealth, usually implying a commitment to greater equality.

Revisionist socialism

The original, fundamentalist goal of socialism was that productive wealth should be owned in common by all, and therefore used for the common benefit. This required the abolition of private property and the transition from a capitalist mode of production to a socialist one, usually through a process of revolutionary change. Capitalism, in this view, is unredeemable: it is a system of class exploitation and oppression that deserves to be abolished altogether, not merely reformed. However, by the end of the nineteenth century, some socialists had come to believe that this analysis of capitalism was defective. The clearest theoretical expression of this belief was found in Eduard Bernstein's *Evolutionary Socialism*

([1898] 1962), which undertook a comprehensive criticism of Marx and the first major attempt at Marxist **revisionism**.

Bernstein's theoretical approach was largely empirical; he rejected Marx's method of analysis – historical materialism – because the predictions Marx had made had proved to be incorrect. Capitalism had shown itself to be both stable and flexible. Rather than class conflict intensifying, dividing capitalist society into 'two great classes' (the bourgeoisie and the proletariat), Bernstein suggested that capitalism was becoming increasingly complex and differentiated. In particular, the ownership of wealth had widened as a result of the introduction of joint stock companies, owned by a number of shareholders, instead of a single powerful industrialist. The ranks of the middle classes had also been swollen by the growing number of salaried employees, technicians, government officials and professional workers, who were neither capitalists nor proletarians. In Bernstein's view, capitalism was no longer a system of naked class oppression. Capitalism could therefore be reformed by the nationalization of major industries and the extension of legal protection and welfare benefits to the working class, a process which Bernstein believed could be achieved peacefully and democratically.

REVISIONISM
The revision or reworking of a political theory that departs from earlier interpretations in an attempt to present a 'corrected' view.

Western socialist parties have been revisionist in practice, if not always in theory, intent on 'taming'

TENSIONS WITHIN... SOCIALISM (1)		
Communism	**VS**	**Social democracy**
scientific socialism	⟷	ethical socialism
fundamentalism	⟷	revisionism
utopianism	⟷	reformism
revolution	⟷	evolution/gradualism
abolish capitalism	⟷	'humanize' capitalism
common ownership	⟷	redistribution
classless society	⟷	ameliorate class conflict
absolute equality	⟷	relative equality
state collectivization	⟷	mixed economy
central planning	⟷	economic management
vanguard party	⟷	parliamentary party
dictatorship of proletariat	⟷	political pluralism
proletarian/people's state	⟷	liberal-democratic state

capitalism rather than abolishing it. In some cases they long retained a formal commitment to fundamentalist goals, as in the UK Labour Party's belief in 'the common ownership of the means of production, distribution and exchange', expressed in clause IV of its 1918 constitution. Nevertheless, as the twentieth century progressed, social democrats dropped their commitment to planning as they recognized the efficiency and vigour of the capitalist market. The Swedish Social Democratic Labour Party formally abandoned planning in the 1930s, as did the West German Social Democrats at the Bad Godesberg Congress of 1959, which accepted the principle 'competition when possible; planning when necessary'. In the UK, a similar bid to embrace revisionism formally in the late 1950s ended in failure when the Labour Party conference rejected the then leader Hugh Gaitskell's attempt to abolish clause IV. Nevertheless, when in power, the Labour Party never revealed an appetite for wholesale nationalization.

The abandonment of planning and comprehensive nationalization left social democracy with three more modest objectives: Social democrats support:

- The *mixed economy*, a blend of public and private ownership that stands between free-market capitalism and state collectivism. Nationalization, when advocated by social democrats, is invariably selective and reserved for the 'commanding heights' of the economy, or industries that are thought to be 'natural monopolies'.
  The 1945–51 Attlee Labour government, for instance, nationalized the major utilities – electricity, gas, coal, steel, the railways and so on – but left most of UK industry in private hands.
- *Economic management*, seeing the need for capitalism to be regulated in order to deliver sustainable growth. After 1945, most social democratic parties were converted to Keynesianism (see p. 55) as a device for controlling the economy and delivering full employment.
- The *welfare state*, viewing it as the principal means of reforming or humanizing capitalism. Its attraction is that it acts as a redistributive mechanism that helps to promote social equality and eradicate poverty. Capitalism no longer needs to be abolished, only modified through the establishment of reformed or welfare capitalism.

An attempt to give theoretical substance to these developments, and in effect update Bernstein, was made by Anthony Crosland (1918–77) in *The Future of Socialism* (1956). He subscribed to **managerialism**, in believing that modern capitalism bore little resemblance to the nineteenth-century model that Marx had had in mind. Crosland suggested that a new class of managers, experts and technocrats had supplanted the old capitalist class and come to dominate all advanced industrial societies, both capitalist and communist.

MANAGERIALISM
The theory that a governing class of managers, technocrats and state officials – those who possess technical and administrative skills – dominates both capitalist and communist societies.

The ownership of wealth had therefore become divorced from its control. Whereas shareholders, who own businesses, were principally concerned with profit, salaried managers, who make day-to-day business decisions, have a broader range of goals, including maintaining industrial harmony and upholding the public image of the company.

Such developments implied that Marxism had become irrelevant: if capitalism could no longer be viewed as a system of class exploitation, the fundamentalist goals of nationalization and planning were simply outdated. Crosland thus recast socialism in terms of politics of social justice, rather than the politics of ownership. Wealth need not be owned in common, because it could be redistributed through a welfare state that is financed by progressive taxation. However, Crosland recognized that economic growth plays a crucial role in the achievement of socialism. A growing economy is essential to generate the tax revenues needed to finance more generous social expenditure, and the prosperous will only be prepared to finance the needy if their own living standards are underwritten by economic growth.

The crisis of social democracy

During the early post-1945 period, Keynesian social democracy – or traditional social democracy – appeared to have triumphed. Its strength was that it harnessed the dynamism of the market without succumbing to the levels of inequality and instability that Marx believed would doom capitalism. Nevertheless, Keynesian social democracy was based on an (arguably) inherently unstable compromise. On the one hand, there was a pragmatic acceptance of the market as the only reliable means of generating wealth. This reluctant conversion to the market meant that social democrats accepted that there was no viable socialist alternative to the market, meaning that the socialist project was reborn as an attempt to reform, not replace, capitalism. On the other hand, the socialist ethic survived in the form of a commitment to social justice. This, in turn, was linked to a weak notion of equality: distributive equality, the idea that poverty should be reduced and inequality narrowed through the redistribution of wealth from rich to poor.

At the heart of Keynesian social democracy there lay a conflict between its commitment to both economic efficiency and egalitarianism. During the 'long boom' of the post-1945 period, social democrats were not forced to confront this conflict because sustained growth, low unemployment and low inflation improved the living standards of all social groups and helped to finance more generous welfare provision. However, as Crosland had anticipated, recession in the 1970s and 1980s created strains within social democracy, polarizing socialist thought into more clearly defined left-wing and right-wing positions. Recession precipitated a 'fiscal crisis of the welfare state', simultaneously increasing demand for welfare support as unemployment re-emerged, and squeezing the tax revenues that financed welfare spending (because fewer people were at work and businesses were less profitable). A difficult question had to be answered: should social democrats attempt to restore efficiency to the market economy, which might mean cutting inflation and possibly taxes, or should they defend the poor and the lower paid by maintaining or even expanding welfare provision?

This crisis of social democracy was intensified in the 1980s and 1990s by a combination of political, social and international factors. In the first place, the electoral viability of social democracy was undermined by deindustrialization and the shrinkage of the traditional working class, the social base of Keynesian social democracy. Whereas in the early post-1945 period the tide of democracy had flowed with progressive politics, since the 1980s it has been orientated increasingly around the interests of what J. K. Galbraith (1992) called the 'contented majority'. Social democratic parties paid a high price for these social and electoral shifts. For instance, the UK Labour Party lost four successive general elections between 1979 and 1992; the SPD in Germany was out of power between 1982 and 1998; and the French Socialist Party suffered crushing defeats, notably in 1993 and 2002. Furthermore, the intellectual credibility of social democracy was badly damaged by the collapse of communism. Not only did this create a world without any significant non-capitalist economic forms, but it also undermined faith in what Anthony Giddens (see p. 329) called the 'cybernetic model' of socialism, in which the state, acting as the brain within society, serves as the principal agent of economic and social reform. In this light, Keynesian social democracy could be viewed as only a more modest version of the 'top-down' state socialism that had been discarded so abruptly in the revolutions of 1989–91.

Neo-revisionism and the 'third way'

Since the 1980s, reformist socialist parties across the globe, but particularly in countries such as the UK, the Netherlands, Germany, Italy, Australia and New Zealand, have undergone a further bout of revisionism, sometimes termed neo-revisionism. In so doing, they have distanced themselves, to a greater or lesser extent, from the principles and commitments of traditional social democracy. The resulting ideological stance has been described in various ways, including 'new' social democracy, the 'third way', the 'radical centre', the 'active centre' and the '*Neue Mitte*' (new middle). However, the ideological significance of neo-revisionism, and its relationship to traditional social democracy in particular and to socialism in general, have been shrouded in debate and confusion. Its central thrust is nevertheless encapsulated in the notion of the third way, highlighting the idea of an alternative to both capitalism and socialism. In its modern form, the third way represents, more specifically, an alternative to old-style social democracy and neoliberalism.

> **THIRD WAY**
> The notion of an alternative form of economics to both state socialism and free-market capitalism, sought at different times by conservatives, socialists and fascists.

Although the third way is (perhaps inherently) imprecise and subject to competing interpretations, certain characteristic third-way themes can nevertheless be identified. The first of these is the belief that

Key concept

Communitarianism

Communitarianism is the belief that the self or person is constituted through the community, in the sense that individuals are shaped by the communities to which they belong and thus owe them a debt of respect and consideration – there are no 'unencumbered selves'. Though clearly at odds with liberal individualism, communitarianism nevertheless has a variety of political forms. *Left-wing* communitarianism holds that community demands unrestricted freedom and social equality (for example, anarchism). *Centrist* communitarianism holds that community is grounded in an acknowledgement of reciprocal rights and responsibilities (for example, social democracy/Tory paternalism). *Right-wing* communitarianism holds that community requires respect for authority and established values (for example, neoconservatism (see p. 88)).

socialism, at least in the form of 'top-down' state intervention, is dead: there is no alternative to what the revised clause IV of the UK Labour Party's 1995 constitution refers to as 'a dynamic market economy'. With this goes a general acceptance of globalization and the belief that capitalism has mutated into an 'information society' or 'knowledge economy'. This general acceptance of the market over the state, and the adoption of a pro-business and pro-enterprise stance, means that the third way attempts to build on, rather than reverse, the neoliberal revolution of the 1980s and 1990s.

The second key third-way belief is its emphasis on community and moral responsibility. Community, of course, has a long socialist heritage, drawing as it does, like fraternity and cooperation, on the idea of a social essence. While the third way accepts many of the economic theories of neoliberalism, it firmly rejects its philosophical basis and its moral and social implications. The danger of market fundamentalism is that it generates a free-for-all that undermines the moral foundations of society. Some versions of the third way, notably the so-called 'Blair project' in the UK, nevertheless attempted to fuse communitarian ideas with liberal ones, creating a form of communitarian liberalism, which in many ways resembled the 'new liberalism' of the late nineteenth century. The cornerstone belief of communitarian liberalism is that rights and responsibilities are intrinsically bound together: all rights must be balanced against responsibilities, and vice versa.

Third, supporters of the third way tend to adopt a consensus view of society, in contrast to socialism's conflict view of society. This is evident, for example, in the tendency of community to highlight ties that bind all members of society, and thus to ignore, or conceal, class differences and economic inequalities. A faith in consensus and social harmony is also reflected in the value framework of the third way, which rejects the either/or approach of conventional moral and ideological thinking, and offers what almost amounts to a non-dualistic

KNOWLEDGE ECONOMY
An economy in which knowledge is supposedly the key source of competitiveness and productivity, especially in the form of information and communication technology.

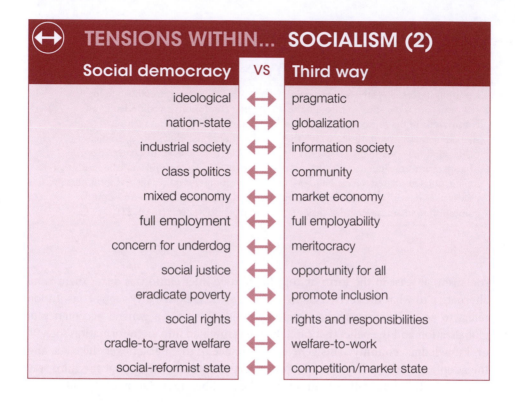

TENSIONS WITHIN... SOCIALISM (2)

Social democracy	VS	Third way
ideological	↔	pragmatic
nation-state	↔	globalization
industrial society	↔	information society
class politics	↔	community
mixed economy	↔	market economy
full employment	↔	full employability
concern for underdog	↔	meritocracy
social justice	↔	opportunity for all
eradicate poverty	↔	promote inclusion
social rights	↔	rights and responsibilities
cradle-to-grave welfare	↔	welfare-to-work
social-reformist state	↔	competition/market state

world-view. Third-way politicians thus typically endorse enterprise *and* fairness, opportunity *and* security, self-reliance *and* interdependence, and so on.

Fourth, the third way has substituted a concern with **social inclusion** for the traditional socialist commitment to equality. This is evident in the stress placed on liberal ideas such as opportunity, and even meritocracy. Egalitarianism is therefore scaled down to a belief in equality of opportunities or 'asset-based egalitarianism', the right of access to assets and opportunities that enable individuals to realise their potential. Third-way proposals for welfare reform therefore typically reject both the neoliberal emphasis on 'standing on your own two feet' and the social democratic belief in 'cradle to grave' welfare. Instead, welfare should be targeted at the 'socially excluded' and should follow the modern liberal approach of 'helping people to help themselves', or as Bill Clinton put it, giving people 'a hand up, not a handout'. Welfare policies should, in particular, aim to widen access to work, in line with the US idea of 'workfare', the belief that welfare support should be conditional on an individual's willingness to seek work and become self-reliant.

Finally, the third way is characterized by new thinking about the proper role of the state. The third way embraces the idea of a **competition state** or market state. The state should therefore concentrate on social

SOCIAL INCLUSION
The aquisition of rights, skills and opportunities that enable citizens to participate fully in their society.

COMPETITION STATE
A state whose principal role is to pursue strategies for national prosperity in conditions of intensifying global competition.

investment, which means improving the infrastructure of the economy and, most important, strengthening the skills and knowledge of the country's workforce. Education rather than social security should therefore be the government's priority, with education being valued not in its own right, because it furthers personal development (the modern liberal view), but because it promotes employability and benefits the economy (the utilitarian or classical liberal view). From this perspective, the government is essentially a cultural actor, whose purpose is to shape or reshape the population's attitudes, values, skills, beliefs and knowledge, rather than to carry out a programme of economic and social engineering. However, there are indications that the trend within social democracy towards revisionism may have been reversed in response to the 2007–9 global financial crisis, as discussed in the following section.

Socialism in a global age

Some have regarded a discussion of socialism in a global age as a pointless exercise. Socialism is dead, and it is largely the dynamics unleashed by globalization that have brought about its demise. From this perspective, globalizing tendencies can be seen to have both brought about the collapse of communism and precipitated a further bout of social-democratic revisionism. Orthodox communism was weakened by the tendency of economic globalization to bolster growth rates in the capitalist West from the 1980s onwards, thereby widening material differentials between capitalism and communism. In conjunction with increased media penetration in eastern Europe, which helped to spread pro-western and pro-capitalist values and appetites, this served to fashion the conditions in which the revolutions of 1989–91 took place. In the case of social democracy, 'accelerated' globalization undermined its economic viability in a variety of ways. These included that traditional social democracy had been based on the assumption that governments can regulate economic activity within their borders, especially through the use of Keynesian strategies designed to stimulate growth and maintain full employment. However, the progressive integration of national economies into a larger, global capitalist system has weakened governments' capacity to manage their economies, perhaps rendering 'national Keynesianism' obsolete. Moreover, intensified global competition created pressure on governments to reduce tax and spending levels – particularly, by reforming the welfare state – and to promote labour flexibility. The advent of neo-revisionism can be understood very much in this context, third-way thinking having largely been shaped by attempts by social democrats to come to terms with globalization (Giddens, 1998). If globalization is an irresistible force, and if globalization is intrinsically linked to neoliberalism, socialism would appear to have been consigned to what Trotsky (see p. 125), in very different circumstances, called the 'dustbin of history'.

However, socialists with a longer sense of history are unlikely to succumb to this despondency. Just as predictions at the beginning of the twentieth century about the inevitable victory of socialism proved to be flawed, so proclamations about the death of socialism made in the early twenty-first century are likely to be unreliable. Indeed, as recently as the 1960s it was free-market liberalism that was considered to be redundant, while socialism appeared to be making irresistible progress. Hopes for the survival of socialism rest largely on the enduring, and perhaps intrinsic, imperfections of the capitalist system. As Ralph Miliband put it in *Socialism for a Sceptical Age* (1995), 'the notion that capitalism has been thoroughly transformed and represents the best that humankind can ever hope to achieve is a dreadful slur on the human race'. In that sense, socialism is destined to survive if only because it serves as a reminder that human development can extend beyond market individualism.

Moreover, globalization may bring opportunities for socialism as well as challenges. Just as capitalism is being transformed by the growing significance of the transnational dimension of economic life, socialism may be in the process of being transformed into a critique of global exploitation and inequality. Indeed, socialism may be particularly well positioned to make sense of the new global age, having long shown an awareness of the pressures and tendencies that have served to create it. For example, Marx and Engels can be seen as the earliest theorists of economic globalization, as the *Communist Manifesto* emphasizes that capitalist development always has a marked transnational character. They thus argued that the desire for profit would drive capitalism to 'strive to tear down every barrier to intercourse' and to 'conquer the whole Earth for its market'.

Marxist and neo-Marxist theories have also been used to highlight asymmetrical tendencies, and therefore deepening divisions, within the modern global system. World-systems theory, devised in particular by Immanuel Wallerstein (1974, 1984), suggested that the world economy is best understood as an interlocking capitalist system which exemplifies, at the international level, many of the features that characterize national capitalism; that is, structural inequalities based on exploitation and a tendency towards instability and crisis that is rooted in economic contradictions. The world-system consists of interrelationships between the 'core', the 'periphery' and the 'semi-periphery'. Such thinking about the inherent inequalities and injustices of global capitalism has been one of the key influences on the anti-globalization, or 'anti-capitalist', movement that has emerged since the 1990s. In these ways, socialism in the twenty-first century may be reborn as global anti-capitalism (see p. 161), a trend that has been particularly apparent since the global financial crisis. A resurgence of leftist radicalism was thus evident in the upsurge of the Occupy movement, which in 2011 organized demonstrations in some 82 countries protesting against the dominance of 'the 1 per cent'.

Evidence of a revival of socialism can also be seen at the national level. In some cases, radical leftist parties have come from seemingly nowhere to challenge mainstream parties of both the centre-left and the centre-right. For example, Syriza (the Coalition of the Radical Left), founded in 2004, became the largest party in the Greek parliament in elections in January and September 2015, its chairman, Alexis Tsipras, becoming prime minister. In Spain, the far-left party Podemos (We can), founded in 2014, gained the third largest number of votes and the second largest number of seats in the 2015 parliamentary elections. In other cases, upsurges of

Key concept

Anti-Politics

'Anti-politics' refers to a rejection of, and/ or alienation from, conventional politicians and political processes, especially mainstream political parties and established representative mechanisms. One manifestation of anti-politics is a decline in civic engagement, as citizens turn away from politics and retreat into private existence. This is reflected most clearly in a fall in voter turnout and a decline in levels of party membership and party activism. However, anti-politics has also spawned new forms of politics, which, in various ways, articulate resentment or hostility towards political structures and offer more 'authentic' alternatives. These include the rise of 'fringe' parties and the emergence of 'populist' political leaders, whose attraction is substantially linked to their image as political 'outsiders' untainted by the exercise of power.

radicalism have occurred within established parties of the centre-left. In the UK, Jeremy Corbyn, a veteran of the Labour Party's hard left, emerged as the surprise victor in the party's 2015 leadership election, while in the USA Bernie Sanders, a self-declared socialist, was only narrowly defeated by Hillary Clinton in the contest to become the Democratic nominee in the 2016 presidential election.

Despite national and regional differences, two wider explanations can be advanced for these developments. The first has been a backlash against the politics of austerity, which was widely adopted as economies fell into recession and tax revenues plummeted in the aftermath of the global financial crisis. In countries such as Greece, Spain and Portugal, this was exacerbated by the terms of bailout arrangements that were negotiated with the EU, the IMF and the European Central Bank. The second factor is that far-left parties and movements have tapped in to the growing mood of anti-establishment radicalism, sometimes called 'anti-politics', that stems, in part, from a narrowing of the ideological divide between left- and right-wing parties. This, in turn, has been one of the consequences of the advance of globalization. In this light, resurgent socialism can be seen as part of the wider rise of populism (see p. 92) since the beginning of the twenty-first century.

(?) QUESTIONS FOR DISCUSSION

- What is distinctive about the socialist view of equality?
- Why do socialists favour collectivism, and how have they tried to promote it?
- Is class politics an essential feature of socialism?
- What are the implications of trying to achieve socialism through revolutionary means?
- How persuasive is the socialist critique of private property?
- What are the implications of trying to achieve socialism through democratic means?
- On what grounds have Marxists predicted the inevitable collapse of capitalism?
- How closely did orthodox communism reflect the classical idea of Marx?
- To what extent is socialism defined by a rejection of capitalism?
- Is social democracy really a form of socialism?
- Is the social-democratic 'compromise' inherently unstable?
- Can there be a 'third way' between capitalism and socialism?

(📖) FURTHER READING

McLellan, D., *Marxism after Marx* (2007). An authoritative and comprehensive account of twentieth-century Marxism and more recent developments that also contains useful biographical information.

Moschonas, G., *In the Name of Social Democracy – The Great Transformation: 1945 to the Present* (2002). An impressive and thorough account of the nature, history and impact of social democracy that focuses on the emergence of 'new social democracy'.

Sassoon, D., *One Hundred Years of Socialism* (2013). A very stylish and detailed account of the life and times of democratic socialist ideas and movements.

Wright, A., *Socialisms: Theories and Practices* (1996). A good, brief and accessible introduction to the basic themes of socialism, highlighting the causes of disagreement within the socialist family.

5 Anarchism

Preview

The word 'anarchy' comes from the Greek *anarkhos* and literally means 'without rule'. The term 'anarchism' has been in use since the French Revolution, and was initially employed in a critical or negative sense to imply a breakdown of civilized or predictable order. In everyday language, anarchy implies chaos and disorder. Needless to say, anarchists themselves fiercely reject such associations. It was not until Pierre-Joseph Proudhon proudly declared in *What Is Property?* ([1840] 1970), 'I am an anarchist', that the word was clearly associated with a positive and systematic set of political ideas.

Anarchist ideology is defined by the central belief that political authority in all its forms, and especially in the form of the state, is both evil and unnecessary. Anarchists therefore look to the creation of a stateless society through the abolition of law and government. In their view, the state is evil because, as a repository of sovereign, compulsory and coercive authority, it is an offence against the principles of freedom and equality. Anarchism is thus characterized by principled opposition to certain forms of social hierarchy. Anarchists believe that the state is unnecessary because order and social harmony do not have to be imposed 'from above' through government. Central to anarchism is the belief that people can manage their affairs through voluntary agreement, without the need for top-down hierarchies or a system of rewards and punishments. However, anarchism draws from two quite different ideological traditions: liberalism and socialism. This has resulted in rival individualist and collectivist forms of anarchism. While both accept the goal of statelessness, they advance very different models of the future anarchist society.

Origins and development

Anarchist ideas have sometimes been traced back to Taoist or Buddhist ideas, to the Stoics and Cynics of Ancient Greece, or to the Diggers of the English Civil War. However, the first, and in a sense classic, statement of anarchist principles was produced by William Godwin (see p. 152) in his *Enquiry Concerning Political Justice* ([1793] 1971), although Godwin never described himself as an anarchist. During the nineteenth century, anarchism was a significant component of a broad but growing socialist movement. In 1864, Proudhon's (see p. 152) followers joined with Marx's (see p. 124) to set up the International Workingmen's Association, or First International. The International collapsed in 1871 because of growing antagonism between Marxists and anarchists, led by Mikhail Bakunin (see p. 153). In the late nineteenth century, anarchists sought mass support among the landless peasants of Russia and southern Europe and, more successfully, through anarcho-syndicalism, among the industrial working classes.

Syndicalism was popular in France, Italy and Spain, and helped to make anarchism a genuine mass movement in the early twentieth century. The powerful CGT union in France was dominated by anarchists before 1914, as was the CNT in Spain, which claimed a membership of over two million during the Civil War. Anarcho-syndicalist movements also emerged in Latin America in the early twentieth century, especially in Argentina and Uruguay, and syndicalist ideas influenced the Mexican Revolution, led by Emiliano Zapata. However, the spread of authoritarianism and political repression gradually undermined anarchism in both Europe and Latin America. The victory of General Franco in the Spanish Civil War (1936–9) brought an end to anarchism as a mass movement. The CNT was suppressed, and anarchists, along with left-wingers in general, were persecuted. The influence of anarchism was also undermined by the success of Lenin and the Bolsheviks in 1917, and thus by the growing prestige of communism (see p. 89) within the socialist and revolutionary movements.

Anarchism is unusual among political ideologies in that it has never succeeded in winning power, at least at the national level. Indeed, as anarchists seek to radically disperse and decentralize political power, this has never been their goal. No society or nation has therefore been re-modelled according to anarchist principles. Hence, it is tempting to regard anarchism as an ideology of less significance than, say, liberalism, socialism, conservatism or fascism, each of which has proved itself capable of achieving power and reshaping societies. The nearest anarchists have come to winning power was during the Spanish Civil War (see p. 149). Consequently, anarchists have looked to historical societies that reflect their principles, such as the cities of Ancient Greece or medieval Europe, or to traditional peasant communes such as the Russian *mir*. Anarchists have also stressed the non-hierarchic and egalitarian

SYNDICALISM

A form of revolutionary trade unionism that focuses on labour syndicates as free associations of workers and emphasizes the use of direct action and the general strike.

nature of many traditional societies – for instance, the Nuer in Africa – and supported experiments in small-scale, communal living within western society.

Anarchism's appeal as a political movement has been restricted by both its ends and its means. The goal of anarchism – the overthrow of the state and dismantling of all forms of political authority – is widely considered to be unrealistic, if not impossible. Most, indeed, view the notion of a stateless society as, at best, a utopian dream. In terms of means, anarchists reject as corrupt, and corrupting, the conventional means of exercising political influence: forming political parties, standing for elections, seeking public office and so on. This does not, however, mean that they reject political organization as such, but rather place their faith in non-hierarchical organizations, possibly supported by mass spontaneity and a popular thirst for freedom. Nevertheless, anarchism refuses to die. Precisely because of its uncompromising attitude to authority and political activism, it has an enduring, and often strong, moral appeal, particularly to the young. This can be seen, for example, in the prominence of anarchist ideas, slogans and groups within the emergent anti-capitalist or anti-globalization movement (as discussed in the final section of this chapter).

Core themes: against statist politics

The defining feature of anarchism is its opposition to hierarchy and domination, with the state often being seen as the paradigmatic form of hierarchy and domination. Anarchists have a preference for a stateless society in which free individuals manage their affairs by voluntary agreement, without compulsion or coercion. However, anarchism has been bedevilled by misleading stereotypes and distortions of various kinds. The most common of these is the idea that anarchism rests on little more than a faith in natural 'goodness', the belief that human beings are, at heart, moral creatures. Anarchists certainly believe that people are capable of leading productive and peaceful lives without the need for rulers or leaders, but this view is rarely sustained simply by optimistic assumptions about human nature (Marshall, 2007). In the first place, anarchists do not share a common view of human nature. For example, despite sharing common individualist assumptions, Godwin stressed rational benevolence, while Max Stirner (see p. 152) emphasized conscious egoism. Second, rather than seeing human nature as fixed or determined, the majority of anarchists believe that human beings are products of their environment, even though they are also capable of changing it. In that sense, anarchists believe that human nature develops through creative and voluntary interaction with others. Third, to the extent that anarchists have a theory of human nature, it can be said to be viewed as realistic, even pessimistic. This is because anarchists are profoundly aware of the corruption inherent in the exercise of power. Indeed, if human nature were naturally good, it is difficult to see how hierarchy and domination, and for that matter the state, could have emerged in the first place.

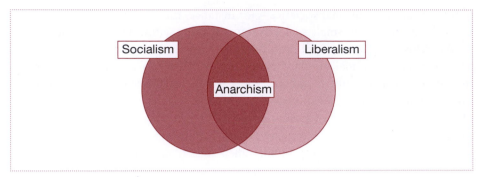

Figure 5.1 The nature of anarchism

An additional feature of anarchism is that it is less a unified and coherent ideology in its own right, and more a point of overlap between two rival ideologies – liberalism and socialism – the point at which both ideologies reach anti-statist conclusions. This is illustrated in Figure 5.1. Anarchism thus has a dual character: it can be interpreted as either a form of 'ultra-liberalism', which resembles extreme liberal individualism (see p. 28), or as a form of 'ultra-socialism', which resembles extreme socialist collectivism (see p. 99). Nevertheless, anarchism is justified in being treated as a separate ideology, in that its supporters, despite drawing on very different political traditions, are united by a series of broader principles and positions. The most significant of these are:

- anti-statism
- natural order
- anti-clericalism
- economic freedom.

Anti-statism

Sébastien Faure, in his four-volume *Encyclopédie anarchiste* (published between 1925 and 1934), defined anarchism as 'the negation of the principle of Authority'. The anarchist case against authority is simple and clear: authority is an offence against the principles of freedom and equality. Authority, based as it is on political inequality and the alleged right of one person to influence the behaviour of others, enslaves, oppresses and limits human life. It damages and corrupts both those who are subject to authority and those who are in authority. Since human beings are free and autonomous creatures, to be subject to authority means to be diminished, to have one's essential nature suppressed and thereby succumb to debilitating dependency. To be in authority is to acquire an appetite for prestige, control and eventually domination. Authority therefore gives rise to a 'psychology of power', based on a pattern of 'dominance and submission', a society in which, according to the US anarchist and social critic Paul Goodman (1911–72), 'many are ruthless and most live in fear' (1977).

PERSPECTIVES ON... **STATE**

LIBERALS see the state as a neutral arbiter among the competing interests and groups in society, a vital guarantee of social order. While classical liberals treat the state as a necessary evil and extol the virtues of a minimal or nightwatchman state, modern liberals recognize the state's positive role in widening freedom and promoting equal opportunities.

CONSERVATIVES link the state to the need to provide authority and discipline and to protect society from chaos and disorder, hence their traditional preference for a strong state. However, whereas traditional conservatives support a pragmatic balance between the state and civil society, neoliberals have called for the state to be 'rolled back', as it threatens economic prosperity and is driven, essentially, by bureaucratic self-interest.

SOCIALISTS have adopted contrasting views of the state. Marxists have stressed the link between the state and the class system, seeing it as either an instrument of class rule or as a means of ameliorating class tensions. Other socialists, however, regard the state as an embodiment of the common good, and thus approve of interventionism in either its social-democratic or state-collectivist form.

ANARCHISTS reject the state outright, believing it to be an unnecessary evil. The sovereign, compulsory and coercive authority of the state is seen as nothing less than legalized oppression operating in the interests of the powerful, propertied and privileged. As the state is inherently evil and oppressive, all states have the same essential character.

FASCISTS, particularly in the Italian tradition, see the state as a supreme ethical ideal, reflecting the undifferentiated interests of the national community, hence their belief in totalitarianism (see p. 207). The Nazis, however, saw the state more as a vessel that contains, or tool that serves, the race or nation.

FEMINISTS have viewed the state as an instrument of male power, the patriarchal state serving to exclude women from, or subordinate them within, the public or 'political' sphere of life. Liberal feminists nevertheless regard the state as an instrument of reform that is susceptible to electoral and other pressures.

ISLAMISTS view the state as an instrument of social and political regeneration, carried out in line with Islamic principles. The Islamic state is a means of 'purifying' Islam, both returning it to its supposed original values and practices, and countering western influence generally. Over time, the Islamic state has increasingly been defined by the predominance given to the enforcement of the *sharia*, even coming to be seen as a *sharia* state.

In practice, the anarchist critique of authority usually focuses on *political* authority, especially when it is backed up by the machinery of the modern state. Anarchism is defined by its radical rejection of state power, a stance that sets anarchism apart from all other political ideologies (with the exception of Marxism).

The flavour of this anarchist critique of law and government is conveyed by one of Pierre-Joseph Proudhon's ([1851] 1923) famous diatribes:

> To be governed is to be watched over, inspected, spied on, directed, legislated, regimented, closed in, indoctrinated, preached at, controlled, assessed, evaluated, censored, commanded; all by creatures that have neither the right, nor the wisdom, nor the virtue.

The state is a *sovereign* body that exercises supreme authority over all individuals and associations living within a defined geographical area. Anarchists emphasize that the authority of the state is absolute and unlimited: law can restrict public behaviour, limit political activity, regulate economic life, interfere with private morality and thinking, and so on. The authority of the state is also *compulsory*. Anarchists reject the liberal notion that political authority arises from voluntary agreement, through some form of 'social contract', and argue instead that individuals become subject to state authority either by being born in a particular country or through conquest. Furthermore, the state is a *coercive* body, whose laws must be obeyed because they are backed up by the threat of punishment. For the Russian-born US anarchist Emma Goldman (1869–1940), government was symbolized by 'the club, the gun, the handcuff, or the prison'. The state can deprive individuals of their property, their liberty and ultimately, through capital punishment, their lives. The state is also *exploitative*, in that it robs individuals of their property through a system of taxation, once again backed up by the force of law and the possibility of punishment. Anarchists often argue that the state acts in alliance with the wealthy and privileged, and therefore serves to oppress the poor and weak. Finally, the state is *destructive*. 'War', as the US anarchist Randolph Bourne (1886–1918) suggested, 'is the health of the State' (1977). Individuals are required to fight, kill and die in wars that are invariably precipitated by a quest for territorial expansion, plunder or national glory by one state at the expense of others.

The basis of this critique of the state lies in the anarchist thinking about human nature. While anarchists emphasize that humanity has a strong libertarian potential, they are also deeply pessimistic about the corrupting influence of political authority and economic inequality. Human beings can be either 'good' or 'evil' depending on the political and social circumstances in which they live. People who would otherwise be cooperative, sympathetic and sociable, become nothing less than oppressive tyrants when raised up above others by power, privilege or wealth. In other words, anarchists replace the liberal warning that 'power tends to corrupt and absolute power corrupts absolutely' (Lord Acton, 1956) with the more radical and alarming warning that power in any shape or form will corrupt absolutely. The state, as a repository of sovereign, compulsory and coercive authority, is therefore nothing less than a concentrated form of evil. The anarchist theory of the state has nevertheless also attracted criticism. Quite apart from concerns about the theory of human nature on which it is based, the assumption that state oppression stems from the corruption of individuals by their political and social circumstances is circular, in that it is unable to explain how political authority arose in the first place.

Natural order

Anarchists regard the state not only as evil, but also as unnecessary. William Godwin sought to demonstrate this by, in effect, turning the most celebrated justification for the state – social contract theory – on its head. The social contract arguments of Hobbes (see p. 84) and Locke (see p. 52) suggest that a stateless society, the 'state of nature', amounts to a civil war of each against all, making orderly and stable life impossible. The source of such strife lies in human nature, which according to Hobbes and Locke is essentially selfish, greedy and potentially aggressive. Only a sovereign state can restrain such impulses and guarantee social order. In short, order is impossible without law. Godwin, in contrast, suggested that human beings are essentially rational creatures, inclined by education and enlightened judgement to live in accordance with truth and universal moral laws. He thus believed that people have a natural propensity to organize their own lives in a harmonious and peaceful fashion. Indeed, in his view it is the corrupting influence of government and unnatural laws, rather than any 'original sin' in human beings, that creates injustice, greed and aggression. Government, in other words, is not the solution to the problem of order, but its cause. Anarchists have often sympathized with the famous opening words of Jean-Jacques Rousseau's (see p. 184) *Social Contract* ([1762] 1913), 'Man was born free, yet everywhere he is in chains'.

At the heart of anarchism lies a distinctive tendency towards utopianism, at least in the sense that utopian thought has the imagination to visualize a society quite different from our own. As pointed out earlier, anarchists believe that human beings are capable of living together peacefully without the need for imposed order. Anarchist thought has thus sought to explain how social order can arise and be sustained in the absence of the machinery of 'law and order'. This has been done in two contrasting but usually interlocking ways. The first way in which anarchists have upheld the idea of natural, as opposed to political, order is through an analysis

Key concept

Utopianism

A utopia (from the Greek *outopia*, meaning 'nowhere', or *eutopia*, meaning 'good place') is usually taken to be perfect, or at least qualitatively better, society. Though utopias of various kinds can be envisaged, most are characterized by the abolition of want, the absence of conflict and the avoidance of

oppression and violence. Utopianism is a style of political theorizing that develops a critique of the existing order by constructing a model of an ideal or perfect alternative. Good examples are anarchism and Marxism. Utopian theories are usually based on assumptions about the unlimited possibilities of human self-development. However, utopianism is often used as a pejorative term to imply deluded or fanciful thinking, a belief in an unrealistic and unachievable goal.

of human nature, or, more accurately, an analysis of the potentialities that reside in human nature. For example, collectivist anarchists have highlighted the human capacity for sociable and cooperative behaviour, while individualist anarchists have drawn attention to the importance of enlightened human reason.

For some anarchists, this potential for spontaneous harmony within human nature is linked to the belief that nature itself, and indeed the universe, is biased in favour of natural order. Anarchists have therefore sometimes been drawn to the ideas of non-western religions such as Buddhism and Daoism, which emphasize interdependence and oneness. An alternative basis for natural order can be found in the notion of ecology, particularly the 'social ecology' of thinkers such as Murray Bookchin (see p. 265). (Social ecology is discussed in Chapter 9 in relation to eco-anarchism.) However, anarchism does not merely stress positive human potentialities. Anarchist theories of human nature are often complex, and acknowledge that rival potentialities reside within the human soul. For instance, in their different ways, Proudhon, Bakunin and Kropotkin (see p. 153) accepted that human beings could be selfish and competitive as well as sociable and cooperative (Morland, 1997). While the human 'core' may be morally and intellectually enlightened, a capacity for corruption lurks within each and every individual.

The second way in which anarchists have supported the idea of natural order is through a stress on the social institutions that foster positive human potential. In this view, human nature is 'plastic', in the sense that it is shaped by the social, political and economic circumstances within which people live. Just as law, government and the state breed a domination/subordination complex, other social institutions nurture respect, cooperation and harmony. Collectivist anarchists thus endorse common ownership or mutualist institutions, while individualist anarchists have supported the market mechanism. Nevertheless, the belief in a stable and peaceful yet stateless society has often been viewed as the weakest and most contentious aspect of anarchist theory. Opponents of anarchism have argued that, however socially enlightened institutions may be, if selfish or negative impulses are basic to human nature and not merely evidence of corruption, the prospect of natural order is simply a delusion. This is why utopianism is most pronounced within the collectivist tradition of anarchism and least pronounced within the individualist tradition, with some anarcho-capitalists rejecting utopianism altogether (Friedman, 1973).

Anti-clericalism

Although the state has been the principal target of anarchist hostility, the same criticisms apply to any other form of compulsory authority. Indeed, anarchists have sometimes expressed as much bitterness towards the church as they have towards the state, particularly in the nineteenth century. This perhaps explains why anarchism has prospered in countries with strong religious traditions, such as Catholic Spain, France, Italy and the countries of Latin America, where it has helped to articulate anti-clerical sentiments.

Anarchist objections to organized religion serve to highlight broader criticisms of authority in general. Religion, for example, has often been seen as the source of authority itself. The idea of God represents the notion of a 'supreme being' who commands ultimate and unquestionable authority. For anarchists such as Proudhon and Bakunin, an anarchist political philosophy had to be based on the rejection of Christianity, because only then could human beings be regarded as free and independent. Moreover, anarchists have suspected that religious and political authority usually work hand in hand. Bakunin proclaimed that 'The abolition of the Church and the State must be the first and indispensable condition of the true liberation of society'. Anarchists view religion as one of the pillars of the state: it propagates an ideology of obedience and submission to both spiritual leaders and earthly rulers. As the Bible says, 'give unto Caesar that which is Caesar's'. Earthly rulers have often looked to religion to legitimize their power, most obviously in the doctrine of the divine right of kings.

Finally, religion seeks to impose a set of moral principles on the individual, and to establish a code of acceptable behaviour. Religious belief requires conformity to standards of 'good' and 'evil', which are defined and policed by figures of religious authority such as priests, imams or rabbis. The individual is thus robbed of moral autonomy and the capacity to make ethical judgements. Nevertheless, anarchists do not reject the religious impulse altogether. There is a clear mystical strain within anarchism. Anarchists can be said to hold an essentially spiritual conception of human nature, a utopian belief in the virtually unlimited possibilities of human self-development and in the bonds that unite humanity, and indeed all living things. Early anarchists were sometimes influenced by millenarianism; indeed, anarchism has often been portrayed as a form of political millenarianism. Modern anarchists have often been attracted to religions such as Daoism and Zen Buddhism, which offer the prospect of personal insight and preach the values of toleration, respect and natural harmony (Christoyannopoulos, 2011).

> **MILLENARIANISM**
> A belief in a thousand-year period of divine rule; political millenarianism offers the prospect of a sudden and complete emancipation from misery and oppression.

Economic freedom

Anarchists have rarely seen the overthrow of the state as an end in itself, but have also been interested in challenging the structures of social and economic life. Bakunin (1973) argued that 'political power and wealth are inseparable'. In the nineteenth century, anarchists usually worked within the working-class movement and subscribed to a broadly socialist philosophy. Capitalism (see p. 97) was understood in class terms: a 'ruling class' exploits and oppresses 'the masses'. However, this 'ruling class' was not, in line with Marxism, interpreted in narrow economic terms, but was seen to encompass all those who command wealth, power or privilege in society. It therefore included kings and princes, politicians and state officials, judges and police officers, and bishops and priests, as well as industrialists and bankers. Bakunin thus argued that, in every developed society, three social groups can be identified: a vast majority who are exploited; a minority who are exploited but also exploit others in equal measure; and 'the supreme governing estate', a small minority of 'exploiters and oppressors pure and simple'. Hence, nineteenth-century anarchists identified themselves with the poor and oppressed and sought to carry out a social revolution in the name of the 'exploited masses', in which both capitalism and the state would be swept away.

However, it is the economic structure of life that most keenly exposes tensions within anarchism. While many anarchists acknowledge a kinship with socialism, based on a common distaste for property and inequality, others have defended property rights and even revered competitive capitalism. This highlights the distinction between the two major anarchist traditions, one of which is collectivist and the other individualist. Collectivist anarchists advocate an economy based on cooperation and collective ownership, while individualist anarchists support the market and private property.

Despite such fundamental differences, anarchists nevertheless agree about their distaste for the economic systems that dominated much of the twentieth century. All anarchists oppose the 'managed capitalism' that flourished in western countries after 1945. Collectivist anarchists argue that state intervention merely props up a system of class exploitation and gives capitalism a human face. Individualist anarchists suggest that intervention distorts the competitive market and creates economies dominated by both public and private monopolies. Anarchists have been even more united in their disapproval of Soviet-style 'state socialism'. Individualist anarchists object to the violation of property rights and individual freedom that, they argue, occurs in a planned economy. Collectivist anarchists argue that 'state socialism' is a contradiction in terms, in that the state merely replaces the capitalist class as the main source of exploitation. Anarchists of all kinds have a preference for an economy in which free individuals manage their own affairs without the need for state ownership or regulation. However, this has allowed them to endorse a number of quite different economic systems, ranging from 'anarcho-communism' to 'anarcho-capitalism'.

Collectivist anarchism

The philosophical roots of collectivist anarchism (sometimes called anarcho-collectivism or social anarchism) lie in socialism rather than liberalism. Anarchist conclusions can be reached by pushing socialist collectivism to its limits. Collectivism is, in essence, the belief that human beings are social animals, better suited to working together for the common good than striving for individual self-interest. Collectivist anarchism, sometimes called social anarchism, stresses the human capacity for social solidarity, or what Kropotkin termed 'mutual aid'. As pointed out earlier, this does not amount to a naïve belief in 'natural goodness', but rather highlights the potential for goodness that resides within all human beings. Human beings are, at heart, sociable, gregarious and cooperative creatures. In this light, the natural and proper relationship between and among people is one of sympathy, affection and harmony. When people are linked together by the recognition of a common humanity, they have no need to be regulated or controlled by government: as Bakunin (1973) proclaimed, 'Social solidarity is the first human law; freedom is the second law'. Not only is government unnecessary but, in replacing freedom with oppression, it also makes social solidarity impossible.

Philosophical and ideological overlaps between anarchism and socialism, particularly Marxist socialism, are evident in the fact that anarchists have often worked within a broad revolutionary socialist movement. For example, the First International, 1864–72, was set up by supporters of Proudhon and Marx. A number of clear theoretical parallels can be identified between collectivist anarchism and Marxism. Both:

- fundamentally reject capitalism, regarding it as a system of class exploitation and structural injustice
- have endorsed revolution as the preferred means of bringing about political change
- exhibit a preference for the collective ownership of wealth and the communal organization of social life
- believe that a fully communist society would be anarchic, expressed by Marx in the theory of the 'withering away' of the state
- agree that human beings have the ultimate capacity to order their affairs without the need for political authority.

Nevertheless, anarchism and socialism diverge at a number of points. This occurs most clearly in relation to parliamentary socialism. Anarchists dismiss parliamentary socialism as a contradiction in terms. Not only is it impossible to reform or 'humanize' capitalism through the corrupt and corrupting mechanisms of government, but also any expansion in the role and responsibilities of the state can only serve to entrench oppression, albeit in the name of equality and social justice. The bitterest disagreement between collectivist anarchists and Marxists centres on their rival conceptions of the transition from capitalism to communism. Marxists have called for a revolutionary 'dictatorship of the proletariat'. They nevertheless argue that this proletarian state will 'wither away' as capitalist class antagonisms abate. In this view, state power is nothing but a reflection of the class system, the state being, in essence, an instrument of class oppression. Anarchists, on the other hand, regard the state as evil and oppressive in its own right: it is, by its very nature, a corrupt and corrupting body. They therefore draw no distinction between bourgeois states and proletarian states. Genuine revolution, for an anarchist, requires not only the overthrow of capitalism but also the immediate and final overthrow of state power. The state cannot be allowed to 'wither away'; it must be abolished. Nevertheless, anarcho-collectivism has taken a variety of forms. The most significant of these are:

- mutualism
- anarcho-syndicalism
- anarcho-communism.

Mutualism

The anarchist belief in social solidarity has been used to justify various forms of cooperative behaviour. At one extreme, it has led to a belief in pure communism, but it has also generated the more modest ideas of **mutualism**, associated with Pierre-Joseph Proudhon. In a sense, Proudhon's libertarian socialism stands between the individualist and collectivist traditions of anarchism, Proudhon's ideas sharing much in common with those of US individualists such as Josiah Warren (see p. 152). In *What Is Property?* ([1840] 1970), Proudhon came up with the famous statement that 'Property is theft', and condemned a system of economic exploitation based on the accumulation of capital. Nevertheless, unlike Marx, Proudhon was not opposed to all forms of private property, distinguishing between property and what he called 'possessions'. In particular, he admired the independence and initiative of small communities of peasants, craftsmen and artisans, especially the watchmakers of Switzerland, who had traditionally managed their affairs on the basis of mutual cooperation. Proudhon therefore sought, through mutualism, to establish a system of property ownership that would avoid exploitation and promote social harmony. Social interaction in such a system would be voluntary, mutually beneficial and harmonious, thus requiring no regulation or interference by government. Proudhon's followers tried to put these ideas into practice by setting up mutual credit banks in France and Switzerland, which provided cheap loans for investors and charged a rate of interest only high enough to cover the cost of running the bank, but not so high that it made a profit.

> **MUTUALISM**
> A system of fair and equitable exchange, in which individuals or groups bargain with one another, trading goods and services without profiteering or exploitation.

Anarcho-syndicalism

Although mutualism and anarcho-communism exerted significant influence within the broader socialist movement in the late nineteenth and early twentieth centuries, anarchism only developed into a mass movement in its own right in the form of anarcho-syndicalism. Syndicalism is a form of revolutionary trade unionism, drawing its name from the French word *syndicat*, meaning union or group. Syndicalism emerged first in France, and was embraced by the powerful CGT union in the period before 1914. Syndicalist ideas spread to Italy, Latin America, the USA and, most significantly, Spain, where the country's largest union, the CNT, supported them.

Syndicalism draws on socialist ideas and advances a theory of stark class war. Workers and peasants are seen to constitute an oppressed class, and industrialists, landlords, politicians, judges and the police are portrayed as exploiters. Workers defend themselves by organizing syndicates or unions, based on particular crafts, industries or professions. In the short term, these syndicates act as conventional trade unions, raising wages, shortening hours and improving working conditions.

POLITICAL IDEOLOGIES IN ACTION . . .
Spain during the Civil War

EVENTS: The Spanish Civil War began in July 1936 with a failed army coup, led by General Franco, against the duly elected Popular Front government. Spain then fell into a civil war which continued until 1939, when Franco and the Nationalists finally prevailed over the Republicans. The outbreak of the Spanish Civil War nevertheless sparked a social revolution, as agrarian and workers' collectives were set up across much of the country, but particularly in Catalonia, Aragon, Andalusia and parts of the Valencian Community. Much of the economy of Spain was put under workers' control, including, from July until October 1936, virtually all production and distribution in Barcelona, the centre of urban collectivization. An estimated eight million people participated directly or indirectly in what became known as the Spanish Revolution.

SIGNIFICANCE: The Spanish Revolution has often been viewed as the greatest ever experiment in anarchism. Dolgoff (1974) claimed that it came closer to realizing the ideal of a free stateless society on a vast scale than any other revolution in history. It certainly corresponded closely to the anarchist conception of social revolution. The collectivization effort was orchestrated, for the most part, by grassroots anarchist and socialist trade unionists, often members of the anarcho-syndicalist CNT or its more radical counterpart, the FAI, or members of the socialist UGT. However, this was essentially a leaderless revolution. None of the leaders of the leftist or trade union organizations called for a revolution. Instead, the collectivizations were a spontaneous response by legions of anonymous labourers to the need to get production on the land and in factories up and running again (Mintz, 2012). The collectives, moreover, operated on the basis of self-management and direct democracy, in line with the principle of 'voluntary authority'.

And yet, the great anarchist experiment was short-lived, lasting barely a year. Rather than succumbing to the pitfalls of leaderless organization, its failure had more to do with the tendency within the CNT–FAI leadership towards collaborationism. Prioritizing the civil war over the revolution, anarchist leaders acted to constrain, isolate and ultimately defeat grassroots opposition to 'governmentalism', helping, in the process, to bring the collectives under government not workers' control. This trend was consolidated by a willingness of anarchist leaders to take ministerial posts in the government, ending the CNT's tradition of independence from political parties and its commitment to revolution through direct action.

However, syndicalists are also revolutionaries, who look forward to the overthrow of capitalism and the seizure of power by the workers. In *Reflections on Violence* ([1908] 1950), Georges Sorel (1847–1922), the influential French syndicalist theorist, argued that such a revolution would come about through a general strike, a 'revolution of empty hands'. Sorel believed that the general strike was a '**political myth**', a symbol of working-class power, capable of inspiring popular revolt.

While syndicalist theory was at times unsystematic and confused, it nevertheless exerted a strong attraction for anarchists who wished to spread their ideas among the masses. As anarchists entered the syndicalist movement, they developed the distinctive ideas of anarcho-syndicalism. Two features of syndicalism inspired particular anarchist enthusiasm. First, syndicalists rejected conventional politics as corrupting and pointless. Working-class power, they believed, should be exerted through **direct action**, boycotts, sabotage and strikes, and ultimately a general strike. Second, anarchists saw the syndicate as a model for the decentralized, non-hierarchic society of the future. Syndicates typically exhibited a high degree of grassroots democracy and formed federations with other syndicates, either in the same area or in the same industry.

POLITICAL MYTH
A belief that has the capacity to provoke political action by virtue of its emotional power rather than through an appeal to reason.

DIRECT ACTION
Political action taken outside the constitutional and legal framework; direct action may range from passive resistance to terrorism.

Although anarcho-syndicalism enjoyed genuine mass support, at least until the Spanish Civil War, it failed to achieve its revolutionary objectives. Beyond the rather vague idea of the general strike, anarcho-syndicalism did not develop a clear political strategy or a theory of revolution. Other anarchists have criticized syndicalism for concentrating too narrowly on short-term trade union goals, and therefore for leading anarchism away from revolution and towards reformism.

Anarcho-communism

In its most radical form, a belief in social solidarity leads in the direction of collectivism and full communism. Sociable and gregarious human beings should lead a shared and communal existence. For example, labour is a social experience, people work in common with fellow human beings and the wealth they produce should therefore be owned in common by the community, rather than by any single individual. In this sense, *all* forms of private property are theft: they represent the exploitation of workers, who alone create wealth, by employers who merely own it. Furthermore, private property encourages selfishness and, particularly offensive to the anarchist, promotes conflict and social disharmony. Inequality in the ownership of wealth fosters greed, envy and resentment, and therefore breeds crime and disorder.

Anarcho-communism stresses the human potential for cooperation, expressed most famously by Peter Kropotkin's theory of 'mutual aid'. Kropotkin attempted to provide a biological foundation for social solidarity via a re-examination of Darwin's theory of evolution. Whereas social thinkers such as Herbert Spencer (1820–1903) had used Darwinism to support the idea that humankind is naturally competitive and aggressive, Kropotkin argued that species are successful precisely because they manage to harness collective energies through cooperation. The process of evolution thus strengthens sociability and favours cooperation over competition. Successful species, such as the human species, must, Kropotkin concluded, have a strong propensity for mutual aid. Kropotkin argued that while mutual aid had flourished in, for example, the city-states of Ancient Greece and medieval Europe, it had been subverted by competitive capitalism, threatening the further evolution of the human species.

Although Proudhon had warned that communism could only be brought about by an authoritarian state, anarcho-communists such as Kropotkin and Errico Malatesta (1853–1932) argued that true communism requires the abolition of the state. Anarcho-communists admire small, self-managing communities along the lines of the medieval city-state or the peasant commune. Kropotkin envisaged that an anarchic society would consist of a collection of largely self-sufficient communes, each owning its wealth in common. From the anarcho-communist perspective, the communal organization of social and economic life has three key advantages. First, as communes are based on the principles of sharing and collective endeavour, they strengthen the bonds of compassion and solidarity, and help to keep greed and selfishness at bay. Second, within communes, decisions are made through a process of participatory or **direct democracy**, which guarantees a high level of popular participation and political equality. Popular self-government is the only form of government that would be acceptable to anarchists. Third, communes are small-scale or 'human-scale' communities, which allow people to manage their own affairs through face-to-face interaction. In the anarchist view, centralization is always associated with depersonalized and bureaucratic social processes.

> **DIRECT DEMOCRACY**
> Popular self-government, characterized by the direct and continuous participation of citizens in the tasks of government.

Individualist anarchism

The philosophical basis of individualist anarchism (sometimes called anarcho-individualism) lies in the liberal idea of the sovereign individual. In many ways, anarchist conclusions are reached by pushing liberal individualism to its logical extreme. For example, William Godwin's anarchism amounts to a form of extreme classical liberalism. At the heart of liberalism is a belief in the primacy of the individual and the central importance of individual freedom. In the classical liberal view, freedom is negative: it consists in the absence of external constraints on the individual. When individualism is taken to its extreme, it therefore implies individual sovereignty: the idea that absolute and unlimited authority resides within each human being. From this perspective, any constraint on the individual is evil; but when this constraint is imposed by the state, by definition a sovereign, compulsory and coercive body, it amounts to an absolute evil. Quite simply, the individual cannot be sovereign in a society ruled by law and government. Individualism and the state are thus irreconcilable principles. As Wolff (1998) put it, 'The autonomous man, insofar as he is autonomous, is not subject to the will of another'.

KEY FIGURES IN... ANARCHISM

William Godwin (1756–1836) A British philosopher and novelist, Godwin developed a thorough-going critique of authoritarianism that amounted to the first full exposition of anarchist beliefs. Adopting an optimism based on the Enlightenment view of human nature as rational and perfectible, based on education and social conditioning, Godwin argued that humanity would become increasingly capable of self-government, meaning that the need for government (and, with it, war, poverty, crime and violence) would disappear. Godwin's chief political work is *Enquiry Concerning Political Justice* (1793).

Josiah Warren (1798–1874) A US individualist anarchist, inventor and musician, Warren was a founding member of the New Harmony experimental community in Indiana. Drawing on the fundamental principle of the 'sovereignty of the individual', Warren advocated a system of 'equitable commerce', which recognized labour as the only legitimate capital and promised to banish both poverty and excessive luxury. His Cincinnati Time Store is sometimes seen as the first experiment in mutualism. Warren's key writings include *Equitable Commerce* (1852) and *True Civilization* (1863).

Max Stirner (1806–56) A German philosopher, Stirner developed an extreme form of individualism, based on egoism, which condemned all checks on personal autonomy. In contrast to other anarchists' stress on moral principles such as justice, reason and community, Stirner emphasized solely the 'ownness' of the human individual, thereby placing the individual self at the centre of the moral universe. Such thinking influenced Nietzsche (see p. 212) and later provided a basis for existentialism. Stirner's most important political work is *The Ego and His Own* (1845).

Pierre-Joseph Proudhon (1809–65) A French social theorist, political activist and largely self-educated printer, Proudhon's writings influenced many nineteenth-century anarchists, socialists and communists. His best-known work, *What Is Property?* (1840), attacked both traditional property rights and collective ownership, and argued instead for mutualism, a cooperative productive system geared towards need rather than profit and organized within self-governing communities. In *The Federal Principle* (1863), Proudhon proposed that such communities should interact on the basis of 'federal' compacts, although this federal state would have minimal functions.

Although these arguments are liberal in inspiration, significant differences exist between liberalism and individualist anarchism. First, while liberals accept the importance of individual liberty, they do not believe this can be guaranteed in a stateless society. Classical liberals argue that a minimal or 'nightwatchman' state is necessary to prevent self-seeking individuals from abusing one another by theft, intimidation, violence or even murder. Law therefore exists to protect freedom, rather than constrain it. Modern liberals take this argument further, and defend

Mikhail Bakunin (1814–76) A Russian political agitator and revolutionary, Bakunin was one of the key proponents of collectivist anarchism and a leading figure within the nineteenth-century anarchist movement. Arguing that political power is intrinsically oppressive and placing his faith in human sociability, Bakunin proposed that freedom could only be achieved through 'collectivism', by which he meant self-governing communities based on voluntary cooperation, the absence of private property, and with rewards reflecting contributions. Bakunin extolled the 'sacred instinct of revolt' and was ferociously anti-theological.

Henry David Thoreau (1817–62) A US author, poet and philosopher, Thoreau's writings had a significant impact on individualist anarchism and, later, on the environmental movement. A follower of transcendentalism, Thoreau's major work, *Walden* (1854), described his two-year 'experiment' in simple living, which emphasized the virtues of self-reliance, contemplation and a closeness to nature. In 'Civil Disobedience' (1849), he defended the validity of conscientious objection to unjust laws, emphasizing that government should never conflict with individual conscience, but he stopped short of explicitly advocating anarchy.

Peter Kropotkin (1842–1921) A Russian geographer and anarchist theorist, Kropotkin's work was imbued with a scientific spirit, based on a theory of evolution that he proposed as an alternative to Darwin's. By seeing 'mutual aid' as the principal means of human and animal development, he claimed to provide an empirical basis for both anarchism and communism, looking to reconstruct society on the basis of self-management and decentralization. Kropotkin's major works include *Mutual Aid* (1902), *The Conquest of Bread* (1892) and *Fields, Factories and Workshops* (1898).

Murray Rothbard (1926–95) A US economist and libertarian thinker, Rothbard advocated 'anarcho-capitalism' based on combining an extreme form of Lockean liberalism with Austrian School free-market economics. Taking the right of total self-ownership to be a 'universal ethic', he argued that economic freedom is incompatible with the power of government and became a fierce enemy of the 'welfare-warfare' state, championing non-intervention in both domestic and foreign affairs. Rothbard's key writings include *Man, Economy and State* (1962), *For a New Liberty* (1978) and *The Ethics of Liberty* (1982).

state intervention on the grounds that it enlarges positive freedom. Anarchists, in contrast, believe that individuals can conduct themselves peacefully, harmoniously and prosperously without the need for government to 'police' society and protect them from their fellow human beings. Anarchists differ from liberals because they believe that free individuals can live and work together constructively because they are rational and moral creatures. Reason and morality dictate that where conflict exists it should be resolved by arbitration or debate, and not by violence.

Second, liberals believe that government power can be 'tamed' or controlled by the development of constitutional and representative institutions. Constitutions claim to protect the individual by limiting the power of government and creating checks and balances among its various institutions. Regular elections are designed to force government to be accountable to the general public, or at least a majority of the electorate. Anarchists dismiss the idea of limited, constitutional or representative government. All laws infringe individual liberty, whether the government that enacts them is constitutional or arbitrary, democratic or dictatorial. In other words, all states are an offence against individual liberty. However, anarcho-individualism has taken a number of forms. The most important of these are:

- egoism
- libertarianism
- anarcho-capitalism.

Egoism

The boldest statement of anarchist convictions built on the idea of the sovereign individual is found in Max Stirner's *The Ego and His Own* ([1845] 1971). Like Marx, the German philosopher Stirner (see p. 152) was deeply influenced by ideas of Hegel (1770–1831), but the two arrived at fundamentally different conclusions. Stirner's theories represent an extreme form of individualism. The term 'egoism' can have two meanings. It can suggest that individuals are essentially concerned about their ego or 'self', that they are self-interested or self-seeking, an assumption that would be accepted by thinkers such as Hobbes or Locke. Self-interestedness, however, can generate conflict among individuals and justify the existence of a state, which would be needed to restrain each individual from harming or abusing others.

In Stirner's view, egoism is a philosophy that places the individual self at the centre of the moral universe. The individual, from this perspective, should simply act as he or she chooses, without any consideration for laws, social conventions, religious or moral principles. Such a position amounts to a form of nihilism. This is a position that clearly points in the direction of both atheism and an extreme form of individualist anarchism. However, as Stirner's anarchism also dramatically turned its back on the principles of the Enlightenment and contained few proposals about how order could be maintained in a stateless society, it had relatively little impact on the emerging anarchist movement. His ideas nevertheless influenced Nietzsche (see p. 212) and twentieth-century existentialism.

> **NIHILISM**
> Literally a belief in nothing; the rejection of all moral and political principles.

Libertarianism

The individualist argument was more fully developed in the USA by libertarian thinkers such as Henry David Thoreau (see p. 153), Lysander Spooner (1808–87), Benjamin Tucker (1854–1939) and Josiah Warren (see p. 152). Thoreau's quest for spiritual truth and self-reliance led him to flee from civilized life and live for several years in virtual solitude, close to nature, an experience described in *Walden* ([1854] 1983). In his most political work, 'Civil Disobedience' ([1849] 1983), Thoreau approved of Jefferson's liberal motto, 'That government is best which governs least', but adapted it to conform with his own anarchist sentiment: 'That government is best which governs not at all'. For Thoreau, individualism leads in the direction of civil disobedience: the individual has to be faithful to his or her conscience and do only what each believes to be right, regardless of the demands of society or the laws made by government. Thoreau's anarchism places individual conscience above the demands of political obligation. In Thoreau's case, this led him to disobey a US government he thought was acting immorally, both in upholding slavery and in waging war against other countries.

Benjamin Tucker took libertarianism further by considering how autonomous individuals could live and work with one another without the danger of conflict or disorder. Two possible solutions to this problem are available to the individualist. The first emphasizes human rationality, and suggests that when conflicts or disagreements develop they can be resolved by reasoned discussion. This, for example, was the position adopted by Godwin, who believed that truth will always tend to displace falsehood. The second solution is to find some sort of mechanism through which the independent actions of free individuals could be brought into harmony with one another. Extreme individualists such as Warren and Tucker believed that this could be achieved through a system of market exchange. Warren thought that individuals have a sovereign right to the property they themselves produce, but are also forced by economic logic to work with others in order to gain the advantages of the division of labour. He suggested that this could be achieved by a system of 'labour-for-labour' exchange, and set up 'time stores' through which one person's labour could be exchanged for a promise to return labour in kind. Tucker argued that 'Genuine anarchism is consistent Manchesterism', referring to the nineteenth-century free-trade, free-market principles of Richard Cobden and John Bright (Nozick, 1974).

LIBERTARIANISM
A belief that the individual should enjoy the widest possible realm of freedom; libertarianism implies the removal of both external and internal constraints upon the individual (see p. 78).

Anarcho-capitalism

The revival of interest in free-market economics in the late twentieth century led to increasingly radical political conclusions. New Right conservatives, attracted to classical economics, wished to 'get government off the back of business' and allow the economy to be disciplined by market forces, rather than managed by an interventionist state. Right-wing libertarians such as Robert Nozick (see p. 85) revived the idea of a minimal state, whose principal function is to protect individual rights. Other thinkers, for instance Ayn Rand (1905–82), Murray Rothbard (see p. 153) and David Friedman (1973), have pushed free-market ideas to their limit and developed a form of anarcho-capitalism. They have argued that government can be abolished and be replaced by unregulated market competition. Property should be owned

 TENSIONS WITHIN... ANARCHISM		
Individualist anarchism	**VS**	**Collectivist anarchism**
ultra-liberalism	⬌	ultra-socialism
extreme individualism	⬌	extreme collectivism
sovereign individual	⬌	social solidarity
civil disobedience	⬌	social revolution
atomism	⬌	organicism
egoism	⬌	communalism
market relations	⬌	social obligations
private property	⬌	common ownership
anarcho-capitalism	⬌	anarcho-communism

by sovereign individuals, who may choose, if they wish, to enter into voluntary contracts with others in the pursuit of self-interest. The individual thus remains free and the market, beyond the control of any single individual or group, regulates all social interaction.

Anarcho-capitalists go well beyond the ideas of free-market liberalism. Liberals believe that the market is an effective and efficient mechanism for delivering most goods, but argue that it also has its limits. Some services, such as the maintenance of domestic order, the enforcement of contracts and protection against external attack, are 'public goods', which must be provided by the state because they cannot be supplied through market competition. Anarcho-capitalists, however, believe that the market can satisfy all human wants. For example, Rothbard (1978) recognized that in an anarchist society individuals will seek protection from one another, but argued that such protection can be delivered competitively by privately owned 'protection associations' and 'private courts', without the need for a police force or a state court system.

Indeed, according to anarcho-capitalists, profit-making protection agencies would offer a better service than the present police force because competition would provide consumers with a choice, ensuring that agencies are cheap, efficient and responsive to consumer needs. Similarly, private courts would be forced to develop a reputation for fairness in order to attract custom from individuals wishing to resolve a conflict. Most important, unlike the authority of public bodies, the contracts thus made with private agencies would be entirely voluntary, regulated only by impersonal market forces. Radical though such proposals may sound, the policy of privatization has already made substantial advances in many western countries. In the USA, several states already use private prisons, and experiments with private courts and arbitration services are well established. In the UK, private prisons and the use of private protection agencies have become commonplace, and schemes such as 'Neighbourhood Watch' have helped to transfer responsibility for public order from the police to the community.

Roads to anarchy

The problem confronting anarchism in terms of political strategy is that if the state is evil and oppressive, any attempt to win government power or even influence government must be corrupting and unhealthy. For example, electoral politics is based on a model of representative democracy, which anarchists firmly reject. Political power is always oppressive, regardless of whether it is acquired through the ballot box or at the point of a gun. Similarly, anarchists are disenchanted by political parties, both parliamentary and revolutionary, because they are bureaucratic and hierarchic organizations. The idea of an anarchist government, an anarchist political party, or an anarchist politician would therefore appear to be contradictions in terms. As there is no conventional 'road to anarchy', anarchists have been forced to explore less orthodox means of political activism. The most significant of these are:

- revolutionary violence
- direct action
- anarcho-pacifism.

Revolutionary violence

In the nineteenth century, anarchist leaders tried to rouse the 'oppressed masses' to insurrection and revolt. Michael Bakunin, for example, led a conspiratorial brotherhood, the Alliance for Social Democracy, and took part in anarchist risings in France and Italy. Other anarchists – for example, Malatesta in Italy, the Russian Populists and Zapata's revolutionaries in Mexico – worked for a peasant revolution. By the end of the nineteenth century, many anarchists had turned their attention to the revolutionary potential of the syndicalist movement, and, during the twentieth century, anarchism increasingly lost support to the better organized and more tightly disciplined communist movement.

Nevertheless, some anarchists continued to place particular emphasis on the revolutionary potential of terrorism and violence. Anarchist violence has been prominent in two periods in particular: in the late nineteenth century, reaching its peak in the 1890s; and again in the 1970s. Anarchists have employed terrorism or 'clandestine violence', often involving bombings or assassinations, designed to create an atmosphere of terror or apprehension. Among its victims were Tsar Alexander II (1881), King Umberto of Italy (1900), Empress Elizabeth of Austria (1898) and Presidents Carnot (1894) of France and McKinley (1901) of the USA. The typical anarchist terrorist was

TERRORISM
The use of violence to induce a climate of fear or terror in order to further political ends; a clearly pejorative and usually subjective term (see p. 314).

either a single individual working alone, such as Emile Henry, who was guillotined in 1894 after placing a bomb in the Café Terminus in Paris, or clandestine groups such as the People's Will in Russia, which assassinated Alexander II. Since the 1990s, anarchism has been linked to political violence through the activities of the so-called Black Blocs, particularly in relation to anti-capitalist or anti-globalization demonstrations.

Practitioners of anarchist violence believe that it always takes place in an ethical and strategic context (Dupuis-Deri, 2014). The anarchist case for the use of violence is distinctive, in that militancy, agitation and sometimes attacks have been thought to be just and fair in themselves and not merely ways of exerting political influence. In the anarchist view, violence is a form of revenge or retribution. Violence originates in the oppression and exploitation that politicians, industrialists, judges, the police and others inflict on the working masses. Anarchist violence thus merely mirrors the everyday violence of society, and directs it towards those who are really guilty. It is therefore a form of 'revolutionary justice'. In addition, violence is a way of raising political consciousness and stimulating the masses to revolt. Russian populists portrayed violence as 'propaganda by the deed', in that it demonstrates the weakness and defencelessness of the ruling class, so helping to stimulate popular insurrection.

However, in practice, anarchist violence has been counter-productive at best. Far from awakening the masses to the reality of their oppression, political violence has normally provoked public horror and outrage. There is little doubt that the association between anarchism and violence has damaged the image of the ideology and therefore its wider appeal. Furthermore, violence and coercion challenge the state on the territory on which its superiority is most clearly overwhelming. Terrorist attacks in the late nineteenth and early twentieth centuries merely encouraged the state to expand and strengthen its repressive machinery, usually with the backing of public opinion.

Direct action

Short of a revolutionary assault on existing society, anarchists have often employed tactics of direct action. Direct action may range from passive resistance to terrorism. Anarcho-syndicalists, for example, refused to engage in conventional, representative politics, preferring instead to exert direct pressure on employers by boycotting their products, sabotaging machinery and organizing strike action. The modern anti-capitalist movement, influenced by anarchism, has also employed strategies of mass popular protest and direct political engagement. From the anarchist point of view, direct action has two advantages. The first is that it is uncontaminated by the processes of government and the machinery of the state. Political discontent and opposition can therefore be expressed openly and honestly; oppositional forces are not diverted in a constitutional direction and cannot be 'managed' by professional politicians.

The second strength of direct action is that it is a form of popular political activism that can be organized on the basis of decentralization and participatory decision-making. This is sometimes seen as the 'new politics', which turns away from established parties, interest groups and representative processes towards a more innovative and theatrical form of protest politics. The clear impact of anarchism can be seen in the tendency of so-called 'new' social movements (such as the feminist, environmental, gay rights and anti-globalization movements) to engage in this form of 'anti-political' politics. Nevertheless, direct action also has its drawbacks. Notably, it may damage public support by leaving political groups and movements that employ it open to the charge of 'irresponsibility' or 'extremism'. Moreover, although direct action attracts media and public attention, it may restrict political influence because it defines the group or movement as a political 'outsider' that is unable to gain access to the process of public policy-making.

> **NEW POLITICS**
> A style of politics that distrusts representative mechanism and bureaucratic processes in favour of strategies of popular mobilization and direct action.

Anarcho-pacifism

In practice, most anarchists see violence as tactically misguided, while others, following Godwin and Proudhon, regard it as abhorrent in principle. These latter anarchists have often been attracted to the principles of non-violence and pacifism developed by the Russian novelist Leo Tolstoy (1828–1910) and Mahatma Gandhi (see p. 185). Although neither of them can properly be classified as anarchists, both, in different ways, expressed ideas that were sympathetic to anarchism. In his political writings, Tolstoy developed the image of a corrupt and false modern civilization. He suggested that salvation could be achieved by living according to religious principles and returning to a simple, rural existence, based on the traditional life-style of the Russian peasantry. For Tolstoy (1937), Christian respect for life required that 'no person would employ violence against anyone, and under no consideration'. Gandhi campaigned against racial discrimination and led the movement for India's independence from the UK, eventually granted in 1947. His political method was based on the idea of *satyagraha*, or non-violent resistance, influenced both by the teachings of Tolstoy and Hindu religious principles.

The principle of non-violence has appealed to anarchists for two reasons. First, it reflects a respect for human beings as moral and autonomous creatures, who are entitled to be treated with compassion and respect. Second, non-violence has been attractive as a political strategy. To refrain from the use of force, especially when subjected to intimidation and provocation, demonstrates the strength and moral purity of one's convictions. However, the anarchists who have been attracted to the principles of pacifism and non-violence have tended to shy away from mass political activism, preferring instead to build model communities that reflect the principles of cooperation and mutual respect. They hope that anarchist ideas will be spread not by political campaigns and demonstrations, but through the stark contrast between the peacefulness and contentment enjoyed within such communities, and the 'quiet desperation', in Thoreau's words, that typifies life in conventional society.

> **PACIFISM**
> A commitment to peace and a rejection of war or violence in any circumstances ('pacific' derives from the Latin and means 'peace-making').

Anarchism in a global age

The success (or failure) of anarchism is difficult to judge because anarchist ideology explicitly rejects mainstream accounts of what constitutes politics and the political. It is nevertheless clear that, despite not existing as a significant political movement for much of the twentieth century, anarchism has stubbornly refused to die. Early signs of an anarchist revival came with the emergence of the New Left (see p. 121) and the New Right, both of which exhibited libertarian tendencies bearing the imprint of anarchist thinking. The New Left encompassed a broad range of movements that were prominent in the 1960s and early 1970s, including student activism, anti-colonialism, feminism and environmentalism. The unifying theme within the New Left was the goal of 'liberation', understood to mean personal fulfilment, and it endorsed an activist style of politics based on popular protest and direct action, clearly influenced by anarchism. The New Right also emphasized the importance of individual freedom, but believed that this could only be guaranteed by market competition. By highlighting what they saw as the evils of state intervention, anarcho-capitalists were prominent in the rediscovery of free-market economics. By emphasizing the coercive and destructive nature of political power, anarchism also helped to counter statist tendencies within other ideologies – notably, socialism, liberalism and conservatism. However, during this period anarchism's significance was less that it provided an ideological basis for acquiring and retaining political power, and more that it challenged, and thereby fertilized, other political creeds.

This nevertheless changed with the upsurge in anti-capitalist protest from the late 1990s onwards. Unlike the New Left activists of the 1960s, who predominantly claimed to be inspired by some form of libertarian socialism (often rooted in Marxist thinking), many contemporary anti-capitalist activists call themselves anarchists. Some have even suggested that this has reversed the process in the period after World War I when anarchism was supplanted by Marxism as the leading form of radical left-wing thinking. But what accounts for this reanimation of anarchism? The most significant factor is that (by virtue of its enduring emphasis on autonomy, participation, decentralization and equality) anarchism has been particularly effective in articulating concerns about the capacity of global capitalism to imprint its values, assumptions and institutions potentially across all parts of the world. It has also offered a style of activism, based on protest, agitation and direct action, through which these concerns can be expressed politically.

The clearest manifestation of this 'new' anarchism has been the activist-based theatrical politics that was first employed during the so-called 'Battle of Seattle' in 1999 (when some 50,000 activists forced the cancellation of the opening ceremony of a World Trade Organization meeting) and has been used in most subsequent anti-capitalist protests. Anarchism's attractiveness to (often young) anti-capitalist activists is bolstered by a variety of factors. These include 'new' anarchism's resistance to compromise for the sake of political expediency, born out of a suspicion of structures and hierarchies of all kinds; its rejection of **consumerism**, symbolized by opposition

CONSUMERISM
A psychic and social phenomenon whereby personal happiness is equated with the consumption of material possessions.

Key concept
Anti-Capitalism

The term 'anti-capitalism' has been associated since the late 1990s with the so-called 'anti-capitalist' (or 'anti-globalization', 'anti-corporate', 'anti-neoliberal', 'alternative globalization' or 'global justice') movement. 'Anti-capitalism' refers to an ideological stance that seeks to expose and contest the discourses and practices of neoliberal globalization, thereby giving a political voice to the disparate range of peoples and groups who have been marginalized or disenfranchised through the rise of global capitalism. However, there is no systematic and coherent 'anti-capitalist' critique of neoliberal globalization, still less a unified vision of an 'anti-capitalist' future. While some in the movement adopt a Marxist-style critique of capitalism, many others seek merely to remove the 'worst excesses' of capitalism, and some simply strive to create 'a better world'.

to 'global goods' and 'brand culture'; and the fact that, in appearing to eschew worked-out strategy and systematic analysis (unlike traditional anarchism), it offers a form of politics that is decidedly 'in the moment'. The theoretical link between anarchism and resistance to globalization, and especially the 'hegemonic' ambitions of the USA, has nevertheless been articulated through the writings of Noam Chomsky (1999, 2003), whose thinking is rooted in anarchist assumptions, especially in that he questions the legitimacy of entrenched power (Chomsky, 2013)

Nevertheless, there are doubts about the extent to which the link between anarchism and resistance to globalization provides the basis for a long-term and meaningful revival of anarchism as a political movement. In the first place, the anarchism that many anti-capitalist protesters espouse is better thought of as an anarchist 'impulse' or an anarchist 'sensibility', in that it does not involve an attempt to deal with anarchism as an ideological system, still less to build on the ideas of 'classic' anarchist thinkers. For example, earlier theoretical debates between anarchists and Marxists about strategy and political organization are entirely alien to the spirit of 'new' anarchism. Thus, although the chief focus of anarchist hostility may have shifted away from the twin targets of the state and industrial capitalism and towards global capitalism, a distinctively anarchist critique of global capitalism has yet to emerge, even in the writings of Chomsky, that corresponds with the 'old-style' anarchist critique of the state.

Second, not only does anarchism operate within a highly diverse and sometimes fragmented anti-capitalist movement, but the anarchist element within this movement is itself highly eclectic. The fact that 'new' anarchism is 'post-ideological' – in that it lacks a theoretical core, and ranges over issues as diverse as pollution and environmental degradation, animal rights, consumerism, urban development, gender relations and global inequality – may help to widen the appeal of the anarchist 'impulse' but, arguably, at the cost of its political effectiveness. Although anarchism may keep alive the idea that a 'better world is possible', it offers few ideas about how that 'better world' would operate or, strategically, how it could be achieved.

(?) QUESTIONS FOR DISCUSSION

- Why do anarchists view the state as evil and oppressive?

- How and why is anarchism linked to utopianism?

- How, and how effectively, have anarchists sustained the idea of natural order?

- Is collectivist anarchism simply an extreme form of socialism?

- How do anarcho-communists and Marxists agree, and over what do they disagree?

- To what extent are anarchism and syndicalism compatible?

- How do individualist anarchists reconcile egoism with statelessness?

- Is anarcho-individualism merely free-market liberalism taken to its logical conclusion?

- To what extent do anarchists disagree about the nature of the future anarchist society?

- How can the political success of anarchism best be judged?

- Why have anarchist ideas been attractive to modern social movements?

- Do anarchists demand the impossible?

(📖) FURTHER READING

Egoumenides, M. *Philosophical Anarchism and Political Obligation* (2014). An analysis of political obligation that challenges the notion of a special relationship between the government and the people from the perspective of philosophical anarchism.

Kinna, R. *Anarchism: A Beginner's Guide* (2009). A clear and insightful introduction to the nature, thinking, tactics and strategies, and various manifestations of anarchism.

Marshall, P., *Demanding the Impossible: A History of Anarchism* (2007). A very comprehensive, authoritative and engagingly enthusiastic account of the full range of anarchist theories and beliefs.

Purkis, J. and Bowen, J. (eds) *Changing Anarchism: Anarchist Theory and Practice in a Global Age* (2004). A wide-ranging collection that reflects on the nature and breadth of contemporary anarchist theory and practice in the light of the changes brought about by globalization.

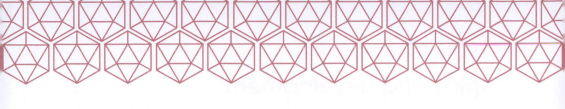

CHAPTER

6 Nationalism

Preview

The word 'nation' has been used since the thirteenth century and derives from the Latin *nasci*, meaning to be born. In the form of *natio*, it referred to a group of people united by birth or birthplace. In its original usage, nation thus implied a breed of people or a racial group, but possessed no political significance. It was not until the late eighteenth century that the term acquired political overtones, as individuals and groups started to be classified as 'nationalists'. The term 'nationalism' was first used in print in 1789 by the anti-Jacobin French priest Augustin Barruel. By the mid-nineteenth century, nationalism was widely recognized as a political doctrine or movement; for example, as a major ingredient of the revolutions that swept across Europe in 1848.

Nationalism can be defined broadly as the belief that the nation is the central principle of political organization. As such, it is based on two core assumptions. First, humankind is naturally divided into distinct nations and, second, the nation is the most appropriate, and perhaps only legitimate, unit of political rule. Classical political nationalism therefore set out to bring the borders of the state into line with the boundaries of the nation. Within so-called nation-states, nationality and citizenship would therefore coincide. However, nationalism is a complex and highly diverse ideological phenomenon. Not only are there distinctive political, cultural and ethnic forms of nationalism, but the political implications of nationalism have also been wide-ranging and sometimes contradictory. Although nationalism has been associated with a principled belief in national self-determination, based on the assumption that all nations are equal, it has also been used to defend traditional institutions and the established social order, as well as to fuel programmes of war, conquest and imperialism. Nationalism, moreover, has been linked to widely contrasting ideological traditions, ranging from liberalism to fascism.

Origins and development

The idea of nationalism was born during the French Revolution. Previously, countries had been thought of as 'realms', 'principalities' or 'kingdoms'. The inhabitants of a country were 'subjects', their political identity being formed by an allegiance to a ruler or ruling dynasty, rather than any sense of national identity or patriotism. However, the revolutionaries in France who rose up against Louis XVI in 1789 did so in the name of the people, and understood the people to be the 'French nation'. Their ideas were influenced by the writings of Jean-Jacques Rousseau (see p. 184) and the new doctrine of popular self-government. Nationalism was therefore a revolutionary and democratic creed, reflecting the idea that 'subjects of the crown' should become 'citizens of France'. The **nation** should be its own master. However, such ideas were not the exclusive property of the French. During the Revolutionary and Napoleonic Wars (1792–1815), much of continental Europe was invaded by France, giving rise to both resentment against France and a desire for **independence**. In Italy and Germany, long divided into a collection of states, the experience of conquest helped to forge, for the first time, a consciousness of national unity, expressed in a new language of nationalism, inherited from France. Nationalist ideas also spread to Latin America in the early nineteenth century, where Simon Bolivar (1783–1830), 'the Liberator', led revolutions against Spanish rule in what was then New Grenada, now the countries of Colombia, Venezuela and Ecuador, as well as in Peru and Bolivia.

NATION
A collection of people bound together by shared values and traditions, a common language, religion and history, and usually occupying the same geographical area (see p. 170).

INDEPENDENCE
The process through which a nation is liberated from foreign rule, usually involving the establishment of sovereign statehood.

In many respects, nationalism developed into the most successful and compelling of political creeds, helping to shape and reshape history in many parts of the world for over two hundred years. The rising tide of nationalism re-drew the map of Europe in the nineteenth century as the autocratic and multinational empires of Turkey, Austria and Russia started to crumble in the face of liberal and nationalist pressure. In

Key concept

Patriotism

Patriotism (from the Latin *patria*, meaning 'fatherland') is a sentiment, a psychological attachment to one's nation, literally a 'love of one's country'. The terms nationalism and patriotism are often confused. Nationalism has a doctrinal character and embodies the belief that the nation is in some way the central principle of political organization. Patriotism provides the affective basis for that belief, and thus underpins all forms of nationalism. It is difficult to conceive of a national group demanding, say, political independence without possessing at least a measure of patriotic loyalty or national consciousness. However, not all patriots are nationalists. Not all of those who identify with, or even love, their nation, see it as a means through which political demands can be articulated.

1848, nationalist uprisings broke out in the Italian states, among the Czechs and the Hungarians, and in Germany, where the desire for national unity was expressed in the creation of the short-lived Frankfurt parliament. The nineteenth century was a period of nation building. Italy, once dismissed by the Austrian Chancellor Metternich as a 'mere geographical expression', became a united state in 1861, the process of **unification** being completed with the acquisition of Rome in 1870. Germany, formerly a collection of 39 states, was unified in 1871, following the Franco-Prussian War.

Nevertheless, it would be a mistake to assume that nationalism was either an irresistible or a genuinely popular movement during this period. Enthusiasm for nationalism was largely restricted to the rising middle classes, who were attracted to the ideas of national unity and constitutional government. Although middle-class nationalist movements kept the dream of national unity or independence alive, they were nowhere strong enough to accomplish the process of nation building on their own. Where nationalist goals were realized, as in Italy and Germany, it was because nationalism coincided with the ambition of rising states such as Piedmont and Prussia. For example, German unification owed more to the Prussian army (which defeated Denmark in 1864, Austria in 1866 and France in 1870–71) than it did to the liberal nationalist movement.

However, by the end of the nineteenth century nationalism had become a truly popular movement, with the spread of flags, national anthems, patriotic poetry and literature, public ceremonies and national holidays. Nationalism became the language of mass politics, made possible by the growth of primary education, mass literacy and the spread of popular newspapers. The character of nationalism also changed. Nationalism had previously been associated with liberal and progressive movements, but was taken up increasingly by conservative and reactionary politicians. Nationalism came to stand for social cohesion, order and stability, particularly in the face of the growing challenge of socialism, which embodied the ideas of social revolution and international working-class solidarity. Nationalism sought to integrate the increasingly powerful working class into the nation, and so to preserve the established social structure. Patriotic fervour was no longer aroused by the prospect of political liberty or democracy, but by the commemoration of past national glories and military victories. Such nationalism became increasingly **chauvinistic** and **xenophobic**. Each nation claimed its own unique or superior qualities, while other nations were regarded as alien, untrustworthy, even menacing. This new climate of popular nationalism helped to fuel policies of imperialism (see p. 166) that intensified dramatically in the 1870s and 1880s and, by the end of the century, had brought most of the world's population

UNIFICATION
The process through which a collection of separate political entities, usually sharing cultural characteristics, are integrated into a single state.

CHAUVINISM
Uncritical and unreasoned dedication to a cause or group, typically based on a belief in its superiority, as in 'national chauvinism' or 'male chauvinism'.

XENOPHOBIA
A fear or hatred of foreigners; pathological ethnocentrism.

Key concept

Imperialism

Imperialism is, broadly, the policy of extending the power or rule of the state beyond its boundaries, typically through the establishment of an empire. In its earliest usage, imperialism was an ideology that supported military expansion and imperial acquisition, usually by drawing on nationalist and racialist doctrines. In its traditional form, imperialism involves the establishment of formal political domination or colonialism and reflects the expansion of state power through a process of conquest and (possibly) settlement. Neo-imperialism (sometimes called neocolonialism) is characterized less by political control and more by economic and ideological domination; it is often seen as a product of structural imbalances in the international economy and/or biases that operate within the institutions of global economic governance.

under European control. It also contributed to a mood of international rivalry and suspicion, which led to world war in 1914.

The end of World War I saw the completion of the process of nation building in central and eastern Europe. At the Paris Peace Conference, US President Woodrow Wilson advocated the principle of national self-determination. The German, Austro-Hungarian and Russian empires were broken up and eight new states created, including Finland, Hungary, Czechoslovakia, Poland and Yugoslavia. These new countries were designed to be nation-states that conformed to the geography of existing national or ethnic groups. However, World War I failed to resolve the serious national tensions that had precipitated conflict in the first place. Indeed, the experience of defeat and disappointment with the terms of the peace treaties left an inheritance of frustrated ambition and bitterness. This was most evident in Germany, Italy and Japan, where fascist or authoritarian movements came to power in the inter-war period by promising to restore national pride through policies of expansion and empire. Nationalism was therefore a powerful factor leading to war in both 1914 and 1939.

During the twentieth century the doctrine of nationalism, which had been born in Europe, spread throughout the globe as the peoples of Asia and Africa rose in opposition to colonial rule. The process of colonialism had involved not only the establishment of political control and economic dominance, but also the importation of western ideas, including nationalism, which began to be used against the colonial masters themselves. Nationalist uprisings took place in Egypt in 1919 and quickly spread throughout the Middle East. The Anglo-Afghan war also broke out in 1919, and rebellions took place in India, the Dutch East Indies and Indochina. After 1945, the map of Africa and Asia was redrawn as the British, French, Dutch and Portuguese empires each disintegrated in the face of nationalist movements that either succeeded in negotiating independence or winning wars of 'national liberation'.

NATION-STATE
A sovereign political association within which citizenship and nationality overlap; one nation within a single state.

EMPIRE
A structure of domination in which diverse cultural, ethnic or nation groups are subjected to a single source of authority.

Anti-colonialism not only witnessed the spread of western-style nationalism to the developing world, but also generated new forms of nationalism. Nationalism in the developing world has embraced a wide range of movements. In China, Vietnam and parts of Africa, nationalism has been fused with Marxism, and national liberation has been regarded not simply as a political goal but as part of a social revolution. Elsewhere, developing-world nationalism has been anti-western, rejecting both liberal democratic and revolutionary socialist conceptions of nationhood. This has been particularly evident in the rise of forms of religious nationalism and especially in the emergence of religious fundamentalism. The relationship between nationalism and religious fundamentalism (see p. 188) is examined later in the chapter, in association with postcolonial nationalism.

Core themes: for the love of country

To treat nationalism as an ideology in its own right is to encounter at least three problems. The first is that nationalism is sometimes classified as a political doctrine rather than a fully-fledged ideology. Whereas, for instance, liberalism, conservatism and socialism constitute complex sets of interrelated ideas and values, nationalism, the argument goes, is at heart the simple belief that the nation is the natural and proper unit of government. The drawback of this view is that it focuses only on what might be regarded as 'classical' **political nationalism**, and ignores the many other, and in some respects no less significant, manifestations of nationalism, such as **cultural nationalism** and **ethnic nationalism**. The core feature of nationalism is therefore not its narrow association with self-government and the nation-state, but its broader link to movements and ideas that in whatever way acknowledge the central importance to political life of the nation.

POLITICAL NATIONALISM
A form of nationalism that regards the nation as a natural political community, usually expressed through the idea of national self-determination.

CULTURAL NATIONALISM
A form of nationalism that places primary emphasis on the regeneration of the nation as a distinctive civilization rather than on self-government.

ETHNIC NATIONALISM
A form of nationalism that is fuelled primarily by a keen sense of ethnic distinctiveness and the desire to preserve it.

Second, nationalism is sometimes portrayed as an essentially psychological phenomenon – usually as loyalty towards one's nation or dislike of other nations – instead of as a theoretical construct. Undoubtedly, one of the key features of nationalism is the potency of its affective or emotional appeal, but to understand it in these terms alone is to mistake the ideology of nationalism for the sentiment of patriotism.

Third, nationalism has a schizophrenic political character. At different times, nationalism has been progressive and reactionary, democratic and authoritarian, rational and irrational, and left-wing and right-wing. It has also been associated with almost all the major ideological traditions. In their different ways, liberals, conservatives, socialists, fascists and even communists have been attracted to nationalism; perhaps only anarchism, by virtue of its outright rejection of the state, is fundamentally at odds with nationalism. Nevertheless, although nationalist doctrines have been used by a bewildering variety of political movements and associated with sometimes diametrically opposed political causes, a bedrock of nationalist ideas and theories can be identified. The most important of these are:

- the nation
- organic community
- self-determination
- culturalism.

The nation

The basic belief of nationalism is that the nation is, or should be, the central principle of political organization. However, much confusion surrounds what nations are and how they can be defined. In everyday language, words such as 'nation', 'state', 'country' and even 'race' are often confused or used as if they are interchangeable. Many political disputes, moreover, are really disputes about whether a particular group of people should be regarded as a nation, and should therefore enjoy the rights and status associated with nationhood. This applies, for instance, to the Tibetans, the Kurds, the Palestinians, the Basques, the Tamils, and so on.

On the most basic level, nations are cultural entities, collections of people bound together by shared values and traditions, in particular a common language, religion and history, and usually occupying the same geographical area. From this point of view, the nation can be defined by 'objective' factors: people who satisfy a requisite set of cultural criteria can be said to belong to a nation; those who do not can be classified as non-nationals or members of foreign nations. However, to define a nation simply as a group of people bound together by a common culture and traditions raises some very difficult questions. Although particular cultural features are commonly associated with nationhood, notably language, religion, ethnicity, history and tradition, there is no blueprint nor any objective criteria that can establish where and when a nation exists.

Language is often taken to be the clearest symbol of nationhood. A language embodies distinctive attitudes, values and forms of expression that produce a sense of familiarity and belonging. German nationalism, for instance, has traditionally been founded on a sense of cultural unity, reflected in the purity and survival of the German language. Nevertheless, at the same time, there are peoples who share the same language without having any conception of a common national identity: Americans, Australians and New Zealanders may speak English as a first language, but certainly do not think of themselves as members of an 'English nation'. Other nations have enjoyed a substantial measure of national unity without possessing

ETHNICITY
A sentiment of loyalty towards a particular population, cultural group or territorial area; bonds that are cultural rather than racial.

a national language, as is the case in Switzerland where, in the absence of a Swiss language, three major languages are spoken: French, German and Italian.

Religion is another major component of nationhood. Religion expresses common moral values and spiritual beliefs. In Northern Ireland, people who speak the same language have been divided along religious lines: most Protestants regard themselves as Unionists and wish to preserve their links with the UK, while many in the Catholic community favour a united Ireland. Islam has been a major factor in forming national consciousness in much of North Africa and the Middle East. On the other hand, religious beliefs do not always coincide with a sense of nationhood. Divisions between Catholics and Protestants in mainland UK do not inspire rival nationalisms, nor has the remarkable religious diversity found in the USA threatened to divide the country into a collection of distinct nations. At the same time, countries such as Poland, Italy, Brazil and the Philippines share a common Catholic faith but do not feel that they belong to a unified 'Catholic nation'.

Nations have also been based on a sense of *ethnic* or, in certain circumstances, *racial* unity. This was particularly evident in Germany during the Nazi period. However, nationalism usually has a cultural rather than a biological basis; it reflects an ethnic unity that may be based on race, but more usually draws on shared values and common cultural beliefs. The nationalism of US blacks, for example, is based less on colour than on their distinctive history and culture. Nations thus usually share a common *history* and *traditions*. Not uncommonly, national identity is preserved by recalling past glories, national independence, the birthdays of national leaders or important military victories. The USA celebrates Independence Day and Thanksgiving; Bastille Day is commemorated in France; in the UK, ceremonies continue to mark Armistice Day. However, nationalist feelings may be based more on future expectations than on shared memories or a common past. This applies in the case of immigrants who have been 'naturalized', and is most evident in the USA, a 'land of immigrants'. The journey of the Mayflower and the War of Independence have no direct relevance for most Americans, whose families arrived centuries after these events occurred.

The cultural unity that supposedly expresses itself in nationhood is therefore very difficult to pin down. It reflects a varying combination of cultural factors, rather than any precise formula. Ultimately, therefore, nations can only be defined 'subjectively', by their members, not by any set of external factors. In this sense, the nation is a psycho-political entity, a group of people who regard themselves as a natural political community and are distinguished by shared loyalty or affection in the form of patriotism. Objective difficulties such as the absence of land, a small population or lack of economic resources are of little significance if a group of people insists on demanding what it sees as 'national rights'. Latvia, for example, became an independent nation in 1991 despite having a population of only 2.6 million (barely half of whom are ethnic Lats), no source of fuel and very few natural resources. Likewise, the Kurdish peoples of the Middle East have nationalist aspirations, even though the Kurds have never enjoyed formal political unity and are at present spread over parts of Turkey, Iraq, Iran and Syria.

PERSPECTIVES ON... NATION

LIBERALS subscribe to a 'civic' view of the nation that places as much emphasis on political allegiance as on cultural unity. Nations are moral entities in the sense that they are endowed with rights, notably an equal right to self-determination.

CONSERVATIVES regard the nation as primarily an 'organic' entity, bound together by a common ethnic identity and a shared history. As the source of social cohesion and collective identity, the nation is perhaps the most politically significant of social groups.

SOCIALISTS tend to view the nation as an artificial division of humankind whose purpose is to disguise social injustice and prop up the established order. Political movements and allegiances should therefore have an international, not a national, character.

ANARCHISTS have generally held that the nation is tainted by its association with the state, and therefore with oppression. The nation is thus seen as a myth, designed to promote obedience and subjugation in the interests of the ruling elite.

FASCISTS view the nation as an organically unified social whole, often defined by race, which gives purpose and meaning to individual existence. However, nations are pitted against one another in a struggle for survival in which some are fitted to succeed and others to go to the wall.

The fact that nations are formed through a combination of objective and subjective factors has given rise to rival concepts of the nation. While all nationalists agree that nations are a blend of cultural and psycho-political factors, they disagree strongly about where the balance between the two lies. On the one hand, 'exclusive' concepts of the nation stress the importance of ethnic unity and a shared history. By viewing national identity as 'given', unchanging and indeed unchangeable, this implies that nations are characterized by common descent and so blurs the distinction between nations and races. Nations are thus held together by '**primordial** bonds', powerful and seemingly innate emotional attachments to a language, religion, traditional way of life and a homeland. To different degrees, conservatives and fascists adopt such a view of the nation. On the other hand, 'inclusive' concepts of the nation, as found in **civic nationalism**, highlight the importance of civic consciousness and patriotic loyalty. From this perspective, nations may be multi-racial, multi-ethnic, multi-religious and so forth. This, in turn, tends to blur the distinction between the nation and the state, and thus between nationality and

> **PRIMORDIALISM**
> The belief that nations are ancient and deep-rooted, fashioned variously out of psychology, culture and biology.
>
> **CIVIC NATIONALISM**
> A form of nationalism that emphasizes political allegiance based on a vision of a community of equal citizens, allowing for significant levels of ethnic and cultural diversity.

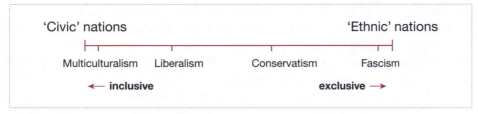

Figure 6.1 Views of the nation

citizenship. Liberals and socialists tend to adopt an inclusive view of the nation. These different approaches to the nation are illustrated in Figure 6.1.

Organic community

Although nationalists may disagree about the defining features of the nation, they are unified by their belief that nations are organic communities. Humankind, in other words, is naturally divided into a collection of nations, each possessing a distinctive character and separate identity. This, nationalists argue, is why a 'higher' loyalty and deeper political significance attaches to the nation than to any other social group or collective body. Whereas, for instance, class, gender, religion and language may be important in particular societies, or may come to prominence in particular circumstances, the bonds of nationhood are more fundamental. National ties and loyalties are found in all societies, they endure over time, and they operate at an instinctual, even primordial, level. Nevertheless, different explanations have been provided for this, the most significant being based on the ideas of primordialism, modernism and constructivism.

Primordialist approaches to nationalism portray national identity as historically embedded: nations are rooted in a common cultural heritage and language that may long pre-date statehood or the quest for independence, and are characterized by deep emotional attachments that resemble kinship ties. All nationalists, in that sense, are primordialists. Anthony Smith (1986) highlighted the importance of primordialism by stressing the continuity between modern nations and pre-modern ethnic communities, which he called 'ethnies'. This implies that there is little difference between ethnicity and nationality, modern nations essentially being updated versions of long-established ethnic communities, although Smith rejected the idea that these proto-nations have existed from time immemorial.

In contrast, *modernist* approaches to nationalism suggests that nation identity is forged in response to changing situations and historical challenges. Ernest Gellner (1983) thus emphasized the degree to which nationalism is linked to modernization, and in particular to the process of industrialization. He stressed that, while pre-modern or 'agro-literate' societies were structured by a network of feudal bonds and loyalties, emerging industrial societies promoted social mobility, self-striving and competition, and so required a new source of cultural cohesion. This was provided by nationalism. Although Gellner's theory suggests that nations coalesced in response to particular social conditions and circumstances, it also implies that the national community is deep-rooted and enduring, as a return to pre-modern loyalties and identities is unthinkable. Benedict Anderson (1983) also portrayed modern nations as a product of socio-economic change, in his case stressing the combined impact of the emergence of capitalism and the advent of modern mass communications, which he dubbed 'print-capitalism'. In his view, the nation is an 'imagined community', in that, within nations, individuals only ever meet a tiny proportion of those with whom they supposedly share a national identity.

The idea that nations are 'imagined', not organic, communities has nevertheless been seized on by critics of nationalism. *Constructivist* approaches to nationalism regard national identity as very largely an ideological construct, usually serving the interests of powerful groups. The Marxist historian Eric Hobsbawm (1983), for example, highlighted the extent to which nations are based on 'invented traditions'. Hobsbawm argued that a belief in historical continuity and cultural purity is invariably a myth, and, what is more, a myth created by nationalism itself. **Constructivism** suggests that nationalism creates nations, not the other way round. In the case of Marxism, nationalism has been viewed as a device through which the ruling class counters the threat of social revolution by ensuring that national loyalty is stronger than class solidarity, thereby binding the working class to the existing power structure.

CONSTRUCTIVISM
The theory that meaning is imposed on the external world by the beliefs and assumptions we hold; reality is a social construct.

Self-determination

Nationalism as a political ideology only emerged when the idea of national community encountered the doctrine of popular **sovereignty**. This occurred during the French Revolution and was influenced by the writings of Jean-Jacques Rousseau, sometimes seen as the 'father' of modern nationalism. Although Rousseau did not specifically address the question of the nation, or discuss the phenomenon of nationalism, his stress on popular sovereignty, expressed in the idea of the '**general will**', was the seed from which nationalist doctrines sprang. As a result of the Polish struggle for independence from Russia, he came to believe that this is vested in a culturally unified people. Rousseau argued that government should be based not on the absolute power of a monarch, but on the indivisible collective will of the entire community. During the French Revolution, these beliefs were reflected in the assertion that the French people were 'citizens' possessed of inalienable rights and duties, no longer merely 'subjects' of the crown. Sovereign power thus resided with the 'French nation'. The form of nationalism that emerged from the French Revolution was

SOVEREIGNTY
The principle of absolute or unrestricted power expressed either as unchallengeable legal authority or unquestionable political power.

GENERAL WILL
The genuine interests of a collective body, equivalent to the common good; the will of all, provided each person acts selflessly.

therefore based on the vision of a people or nation governing itself. In other words, the nation is not merely a natural community: it is a natural *political* community.

In this tradition of nationalism, nationhood and statehood are intrinsically linked. The litmus test of national identity is the desire to attain or maintain political independence, usually expressed in the principle of national self-determination. The goal of nationalism is therefore the founding of a 'nation-state'. To date, this has been achieved in one of two ways. First, it may involve a process of unification. German history, for instance, has repeatedly witnessed unification. This occurred in medieval times under Charlemagne through the Holy Roman Empire; in the nineteenth century under Bismarck; and when the 'two Germanies' (East Germany and West Germany) were reunited in 1990. Second, nation-states can be created through the achievement of independence. For example, much of Polish history has witnessed successive attempts to achieve independence from the control of various foreign powers. Poland ceased to exist in 1793 when the Poles were partitioned by Austria, Russia and Prussia. Recognized by the Treaty of Versailles of 1919, Poland was proclaimed in 1918 and became an independent republic. However, in accordance with the Nazi–Soviet Pact of 1939, Poland was invaded by Germany and repartitioned, this time between Germany and the Soviet Union. Although Poland achieved formal independence in 1945, for much of the post-war period it remained firmly under Soviet control. The election of a non-communist government in 1989 therefore marked a further liberation of the country from foreign control.

For nationalists, the nation-state is the highest and most desirable form of political organization. The great strength of the nation-state is that it offers the prospect of both cultural cohesion and political unity. When a people who share a common cultural or ethnic identity gain the right to self-government, nationality and citizenship coincide. Moreover, nationalism legitimizes the authority of government. Political sovereignty in a nation-state resides with the people or the nation itself. Consequently, nationalism represents the notion of popular self-government, the idea that government is carried out either by the people or for the people, in accordance with their 'national interest'. This is why nationalists believe that the forces that have created a world of independent nation-states are natural and irresistible, and that no other social group could constitute a meaningful political community. The nation-state, in short, is the only viable political unit.

However, it would be misleading to suggest that nationalism is always associated with the nation-state or is necessarily linked to the idea of self-determination. Some nations, for instance, may be satisfied with a measure of political autonomy that stops short of statehood and full independence. This can be seen in the case of Welsh nationalism in the UK, and Breton and Basque nationalism in France. Nationalism is thus not always associated with **separatism**, but may instead be expressed through federalism (see p. 39) or devolution. Nevertheless, it is unclear whether devolution, or even

> **SEPARATISM**
> The quest to secede from a larger political formation with a view to establishing an independent state.

federalism, establishes a sufficient measure of self-government to satisfy nationalist demands. The granting of wide-ranging powers to the Basque region of Spain has failed to end ETA's separatist campaign. Similarly, the creation of a Scottish Parliament in the UK in 1999 has not ended the Scottish National Party's (SNP's) campaign to achieve an independent Scotland, which continues despite the failure of the 2015 independence referendum.

Culturalism

Although 'classical' nationalism is associated with political goals – most commonly the pursuit, or defence, of independent statehood – other forms of nationalism are related more closely to ethnocultural aspirations and demands. This applies particularly in the case of cultural nationalism and ethnic nationalism. Cultural nationalism is a form of nationalism that emphasizes the strengthening or defence of cultural identity over overt political demands. Its principal stress is on the regeneration of the nation as a distinctive civilization, with the state being viewed as a peripheral, if not as an alien, entity. Whereas political nationalism is 'rational' and may be principled, cultural nationalism tends to be 'mystical', in that it is based on a romantic belief in the nation as a unique historical and organic whole. Typically, cultural nationalism is a 'bottom-up' form of nationalism that draws more on popular rituals, traditions and legends than on elite or 'higher' culture. Although it usually has an anti-modern character, cultural nationalism may also serve as an agent of modernization, providing a people with a means of 'recreating' itself.

Whereas Rousseau is commonly seen as the 'father' of political nationalism, Johann Herder (see p. 184) is usually viewed as the architect of cultural nationalism. Herder, together with writers such as Johann Fichte (1762–1814) and Friedrich Jahn (1778–1852), highlighted what they believed to be the uniqueness and superiority of German culture, in contrast to the ideas of the French Revolution. Herder believed that each nation possesses a *Volksgeist* which reveals itself in songs, myths and legends, and provides a nation with its source of creativity. Herder's nationalism therefore amounts to a form of **culturalism**. In this light, the role of nationalism is to develop an awareness and appreciation of national traditions and collective memories rather than to provide the basis for an overtly political quest for statehood. The tendency for nationalism to be expressed through cultural regeneration was particularly marked in nineteenth-century Germany, where it was reflected in the revival of folk traditions and the rediscovery of German myths and legends. The Brothers Grimm, for example, collected and published German folk tales, and the composer Richard Wagner (1813–83) based many of his operas on ancient myths.

Although cultural nationalism has often emerged within a European context, with early German nationalism sometimes being viewed as its archetypal form,

VOLKSGEIST
(German) Literally, the spirit of the people; the organic identity of a people reflected in their culture and particularly in their language.

CULTURALISM
The belief that human beings are culturally-defined creatures, culture being the universal basis for personal and social identity.

cultural nationalism has been found in many parts of the world. It was, for instance, evident in black nationalism in the USA, as articulated by figures such as Marcus Garvey (see p. 185) and by groups such as the Black Panthers and the Black Muslims (later the Nation of Islam). Similarly, it has been apparent in India, in forms of nationalism that have been based on the image of India as a distinctively Hindu civilization. It is also evident in modern China in the increasing prominence given by party and state officials to the idea of 'Chineseness', expressed, among other things, in a revival of traditional cultural practices and an emphasis on 'Chinese' principles and moral values.

However, there has been disagreement about the implications of viewing nations primarily as cultural communities rather than political communities. On the one hand, cultural forms of nationalism have been viewed as being tolerant and consistent with progressive political goals, in which case it clearly differs from ethnic nationalism, even though the terms 'culture' and 'ethnicity' overlap. Ethnicity refers to loyalty towards a distinctive population, cultural group or territorial area. The term is complex because it has both racial and cultural overtones. Members of ethnic groups are often seen, correctly or incorrectly, to have descended from common ancestors, suggesting that ethnic groups are extended kinship groups, united by blood. A further indication of ethnic belonging is a link with an ancient or historic territory, a 'homeland', as in the case of Zionism (see p. 176). As it is not possible to 'join' an ethnic group (except perhaps through intermarriage), ethnic nationalism has a clearly exclusive character and tends to overlap with

⟷ TENSIONS WITHIN... NATIONALISM (1)

Civic nationalism	VS	Ethnocultural nationalism
political nation	⟷	cultural/historical nation
inclusive	⟷	exclusive
universalism	⟷	particularism
equal nations	⟷	unique nations
rational/principled	⟷	mystical/emotional
national sovereignty	⟷	national 'spirit'
voluntaristic	⟷	organic
based on citizenship	⟷	based on descent
civic loyalty	⟷	ethnic allegiance
cultural diversity	⟷	cultural unity

Key concept

Zionism

Zionism (*Zion* is Hebrew for the Kingdom of Heaven) is the movement for the establishment of a Jewish homeland, usually seen as being located in Palestine. The idea was first advanced in 1897 by Theodore Herzl (1860–1904) at the World Zionist Congress in Basle, as the only means of protecting the Jewish people from persecution. Early Zionists had secularist and nationalistic aspirations, often associated with socialist sympathies. Since the foundation of the state of Israel in 1948, however, Zionism has come to be associated both with the continuing promise of Israel to provide a home for all Jews, and with attempts to promote sympathy for Israel and defend it against its enemies. In the latter sense, it has been recruited to the cause of fundamentalism, and, according to Palestinians, it has acquired an expansionist, anti-Arab character.

racism (see p. 210). On the other hand, cultural and ethnic forms of nationalism have been viewed as closely related, even as part of the same phenomenon, commonly termed 'ethnocultural nationalism'. In this view, a distinction is drawn between inclusive or 'open' political nationalism and exclusive or 'closed' cultural nationalism. Cultural nationalism, from this perspective, is often taken to be, either implicitly or explicitly, chauvinistic or hostile towards other nations or minority groups, being fuelled by a mixture of pride and fear. To the extent that cultural nationalism is associated with demands for assimilation and cultural 'purity', it becomes incompatible with multiculturalism (the relationship between multiculturalism and nationalism is examined in greater depth in Chapter 11).

Types of nationalism

Political nationalism is a highly complex phenomenon, being characterized more by ambiguity and contradictions than by a single set of values and goals. For example, nationalism has been both liberating and oppressive: it has brought about self-government and freedom, and it has led to conquest and subjugation. Nationalism has been both progressive and regressive: it has looked to a future of national independence or national greatness, and it has celebrated past national glories and entrenched established identities. Nationalism has also been both rational and irrational: it has appealed to principled beliefs, such as national self-determination, and it has bred from non-rational drives and emotions, including ancient fears and hatreds. This ideological shapelessness is a product of a number of factors. Nationalism has emerged in very different historical contexts, been shaped by contrasting cultural inheritances, and it has been used to advance a wide variety of political causes and aspirations. However, it also reflects the capacity of nationalism to fuse with and absorb other political doctrines and ideas, thereby creating a series of rival nationalist traditions. The most significant of these traditions are:

- liberal nationalism
- conservative nationalism
- expansionist nationalism
- anti-colonial and postcolonial nationalism.

Liberal nationalism

Liberal nationalism is the oldest form of nationalism, dating back to the French Revolution and embodying many of its values. Its ideas spread quickly through much of Europe and were expressed most clearly by Giuseppe Mazzini (see p. 184), often thought of as the 'prophet' of Italian unification. They also influenced the remarkable exploits of Simon Bolivar, who led the Latin American independence movement in the early nineteenth century and expelled the Spanish from much of Hispanic America. Woodrow Wilson's (see p. 184) 'Fourteen Points', proposed as the basis for the reconstruction of Europe after the First World War, were also based on liberal nationalist principles. Moreover, many twentieth-century anti-colonial leaders were inspired by liberal ideas, as in the case of Sun Yat-Sen (1866–1925), one of the leaders of China's 1911 Revolution, and Jawaharlal Nehru (1889–1964), the first prime minister of India.

The ideas of liberal nationalism were clearly shaped by J.-J. Rousseau's defence of popular sovereignty, expressed in particular in the notion of the 'general will'. As the nineteenth century progressed, the aspiration for popular self-government was fused progressively with liberal principles. This fusion was brought about by the fact that the multinational empires against which nationalists fought were also autocratic and oppressive. Mazzini, for example, wished the Italian states to unite, but this also entailed throwing off the influence of autocratic Austria. For many European revolutionaries in the mid-nineteenth century, liberalism and nationalism were virtually indistinguishable. Indeed, their nationalist creed was largely forged by applying liberal ideas, initially developed in relation to the individual, to the nation and to international politics.

Liberalism was founded on a defence of individual freedom, traditionally expressed in the language of rights. Nationalists believed nations to be sovereign entities, entitled to liberty, and also possessing rights, the most important being the right of self-determination. Liberal nationalism is therefore a liberating force in two senses. First, it opposes all forms of foreign domination and oppression, whether by multinational empires or colonial powers. Second, it stands for the ideal of self-government, reflected in practice in a belief in constitutionalism (see p. 37) and representation. Woodrow Wilson, for example, argued in favour of a Europe composed not only of nation-states, but also one in which political democracy rather than autocracy ruled. For him, only a democratic republic, on the US model, could be a genuine nation-state.

Furthermore, liberal nationalists believe that nations, like individuals, are equal, at least in the sense that they are equally entitled to the right of self-determination. The ultimate goal of liberal nationalism is, therefore, the construction of a world

Key concept

Internationalism

Internationalism is the theory or practice of politics based on transnational or global cooperation. It is rooted in universalist assumptions about human nature that put it at odds with political nationalism, the latter emphasizing the degree to which political identity is shaped by nationality. However, internationalism is compatible with nationalism in the sense that it calls for cooperation or solidarity between or among pre-existing nations, rather than for the removal or abandonment of national identities altogether. Internationalism thus differs from cosmopolitanism (see p. 191), the latter implying the displacement of national allegiances by global allegiances. 'Weak' forms of internationalism can be seen in doctrines such as feminism, racism and religious fundamentalism, which hold that national ties are secondary to other political bonds. 'Strong' forms of internationalism have usually drawn on the universalist ideas of either liberalism or socialism.

of independent nation-states, not merely the unification or independence of a particular nation. John Stuart Mill (see p. 53) expressed this as the principle that 'the boundaries of government should coincide in the main with those of nationality'. Mazzini formed the clandestine organization 'Young Italy' to promote the idea of a united Italy, but he also founded 'Young Europe' in the hope of spreading nationalist ideas throughout the continent. At the Paris Peace Conference, Woodrow Wilson advanced the principle of self-determination not simply because the break-up of the European empire served US national interests, but because he believed that the Poles, Czechs, Hungarians and so on all had the same right to political independence that Americans already enjoyed.

Liberals also believe that the principle of balance or natural harmony applies to the nations of the world, not just to individuals within society. The achievement of national self-determination is a means of establishing a peaceful and stable international order. Wilson believed that the First World War had been caused by an 'old order', dominated by autocratic and militaristic empires. Democratic nation-states, on the other hand, would respect the national sovereignty of their neighbours and have no incentive to wage war or subjugate others. For a liberal, nationalism does not divide nations from one another, promoting distrust, rivalry and possibly war. Rather, it is a force that is capable of promoting both unity within each nation and brotherhood among all nations on the basis of mutual respect for national rights and characteristics. At heart, liberalism looks beyond the nation to the ideas of cosmopolitanism (see p. 176) and internationalism (see p. 178).

Liberal internationalism is grounded in a fear of an international 'state of nature'. Liberals have long accepted that national self-determination is a mixed blessing. While it preserves self-government and forbids foreign control, it also creates a world of sovereign nation-states in which each nation has the freedom to pursue its own interests, possibly at the expense of other nations. Liberal

TENSIONS WITHIN... NATIONALISM (2)

Liberal nationalism	VS	Expansionist nationalism
national self-determination	↔	national chauvinism
inclusive	↔	exclusive
voluntaristic	↔	organic
progressive	↔	reactionary
rational/principled	↔	emotional/instinctive
human rights	↔	national interest
equal nations	↔	hierarchy of nations
constitutionalism	↔	authoritarianism
ethnic/cultural pluralism	↔	ethnic/cultural purity
cosmopolitanism	↔	imperialism/militarism
collective security	↔	power politics
supranationalism	↔	international anarchy

nationalists have certainly accepted that constitutionalism and democracy reduce the tendency towards militarism and war, but when sovereign nations operate within conditions of 'international anarchy', self-restraint alone may not be sufficient to ensure what Kant (see p. 52) called 'perpetual peace'. Liberals have generally proposed two means of preventing a recourse to conquest and plunder. The first is national interdependence, aimed at promoting mutual understanding and cooperation. This is why liberals have traditionally supported the policy of **free trade**: economic interdependence means that the material costs of international conflict are so great that warfare becomes virtually unthinkable. Second, Liberals have proposed that national ambition should be checked by the construction of international organizations capable of bringing order to an otherwise lawless international scene. This explains Woodrow Wilson's support for the first, if flawed, experiment in world government, the League of Nations, set up in 1919, and far wider support for its successor, the United Nations, founded by the San Francisco Conference of 1945. Liberals have looked to these bodies to establish a law-governed state system to make possible the peaceful resolution of international conflicts.

FREE TRADE
A system of trading between states that is unrestricted by tariffs or other forms of protectionism.

However, critics of liberal nationalism have sometimes suggested that its ideas are naïve and romantic. Liberal nationalists see the progressive and liberating face of nationalism; their nationalism is rational and tolerant. However, they perhaps ignore the darker face of nationalism, the irrational bonds or **tribalism** that distinguish 'us' from a foreign and threatening 'them'. Liberals see nationalism as a universal principle, but have less understanding of the emotional power of nationalism, which has, in times of war, persuaded individuals to kill or die for their country, regardless of the justice of their nation's cause. Liberal nationalism is also misguided in its belief that the nation-state is the key to political and international harmony. The mistake of Wilsonian nationalism was the belief that nations live in convenient and discrete geographical areas, and that states can be constructed that coincide with these areas. In practice, all so-called 'nation-states' comprise a range of linguistic, religious, ethnic or regional groups, some of which may also consider themselves to be 'nations'. For example, in 1918 the newly created nation-states of Czechoslovakia and Poland contained a significant number of German speakers, and Czechoslovakia itself was a fusion of two major ethnic groups: the Czechs and the Slovaks. The former Yugoslavia, also created by Versailles, contained a bewildering variety of ethnic groups – Serbs, Croats, Slovenes, Bosnians, Albanians and so on – which have subsequently realized their aspiration for nationhood. In fact, the ideal of a politically unified and culturally homogeneous nation-state can only be achieved by forcibly deporting minority groups and imposing an outright ban on immigration.

> **TRIBALISM**
> Group behaviour characterized by insularity and exclusivity, typically fuelled by hostility towards rival groups.

Conservative nationalism

In the early nineteenth century, conservatives regarded nationalism as a radical and dangerous force, a threat to order and political stability. However, as the century progressed, conservative statesmen such as Disraeli, Bismarck and even Tsar Alexander III became increasingly sympathetic towards nationalism, seeing it as a natural ally in maintaining social order and defending traditional institutions. In the modern period, nationalism has become an article of faith for most conservatives in most parts of the world.

Conservative nationalism tends to develop in established nation-states, rather than in those that are in the process of nation building. Conservatives care less for the principled nationalism of universal self-determination and more about the promise of social cohesion and public order embodied in the sentiment of national patriotism. For conservatives, society is organic: they believe that nations emerge naturally from the desire of human beings to live with others who possess the same views, habits and appearance as themselves. Human beings are thought to be limited and imperfect creatures, who seek meaning and security within the national community. Therefore, the principal goal of conservative nationalism is to maintain national unity by fostering patriotic loyalty and 'pride in one's country', especially in the face of the divisive idea of class solidarity preached by socialists. Indeed, by incorporating the working class into the nation, conservatives have often seen nationalism as the antidote to social revolution. Charles de Gaulle, French president 1959–69, harnessed nationalism to the conservative cause in France with particular skill. De Gaulle appealed to national pride by pursuing an independent, even anti-American, defence and foreign policy, and by attempting to restore order and authority to social life and build up a powerful state. In some respects, Thatcherism in the UK amounted to a British form of Gaullism, in that it fused an appeal based on nationalism, or at least national independence within Europe, with the promise of strong government and firm leadership.

The conservative character of nationalism is maintained by an appeal to tradition and history; nationalism thereby becomes a defence for traditional institutions and a traditional way of life. Conservative nationalism is essentially nostalgic and backward-looking, reflecting on a past age of national glory or triumph. This is evident in the widespread tendency to use ritual and commemoration to present past military victories as defining moments in a nation's history. It is also apparent in the use of traditional institutions as symbols of national identity. This occurs in the case of British, or, more accurately, English nationalism, which is closely linked to the institution of monarchy. Britain (plus Northern Ireland) is the United Kingdom, its national anthem is 'God Save the Queen', and the royal family plays a prominent role in national celebrations such as Armistice Day, and on state occasions such as the opening of Parliament.

Conservative nationalism is particularly prominent when the sense of national identity is felt to be threatened or in danger of being lost. The issues of immigration and supranationalism have therefore helped to keep this form of nationalism alive in many modern states. Conservative reservations about immigration stem from the belief that cultural diversity leads to instability and conflict. As stable and successful societies must be based on shared values and a common culture, immigration, particularly from societies with different religious and other traditions, should either be firmly restricted or minority ethnic groups should be encouraged to assimilate into the culture of the 'host' society. This puts conservative nationalism clearly at odds with multiculturalism (as discussed in Chapter 10). Conservative nationalists are also concerned about the threat that supranational bodies, such as the EU, pose to national identity and so to the cultural bonds of society. This is expressed in the UK in the form of 'Euroscepticism', particularly strong within the Conservative Party, with similar views being expressed in continental Europe by a variety of far right groups such as the French National Front. Eurosceptics not only defend sovereign national institutions and a distinctive national currency on the grounds that they are vital symbols of national identity, but also warn that the 'European project' is

THATCHERISM
The free-market/strong state ideological stance associated with Margaret Thatcher; the UK version of the New Right political project.

SUPRANATIONALISM
The ability of bodies with transnational or global jurisdictions to impose their will on nation-states.

fatally misconceived because a stable political union cannot be forged out of such national, language and cultural diversity.

Although conservative politicians and parties have derived considerable political benefit from their appeal to nationalism, opponents have sometimes pointed out that their ideas are based on misguided assumptions. In the first place, conservative nationalism can be seen as a form of elite manipulation. The 'nation' is invented and certainly defined by political leaders who may use it for their own purposes. This is most evident in times of war or international crisis, when the nation is mobilized to fight for the 'fatherland' by emotional appeals to patriotic duty. Furthermore, conservative nationalism may also serve to promote intolerance and bigotry. By insisting on the maintenance of cultural purity and established traditions, conservatives may portray immigrants, or foreigners in general, as a threat, and in the process promote, or at least legitimize, racist and xenophobic fears. The revival of national conservatism in the twenty-first century is discussed on p. 92.

Expansionist nationalism

In many countries the dominant image of nationalism is one of aggression and militarism, quite the opposite of a principled belief in national self-determination. The aggressive face of nationalism became apparent in the late nineteenth century as European powers indulged in a 'scramble for Africa' in the name of national glory and their 'place in the sun'. The imperialism of the late nineteenth century differed from earlier periods of colonial expansion in that it was supported by a climate of popular nationalism: national prestige was linked increasingly to the possession of an empire and each colonial victory was greeted by demonstrations of public approval. In the UK, a new word, jingoism, was coined to describe this mood of popular nationalism. In the early twentieth century, the growing rivalry of the European powers divided the continent into two armed camps, the Triple Entente, comprising the UK, France and Russia, and the Triple Alliance, containing Germany, Austria and Italy. When world war eventually broke out in August 1914, after a prolonged arms race and a succession of international crises, it provoked public rejoicing in all the major cities of Europe. Aggressive and expansionist nationalism reached its high point in the inter-war period when the authoritarian or fascist regimes of Japan, Italy and Germany embarked on policies of imperial expansion and world domination, eventually leading to war in 1939.

What distinguished this form of nationalism from earlier liberal nationalism was its chauvinism, a term derived from the name of Nicolas Chauvin, a French soldier who had been fanatically devoted to Napoleon I. Nations are not thought to be equal in their right to self-determination; rather, some nations are believed to possess characteristics or qualities that make them superior to others. Such ideas were clearly

MILITARISM
The achievement of ends by military means, or the extension of military ideas, values and practices to civilian society.

JINGOISM
A mood of nationalist enthusiasm and public celebration provoked by military expansion or imperial conquest.

evident in European imperialism, which was justified by an ideology of racial and cultural superiority. In nineteenth-century Europe it was widely believed that the 'white' peoples of Europe and America were intellectually and morally superior to the 'black', 'brown' and 'yellow' peoples of Africa and Asia. Indeed, Europeans portrayed imperialism as a moral duty: colonial peoples were the 'white man's burden'. Imperialism supposedly brought the benefits of civilization, and in particular Christianity, to the less fortunate and less sophisticated peoples of the world.

More particular varieties of national chauvinism have developed in the form of pan-nationalism. In Russia this took the form of pan-Slavism, sometimes called Slavophile nationalism, which was particularly strong in the late nineteenth and early twentieth centuries. The Russians are Slavs, and enjoy linguistic and cultural links with other Slavic peoples in eastern and south-eastern Europe. Pan-Slavism was defined by the goal of Slavic unity, which many Russian nationalists believed to be their country's historic mission. In the years before 1914, such ideas brought Russia into growing conflict with Austro-Hungary for control of the Balkans. The chauvinistic character of pan-Slavism derived from the belief that the Russians are the natural leaders of the Slavic people, and that the Slavs are culturally and spiritually superior to the peoples of central or western Europe. Pan-Slavism is therefore both anti-western and anti-liberal. Forms of pan-Slavism have been re-awakened since 1991 and the collapse of communist rule in Russia.

Traditional German nationalism also exhibited a marked chauvinism, which was born out of defeat in the Napoleonic Wars. Writers such as Johann Fichte and Friedrich Jahn reacted strongly against France and the ideals of its revolution, emphasizing instead the uniqueness of German culture and its language, and the racial purity of its people. After unification in 1871, German nationalism developed a pronounced chauvinistic character with the emergence of pressure groups such as the Pan-German League and the Navy League, which campaigned for closer ties with German-speaking Austria and for a German empire, Germany's 'place in the sun'. Pan-Germanism was an expansionist and aggressive form of nationalism that envisaged the creation of a German-dominated Europe. German chauvinism found its highest expression in the racialist and anti-Semitic doctrines developed by the Nazis. The Nazis adopted the expansionist goals of pan-Germanism with enthusiasm, but justified them in the language of biology rather than politics. This is examined more fully in Chapter 7, in connection with racism.

National chauvinism breeds from a feeling of intense, even hysterical nationalist enthusiasm. The individual as a separate, rational being is swept away on a tide of patriotic emotion, expressed in the desire for aggression, expansion and war. Charles Maurras (see p. 185) called such intense patriotism 'integral nationalism': individuals and independent groups lose their identity within an all-powerful 'nation', which has an existence and meaning beyond the life of any single individual. Such militant nationalism is often accompanied by militarism.

PAN-NATIONALISM
A style of nationalism that is dedicated to unifying a disparate people either through expansionism or political solidarity ('pan' means all or every).

KEY FIGURES IN... NATIONALISM

Jean-Jacques Rousseau (1712–78) A Geneva-born French moral and political philosopher, Rousseau is commonly viewed as the architect of political nationalism, but also influenced liberal, socialist, anarchist and, some claim, fascist thought. In *The Social Contract* (1762), Rousseau argued that 'natural man' could only throw off the corruption, exploitation and domination imposed by society and regain the capacity for moral choice through a radical form of democracy, based on the 'general will'. This subordinates the individual to the collective and promises political liberty and equality for all.

Johann Gottfried Herder (1744–1803) A German poet, critic and philosopher, Herder is often portrayed as the 'father' of cultural nationalism. A leading intellectual opponent of the Enlightenment, Herder's emphasis on the nation as an organic group characterized by a distinctive language, culture and 'spirit' helped both to found cultural history and to give rise to a form of nationalism that emphasizes the intrinsic value of the national culture. Herder's major work was *Reflections on the Philosophy of the History of Mankind* (1784–91).

Guiseppe Mazzini (1805–72) An Italian nationalist, often portrayed as the 'prophet' of Italian unification. Mazzini practised a form of liberal nationalism that fused a belief in the nation as a distinctive language and cultural community with the principles of liberal republicanism. In this view, nations are effectively sublimated individuals endowed with the right to self-government, a right to which all nations are equally entitled. Mazzini was also one of the earliest thinkers to link nationalism to the prospect of perpetual peace.

Woodrow Wilson (1856–1924) A US historian and political scientist and later politician, Wilson was the 28th president of the USA (1913–21). His 'Fourteen Points', laid down in 1918 as the basis for peace after World War I, proposed to reconstruct Europe according to the principle of national self-determination, and to ban secret diplomacy, expand trade and achieve security through a 'general association of nations'. Wilsonian liberalism is usually associated with the idea that constructing a world of democratic nation-states (modelled on the USA) is the surest way of preventing war.

Military glory and conquest are the ultimate evidence of national greatness and have been capable of generating intense feelings of nationalist commitment. The civilian population is, in effect, militarized: it is infected by the martial values of absolute loyalty, complete dedication and willing self-sacrifice. When the honour or integrity of the nation is in question, the lives of ordinary citizens become unimportant. Such emotional intensity was amply demonstrated in August 1914, and perhaps also underlies the emotional power of *jihad* (crudely defined as 'holy war') from the viewpoint of militant Islamist groups.

Charles Maurras (1868–1952) A French political thinker and leading figure within the political movement *Action Française*, Maurras was a key exponent of right-wing nationalism and an influence on fascism. His idea of 'integral nationalism' emphasized the organic unity of the nation, fusing a clearly illiberal rejection of individualism with a stress on hierarchy and traditional institutions (in his case, the French monarchy and the Roman Catholic Church). His insular and exclusionary nationalism articulated hostility towards, among others, Protestants, Jews, Freemasons and foreigners in general.

Mohandas Karamchand Gandhi (1869–1948) An Indian spiritual and political leader (called *Mahatma*, 'Great Soul'), Gandhi campaigned tirelessly for Indian independence, which was finally achieved in 1947. His ethic of non-violent resistance, *satyagraha*, reinforced by his ascetic lifestyle, gave the movement for Indian independence enormous moral authority. Derived from Hinduism, Gandhi's political philosophy was based on the assumption that the universe is regulated by the primacy of truth, or satya, and that humankind is 'ultimately one'. Gandhi was a trenchant opponent of both Hindu and Muslim sectarianism.

Marcus Garvey (1887–1940) A Jamaican political thinker and activist, and founder of the Universal Negro Improvement Association, Garvey was an early advocate of black nationalism. Placing a particular emphasis on establishing black pride, Garvey's vision of Africa as a 'homeland' provided the basis for a pan-African philosophy and an associated political movement. Although his call for a return to Africa to 'redeem' it from European colonialism was largely ignored, his views provided the basis for the later Black Power movement and helped to inspire Rastafarianism.

Frantz Fanon (1925–61) A Martinique-born French revolutionary theorist, Fanon is best known for his views on the anti-colonial struggle. In his classic work on decolonization, *The Wretched of the Earth* (1965), he drew on psychiatry, politics, sociology and the existentialism of Jean-Paul Sartre in arguing that only total revolution and absolute violence can help black or colonized people to liberate themselves from the social and psychological scars of imperialism. Fanon's other works include *Black Skin, White Masks* (1952) and *Towards the African Revolution* (1964).

National chauvinism has a particularly strong appeal for the isolated and powerless, for whom nationalism offers the prospect of security, self-respect and pride. Militant or integral nationalism requires a heightened sense of belonging to a distinct national group. Such intense nationalist feeling is often stimulated by 'negative integration', the portrayal of another nation or race as a threat or an enemy. In the face of the enemy, the nation draws together and experiences an intensified sense of its own identity and importance. National chauvinism therefore breeds from a clear distinction between 'them' and 'us'. There has to be a 'them' to deride or hate

POLITICAL IDEOLOGIES IN ACTION . . .
Independence for India and Pakistan

Events: On 15 August 1947, the Indian Independence Act took effect, providing for the creation of two new sovereign states in the form of India and Pakistan. In so doing, it brought to an end 200 years of British rule. The unravelling of the British Raj occurred at a pace that defied most participants' expectations, coming, as it did, less than two years after the British empire in Asia had survived the challenge of Japanese expansionism. The partition of the Indian subcontinent into two independent countries nevertheless had dramatic repercussions, sparking a frantic scramble as millions of Indian Muslims fled to Pakistan, while many Hindus and Sikhs headed in the opposite direction. Around half a million people died in the violence, and 10–15 million were left as refugees.

Significance: Independence for India and Pakistan is widely interpreted as a consequence of the rising tide of nationalism, Britain's hand having been forced by the emergence of an independence movement that threatened to make the maintenance of empire politically and economically unfeasible. The most influential body campaigning for independence was the Indian National Congress, founded in 1883, which pursued a moderate strategy. During the 1920s, Congress was converted to Gandhi's policy of non-violent civil resistance, its protests and demonstrations escalating significantly during World War II, especially with the instigation of the 'Quit India' campaign in 1942. Although formally a secular party that had previously attracted support from Hindus and Muslims, from the late 1930s onwards Congress developed a more pronounced Hindu orientation, as the various Muslim political groupings came to be effectively dominated by Muhammad Ali Jinnah's Muslim League.

Nevertheless, factors other than rising nationalism also helped to support the cause of independence. These included the success of the Labour Party, traditionally committed to Indian self-rule, in the 1945 UK general election; the need for the UK, exhausted by war, to focus on issues closer to home; and the USA's firm opposition to a continuation of European colonialism. The Hindu–Muslim violence that came in the wake of independence has also provoked debate. Although sometimes seen as evidence of the hatred and tribalism that, critics allege, lie under the surface of nationalism, it is perhaps better understood as a consequence of the British policy of divide and rule, which politicized religious differences between groups that had previously lived together in conditions of relative peace.

in order to forge a sense of 'us'. In politics, national chauvinism has commonly been reflected in racist ideologies, which divide the world into an 'in group' and an 'out group', in which the 'out group' becomes a scapegoat for all the misfortunes and frustrations suffered by the 'in group'. It is therefore no coincidence that chauvinistic political creeds are a breeding ground for racist ideas. Both pan-Slavism and pan-Germanism, for example, have been characterized by virulent anti-Semitism (see p. 210).

Anti-colonial and postcolonial nationalism

Nationalism may have been born in Europe, but it became a worldwide phenomenon thanks to imperialism. The experience of colonial rule helped to forge a sense of nationhood and a desire for 'national liberation' among the peoples of Asia and Africa, and gave rise to a specifically anti-colonial form of nationalism. During the twentieth century, the political geography of much of the world was transformed by anti-colonialism. Although Versailles applied the principle of self-determination to Europe, it was conveniently ignored in other parts of the world, where German colonies were simply transferred to UK and French control. However, during the inter-war period, independence movements increasingly threatened the overstretched empires of the UK and France. The final collapse of the European empires came after World War II. In some cases, a combination of mounting nationalist pressure and declining domestic economic performance persuaded colonial powers to depart relatively peacefully, as occurred in India and Pakistan in 1947 (see p. 186) and in Malaysia in 1957. However, decolonization in the post-1945 period was often characterized by revolution, and sometimes periods of armed struggle. This occurred, for instance, in the case of China, 1937–45 (against Japan), Algeria, 1954–62 (against France), and Vietnam, 1946–54 (against France) and 1964–75 (against USA).

In a sense, the colonizing Europeans had taken with them the seed of their own destruction: the doctrine of nationalism. For example, it is notable that many of the leaders of independence or liberation movements were western educated. It is therefore not surprising that anti-colonial movements sometimes articulated their goals in the language of liberal nationalism, reminiscent of Mazzini or Woodrow Wilson. However, emergent African and Asian nations were in a very different position from the newly created European states of the nineteenth and early twentieth centuries. For these African and Asian nations, the quest for political independence was closely related to their awareness of economic under-development and their subordination to the industrialized states of Europe and North America. Anti-colonialism thus came to express the desire for national liberation in both political and economic terms, and this has left its mark on the form of nationalism practised in the developing world. Some forms of anti-colonial nationalism nevertheless distanced themselves more clearly from western political traditions by constructing non-European models of national liberation. This had a

Key concept

Religious Fundamentalism

Religious fundamentalism is defined by the belief that religion cannot and should not be confined to the private sphere, but finds its highest and proper expression in the politics of popular mobilization and social regeneration. Although often related, religious fundamentalism should not be equated with scriptural literalism, as the 'fundamentals' of a creed are often extracted through a process of 'dynamic' interpretation by a charismatic leader. Religious fundamentalism also differs from ultra-orthodoxy, in that it advances a programme of moral and political regeneration of society in line with religious principles, as opposed to a retreat from corrupt secular society into the purity of faith-based communal living. Ruthven (2007) associated religious fundamentalism with a 'search for meaning' in a world of growing doubt and uncertainty.

range of implications, however. For example, Gandhi (see p. 185) advanced a political philosophy that fused Indian nationalism with an ethic of non-violence and self-sacrifice that was ultimately rooted in Hinduism. 'Home rule' for India was thus a spiritual condition, and not merely a political one, a stance underpinned by Gandhi's anti-industrialism, famously embodied in his wearing of home-spun clothes. In contrast, Frantz Fanon (see p. 185) emphasized links between the anti-colonial struggle and violence. His theory of imperialism stressed the psychological dimension of colonial subjugation. For Fanon (1965), colonization was not simply a political process, but also one through which a new 'species' of human is created. He argued that only the cathartic experience of violence is powerful enough to bring about this psycho-political regeneration.

However, most of the leaders of Asian and African anti-colonial movements were attracted to some form of socialism, ranging from the moderate and peaceful ideas represented by Gandhi and Nehru in India, to the revolutionary Marxism espoused by Mao Zedong in China, Ho Chi Minh in Vietnam and Fidel Castro in Cuba. On the surface, socialism is more clearly related to internationalism than to nationalism. This reflects the stress within socialism, first, on social class, class loyalties having an intrinsically transnational character, and, at a deeper level, on the idea of a common humanity. Marx (see p. 124) thus declared in the *Communist Manifesto* that 'working men have no country'.

Socialist ideas nevertheless appealed powerfully to nationalists in the developing world. This was partly because socialism embodies values such as community and cooperation that are deeply entrenched in traditional, preindustrial societies. More important, socialism, and in particular Marxism, provided an analysis of inequality and exploitation through which the colonial experience could be understood and colonial rule challenged. During the 1960s and 1970s, in particular, developing-world nationalists were drawn to revolutionary Marxism, influenced by the belief that colonialism is in practice an extended form of class oppression.

Lenin (see p. 124) had earlier provided the basis for such a view by portraying imperialism as essentially an economic phenomenon, a quest for profit by capitalist countries seeking investment opportunities, cheap labour and raw materials, and secure markets (Lenin, [1916] 1970). The class struggle thus became a struggle against colonial exploitation and oppression. As a result, the overthrow of colonial rule implied not only political independence, but also a social revolution which would bring about economic as well as political emancipation.

In some cases, developing-world regimes have openly embraced Marxist-Leninist principles. On achieving independence, China, North Korea, Vietnam and Cambodia moved swiftly to seize foreign assets and nationalize economic resources. They founded one-party states and centrally planned economies, closely following the Soviet model. In other cases, states in Africa and the Middle East have developed a less ideological form of nationalistic socialism, as has been evident in Algeria, Libya, Zambia, Iraq and South Yemen. The 'socialism' proclaimed in such countries usually took the form of an appeal to a unifying national cause or interest, in most cases economic or social development, as in the case of so-called 'African socialism', embraced, for instance, by Tanzania, Zimbabwe and Angola.

The postcolonial period has thrown up quite different forms of nationalism, however. With the authority of socialism and especially the attraction of Marxism-Leninism, declining significantly since the 1970s, nation building in the postcolonial period has been shaped increasingly by the rejection of western ideas and culture more than by the attempt to reapply them. If the West is regarded as the source of oppression and exploitation, postcolonial nationalism must seek an anti-western voice. In part, this has been a reaction against the dominance of western, and particularly US, culture and economic power in much of the developing world.

The principal vehicle for expressing such views has been religious fundamentalism. Although Islam in particular has thrown up a comprehensive programme of political renewal, in the form of Islamism (discussed in Chapter 11), most fundamentalist religious movements have been more narrowly concerned with helping to clarify or redefine national or ethnic identity, examples being associated with Hinduism, Sikhism, Judaism and Buddhism. Hindu fundamentalism has been expressed in calls for the 'Hinduization' of Muslim, Sikh and other communities in India. The Bharatiya Janata Party (BJP) has been the largest party in the Indian parliament since 1996, articulating, as it does, the newly prosperous middle classes' ambivalence towards modernity and, particularly, its concerns about a weakening of national identity. The more radical World Hindu Council preaches 'India for the Hindus', while its parent body, the RSS (Rashtriya Swayamsevak Sangh), aims to create a 'Greater India', stretching from Burma to Iraq. Sikh fundamentalism is associated with the struggle to found an independent nation-state, 'Khalistan', located in present-day Punjab, with Sikhism as the state religion and its government obliged to ensure its unhindered flourishing. Jewish fundamentalists have transformed Zionism into a defence of the 'Greater Land of Israel', characterized by territorial aggressiveness. In the case of Israel's best-known fundamentalist group,

Gushmun Emunim (Bloc of the Faithful), this has been expressed in a campaign to build Jewish settlements in territory occupied in the Six-Day War of 1967. Buddhist nationalism has been evident in both Sri Lanka and Burma, in the former case being associated with the 'Sinhalization' of national identity and the war waged against Tamil separatism, finally crushed in 2009.

Nationalism in a global age

One of the ironies of nationalism is that just as it was completing its greatest accomplishment – bringing about the collapse of the world's major empires (the last of which, the Soviet empire, was destroyed by the revolutions of 1989–91) – the nation-state was being undermined, some would say fatally, by the advance of globalization (see p. 20). The challenges that globalization has posed to nationalism have been many and varied. They include the tendency of economic globalization to diminish the nation-state's capacity to function as an autonomous economic unit, and the trend for cultural globalization to weaken the cultural distinctiveness of the nation-state.

However, two developments deserve particular attention. First, the growth of global interconnectedness, the process that lies at the heart of globalization, has arguably reconfigured our sense of political community and, in the process, expanded our moral sensibilities. This has led some to suggest that nationalism is in the process of being superseded by cosmopolitanism (see p. 191). In this view, the narrowing of political allegiances and moral responsibilities only to people within our own society has become increasingly unsustainable in a world characterized by interconnectedness and interdependence. Transborder information and communication flows, particularly the impact of television, means that the 'strangeness' or 'remoteness' of people and societies on the other side of the globe has substantially diminished. This is the sense in which the world has 'shrunk'. Although political cosmopolitanism is widely viewed as an unfeasible and (because it is linked to the possibly tyrannical notion of world government) undesirable, a form of moral cosmopolitanism may be developing through which people view themselves as global citizens, rather than as merely national citizens. **Ethical nationalism** has thus been eroded as we recognize that, increasingly, we live in a world of global cause and effect. For example, purchasing decisions in one part of the world affect job opportunities, working conditions and poverty levels in other parts of the world. For cosmopolitans, this reflects a recognition that national divisions have always

ETHICAL NATIONALISM
The theory that the rights of, and obligations towards, members of one's own nation should enjoy moral priority over those related to members of other nations: a stance that implies moral relativism.

been arbitrary and are sustained largely by ignorance, suggesting that humankind has the capacity to evolve beyond nationalism.

Second, the advent of a global age has affected nationalism because it has been accompanied by an upsurge in international migration, greatly increasing levels of cultural and ethnic diversity in most, if not all,

Key concept

Cosmopolitanism

Cosmopolitanism literally means a belief in a *cosmopolis* or 'world state'. *Moral* cosmopolitanism is the belief that the world constitutes a single moral community, in that people have obligations (potentially) towards all other people in the world, regardless of nationality, religion, ethnicity and so on. All forms of moral cosmopolitanism are based on a belief that every individual is of equal moral worth, most commonly linked to the doctrine of human rights (see p. 58). *Political* cosmopolitanism (sometimes called 'legal' or 'institutional' cosmopolitanism) is the belief that there should be global political institutions, and possibly a world government. However, most modern political cosmopolitans favour a system in which authority is divided between global, national and local levels.

modern societies. The culturally cohesive nation-state may therefore have become a thing of the past, meaning that national identity is in the process of being displaced by rival forms of identity, linked, for instance, to ethnicity, culture or religion. The increase in international migration in recent decades has been fuelled by war, ethnic conflict and political upheaval, particularly in parts of Africa, the Middle East and central Asia, and by the tendency of economic globalization to 'pull' people from their countries of origin through the prospect of better job opportunities and higher living standards elsewhere. The general consequence of this has sometimes been portrayed as a shift from nationalism to multiculturalism, although this may also be viewed as the emergence of multicultural nationalism. In some respects, nevertheless, political identities have been reshaped in ways that are difficult to accommodate within the traditional bounds of nationalism. This applies, for instance, in the case of the growth of **transnational communities**, which challenge the nation-state ideal by weakening the link between politico-cultural identity and a specific territory or 'homeland'. Transnational communities can therefore be thought of as 'deterritorialized nations' or 'global tribes'. Nevertheless, transnational communities typically have multiple attachments, as allegiances to a country of origin do not preclude the formation of attachments to a country of settlement, creating a form of 'differentiated' citizenship.

However, there is little empirical evidence to suggest that predictions of the death of nationalism are close to being realized. For example, although international organizations – ranging from the UN and the EU to the WTO and the IMF – have undoubtedly become more important in terms of global policy-making, none of them, including the EU (the only one to have some form of democratic framework), has come anywhere close to rivalling the nation-state in terms of its ability to attract political affiliation or emotional allegiance, still less love. Indeed, there are reasons to believe that the advent of a global age may be leading to a revival, rather than a decline, of nationalism. The resurgence

TRANSNATIONAL COMMUNITY

A community whose cultural identity, political allegiances and psychological orientations cut across or transcend national borders.

of nationalism since the final decades of the twentieth century can be explained in at least three ways.

First, increased national self-assertion has become a strategy of growing significance for powerful states, especially in the light of the fluid nature of world order in the post-Cold War world. Nationalism has thus, once again, proved its capacity for investing the drive for economic and political development with an ideological impetus rooted in a vision of strength, unity and pride. For instance, China's remarkable economic revival has been accompanied by clear evidence of rising nationalism – apparent, among other things, in increased pressure being brought to bear on Taiwan, and in a firm and sometimes forceful response to independence movements in Tibet and Xinjiang. Similar tendencies have been found in India, particularly associated with Hindu nationalism, as well as in Russia.

Second, from the 1990s onwards, forms of cultural, and particularly ethnic, nationalism have flourished. This was evident in a series of wars in the former Yugoslavia, which also featured programmes of '**ethnic cleansing**' and the worst massacres in Europe since World War II. Other examples of ethnic assertiveness include secessionist uprisings in Chechnya and elsewhere in the Caucasus, and the genocidal bloodshed that broke out in Rwanda in 1994, when between 800,000 and one million Tutsis and moderate Hutus were slaughtered in an uprising by militant Hutus.

> **ETHNIC CLEANSING**
> A euphemism that refers to the forcible expulsion of an ethnic group or groups in the cause of racial purity, often involving genocidal violence.

Finally, there is clear evidence that nationalism has revived as a reaction *against* globalization and the deep economic, cultural and political changes it brings about. Nationalism has often prospered in conditions of fear, insecurity and social dislocation, its strength being its capacity to stand for unity and certainty. The forms of nationalism that develop in such circumstances provide ideological opportunities for generally right-wing parties or movements to mount campaigns against conventional politics. This has been most apparent since the 1980s in the rise of far right anti-immigration parties, such as the Front National in France, the Freedom Party in Austria, Alternative for Germany, the Northern League in Italy and the Danish People's Party. Perhaps the most dramatic demonstration of the potency of this form of nationalism came with the victory of the Leave camp in the UK's 2016 referendum on EU membership. Where nationalism draws from anxieties about immigration, national identity tends to be defined in terms of a backward-looking and culturally – and perhaps ethnically – 'pure' model. In these cases, nationalism is defined by its rejection of diversity and cultural mixing.

? QUESTIONS FOR DISCUSSION

- Do nations develop 'naturally', or are they, in some sense, invented?
- Why have nations and states often been confused?
- Is any group of people entitled to define itself as a 'nation'?
- How does nationalism differ from racism?
- To what extent is nationalism compatible with ethnic and cultural diversity?
- In what sense is liberal nationalism principled?
- Why have liberals viewed nationalism as the antidote to war?
- Are all conservatives nationalists? If so, why?
- Why has nationalism so often been associated with expansionism, conquest and war?
- To what extent is nationalism a backward-looking ideology?
- Why and how has developing-world nationalism differed from nationalism in the developed world?
- Has globalization made nationalism irrelevant?

📖 FURTHER READING

Brown, D., *Contemporary Nationalism: Civic, Ethnocultural and Multicultural Politics* (2000). A clear and stimulating account of differing approaches to nationalism and of the contrasting forms of modern nationalist politics.

Hearn, J., *Rethinking Nationalism: A Critical Introduction* (2006). An innovative and wide-ranging study of nationalism that critically reviews approaches to the nature and origins of nationalism.

Özkirimli, U., *Theories of Nationalism,* 2nd edition (2017). A clear and genuinely international account of classical and modern contributions to debates about nationalism.

Spencer, P. and Wollman, H., *Nationalism: A Critical Introduction* (2002). A very useful survey of classical and contemporary approaches to nationalism that addresses all the key issues, theories and debates.

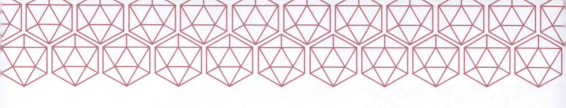

7 Fascism

Preview

The term 'fascism' derives from the Italian word *fasces*, meaning a bundle of rods with an axe-blade protruding that signified the authority of magistrates in Imperial Rome. By the 1890s, the word *fascia* was being used in Italy to refer to a political group or band, usually of revolutionary socialists. It was not until Mussolini employed the term to describe the paramilitary armed squads he formed during and after the First World War that *fascismo* acquired a clearly ideological meaning.

The defining theme of fascism is the idea of an organically unified national community, embodied in a belief in 'strength through unity'. The individual, in a literal sense, is nothing; individual identity must be entirely absorbed into the community or social group. The fascist ideal is that of the 'new man', a hero, motivated by duty, honour and self-sacrifice, prepared to dedicate his life to the glory of his nation or race, and to give unquestioning obedience to a supreme leader. In many ways, fascism constitutes a revolt against the ideas and values that dominated western political thought from the French Revolution onwards; in the words of the Italian fascists' slogan: '1789 is Dead'. Values such as rationalism, progress, freedom and equality were thus overturned in the name of struggle, leadership, power, heroism and war. Fascism therefore has a strong 'anti-character': it is anti-rational, anti-liberal, anti-conservative, anti-capitalist, anti-bourgeois, anti-communist and so on.

Fascism has nevertheless been a complex historical phenomenon, encompassing, many argue, two distinct traditions. Italian fascism was essentially an extreme form of statism that was based on absolute loyalty towards a 'totalitarian' state. In contrast, German fascism, or Nazism, was founded on racial theories, which portrayed the Aryan people as a 'master race' and advanced a virulent form of anti-Semitism.

Origins and development

Whereas liberalism, conservatism and socialism are nineteenth-century ideologies, fascism is a child of the twentieth century, some would say specifically of the period between the two world wars. Indeed, fascism emerged very much as a revolt against modernity, against the ideas and values of the Enlightenment and the political creeds that it spawned. The Nazis in Germany, for instance, proclaimed that '1789 is Abolished'. In Fascist Italy, slogans such as 'Believe, Obey, Fight' and 'Order, Authority, Justice' replaced the more familiar principles of the French Revolution, 'Liberty, Equality and Fraternity'. Fascism came not only as a 'bolt from the blue', as O'Sullivan (1983) put it, but also attempted to make the political world anew, quite literally to root out and destroy the inheritance of conventional political thought.

Although the major ideas and doctrines of fascism can be traced back to the nineteenth century, they were fused together and shaped by World War I and its aftermath, in particular by a potent mixture of war and revolution. Fascism emerged most dramatically in Italy and Germany. In Italy, a Fascist Party was formed in 1919, its leader, Benito Mussolini (see p. 213), was appointed prime minister in 1922 against the backdrop of the March on Rome (see p. 206), and by 1926 a one-party fascist state had been established. The National Socialist German Workers' Party, known as the Nazis, was also formed in 1919 and, under the leadership of Adolf Hitler (see p. 213), it consciously adopted the style of Mussolini's Fascists. Hitler was appointed German chancellor in 1933 and in little over a year had turned Germany into a Nazi dictatorship. During the same period, democracy collapsed or was overthrown in much of Europe, often being supplanted by right-wing, authoritarian or openly fascist regimes, especially in eastern Europe. Regimes that bear some relationship to fascism have also developed outside Europe, notably in the 1930s in Imperial Japan and in Argentina under Perón (1945–55).

The origins and meaning of fascism have provoked considerable historical interest and often fierce disagreements. No single factor can, on its own, account for the rise of fascism; rather, fascism emerged out of a complex range of historical forces that were present during the inter-war period. In the first place, democratic government had only recently been established in many parts of Europe, and democratic political values had not replaced older, autocratic ones. Moreover, democratic governments, representing a coalition of interests or parties, often appeared weak and unstable when confronted by economic or political crises. In this context, the prospect of strong leadership brought about by personal rule cast a powerful appeal. Second, European society had been disrupted by the experience of industrialization, which had particularly threatened a lower middle class of shopkeepers, small businessmen, farmers and craftsmen, who were squeezed between the growing might of big business, on the one hand, and the rising power of organized labour, on the other. Fascist movements drew their membership and support largely from such lower middle-class elements. In a sense, fascism was an 'extremism of the centre' (Lipset, 1983), a revolt of the lower middle classes, a fact that helps to explain the hostility of fascism to both capitalism and communism.

Third, the period after World War I was deeply affected by the Russian Revolution and the fear among the propertied classes that social revolution was about to spread throughout Europe. Fascist groups undoubtedly drew both financial and political support from business interests. As a result, Marxist historians have interpreted fascism as a form of counter-revolution, an attempt by the bourgeoisie to cling on to power by lending support to fascist dictators. Fourth, the world economic crisis of the 1930s often provided a final blow to already fragile democracies. Rising unemployment and economic failure produced an atmosphere of crisis and pessimism that could be exploited by political extremists and demagogues. Finally, World War I had failed to resolve international conflicts and rivalries, leaving a bitter inheritance of frustrated nationalism and the desire for revenge. Nationalist tensions were strongest in those 'have not' nations that had either, like Germany, been defeated in war, or had been deeply disappointed by the terms of the Versailles peace settlement; for example, Italy and Japan. In addition, the experience of war itself had generated a particularly militant form of nationalism and imbued it with militaristic values.

Fascist regimes were not overthrown by popular revolt or protest but by defeat in World War II. Since 1945, fascist movements have achieved only marginal success, encouraging some to believe that fascism was a specifically inter-war phenomenon, linked to the unique combination of historical circumstances that characterized that period (Nolte, 1965). Others, however, regard fascism as an ever-present danger, seeing its roots in human psychology, or as Erich Fromm (1984) called it, 'the fear of freedom'. Modern civilization has produced greater individual freedom but, with it, the danger of isolation and insecurity. At times of crisis, individuals may therefore flee from freedom, seeking security in submission to an all-powerful leader or a totalitarian state. Political instability or an economic crisis could therefore produce conditions in which fascism could revive. Fears, for example, have been expressed about the growth of neofascism in parts of eastern Europe following the collapse of communist rule (1989–91). The prospects for fascism in the light of the advance of globalization (see p. 20) are discussed in the final section of the chapter.

Core themes: strength through unity

Fascism is a difficult ideology to analyse, for at least two reasons. First, it is sometimes doubted if fascism can be regarded, in any meaningful sense, as an ideology. Lacking a rational and coherent core, fascism appears to be, as Hugh Trevor-Roper put it, 'an ill-assorted hodge-podge of ideas' (Woolf, 1981). Hitler, for instance, preferred to describe his ideas as a *Weltanschauung*, rather than a systematic ideology. In this sense, a world-view is a complete, almost religious, set of attitudes that demand commitment and faith,

WELTANSCHAUUNG
(German) Literally, a 'world-view'; a distinctive, even unique, set of presuppositions that structure how a people understands and engages emotionally with the world.

rather than invite reasoned analysis and debate. Fascists were drawn to ideas and theories less because they helped to make sense of the world, in rational terms, but more because they had the capacity to stimulate political activism. Fascism may thus be better described as a political movement or even a political religion, rather than an ideology.

Second, so complex has fascism been as a historical phenomenon that it has been difficult to identify its core principles or a 'fascist minimum', sometimes seen as generic fascism. Where does fascism begin and where does it end? Which movements and regimes can be classified as genuinely fascist? Doubt, for instance, has been cast on whether Imperial Japan, Vichy France, Franco's Spain, Perón's Argentina and even Hitler's Germany can be classified as fascist. Controversy surrounds the relationship between modern radical right groups, such as the *Front National* in France and the British National Party in the UK, and fascism: are these groups 'fascist', 'neofascist', 'post-fascist', 'extreme nationalist' or whatever?

Among the attempts to define the ideological core of fascism have been Ernst Nolte's (1965) theory that it is a 'resistance to transcendence', A. J. Gregor's (1969) belief that it looks to construct 'the total charismatic community', Roger Griffin's (1993) assertion that it constitutes 'palingenetic ultranationalism' (palingenesis meaning rebirth) and Roger Eatwell's (2003) assertion that it is a 'holistic-national radical Third Way'. While each of these undoubtedly highlights an important feature of fascism, it is difficult to accept that any single-sentence formula can sum up a phenomenon as resolutely shapeless as fascist ideology. Perhaps the best we can hope to do is to identify a collection of themes that, when taken together, constitute fascism's structural core. The most significant of these include:

- anti-rationalism
- struggle
- leadership and elitism
- socialism
- ultranationalism.

Anti-rationalism

Although fascist political movements were born out of the upheavals that accompanied World War I, they drew on ideas and theories that had been circulating since the late nineteenth century. Among the most significant of these were anti-rationalism and the growth of counter-Enlightenment thinking generally. The Enlightenment, based on the ideas of universal reason, natural goodness and inevitable progress, was committed to liberating humankind from the darkness of irrationalism and superstition. In the late nineteenth century, however, thinkers had started to highlight the limits of human reason and draw attention to other, perhaps more powerful, drives and impulses. For instance, Friedrich Nietzsche (see p. 212) proposed that human beings are motivated by powerful emotions, their 'will' rather than the rational mind, and in particular by what he called the 'will to power'. In *Reflections on Violence* ([1908] 1950), the French syndicalist Georges Sorel (1847–1922) highlighted the importance of 'political myths', and especially the 'myth of the general strike', which are not passive descriptions of political reality but 'expressions of the will' that engaged the emotions and provoked action. Henri Bergson (1859–1941), the French philosopher, advanced the theory of vitalism. This suggests that the purpose of human existence is therefore to give expression to the life force, rather than to allow it to be confined or corrupted by the tyranny of cold reason or soulless calculation.

Although anti-rationalism does not necessarily have a right-wing or proto-fascist character, fascism gave political expression to the most radical and extreme forms of counter-Enlightenment thinking. Anti-rationalism has influenced fascism in a number of ways. In the first place, it gave fascism a marked anti-intellectu-alism, reflected in a tendency to despise abstract thinking and revere action. For example, Mussolini's favourite slogans included 'Action not Talk' and 'Inactivity Is Death'. Intellectual life was devalued, even despised: it is cold, dry and lifeless. Fascism, instead, addresses the soul, the emotions, the instincts. Its ideas possess little coherence or rigour, but seek to exert a mythic appeal. Its major ideologists, in particular Hitler and Mussolini, were essentially propagandists, interested in ideas and theories largely because of their power to elicit an emotional response and spur the masses to action. Fascism thus practises the 'politics of the will'.

Second, the rejection of the Enlightenment gave fascism a predominantly nega-tive or destructive character. Fascists, in other words, have often been clearer about what they oppose than what they support. Fascism thus appears to be an 'anti-philosophy': it is anti-rational, anti-liberal, anti-conservative, anti-capitalist, anti-bourgeois, anti-communist and so on. In this light, some have portrayed fascism as an example of nihilism. Nazism, in particular, has been described as a 'revolution of nihilism'. However, fascism is not merely the negation of established beliefs and principles. Rather, it is an attempt to reverse the heritage of the Enlightenment. It represents the darker underside of the western political tradition, the central and enduring values of which were not abandoned but rather transformed or turned upside-down. For example, in fascism, 'freedom' came to mean unquestioning submission, 'democracy' was equated with absolute dictatorship, and 'progress' implied constant struggle and war. Moreover, despite an undoubted inclination towards nihilism, war and even death, fascism saw itself as a creative force, a means of constructing a new civilization through 'creative destruction'. Indeed, this conjunction of birth and death, creation and destruction, can be seen as one of the characteristic features of the fascist world-view.

Third, by abandoning the standard of universal reason, fascism has placed its faith entirely in history, culture and the idea of organic community. Such a community is shaped not by the calculations and

VITALISM
The theory that living organisms derive their characteristic properties from a universal 'life-force'; vitalism implies an emphasis upon instinct and impulse rather than intellect and reason.

interests of rational individuals but by innate loyalties and emotional bonds forged by a common past. In fascism, this idea of organic unity is taken to its extreme. The national community, or as the Nazis called it, the *Volksgemeinschaft*, was viewed as an indivisible whole, all rivalries and conflicts being subordinated to a higher, collective purpose. The strength of the nation or race is therefore a reflection of its moral and cultural unity. This prospect of unqualified social cohesion was expressed in the Nazi slogan, 'Strength through Unity'. The revolution that fascists sought was thus 'revolution of the spirit', aimed at creating a new type of human being (always understood in male terms). This was the 'new man' or 'fascist man', a hero, motivated by duty, honour and self-sacrifice, and prepared to dissolve his personality in that of the social whole.

Struggle

The ideas that the UK biologist Charles Darwin (1809–82) developed in *On the Origin of Species* ([1859] 1972), popularly known as the theory of '**natural selection**', had a profound effect not only on the natural sciences, but also, by the end of the nineteenth century, on social and political thought. The notion that human existence is based on competition or struggle was particularly attractive in the period of intensifying international rivalry that eventually led to war in 1914. Social Darwinism also had a considerable impact on emerging fascism. In the first place, fascists regarded struggle as the natural and inevitable condition of both social and international life. Only competition and conflict guarantee human progress and ensure that the fittest and strongest will prosper. As Hitler told German officer cadets in 1944, 'Victory is to the strong and the weak must go to the wall.' If the testing ground of human existence is competition and struggle, then the ultimate test is war, which Hitler described as 'an unalterable law of the whole of life'. Fascism is perhaps unique among political ideologies in regarding war as good in itself, a view reflected in Mussolini's belief that 'War is to men what maternity is to women.'

Darwinian thought also invested fascism with a distinctive set of political values, which equate 'goodness' with strength, and 'evil' with weakness. In contrast to traditional humanist or religious values, such as caring, sympathy and compassion, fascists respect a very different set of martial values: loyalty, duty, obedience and self-sacrifice. When the victory of the strong is glorified, power and strength are worshipped for their own sake. Similarly, weakness is despised and the elimination of the weak and inadequate is positively welcomed: they must be sacrificed for the common good, just as the survival of a species is more important than the life of any single member of that species. Weakness and disability must therefore not be tolerated; they should be removed. This was illustrated most graphically by the programme of **eugenics**, introduced by the Nazis in Germany,

NATURAL SELECTION
The theory that species go through a process of random mutations that fits some to survive (and possibly thrive) while others become extinct.

EUGENICS
The theory or practice of selective breeding, achieved either by promoting procreation amongst 'fit' members of a species or by preventing procreation by the 'unfit'.

whereby mentally and physically handicapped people were first forcibly sterilized and then, between 1939 and 1941, systematically murdered. The attempt by the Nazis to exterminate European Jewry from 1941 onwards was, in this sense, an example of racial eugenics.

Finally, fascism's conception of life as an 'unending struggle' gave it a restless and expansionist character. National qualities can only be cultivated through conflict and demonstrated by conquest and victory. This was clearly reflected in Hitler's foreign policy goals, as outlined in *Mein Kampf* ([1925] 1969): '*Lebensraum* [living space] in the East', and the ultimate prospect of world domination. Once in power in 1933, Hitler embarked on a programme of rearmament in preparation for expansion in the late 1930s. Austria was annexed in the *Anschluss* of 1938; Czechoslovakia was dismembered in the spring of 1939; and Poland invaded in September 1939, provoking war with the UK and France. In 1941, Hitler launched Operation Barbarossa, the invasion of the Soviet Union. Even when facing imminent defeat in 1945, Hitler did not abandon social Darwinism, but declared that the German nation had failed him and gave orders, never fully carried out, for a fight to the death and, in effect, the annihilation of Germany.

Leadership and elitism

Fascism also stands apart from conventional political thought in its radical rejection of equality. Fascism is deeply elitist and fiercely patriarchal; its ideas were founded on the belief that absolute leadership and **elitism** are natural and desirable. Human beings are born with radically different abilities and attributes, a fact that emerges as those with the rare quality of leadership rise, through struggle, above those capable only of following. Fascists believe that society is composed, broadly, of three kinds of people. First, and most important, there is a supreme, all-seeing leader who possesses unrivalled authority. Second, there is a 'warrior' elite, exclusively male and distinguished, unlike traditional elites, by its heroism, vision and the capacity for self-sacrifice. In Germany, this role was ascribed to the SS, which originated as a bodyguard but developed during Nazi rule into a state within a state. Third, there are the masses, who are weak, inert and ignorant, and whose destiny is unquestioning obedience.

Such a pessimistic view of the capabilities of ordinary people puts fascism starkly at odds with the ideas of liberal democracy (see p. 40). Nevertheless, the idea of supreme leadership was also associated with a distinctively fascist, if inverted,

ELITISM A belief in rule by an elite or minority; elite rule may be thought to be desirable (the elite having superior talents or skills) or inevitable, (egalitarianism simply being impractical).

notion of democratic rule. The fascist approach to leadership, especially in Nazi Germany, was crucially influenced by Friedrich Nietzsche's idea of the *Übermensch*, the 'over-man' or 'superman', a supremely gifted or powerful individual. Most fully developed in *Thus Spoke Zarathustra* ([1884] 1961), Nietzsche portrayed the 'superman' as an individual who rises above the 'herd instinct' of conventional morality

PERSPECTIVES ON... AUTHORITY

LIBERALS believe that authority arises 'from below' through the consent of the governed. Though a requirement of orderly existence, authority is rational, purposeful and limited, a view reflected in a preference for legal-rational authority and public accountability.

CONSERVATIVES see authority as arising from natural necessity, being exercised 'from above' by virtue of the unequal distribution of experience, social position and wisdom. Authority is beneficial as well as necessary, in that it fosters respect and loyalty, and promotes social cohesion.

SOCIALISTS, typically, are suspicious of authority, which is regarded as implicitly oppressive and generally linked to the interests of the powerful and privileged. Socialist societies have nevertheless endorsed the authority of the collective body, however expressed, as a means of checking individualism and greed.

ANARCHISTS view all forms of authority as unnecessary and destructive, equating authority with oppression and exploitation. Since there is no distinction between authority and naked power, all checks on authority and all forms of accountability are entirely bogus.

FASCISTS regard authority as a manifestation of personal leadership or charisma, a quality possessed by unusually gifted (if not unique) individuals. Such charismatic authority is, and should be, absolute and unquestionable, and is thus implicitly, and possibly explicitly, totalitarian in character.

and lives according to his own will and desires. Fascists, however, turned the superman ideal into a theory of supreme and unquestionable political leadership. Fascist leaders styled themselves simply as 'the Leader' – Mussolini proclaimed himself to be *Il Duce*, while Hitler adopted the title *Der Führer* – precisely in order to emancipate themselves from any constitutionally defined notion of leadership. In this way, leadership became exclusively an expression of **charismatic** authority emanating from the leader himself. While constitutional, or, in Max Weber's term, legal-rational authority operates within a framework of laws or rules, charismatic authority is potentially unlimited. As the leader was viewed as a uniquely gifted individual, his authority was absolute. At the Nuremburg Rallies, the Nazi faithful thus chanted 'Adolf Hitler is Germany, Germany is Adolf Hitler.' In Italy, the principle that 'Mussolini is always right' became the core of fascist dogma.

CHARISMA
Charm or personal power; the ability to inspire loyalty, emotional dependence or even devotion in others.

The 'leader principle' (in German, the *Führerprinzip*), the principle that all authority emanates from the leader personally, thus became the guiding principle of the fascist state. Intermediate institutions such as elections, parliaments and parties were either abolished or weakened to prevent them from challenging or distorting the leader's will. This principle of absolute leadership was underpinned by the belief that the leader possesses a monopoly of ideological wisdom: the leader, and the leader alone, defines the destiny of his people, their 'real' will, their 'general will'. A Nietzschean theory of leadership thus coincided with a Rousseauian belief in a single, indivisible public interest. In this light, a genuine democracy is an absolute dictatorship, absolutism and popular sovereignty being fused into a form of '**totalitarian democracy**' (Talmon, 1952). The role of the leader is to awaken the people to their destiny, to transform an inert mass into a powerful and irresistible force. Fascist regimes therefore exhibited populist-mobilizing features that set them clearly apart from traditional dictatorships. Whereas traditional dictatorships aimed to exclude the masses from politics, totalitarian dictatorships set out to recruit them into the values and goals of the regime through constant propaganda and political agitation. In the case of fascist regimes, this was reflected in the widespread use of plebiscites, rallies and popular demonstrations.

Socialism

At times, both Mussolini and Hitler portrayed their ideas as forms of 'socialism'. Mussolini had previously been an influential member of the Italian Socialist Party and editor of its newspaper, *Avanti*, while the Nazi Party espoused a philosophy it called 'national socialism'. To some extent, undoubtedly, this represented a cynical attempt to elicit support from urban workers. Nevertheless, despite obvious ideological rivalry between fascism and socialism, fascists did have an affinity for certain socialist ideas and positions. In the first place, lower-middle-class fascist activists had a profound distaste for large-scale capitalism, reflected in a resentment towards big business and financial institutions. For instance, small shopkeepers were under threat from the growth of department stores, the small-holding peasantry was losing out to large-scale farming, and small businesses were increasingly in hock to the banks. Socialist or 'leftist' ideas were therefore prominent in German grassroots organizations such as the SA, or Brownshirts, which recruited significantly from among the lower middle classes. Second, fascism, like socialism, subscribes to collectivism (see p. 99), putting it at odds with the 'bourgeois' values of capitalism. Fascism places the community above the individual; Nazi coins, for example, bore the inscription 'Common Good before Private Good'. Capitalism, in contrast, is based on the pursuit of self-interest and therefore threatens to undermine the cohesion of the nation or race. Fascists also despise the materialism that capitalism fosters: the desire for wealth or profit runs counter to the idealistic vision of national regeneration or world conquest that inspires fascists.

TOTALITARIAN DEMOCRACY
An absolute dictatorship that masquerades as a democracy, typically based on the leader's claim to a monopoly of ideological wisdom.

Third, fascist regimes often practised socialist-style economic policies designed to regulate or control capitalism. Capitalism was thus subordinated to the ideological objectives of the fascist state. As Oswald Mosley (1896–1980), leader of the British Union of Fascists, put it, 'Capitalism is a system by which capital uses the nation for its own purposes. Fascism is a system by which the nation uses capital for its own purposes.' Both the Italian and German regimes tried to bend big business to their political ends through policies of nationalization and state regulation. For example, after 1939, German capitalism was reorganized under Hermann Göring's Four Year Plan, deliberately modelled on the Soviet idea of Five Year Plans.

However, the notion of fascist socialism has severe limitations. For instance, 'leftist' elements within fascist movements, such as the SA in Germany and Sorelian revolutionary syndicalists in Italy, were quickly marginalized once fascist parties gained power, in the hope of cultivating the support of big business. This occurred most dramatically in Nazi Germany, through the purge of the SA and the murder of its leader, Ernst Rohm, in the 'Night of the Long Knives' in 1934. Marxists have thus argued that the purpose of fascism was to salvage capitalism rather than to subvert it. Moreover, fascist ideas about the organization of economic life were, at best, vague and sometimes inconsistent; pragmatism (see p. 9), not ideology, determined fascist economic policy. Finally, anti-communism was more prominent within fascism than anti-capitalism. A core objective of fascism was to seduce the working class away from Marxism and Bolshevism, which preached the insidious, even traitorous, idea of international working-class solidarity and upheld the misguided values of cooperation and equality. Fascists were dedicated to national unity and integration, and so wanted the allegiances of race and nation to be stronger than those of social class.

Ultranationalism

Fascism embraced an extreme version of chauvinistic and expansionist nationalism. This tradition regarded nations not as equal and interdependent entities, but as rivals in a struggle for dominance. Fascist nationalism did not preach respect for distinctive cultures or national traditions, but asserted the superiority of one nation over all others. In the explicitly racial nationalism of Nazism this was reflected in the ideas of **Aryanism**. Between the wars, such militant nationalism was fuelled by an inheritance of bitterness and frustration, which resulted from World War I and its aftermath.

ARYANISM
The belief that the Aryans, or German people, are a 'master race', destined for world domination.

INTEGRAL NATIONALISM
An intense, even hysterical, form of nationalist enthusiasm, in which individual identity is absorbed within the national community.

Fascism seeks to promote more than mere patriotism (see p. 164); it wishes to establish an intense and militant sense of national identity, which Charles Maurras (see p. 185) called '**integral nationalism**'. Fascism embodies a sense of messianic or fanatical mission: the prospect of national regeneration and the rebirth of national pride. Indeed, the popular appeal that fascism has exerted has largely been based on the promise of national greatness. According to Griffin (1993), the mythic core of generic fascism is the conjunction of the ideas of 'palingenesis', or recurrent rebirth, and 'populist ultranationalism'. All fascist movements therefore highlight the moral bankruptcy and cultural decadence of modern society, but proclaim the possibility of rejuvenation, offering the image of the nation 'rising phoenix-like from the ashes'. Fascism thus fuses myths about a glorious past with the image of a future characterized by renewal and reawakening, hence the idea of the 'new' man. In Italy, this was reflected in attempts to recapture the glories of Imperial Rome; in Germany, the Nazi regime was portrayed as the 'Third Reich', in succession to Charlemagne's 'First Reich' and Bismarck's 'Second Reich'.

However, in practice, national regeneration invariably meant the assertion of power over other nations through expansionism, war and conquest. Influenced by social Darwinism and a belief in national and sometimes racial superiority, fascist nationalism became inextricably linked to militarism and imperialism. Nazi Germany looked to construct a 'Greater Germany' and build an empire stretching into the Soviet Union – *Lebensraum* in the East'. Fascist Italy sought to found an African empire through the invasion of Abyssinia in 1934. Imperial Japan occupied Manchuria in 1931 in order to found a 'co-prosperity' sphere in a new Japanese-led Asia. These empires were to be **autarkic**, based on strict self-sufficiency. In the fascist view, economic strength is based on the capacity of the nation to rely solely on resources and energies it directly controls. Conquest and expansionism are therefore a means of gaining economic security as well as national greatness. National regeneration and economic progress are therefore intimately tied up with military power.

> **AUTARKY**
> Economic self-sufficiency, brought about either through expansionism aimed at securing markets and sources of raw materials, or by withdrawal from the international economy.

Fascism and the state

> **STATISM**
> The belief that the state is the most appropriate means of resolving problems and of guaranteeing economic and social development.
>
> **RACE**
> A collection of people who share a common genetic inheritance and are thus distinguished from others by biological factors.

Although it is possible to identify a common set of fascist values and principles, Fascist Italy and Nazi Germany nevertheless represented different versions of fascism and were inspired by distinctive and sometimes rival beliefs. Fascist regimes and movements have therefore corresponded to one of two major traditions, as illustrated in Figure 7.1. One, following Italian fascism, emphasizes the ideal of an all-powerful or totalitarian state, in the form of extreme **statism**. The other, reflected in German Nazism or national socialism, stresses the importance of **race** and racism (see p. 210).

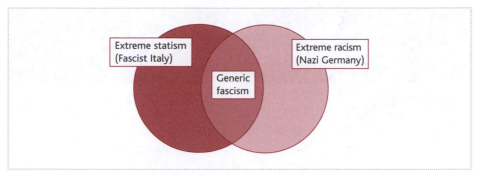

Figure 7.1   Types of fascism

The totalitarian ideal

Totalitarianism (see p. 207) is a controversial concept. The height of its popularity came during the Cold War period, when it was used to draw attention to parallels between fascist and communist regimes, highlighting the brutal features of both. As such, it became a vehicle for expressing anti-communist views and, in particular, hostility towards the Soviet Union. Nevertheless, totalitarianism remains a useful concept for the analysis of fascism. Generic fascism tends towards totalitarianism in at least three respects. First, the extreme collectivism that lies at the heart of fascist ideology, the goal of the creation of 'fascist man' – loyal, dedicated and utterly obedient – effectively obliterates the distinction between 'public' and 'private' existence. The good of the collective body, the nation or the race, is placed firmly before the good of the individual: collective egoism consumes individual egoism. Second, as the fascist leader principle invests the leader with unlimited authority, it violates the liberal idea of a distinction between the state and civil society. An unmediated relationship between the leader and his people implies active participation and total commitment on the part of citizens; in effect, the politicization of the masses. Third, the **monistic** belief in a single value system, and a single source of truth, places fascism firmly at odds with the notions of pluralism (see p. 290) and civil liberty. However, the idea of an all-powerful state has particular significance for Italian fascism.

The essence of Italian fascism was a form of state worship. In a formula regularly repeated by Mussolini, Giovanni Gentile (see p. 212) proclaimed: 'Everything for the state; nothing against the state; nothing outside the state.' The individual's political obligations are thus absolute and all-encompassing. Nothing less than unquestioning obedience and constant devotion are required of the citizen. This fascist theory of the state has sometimes been associated with the ideas of the German philosopher Hegel (1770–1831). Hegel portrayed the state as an ethical idea, reflecting the altruism and mutual sympathy of its members. In this view, the state is capable of motivating and inspiring individuals to act in the common

> **MONISM**
> A belief in only one theory or value; monism is reflected politically in enforced obedience to a unitary power and is thus implicitly totalitarian.

POLITICAL IDEOLOGIES IN ACTION . . .
The March on Rome

EVENTS: The period 27–29 October 1922 witnessed a political crisis in Italy that brought Mussolini and the Fascist Party to power. Taking advantage of fears of an imminent 'red' threat, on 27 October about 26,000 fascist troops started to gather outside Rome, cutting off lines of communication to the capital and preparing for a march on Rome. On 28 October, the king, Victor Emmanuel III, refused Prime Minister Luigi Facta's call for a decree introducing martial law, despite the fact that regular troops greatly outnumbered fascist forces and were better trained and equipped. The king then summonsed Mussolini to Rome and asked him to form a ministry. The March on Rome duly went ahead on 29 October, celebrating a transfer of power that had, effectively, already taken place. Arriving in Rome by train on the same day, Mussolini took up his appointment and started to form a cabinet.

SIGNIFICANCE: The transfer of power that occurred in Italy in late October 1922 can be said, in important ways, to have occurred within the existing constitutional framework. It did not amount to a seizure of power, as such, and it did not, in itself, alter the distribution of constitutional power. Mussolini's fascist dictatorship was constructed in the succeeding years. That said, fascist intimidation in October 1922 undoubtedly played a major role in shaping events, but it was a challenge that the Italian state clearly had the ability to resist. The crucial factor in explaining Mussolini's appointment may therefore be that Victor Emmanuel personally, and Italy's political, economic and social establishment, more widely, lacked the political will to use this ability, whether this was through panic, weakness or self-interest.

However, despite the complexities and confusions surrounding the events of October 1922, the March on Rome was speedily reinterpreted by fascist historians as a glorious national revolution. The emphasis was placed not on the surrender of the regime, but on the image of Mussolini's strength, buoyed up by a spontaneous uprising of the Italian people. The March on Rome thus became the founding myth of the Mussolini regime, giving it popular legitimacy and instilling the idea that it had purged a despised parliamentary system. Although regimes of all ideological complexions are prone to rewrite history, the March on Rome perhaps illustrates fascism's unusual appetite for myth-making, based on an acute awareness of the power of symbolism and emotion.

Key concept
Totalitarianism

Totalitarianism is an all-encompassing system of political rule that is typically established by pervasive ideological manipulation and open terror and brutality. It differs from autocracy, authoritarianism and traditional dictatorship in that it seeks 'total power' through the politicization of every aspect of social and personal existence. Totalitarianism thus implies the outright abolition of civil society: the abolition of 'the private'. Fascism and communism have sometimes been seen as left- and right-wing forms of totalitarianism, based on their rejection of toleration, pluralism and the open society. However, radical thinkers such as Marcuse (see p. 125) have claimed that liberal democracies also exhibit totalitarian features.

interest, and Hegel thus believed that higher levels of civilization would only be achieved as the state itself developed and expanded. Hegel's political philosophy therefore amounted to an uncritical reverence for the state, expressed in practice in firm admiration for the autocratic Prussian state of his day.

In contrast, the Nazis did not venerate the state as such, but viewed it as a means to an end. Hitler, for instance, described the state as a mere 'vessel', implying that creative power derives not from the state but from the race, the German people. Alfred Rosenberg (see p. 213) dismissed the idea of the 'total state', describing the state instead as an 'instrument of the National Socialist *Weltanschauung*'. However, there is little doubt that the Hitler regime came closer to realizing the totalitarian ideal in practice than did the Mussolini regime. Although it seethed with institutional and personal rivalries, the Nazi state was brutally effective in suppressing political opposition, and succeeded in extending political control over the media, art and culture, education and youth organizations. By comparison, despite its formal commitment to totalitarianism, the Italian state operated, in some ways, like a traditional or personalized dictatorship rather than a totalitarian dictatorship. For example, the Italian monarchy survived throughout the fascist period; many local political leaders, especially in the south, continued in power; and the Catholic Church retained its privileges and independence throughout the fascist period.

Corporatism

Although Italian fascists revered the state, this did not extend to an attempt to collectivize economic life. Fascist economic thought was seldom systematic, reflecting the fact that fascists sought to transform human consciousness rather than social structures. Its distinguishing feature was the idea of corporatism, which Mussolini portrayed as the 'third way', an alternative to both capitalism and socialism. This was a common theme in fascist thought, also embraced by Mosley in the UK and Perón in Argentina. Corporatism opposes both the free market and central planning: the former leads to the unrestrained pursuit of profit by individuals, while the latter is linked to the divisive idea of class war. In contrast, corporatism is based on the belief that business and labour are bound together in an organic

Key concept

Corporatism

Corporatism, in its broadest sense, is a means of incorporating organized interests into the processes of government. There are two faces of corporatism. *Authoritarian* corporatism (closely associated with Fascist Italy) is an ideology and an economic form. As an ideology, it offers an alternative to capitalism and socialism based on holism and group integration. As an economic form, it is characterized by the extension of direct political control over industry and organized labour. *Liberal* corporatism ('neocorporatism' or 'societal' corporatism) refers to a tendency found in mature liberal democracies for organized interests to be granted privileged and institutional access to policy formulation. In contrast to its authoritarian variant, liberal corporatism strengthens groups rather than government.

and spiritually unified whole. This holistic vision was based on the assumption that social classes do not conflict with one another, but can work in harmony for the common good or national interest. Such a view was influenced by traditional Catholic social thought, which, in contrast to the Protestant stress on the value of individual hard work, emphasizes that social classes are bound together by duty and mutual obligations.

Social harmony between business and labour offers the prospect of both moral and economic regeneration. However, class relations have to be mediated by the state, which is responsible for ensuring that the national interest takes precedence over narrow sectional interests. Twenty-two corporations were set up in Italy in 1927, each representing employers, workers and the government. These corporations were charged with overseeing the development of all the major industries in Italy. The 'corporate state' reached its peak in 1939, when a Chamber of Fasces and Corporations was created to replace the Italian parliament. Nevertheless, there was a clear divide between corporatist theory and the reality of economic policy in Fascist Italy. The 'corporate state' was little more than an ideological slogan, corporatism in practice amounting, effectively, to an instrument through which the fascist state controlled major economic interests. Working-class organizations were smashed and private businesses were intimidated.

Modernization

The state also exerted a powerful attraction for Mussolini and Italian fascists because they saw it as an agent of modernization. Italy was less industrialized than many of its European neighbours, notably the UK, France and Germany, and many fascists equated national revival with economic modernization. All forms of fascism tend to be backward-looking, highlighting the glories of a lost era of national greatness; in Mussolini's case, Imperial Rome. However, Italian fascism was also distinctively forward-looking, extolling the virtues of modern technology and industrial life, and looking to construct an advanced industrial society. This tendency within

Italian fascism is often linked to the influence of **futurism**, led by Filippo Marinetti (1876–1944). After 1922, Marinetti and other leading futurists were absorbed into fascism, bringing with them a belief in dynamism, a cult of the machine and a rejection of the past. For Mussolini, the attraction of an all-powerful state was, in part, that it would help Italy break with backwardness and tradition, and become a future-orientated industrialized country.

> **FUTURISM**
> An early twentieth-century movement in the arts that glorified factories, machinery and industrial life generally.

Fascism and racism

Not all forms of fascism involve overt racism, and not all racists are necessarily fascists. Italian fascism, for example, was based primarily on the supremacy of the fascist state over the individual, and on submission to the will of Mussolini. It was therefore a **voluntaristic** form of fascism, in that, at least in theory, it could embrace all people regardless of race, colour or, indeed, country of birth. When Mussolini passed anti-Semitic laws after 1937, he did so largely to placate Hitler and the Germans, rather than for any ideological purpose. Nevertheless, fascism has often coincided with, and bred from, racist ideas. Indeed, some argue that its emphasis on militant nationalism means that all forms of fascism are either hospitable to racism or harbour implicit or explicit racist doctrines (Griffin, 1993). Nowhere has this link between race and fascism been so evident as in Nazi Germany, where official ideology at times amounted to little more than hysterical, pseudo-scientific anti-Semitism (see p. 211).

The politics of race

The term 'race' implies that there are meaningful biological or genetic differences among human beings. While it may be possible to drop one national identity and assume another by a process of 'naturalization', it is impossible to change one's race, determined as it is at birth, indeed before birth, by the racial identity of one's parents. The symbols of race – skin tone, hair colour, physiognomy and blood – are thus fixed and unchangeable. The use of racial terms and categories became commonplace in the West during the nineteenth century as imperialism brought the predominantly 'white' European races into increasingly close contact with the 'black', 'brown' and 'yellow' races of Africa and Asia.

However, racial categories largely reflect cultural stereotypes and enjoy little, if any, scientific foundation. The broadest racial classifications – for example those based on skin colour – white, brown, yellow and so on – are at best misleading and at worst simply arbitrary. More detailed and ambitious racial theories, such as those of the Nazis, simply produced anomalies, one of the most glaring being that Adolf Hitler himself

> **VOLUNTARISM**
> A theory that emphasizes free will and personal commitment, rather than any form of determinism.

Key concept

Racism

Racism ('racism' and 'racialism' are now generally treated as synonymous) is, broadly, the belief that political or social conclusions can be drawn from the idea that humankind is divided into biologically distinct races. Racist theories are thus based on two assumptions. The first is that there are fundamental genetic, or species-type, differences among the peoples of the world – racial differences matter. The second is that these genetic divisions are reflected in cultural, intellectual and/or moral differences, making them politically or socially significant. Political racism is manifest in calls for racial segregation (for example, apartheid) and in doctrines of 'blood' superiority or inferiority (for example, Aryanism or anti-Semitism). 'Institutionalized' racism operates through the norms and values of an institution.

certainly did not fit the racial stereotype of the tall, broad-shouldered, blond-haired, blue-eyed Aryan commonly described in Nazi literature.

The core assumption of racism is that political and social conclusions can be drawn from the idea that there are innate or fundamental differences between the races of the world. At heart, genetics determines politics: racist political theories can be traced back to biological assumptions, as illustrated in Figure 7.2. A form of implicit racism has been associated with conservative nationalism. This is based on the belief that stable and successful societies must be bound together by a common culture and shared values. For example, Enoch Powell in the UK in the 1960s and Jean-Marie Le Pen in France since the 1980s have argued against 'non-white' immigration into their countries on the grounds that the distinctive traditions and culture of the 'white' host community would be threatened.

However, more systematic and developed forms of racism are based on explicit assumptions about the nature, capacities and destinies of different racial groups. In many cases, these assumptions have had a religious basis. For example, nineteenth-century European imperialism was justified, in part, by the alleged superiority of the Christian peoples of Europe over the 'heathen' peoples of Africa and Asia.

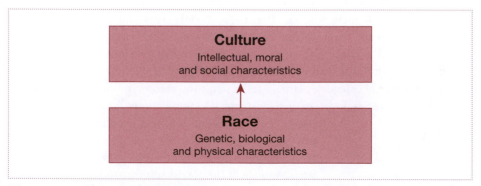

Figure 7.2   The nature of racism

Biblical justification was also offered for doctrines of racial segregation preached by the Ku Klux Klan, formed in the USA after the American Civil War, and by the founders of the **apartheid** system, which operated in South Africa from 1948 until 1993. In Nazi Germany, however, racism was rooted in biological, and therefore quasi-scientific, assumptions. Biologically based racial theories, as opposed to those that are linked to culture or religion, are particularly militant and radical because they make claims about the essential and inescapable nature of a people that are supposedly backed up by the certainty and objectivity of scientific belief.

> **APARTHEID**
> (Afrikaans) Literally, 'apartness'; a system of racial segregation practised in South Africa after 1948.

Nazi race theories

Nazi ideology was fashioned out of a combination of racial anti-Semitism and social Darwinism. Anti-Semitism had been a force in European politics, especially in eastern Europe, since the dawn of the Christian era. Its origins were largely theological: the Jews were responsible for the death of Christ, and in refusing to convert to Christianity they were both denying the divinity of Jesus and endangering their own immortal souls. The association between the Jews and evil was therefore not a creation of the Nazis, but dated back to the Christian Middle Ages, a period when the Jews were first confined in ghettoes and excluded from respectable society. However, anti-Semitism intensified in the late nineteenth century. As nationalism and imperialism spread throughout Europe, Jews were subjected to increasing persecution in many countries. In France, this led to the celebrated Dreyfus affair, 1894–1906; and, in Russia, it was reflected in a series of pogroms carried out against the Jews by the government of Alexander III.

The character of anti-Semitism also changed during the nineteenth century. The growth of a 'science of race', which applied pseudo-scientific ideas to social and political issues, led to Jewish people being thought of as a race rather than a religious, economic or cultural group. Thereafter, they were defined inescapably

Key concept

Anti-Semitism

By tradition, Semites are descendants of Shem, son of Noah, and include most of the peoples of the Middle East. Anti-Semitism refers specifically to prejudice against or hatred towards the Jews. In its earliest systematic form, anti-Semitism had a religious character, reflecting the hostility of Christians towards the Jews, based on their complicity in the murder of Jesus and their refusal to acknowledge him as the Son of God. Economic anti-Semitism developed from the Middle Ages onwards, expressing a distaste for the Jews as moneylenders and traders. The nineteenth century saw the birth of racial anti-Semitism in the works of Richard Wagner and H. S. Chamberlain, who condemned the Jewish peoples as fundamentally evil and destructive. Such ideas provided the ideological basis for German Nazism and found their most grotesque expression in the Holocaust.

KEY FIGURES IN... FASCISM

Joseph Arthur Gobineau (1816–82) A French social theorist, Gobineau is widely viewed as the architect of modern racial theory. In his major work, *Essay on the Inequality of the Human Races* ([1853–55] 1970), Gobineau advanced a 'science of history' in which the strength of civilizations was seen to be determined by their racial composition. In this, 'white' people – and particularly the 'Aryans' (the Germanic peoples) – were superior to 'black', 'brown' and 'yellow' people, and miscegenation (racial mixing) was viewed as a source of corruption and civilizational decline.

Friedrich Nietzsche (1844–1900) A German philosopher, Nietzsche's complex and ambitious work stressed the importance of will, especially the 'will to power', and influenced anarchism and feminism, as well as fascism. Anticipating modern existentialism, he emphasized that people create their own world and make their own values, expressed in the idea that 'God is dead'. In *Thus Spoke Zarathustra* ([1884] 1961), Neitzsche emphasized the role of the *Übermensch,* crudely translated as the 'supermen', who alone are unrestrained by conventional morality. His other works include *Beyond Good and Evil* (1886).

Houston Stewart Chamberlain (1855–1929) A British-born German writer, Chamberlain played a major role in popularizing racial theories, having a major impact on Hitler and the Nazis. In *Foundations of the Nineteenth Century* ([1899] 1913), largely based on the writings of Gobineau, Chamberlain used the term 'Aryan race' to describe almost all the peoples of Europe, but portrayed the 'Nordic' or 'Teutonic' peoples (by which he meant the Germans) as its supreme element, with the Jewish people being their implacable enemy.

Giovanni Gentile (1875–1944) An Italian idealist philosopher, Gentile was a leading figure in the Fascist government, 1922–9, and is sometimes called the 'philosopher of fascism'. Strongly influenced by the ideas of Hegel, Gentile advanced a radical critique of individualism, based on an 'internal' dialectic in which distinctions between subject and object, and between theory and practice, are transcended. In political terms, this implied the establishment of an all-encompassing state that would abolish the division between public and private life once and for all.

by biological factors such as hair colour, facial characteristics and blood. Anti-Semitism was therefore elaborated into a racial theory, which assigned to the Jewish people a pernicious and degrading racial stereotype. The first attempt to develop a scientific theory of racism was undertaken by Joseph-Arthur Gobineau (see p. 212). Gobineau argued that there is a hierarchy of races, with very different qualities and characteristics. The most developed and creative race is the 'white peoples', whose highest element Gobineau referred to as the 'Aryans'. Jewish people,

Benito Mussolini (1883–1945) An Italian politician, Mussolini founded the Fascist Party in 1919 and was the leader of Italy from 1922 to 1943. Claiming to be the founder of fascism, Mussolini's political philosophy drew on the work of Plato, Sorel, Nietzsche and Vilfredo Pareto, and stressed that human existence is only meaningful if it is sustained and determined by the community. This required the construction of a 'totalitarian' state, based on the principle that no human or spiritual values exist or have meaning outside the state.

Adolf Hitler (1889–1945) An Austrian-born German politician, Hitler became leader of the Nazi Party (German National Socialist Workers' Party) in 1921 and was the German leader from 1933 to 1945. Largely expressed in *Mein Kampf* [*My Struggle*] (1925), Hitler's world-view drew expansionist German nationalism, racial anti-Semitism and a belief in relentless struggle together in a theory of history that highlighted the endless battle between the Germans and the Jews. Under Hitler, the Nazis sought German world domination and, after 1941, the wholesale extermination of the Jewish people.

Alfred Rosenberg (1895–1946) A German politician and wartime Nazi leader, Rosenberg was a major intellectual influence on Hitler and the Nazi Party. In *The Myth of the Twentieth Century* (1930), Rosenberg developed the idea of the 'race-soul', arguing that race is the key to a people's destiny. His hierarchy of racial attributes allowed him to justify both Nazi expansionism (by emphasizing the superiority of the 'Aryan' race) and Hitler's genocidal policies (by portraying Jews as fundamentally 'degenerate', along with 'sub-human' Slavs, Poles and Czechs).

on the other hand, were thought to be fundamentally uncreative. Unlike the Nazis, however, Gobineau was a pessimistic racist, believing that, by his day, intermarriage had progressed so far that the glorious civilization built by the Aryans had already been corrupted beyond repair.

The doctrine of racial anti-Semitism entered Germany through Gobineau's writing and took the form of Aryanism, a belief in the biological superiority of the Aryan peoples. These ideas were taken up by the composer Richard Wagner and his UK-born son-in-law, H. S. Chamberlain (see p. 212), whose writings had an enormous impact on Hitler and the Nazis. Chamberlain defined the highest race more narrowly as the 'Teutons', clearly understood to mean the German peoples. All cultural development was ascribed to the German way of life, while Jewish people were described as 'physically, spiritually and morally degenerate'. Chamberlain presented history as a confrontation between the Teutons and the Jews, and therefore prepared the ground for Nazi race theory, which portrayed Jewish people as a universal scapegoat for all of Germany's misfortunes. The Nazis blamed the Jews for Germany's defeat in 1918; they were responsible for its humiliation at Versailles; they were behind the financial power of the banks and big business that enslaved the lower middle classes; and their influence was exerted through the working-class movement and the threat of social revolution. In Hitler's view, the Jews were responsible for an international conspiracy of capitalists and communists, whose prime objective was to weaken and overthrow the German nation.

Nazism, or national socialism, portrayed the world in pseudo-religious, pseudo-scientific terms as a struggle for dominance between the Germans and the Jews, representing, respectively, the forces of 'good' and 'evil'. Hitler himself divided the races of the world into three categories:

- The first, the Aryans, were the *Herrenvolk*, the 'master race'; Hitler described the Aryans as the 'founders of culture' and literally believed them to be responsible for all creativity, whether in art, music, literature, philosophy or political thought.
- Second, there were the 'bearers of culture', peoples who were able to utilize the ideas and inventions of the German people, but were themselves incapable of creativity.
- At the bottom were the Jews, who Hitler described as the 'destroyers of culture', pitted in an unending struggle against the noble and creative Aryans.

Hitler's Manichaean world view was therefore dominated by the idea of conflict between good and evil, reflected in a racial struggle between the Germans and the Jews, a conflict that could only end in either Aryan world domination (and the elimination of the Jews) or the final victory of the Jews (and the destruction of Germany).

This ideology took Hitler and the Nazis in appalling and tragic directions. In the first place, Aryanism, the conviction that the Aryans are a uniquely creative 'master race', dictated a policy of expansionism and war. If the Germans are racially superior, other races are biologically relegated to an inferior and subservient position. Nazi ideology therefore dictated an aggressive foreign policy in pursuit of a racial empire and, ultimately, world domination. Second, the Nazis believed that Germany could never be secure so long as its arch-enemies, the Jews, continued to exist. The Jews had to be persecuted, indeed they deserved to be persecuted, because they represented evil. The Nuremburg Laws, passed in 1935, prohibited both marriage and sexual relations between Germans and Jews. After *Kristallnacht* ('The Night of Broken

MANICHAEANISM
A third-century Persian religion that presented the world in terms of conflict between light and darkness, and good and evil.

Glass') in 1938, Jewish people were effectively excluded from the economy. However, Nazi race theories drove Hitler from a policy of persecution to one of terror and, eventually, **genocide** and racial extermination. In 1941, with a world war still to be won, the Nazi regime embarked on what it called the 'final solution', an attempt to exterminate the Jewish population of Europe in an unparalleled process of mass murder, which led to the death of some six million Jewish people.

Peasant ideology

A further difference between the Italian and German brands of fascism is that the latter advanced a distinctively anti-modern philosophy. While Italian fascism was eager to portray itself as a modernizing force and to embrace the benefits of industry and technology, Nazism reviled much of modern civilization as decadent and corrupt. This applied particularly in the case of urbanization and industrialization. In the Nazi view, the Germans are in truth a peasant people, ideally suited to a simple existence lived close to the land and ennobled by physical labour. However, life in overcrowded, stultifying and unhealthy cities had undermined the German spirit and threatened to weaken the racial stock. Such fears were expressed in the 'Blood and Soil' ideas of the Nazi Peasant Leader Walter Darré, which blended Nordic racism with rural romanticism to create a peasant philosophy that prefigured many of the ideas of ecologism (discussed in Chapter 9). They also explain why the Nazis extolled the virtues of *Kultur*, which embodied the folk traditions and craft skills of the German peoples, over the essentially empty products of western civilization. This peasant

GENOCIDE
The attempt to destroy, in whole or in part, a national, ethnic, racial or religious group.

Fascism	VS	Nazism
state worship	↔	state as vessel
chauvinist nationalism	↔	extreme racism
voluntarism	↔	essentialism
national greatness	↔	biological superiority
organic unity	↔	racial purity/eugenics
pragmatic anti-Semitism	↔	genocidal anti-Semitism
futurism/modernism	↔	peasant ideology
corporatism	↔	war economy
colonial expansion	↔	world domination

ideology had important implications for foreign policy. In particular, it helped to fuel expansionist tendencies by strengthening the attraction of *Lebensraum*. Only through territorial expansion could overcrowded Germany acquire the space to allow its people to resume their proper, peasant existence.

This policy was based on a deep contradiction, however. War and military expansion, even when justified by reference to a peasant ideology, cannot but be pursued through the techniques and processes of a modern industrial society. The central ideological goals of the Nazi regime were conquest and empire, and these dictated the expansion of the industrial base and the development of the technology of warfare. Far from returning the German people to the land, the Hitler period witnessed rapid industrialization and the growth of the large towns and cities so despised by the Nazis. Peasant ideology thus proved to be little more than rhetoric. Militarism also brought about significant cultural shifts. While Nazi art remained fixated with simplistic images of small-town and rural life, propaganda constantly bombarded the German people with images of modern technology, from the Stuka dive-bomber and Panzer tank to the V1 and V2 rockets.

Fascism in a global age

Some commentators have argued that fascism, properly understood, did not survive into the second half of the twentieth century, still less continue into an age shaped by globalization. In the classic analysis by Ernst Nolte (1965), for instance, fascism is seen as a historically specific revolt against modernization, linked to the desire to preserve the cultural and spiritual unity of traditional society. Since this moment in the modernization process has passed, all references to fascism should be made in the past tense. Hitler's suicide in the Führer bunker in April 1945, as the Soviet Red Army approached the gates of Berlin, may therefore have marked the *Götterdämmerung* of fascism, its 'twilight of the gods'. Such interpretations, however, have been far less easy to advance in view of the revival of fascism, or at least of fascist-type movements, in the final decades of the twentieth century and beyond, although these movements have adopted very different strategies and styles.

In some respects, the historical circumstances since the late twentieth century bear out some of the lessons of the inter-war period, namely, that fascism breeds in conditions of crisis, uncertainty and disorder. Steady economic growth and political stability in the early post-1945 period had proved a very effective antidote to the politics of hatred and resentment so often associated with the extreme right. However, uncertainty in the world economy and growing disillusionment with the capacity of established parties to tackle political and social problems have opened up opportunities for right-wing extremism, usually drawing on fears associated with immigration and the weakening of national identity. The end of the Cold War and the advance of globalization have, in some ways, strengthened these factors.

The end of communist rule in eastern Europe allowed long-suppressed national rivalries and racial hatreds to re-emerge, giving rise, particularly in the former Yugoslavia, to forms of extreme nationalism that have exhibited fascist-type features. Globalization, for its part, has contributed to the growth of insular, ethnically or racially based forms of nationalism by weakening the nation-state and so undermining civic forms of nationalism. Some, for instance, have drawn parallels between the rise of religious fundamentalism (see p. 188) and the rise of fascism, even seeing militant Islam as a form of 'Islamo-fascism'.

On the other hand, although far right and anti-immigration groups have taken up themes that are reminiscent of 'classical' fascism, the circumstances that have shaped them and the challenges they confront are very different from those found during the post-World War I period. For instance, instead of building on a heritage of European imperialism, the modern far right is operating in a context of post-colonialization. Multiculturalism has also advanced so far in many western societies that the prospect of creating ethnically or racially pure 'national communities' appears to be entirely unrealistic. Similarly, traditional class divisions, so influential in shaping the character and success of inter-war fascism, have given way to the more complex and pluralized 'post-industrial' social formations. Finally, economic globalization acts as a powerful constraint on the growth of classical fascist movements. So long as global capitalism continues to weaken the significance of national borders, the idea of national rebirth brought about through war, expansionism and autarky will appear to belong, firmly, to a bygone age.

However, what kind of fascism do modern fascist-type parties and groups espouse? While certain, often underground, groups continue to endorse a militant or revolutionary fascism that harks back proudly to Hitler or Mussolini, most of the larger parties and movements claim either to have broken ideologically with their past or deny that they are or ever have been fascist. For want of a better term, the latter can be classified as 'neofascist'. The principal way in which groups such as the French *Front National*, the Freedom Party in Austria, the *Alleanza Nazionale* in Italy and anti-immigration groups in the Netherlands, Belgium and Denmark claim to differ from fascism is in their acceptance of political pluralism and electoral democracy. In other words, 'democratic fascism' is fascism divorced from principles such as absolute leadership, totalitarianism and overt racism. In some respects, this 'de-ideologized' form of fascism may be well positioned to prosper in a context of globalization. For one thing, in reaching an accommodation with liberal democracy it appears to have buried its past and is no longer tainted with the barbarism of the Hitler and Mussolini period. For another, it still possesses the ability to advance a politics of organic unity and social cohesion in the event of political instability and social dislocation brought about by further, and perhaps deeper, crises in the global capitalist system.

? QUESTIONS FOR DISCUSSION

- Was fascism merely a product of the specific historical circumstances of the inter-war period?

- Is there such a thing as a 'fascist minimum', and if so, what are its features?

- How has anti-rationalism shaped fascist ideology?

- Why do fascists value struggle and war?

- How can the fascist leader principle be viewed as a form of democracy?

- Is fascism simply an extreme form of nationalism?

- In what sense is fascism a revolutionary creed?

- To what extent can fascism be viewed as a blend of nationalism and socialism?

- Why and how is fascism linked to totalitarianism?

- Are all fascists racists, or only some of them?

- Why and how have some fascists objected to capitalism?

- To what extent is modern 'neofascism' a genuine form of fascism?

- Is fascism dead?

📖 FURTHER READING

Eatwell, R., *Fascism: A History* (2003). A thorough, learned and accessible history of fascism that takes ideology to be important; covers both inter-war and postwar fascisms.

Griffin, R. (ed.), *International Fascism: Theories, Causes and the New Consensus* (1998). A collection of essays that examine contrasting interpretations of fascism but arrive at a 'state of the art' theory.

Neocleous, M., *Fascism* (1997). A short and accessible overview of fascism that situates it within the contradictions of modernity and capitalism.

Passmore, K., *Fascism: A Very Short Introduction* (2014). A lucid and stimulating introduction to the nature and causes of fascism.

CHAPTER

8 Feminism

Preview

As a political term, 'feminism' was a twentieth-century invention and has only been a familiar part of everyday language since the 1960s. ('Feminist' was first used in the nineteenth century as a medical term to describe either the feminization of men or the masculinization of women.) In modern usage, feminism is invariably linked to the women's movement and the attempt to advance the social role of women.

Feminist ideology is defined by two basic beliefs: that women are disadvantaged because of their sex; and that this disadvantage can and should be overthrown. In this way, feminists have highlighted what they see as a political relationship between the sexes, the supremacy of men and the subjection of women in most, if not all, societies. In viewing gender divisions as 'political', feminists challenged a 'mobilization of bias' that has traditionally operated within political thought, by which generations of male thinkers, unwilling to examine the privileges and power their sex had enjoyed, had succeeded in keeping the role of women off the political agenda.

Nevertheless, feminism has also been characterized by a diversity of views and political positions. The women's movement, for instance, has pursued goals that range from the achievement of female suffrage and an increase in the number of women in elite positions in public life, to the legalization of abortion, and the ending of female circumcision. Similarly, feminists have embraced both revolutionary and reformist political strategies, and feminist theory has both drawn on established political traditions and values, notably liberalism and socialism, and, in the form of radical feminism, rejected conventional political ideas and concepts. However, feminist ideology has long since ceased to be confined to these 'core' traditions, modern feminist thought focusing on new issues and characterized, generally, by a more radical engagement with the politics of difference.

Origins and development

Although the term 'feminism' may be of recent origin, feminist views have been expressed in many different cultures and can be traced back as far as the ancient civilizations of Greece and China. Christine de Pisan's *Book of the City of Ladies*, published in Italy in 1405, foreshadowed many of the ideas of modern feminism in recording the deeds of famous women of the past and advocating women's right to education and political influence. Nevertheless, it was not until the nineteenth century that an organized women's movement developed. The first text of modern feminism is usually taken to be Mary Wollstonecraft's (see p. 236) *A Vindication of the Rights of Woman* ([1792] 1967), written against the backdrop of the French Revolution. By the mid-nineteenth century, the women's movement had acquired a central focus: the campaign for female suffrage, the right to vote, which drew inspiration from the progressive extension of the franchise to men. This period is usually referred to as **first-wave feminism**, and was characterized by the demand that women should enjoy the same legal and political rights as men. Female suffrage was its principal goal because it was believed that if women could vote, all other forms of sexual discrimination or prejudice would quickly disappear.

The women's movement was strongest in those countries where political democracy was most advanced; women demanded rights that in many cases were already enjoyed by their husbands and sons. In the USA, a women's movement emerged during the 1840s, inspired in part by the campaign to abolish slavery. The famous Seneca Falls convention, held in 1848, marked the birth of the US women's rights movement. It adopted a Declaration of Sentiments, written by Elizabeth Cady Stanton (1815–1902), which deliberately drew on the language and principles of the Declaration of Independence and called, among other things, for female suffrage. The National Women's Suffrage Association, led by Stanton and Susan B. Anthony (1820–1906), was set up in 1869 and merged with the more conservative American Women's Suffrage Association in 1890. Similar movements developed in other western countries. In the UK, an organized movement developed during the 1850s and, in 1867, the House of Commons defeated the first attempt to introduce female suffrage, an amendment to the Second Reform Act, proposed by John Stuart Mill (see p. 53). The UK suffrage movement adopted increasingly militant tactics after the formation in 1903 of the Women's Social and Political Union, led by Emmeline Pankhurst (1858–1928) and her daughter Christabel (1880–1958). From their underground base in Paris, the Pankhursts coordinated a campaign of direct action in which 'suffragettes' carried out wholesale attacks on property and mounted a series of well-publicized public demonstrations.

FIRST-WAVE FEMINISM
The early form of feminism which developed in the mid-nineteenth century and was based on the pursuit of sexual equality in the areas of political and legal rights, particularly suffrage rights.

'First-wave' feminism ended with the achievement of female suffrage, introduced first in New Zealand in 1893. The Nineteenth Amendment of the US Constitution granted the vote to American women in 1920. The franchise was extended to women in the UK in 1918, but they did not achieve equal voting rights with men for a further decade. Ironically, in many ways, winning the right to vote weakened and undermined the women's movement. The struggle for female suffrage had united and inspired the movement, giving it a clear goal and a coherent structure. Furthermore, many activists naïvely believed that in winning suffrage rights, women had achieved full emancipation. It was not until the 1960s that the women's movement was regenerated, with the emergence of feminism's 'second wave'.

The publication in 1963 of Betty Friedan's *The Feminine Mystique* did much to relaunch feminist thought. Friedan (see p. 236) set out to explore what she called 'the problem with no name', the frustration and unhappiness many women experienced as a result of being confined to the roles of housewife and mother. **Second-wave feminism** acknowledged that the achievement of political and legal rights had not solved the 'women's question'. Indeed, feminist ideas and arguments became increasingly radical, and at times revolutionary. Books such as Kate Millett's *Sexual Politics* (1970) and Germaine Greer's *The Female Eunuch* (1970) pushed back the borders of what had previously been considered to be 'political' by focusing attention on the personal, psychological and sexual aspects of female oppression. The goal of second-wave feminism was not merely political emancipation but 'women's liberation', reflected in the ideas of the growing Women's Liberation Movement. Such a goal could not be achieved by political reforms or legal changes alone, but demanded, modern feminists argued, a more far-reaching and perhaps revolutionary process of social change.

Since the first flowering of radical feminist thought in the late 1960s and early 1970s, feminism has developed into a distinctive and established ideology, whose ideas and values challenge the most basic assumptions of conventional political thought. Feminism has succeeded in establishing **gender** and gender perspectives as important themes in a range of academic disciplines, and in raising consciousness about gender issues in public life in general. By the 1990s, feminist organizations existed in all western countries and most parts of the developing world. However, two processes have accompanied these developments. The first is a process of deradicalization, whereby there has been a retreat from the sometimes uncompromising positions that characterized feminism in the early 1970s. This has led to the popularity of the idea of 'postfeminism', which suggests that, as feminist goals have been largely achieved, the women's movement has moved 'beyond feminism'. The second process is one of fragmentation. Instead of simply losing its radical or critical edge, feminist thinking has gone through a process of radical diversification, making it difficult, and perhaps impossible, any longer to identify 'common ground' within feminism. In addition to the 'core' feminist traditions – liberal, socialist/Marxist and **radical feminism** – must

SECOND-WAVE FEMINISM
The form of feminism that emerged in the 1960s and 1970s, and was characterized by a more radical concern with 'women's liberation', including, and perhaps especially, in the private sphere.

GENDER
A social and cultural distinction between males and females, as opposed to sex, which refers to biological and therefore ineradicable differences between women and men.

RADICAL FEMINISM
A form of feminism that holds gender divisions to be the most politically significant of social cleavages, and believes that they are rooted in the structures of domestic life.

now be added postmodern feminism, psychoanalytical feminism, black feminism, lesbian feminism, transfeminism and so on.

Core themes: the politics of the personal

Until the 1960s, the idea that feminism should be regarded as an ideology in its own right would have been highly questionable. It is more likely that feminism would have been viewed as a sub-set of liberalism and socialism, the point at which the basic values and theories of these two ideologies can be applied to gender issues. The rise of radical feminism changed this, in that radical feminists proclaimed the central political importance of gender divisions, something that no conventional ideology could accept. Conventional ideologies were therefore viewed as inadequate vehicles for advancing the social role of women, and even, at times, criticized for harbouring patriarchal attitudes and assumptions. However, the emergent ideology of feminism was a cross-cutting ideology, encompassing, from the outset, three broad traditions: **liberal feminism**; Marxist or **socialist feminism**; and radical feminism. In addition, the 'core' feminist traditions each contain rival tendencies and have spawned hybrid or 'dual-system' feminisms (such as the attempt to blend radical feminism with certain Marxist ideas), and new feminist traditions have emerged, particularly since the 1980s. It is thus easy to dismiss feminism as hopelessly fragmented, to argue that it is characterized more by disagreement than by agreement. A range of 'common ground' themes can nevertheless be identified within feminism. The most important of these are:

LIBERAL FEMINISM
A form of feminism that is grounded in the belief that sexual differences are irrelevant to personal worth, and calls for equal rights for women and men in the public sphere.

SOCIALIST FEMINISM
A form of feminism that links the subordination of women to the dynamics of the capitalist economic system, emphasizing that women's liberation requires a process of radical social change.

- redefining 'the political'
- patriarchy
- sex and gender
- equality and difference.

Redefining 'the political'

Traditional notions of what is 'political' locate politics in the arena of public rather than private life. Politics has usually been understood as an activity that takes place within a 'public sphere' of government institutions, political parties, pressure groups and public debate. Family life and personal relationships have normally been thought to be part of a 'private sphere', and therefore to be 'non-political'. Modern feminists, on the other hand, insist that politics is an activity that takes place within all social groups and is not merely confined to the affairs of government or other public bodies. Politics exists whenever and wherever social conflict is found. Kate Millett (1970), for example, defined politics as 'power-structured relationships, arrangements whereby one group of persons is controlled by another'. The relationship between government and its citizens is therefore clearly political, but so is the relationship between employers and workers within a firm, and also relationships in the family, between husbands and wives, and between parents and children.

The definition of what is 'political' is not merely of academic interest. Feminists argue that sexual inequality has been preserved precisely because the sexual division of labour that runs through society has been thought of as 'natural' rather than 'political'. Traditionally, the public sphere of life, encompassing politics, work, art and literature, has been the preserve of men, while women have been confined to an essentially private existence, centred on the family and domestic responsibilities, as illustrated in Figure 8.1. If politics takes place only within the public sphere, the role of women and the question of sexual equality are issues of little or no political importance. Women, restricted to the private role of housewife and mother, are in effect excluded from politics.

Feminists have therefore sought to challenge the divide between 'public man' and 'private woman' (Elshtain, 1993). However, they have not always agreed about what it means to break down the public/private divide, about how it can be achieved, or about how far it is desirable. Radical feminists have been the keenest opponents of the idea that politics stops at the front door, proclaiming instead that 'the personal is the political'. Female oppression is thus thought to operate in all walks of life, and in many respects originates in the family itself. Radical feminists have therefore been concerned to analyse what can be called 'the politics of everyday life'. This includes the process of conditioning in the family, the distribution of housework and other domestic responsibilities, and the politics of personal and sexual conduct. For some feminists, breaking down the public/private divide implies transferring the responsibilities of private life to the state or other public bodies. For example, the burden of child-rearing on women could be relieved by more generous welfare support for families or the provision of nursery schools or crèches at work. Socialist feminists have also viewed the private sphere as political, in that they have linked women's roles within the conventional family to the maintenance of the capitalist economic

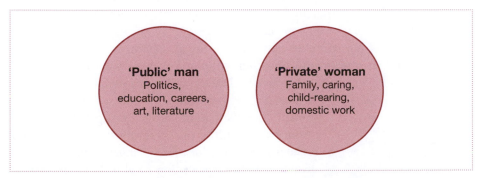

Figure 8.1 The sexual division of labour

system. However, although liberal feminists object to restrictions on women's access to the public sphere of education, work and political life, they also warn against the dangers of politicizing the private sphere, which, according to liberal theory, is a realm of personal choice and individual freedom.

Patriarchy

Feminists believe that gender, like social class, race or religion, is a politically significant social cleavage. Indeed, radical feminists argue that gender is the deepest and most politically important of social divisions. Feminists have therefore advanced a theory of 'sexual politics', in much the same way that socialists have preached the idea of 'class politics'. They also refer to 'sexism' as a form of oppression, drawing a conscious parallel with 'racism' or racial oppression. However, conventional political theory has traditionally ignored sexual oppression and failed to recognize gender as a politically significant category. As a result, feminists have been forced to develop new concepts and theories to convey the idea that society is based on a system of sexual inequality and oppression.

Feminists use the concept of 'patriarchy' to describe the power relationship between women and men. The term literally means 'rule by the father' (*pater* meaning father in Latin). Some feminists employ patriarchy only in this specific and limited sense, to describe the structure of the family and the dominance of the husband-father within it, preferring to use broader terms such as 'male supremacy' or 'male dominance' to describe gender relations in society at large. However, feminists believe that the dominance of the father within the family symbolizes male supremacy in all other institutions. Many would argue, moreover, that the patriarchal family lies at the heart of a systematic process of male domination, in that it reproduces male dominance in all other walks of life: in education, at work and in politics. Patriarchy is therefore commonly used in a broader sense to mean quite simply 'rule by men', both within the family and outside. Millett (1970), for instance described 'patriarchal government' as an institution whereby 'that half of the populace which is female is controlled by that half which is male'. She suggested that patriarchy contains two principles: 'male shall dominate female, elder male shall dominate younger'. A patriarchy is therefore a hierarchic society, characterized by both sexual and generational oppression.

The concept of patriarchy is, nevertheless, broad. Feminists may believe that men have dominated women in all societies, but accept that the forms and degree of oppression have varied considerably in different cultures and at different times.

PATRIARCHY
Literally, rule by the father; often used more generally to describe the dominance of men and subordination of women in society at large.

At least in western countries, the social position of women improved significantly during the twentieth century as a result of the achievement of the vote and broader access to education, changes in marriage and divorce law, the legalization of abortion (see p. 226) and so on. However, in parts of the developing world,

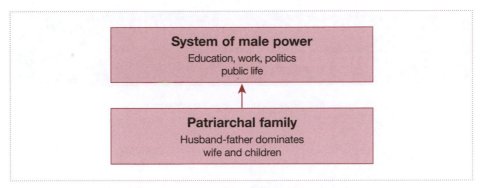

Figure 8.2   Radical feminist view of patriarchy

patriarchy still assumes a cruel, even gruesome, form: 80 million women, mainly in Africa, are subjected to the practice of circumcision; bride murders still occur in India; and the persistence of the dowry system ensures that female children are often unwanted and sometimes allowed to die.

Feminists do not have a single or simple analysis of patriarchy, however. Liberal feminists, to the extent that they use the term, use it to draw attention to the unequal distribution of rights and entitlements in society at large. The face of patriarchy they highlight is therefore the under-representation of women in senior positions in politics, business, the professions and public life generally. Socialist feminists tend to emphasize the economic aspects of patriarchy. In their view, patriarchy operates in tandem with capitalism, gender subordination and class inequality being interlinked systems of oppression. Some socialist feminists, indeed, reject the term altogether, on the grounds that gender inequality is merely a consequence of the class system: capitalism, not patriarchy, is the issue. Radical feminists, on the other hand, place considerable stress on patriarchy. They see it as a systematic, institutionalized and pervasive form of male power that is rooted in the family. Patriarchy thus expresses the belief that the pattern of male domination and female subordination that characterizes society at large is, essentially, a reflection of the power structures that operate within domestic life, as illustrated in Figure 8.2.

Sex and gender

The most common of all anti-feminist arguments, often associated with conservatives, asserts that gender divisions in society are 'natural': women and men merely fulfil the social roles for which nature designed them. A woman's physical and anatomical make-up thus suits her to a subordinate and domestic role in society; in short, 'biology is destiny'. The biological factor that is most frequently linked to women's social position is their capacity to bear children. Without doubt, childbearing is unique to the female sex, together with the fact that women menstruate and

POLITICAL IDEOLOGIES IN ACTION . . .
Legalizing abortion

EVENTS: In January 1973, the US Supreme Court made a landmark decision on abortion. In *Roe v. Wade*, the Court ruled that criminal laws which prohibit abortion except to save the life of the mother are unconstitutional violations of the right to privacy as protected by the Fourteenth Amendment. Although the Supreme Court judgement had a particularly high profile, it came in the context of a wider shift in favour of legalized abortion. Between 1950 and 1985, abortion was legalized in almost all developed states, although the circumstances in which it could take place and the timescales applied to it differed, sometimes significantly. Currently, about 25 per cent of the world's population live in countries where abortion remains illegal or access to it is highly restrictive, mainly in Latin America, Africa and Asia.

SIGNIFICANCE: The legalization of abortion across much of the world during the second half of the twentieth century was largely a consequence of the campaigning efforts of the women's movement and of feminism's success in reshaping attitudes and values, operating in tandem with concerns over health and medicine. Indeed, in the early 1970s abortion emerged as almost the defining issue of second-wave feminism. The fundamental feminist argument in favour of abortion is that women have a basic and inalienable right to limit their reproduction. However, there is no single feminist theory of abortion. Liberal feminists understand the issue in terms of individual freedom of choice (hence the idea that they are 'pro-choice') and effective access to the public realm. Radical feminists, for their part, have stressed that abortion symbolizes women's sexual and reproductive self-determination, also warning that restricting access to abortion helps to promote patriarchy by institutionalizing motherhood.

Since the late 1970s, abortion has lost its central place in the concerns of western feminism, largely because abortion law has been liberalized, but also because some have seen the issue as less morally and ideological straightforward. Nevertheless, since the 1980s abortion has been a major political battleground, particularly in the USA, through the tendency of the New Right's politics of morality to coalesce around a 'pro-life' opposition to abortion. This reflects the emergence of an important tendency within US conservatism which is inspired by religious belief and especially the ideas of evangelical Protestantism. However, the extent to which it has been able to 'roll back' abortion law has been limited.

have the capacity to suckle babies. However, feminists insist that in no way do such biological facts necessarily disadvantage women nor determine their social destiny. Women may be mothers, but they need not accept the responsibilities of motherhood: nurturing, educating and raising children by devoting themselves to home and family. The link between childbearing and child-rearing is cultural rather than biological: women are *expected* to stay at home, bring up their children and look after the house because of the structure of traditional family life. Domestic responsibilities could be undertaken by the husband, or they could be shared equally between husband and wife in so-called 'symmetrical families'. Moreover, child-rearing could be carried out by the community or the state, or it could be undertaken by relatives, as in 'extended' families.

Feminists have traditionally challenged the idea that biology is destiny by drawing a sharp distinction between sex and gender. 'Sex', in this sense, refers to biological differences between females and males; these differences are natural

PERSPECTIVES ON... GENDER

LIBERALS have traditionally regarded differences between women and men as being of entirely private or personal significance. In public and political life, all people are considered as individuals, gender being as irrelevant as ethnicity or social class. In this sense, individualism is 'gender-blind'.

CONSERVATIVES have traditionally emphasised the social and political significance of gender divisions, arguing that they imply that the sexual division of labour between women and men is natural and inevitable. Gender is thus one of the factors that gives society its organic and hierarchical character.

SOCIALISTS, like liberals, have rarely treated gender as a politically significant category. When gender divisions are significant it is usually because they reflect and are sustained by deeper economic and class inequalities.

FASCISTS view gender as a fundamental division within humankind. Men naturally monopolize leadership and decision-making, while women are suited to an entirely domestic, supportive and subordinate role.

FEMINISTS usually see gender as a cultural or political distinction, in contrast to biological and ineradicable sexual differences. Gender divisions are therefore a manifestation of male power. Difference feminists may nevertheless believe that gender differences reflect a psycho-biological gulf between female and male attributes and sensibilities.

ISLAMISTS have an ultra-conservative view of gender roles, typically characterized by male 'guardianship' over the family, the observation by women of a strict dress code, and restrictions on women's access to aspects of public life.

and therefore are unalterable. The most important sex differences are those that are linked to reproduction. 'Gender', on the other hand, is a cultural term; it refers to the different roles that society ascribes to women and men. Gender differences are typically imposed through contrasting stereotypes of 'masculinity' and 'femininity'. As Simone de Beauvoir (see p. 236) pointed out, 'Women are made, they are not born'. Patriarchal ideas blur the distinction between sex and gender, and assume that all social distinctions between women and men are rooted in biology or anatomy. Feminists, in contrast, usually deny that there is a necessary or logical link between sex and gender, and emphasize that gender differences are socially, or even politically, constructed.

Most feminists believe that sex differences between women and men are relatively minor and neither explain nor justify gender distinctions. As a result, human nature is thought to be **androgynous**. All human beings, regardless of sex, possess the genetic inheritance of a mother and a father, and therefore embody a blend of both female and male attributes or traits. Such a view accepts that sex differences are biological facts of life but insists that they have no social, political or economic significance. Women and men should not be judged by their sex, but as individuals, as 'persons'. The goal of feminism is therefore the achievement of genderless 'personhood'. Establishing a concept of gender that is divorced from biological sex had crucial significance for feminist theory. Not only did it highlight the possibility of social change – socially constructed identities can be reconstructed or even demolished – but it also drew attention to the processes through which women had been 'engendered' and therefore oppressed.

Although most feminists have regarded the sex/gender distinction as empowering, others have attacked it. These attacks have been launched from two main directions. The first, advanced by so-called '**difference feminists**', suggests that there are profound and perhaps ineradicable differences between women and men. From this '**essentialist**' perspective, accepted by some but by no means all difference feminists, social and cultural characteristics are seen to reflect deeper biological differences. The second attack on the sex/gender distinction challenges the categories themselves. Postmodern feminists have questioned whether 'sex' is as clear-cut a biological distinction as is usually assumed. For example, the features of 'biological womanhood' do not apply to many who are classified as women: some women cannot bear children, some women are not sexually attracted to men, and so on. If there is a biology–culture continuum rather than a fixed biological/cultural divide, the categories 'female' and 'male' become more or less arbitrary, and the concepts of sex and gender become hopelessly entangled. An alternative approach to gender

ANDROGYNY
The possession of both male and female characteristics; used to imply that human beings are sexless 'persons' in the sense that sex is irrelevant to their social role or political status.

DIFFERENCE FEMINISM
A form of feminism which holds that there are deep and possibly ineradicable differences between women and men, whether these are rooted in biology, culture or material experience.

ESSENTIALISM
The belief that biological factors are crucial in determining psychological and behavioural traits.

TRANSFEMINISM
A form of feminism that rejects the idea of fixed identities and specifically avows gender and sexual ambiguity.

has been advanced by the trans movement, which seeks to explode the dualistic conception of gender, in which divides the human world is tidily divided into female and male parts. Such thinking is examined later in the chapter, in connection with **transfeminism**.

Equality and difference

Although the goal of feminism is the overthrow of patriarchy and the ending of sexist oppression, feminists have sometimes been uncertain about what this means in practice and how it can be brought about. Traditionally, women have demanded equality with men, even to the extent that feminism is often characterized as a movement for the achievement of sexual equality. However, the issue of equality has also exposed major faultlines within feminism: feminists have embraced contrasting notions of equality and some have entirely rejected equality in favour of the idea of difference. Liberal feminists champion legal and political equality with men. They have supported an equal rights agenda, which would enable women to compete in public life on equal terms with men, regardless of sex. Equality thus means equal access to the public realm. Socialist feminists, in contrast, argue that equal rights may be meaningless unless women also enjoy social equality. Equality, in this sense, has to apply in terms of economic power, and so must address issues such as the ownership of wealth, pay differentials and the distinction between waged and unwaged labour. Radical feminists, for their part, are primarily concerned about equality in family and personal life. Equality must therefore operate, for example, in terms of child care and other domestic responsibilities, the control of one's own body, and sexual expression and fulfilment.

Despite tensions between them, these egalitarian positions are united in viewing gender differences in a negative light. **Equality feminism** links 'difference' to patriarchy, seeing it as a manifestation of oppression or subordination. From this viewpoint, the feminist project is defined by the desire to liberate women *from* 'difference'. However, other feminists champion difference rather than equality. Difference feminists regard the very notion of equality as either misguided or simply undesirable. To want to be

EQUALITY FEMINISM
A form of feminism that aspires to the goal of sexual equality, whether this is defined in terms of formal rights, the control of resources, or personal power.

'PRO-WOMAN' FEMINISM
A form of feminism that advances a positive image of women's attributes and propensities, usually stressing creativity, caring and human sympathy, and cooperation.

equal to a man implies that women are 'male identified', in that they define their goals in terms of what men are or what men have. The demand for equality therefore embodies a desire to be 'like men'. Although feminists seek to overthrow patriarchy, many warn against the danger of modelling themselves on men, which would require them, for example, to adopt the competitive and aggressive behaviour that characterizes male society. For many feminists, liberation means achieving fulfilment as women; in other words, being 'female identified'.

Difference feminists are thus often said to subscribe to a '**pro-woman**' position, which accepts that sex differences have political and social importance. This is based on the essentialist belief that women and men are fundamentally different at a psycho-biological level. The aggressive and competitive nature of men and the creative and empathetic character of women are thought to reflect deeper hormonal and other genetic differences, rather than simply the structure of society. To idealize androgyny or personhood and ignore sex differences is therefore a mistake. Women should recognize and celebrate the distinctive characteristics of the female sex; they should seek liberation *through* difference, as developed and fulfilled women, not as sexless 'persons'. In the form of cultural feminism, this has lead to an emphasis on women's crafts, art and literature, and on experiences that are unique to women and promote a sense of 'sisterhood', such as childbirth, motherhood and menstruation.

> **CULTURAL FEMINISM**
> A form of feminism that emphasizes an engagement with a woman-centred culture and life-style, and is typically repelled by the corrupting and aggressive male world of political activism.

Types of feminism

Feminism is a cross-cutting ideology. The rival traditions of feminism have largely emerged out of established ideologies or theories, most obviously liberalism and socialism, but also, more recently, ideas such as postmodernism (see p. 59) and psychoanalysis. Such ideologies and theories have served as vehicles for advancing the social role of women because they are generally sympathetic towards equality. Hierarchical or elitist ideologies or theories, in contrast, are associated more commonly with anti-feminism. For instance, traditional conservatism holds that the patriarchal structure of society and the sexual division of labour between 'public' man and 'private' woman is natural and inevitable. Women are born to be housewives and mothers, and rebellion against this fate is both pointless and wrong. At best, conservatives can argue that they support sexual equality on the grounds that women's family responsibilities are every bit as important as men's public duties. Women and men are therefore 'equal but different'.

Forms of reactionary feminism have also developed in certain circumstances. This has occurred when the traditional status and position of women has been threatened by rapid social or cultural change. So-called Islamic feminism has this character. In Islamic states, such as Iran, Pakistan and Sudan, the imposition of *sharia* law (see p. 312) and the return to traditional moral and religious principles have sometimes been portrayed as a means of enhancing the status of women, threatened by the spread of western attitudes and values. From this perspective, the veil and other dress codes, and the exclusion of women from public life, have been viewed by some Muslim women as symbols of liberation. Iran is a particularly complex example of this, in that the reimposition of traditionalist values and female dress codes since the 1979 Islamic Revolution (see p. 303) has gone hand in hand with, for instance, a dramatic increase in female participation in higher education. However, from the perspective of conventional feminism, reactionary feminism is simply a contradiction in terms, reflecting the misguided belief that the traditional public/private divide genuinely afforded women status and protection. Indeed, it provides evidence of the ideological power of patriarchy, through its capacity to recruit women into their own oppression. The major traditions within feminism are the following:

- liberal feminism
- socialist feminism
- radical feminism
- third-wave feminism and beyond.

Liberal feminism

Early feminism, particularly the 'first wave' of the women's movement, was deeply influenced by the ideas and values of liberalism. The first major feminist text, Wollstonecraft's *A Vindication of the Rights of Woman* ([1792] 1967), argued that women should be entitled to the same rights and privileges as men on the grounds that they are 'human beings'. She claimed that the 'distinction of sex' would become unimportant in political and social life if women gained access to education and were regarded as rational creatures in their own right. John Stuart Mill's *On the Subjection of Women* ([1869] 1970), written in collaboration with Harriet Taylor, proposed that society should be organized according to the principle of 'reason', and that 'accidents of birth' such as sex should be irrelevant. Women would there-fore be entitled to the rights and liberties enjoyed by men and, in particular, the right to vote.

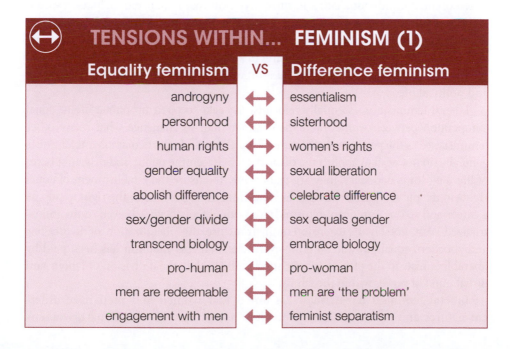

TENSIONS WITHIN... FEMINISM (1)

Equality feminism	VS	Difference feminism
androgyny	↔	essentialism
personhood	↔	sisterhood
human rights	↔	women's rights
gender equality	↔	sexual liberation
abolish difference	↔	celebrate difference
sex/gender divide	↔	sex equals gender
transcend biology	↔	embrace biology
pro-human	↔	pro-woman
men are redeemable	↔	men are 'the problem'
engagement with men	↔	feminist separatism

'Second-wave' feminism also has a significant liberal component. Liberal feminism has dominated the women's movement in the USA; for instance, the publication of Betty Friedan's *The Feminine Mystique* marked the resurgence of feminist thought in the 1960s. The 'feminine mystique' to which Friedan referred is the cultural myth that women seek security and fulfilment in domestic life and 'feminine' behaviour, a myth that serves to discourage women from entering employment, politics and public life in general. She highlighted what she called 'the problem with no name', by which she meant the sense of despair and deep unhappiness many women experience because they are confined to a domestic existence and are thus unable to gain fulfilment in a career or through political life. In 1966, Friedan helped to found and became the first leader of the National Organization of Women (NOW), which has developed into a powerful pressure group and the largest women's organization in the world.

The philosophical basis of liberal feminism lies in the principle of individualism (see p. 27), the belief that the human individual is all-important and therefore that all individuals are of equal moral worth. Individuals are entitled to equal treatment, regardless of their sex, race, colour, creed or religion. If individuals are to be judged, it should be on rational grounds, on the content of their character, their talents, or their personal worth. Liberals express this belief in the demand for equal rights: all individuals are entitled to participate in, or gain access to, public or political life. Any form of discrimination against women in this respect should therefore be prohibited. Wollstonecraft, for example, insisted that education, in her day the province of men, should be opened up to women. J. S. Mill argued in favour of equal citizenship and political rights. Indeed, the entire suffrage movement was based on liberal individualism and the conviction that female emancipation would be brought about once women enjoyed equal voting rights with men. Liberal feminist groups therefore aim to break down the remaining legal and social pressures that restrict women from pursuing careers and being politically active. They seek, in particular, to increase the representation of women in senior positions in public and political life.

Liberal feminism is essentially reformist: it seeks to open up public life to equal competition between women and men, rather than to challenge what many other feminists see as the patriarchal structure of society itself. In particular, liberal feminists generally do not wish to abolish the distinction between the public and private spheres of life. Reform is necessary, they argue, but only to ensure the establishment of equal rights in the public sphere: the right to education, the right to vote, the right to pursue a career and so on. Significant reforms have undoubtedly been achieved in the industrialized West, notably the extension of the franchise, the 'liberalization' of divorce law and abortion, equal pay and so on. Nevertheless, far less attention has been paid by liberal feminists to the private sphere, specifically to the sexual division of labour and distribution of power within the family.

Liberal feminists have usually assumed that women and men have different natures and inclinations, and therefore accept that, at least in part, women's leaning towards family and domestic life is influenced by natural impulses and so reflects a willing choice. This certainly applied in the case of nineteenth-century feminists, who regarded the traditional structure of family life as 'natural', but it is also evident in the work of modern liberal feminists such as Friedan. In *The Second Stage* (1983) Friedan discussed the problem of reconciling the achievement of 'personhood', made possible by opening up broader opportunities for women in work and public life, with the need for love, represented by children, home and the family. Friedan's emphasis on the continuing and central importance of the family in women's lives has been criticized by more radical feminists for contributing to a 'mystique of motherhood'. Others have condemned it for suggesting that women can 'have it all', being successful in terms of career advancement as well as in terms of motherhood and homemaking.

Finally, the demand for equal rights, which lies at the core of liberal feminism, has principally attracted those women whose education and social backgrounds equip them to take advantage of wider educational and career opportunities. For example, nineteenth-century feminists and the leaders of the suffrage movement were usually educated, middle-class women who had the opportunity to benefit from the right to vote, pursue a career or enter public life. The demand for equal rights assumes that all women would have the opportunity to take advantage of, for example, better educational and economic opportunities. In reality, women are judged not only by their talents and abilities, but also by social and economic factors. If emancipation simply means the achievement of equal rights and opportunities for women and men, other forms of social disadvantage – for example, those linked to social class and race – are ignored. Liberal feminism may therefore reflect the interests of white, middle-class women in developed societies but fail to address the problems of working-class women, black women and women in the developing world.

Socialist feminism

Although some early feminists subscribed to socialist ideas, socialist feminism only became prominent in the second half of the twentieth century. In contrast to their liberal counterparts, socialist feminists have not believed that women simply face political or legal disadvantages that can be remedied by equal legal rights or the achievement of equal opportunities. Rather, they argue that the relationship between the sexes is rooted in the social and economic structure itself, and that nothing short of profound social change, some would say a social revolution, can offer women the prospect of genuine emancipation.

The central theme of socialist feminism is that patriarchy can only be understood in the light of social and economic factors. The classic statement of this argument was developed in Friedrich Engels' *The Origins of the Family, Private Property and the State* ([1884] 1976). Engels suggested that the position of women in society had changed fundamentally with the development of capitalism and the institution of private property. In pre-capitalist societies, family life had been communistic, and 'mother right' – the inheritance of property and social position through the female line – was widely observed. Capitalism, however, being based on the ownership of private property by men, had overthrown 'mother right' and brought about what Engels called 'the world historical defeat of the female sex'. Like many subsequent socialist feminists, Engels believed that female oppression operates through the institution of the family. The 'bourgeois family' is patriarchal and oppressive because men wish to ensure that their property will be passed on only to *their* sons. Men achieve undisputed paternity by insisting on monogamous marriage, a restriction that is rigorously applied to wives, depriving them of other sexual partners but, as Engels noted, is routinely ignored by their husbands. Women are compensated for this repression by the development of a 'cult of femininity', which extols the attractions of romantic love but, in reality, is an organized hypocrisy designed to protect male privileges and property. Other socialist feminists have proposed that the traditional, patriarchal family should be replaced by a system of communal living and 'free love', as advocated by early utopian socialists such as Charles Fourier (1772–1837) and Robert Owen (see p. 124).

Most socialist feminists agree that the confinement of women to a domestic sphere of housework and motherhood serves the economic interests of capitalism. Some have argued that women constitute a 'reserve army of labour', which can be recruited into the workforce when there is a need to increase production, but easily shed and returned to domestic life during a depression, without imposing a burden on employers or the state. At the same time, women's domestic labour is vital to the health and efficiency of the economy. In bearing and rearing children, women are producing the next generation of capitalism's workers. Similarly, in their role as housewives, women relieve men of the burden of housework and child-rearing, allowing them to concentrate their time and energy on paid and productive employment. The traditional family provides the worker with a powerful incentive to find and keep a job because he has a wife and children to support. The family also provides male workers with a necessary cushion against the alienation and frustrations of life as 'wage slaves'. Male 'breadwinners' enjoy high status within the family and are relieved of the burden of 'trivial' domestic labour.

Although socialist feminists agree that the 'women's question' cannot be separated from social and economic life, they are profoundly divided about the nature of that link. Gender divisions clearly cut across class cleavages, creating tension within socialist feminist analysis about the relative importance of gender and social class, and raising particularly difficult questions for Marxist feminists. Orthodox Marxists insist on the primacy of class politics over sexual politics. This suggests that class exploitation is a deeper and more significant process than sexual oppression. It also suggests that women's emancipation will be a by-product of a social revolution in which capitalism is overthrown and replaced by socialism. Women seeking liberation should therefore recognize that the 'class war' is more important than the 'sex war'. Such an analysis suggests that feminists should devote their energies to the labour movement rather than support a separate and divisive women's movement.

However, modern socialist feminists have found it increasingly difficult to accept the primacy of class politics over sexual politics. In part, this was a consequence of the disappointing progress that had been made by women in state-socialist societies such as the Soviet Union, suggesting that socialism does not, in itself, end patriarchy. For modern socialist feminists, sexual oppression is every bit as important as class exploitation. Many of them subscribe to a form of neo-Marxism, which accepts the interplay of economic, social, political and cultural forces in society. They therefore refuse to analyse the position of women in simple economic terms and have, instead, given attention to the cultural and ideological roots of patriarchy. For example, Juliet Mitchell (1971), suggested that women fulfil four social functions: (1) they are members of the workforce and are active in production; (2) they bear children and thus reproduce the human species; (3) they are responsible for socializing children; and (4) they are sex objects. From this perspective, liberation requires that women achieve emancipation in each of these areas, and not merely that the capitalist class system is replaced by socialism.

Radical feminism

One of the distinctive features of second-wave feminism is that many feminist writers moved beyond the perspectives of existing political ideologies. Gender differences in society were regarded for the first time as important in themselves,

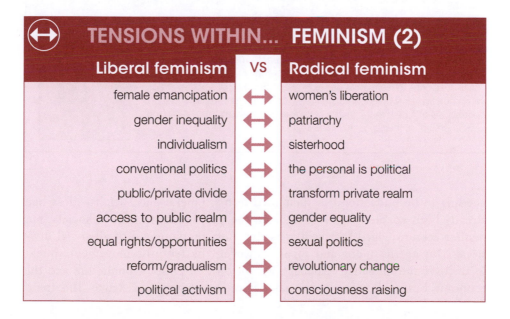

⬌ TENSIONS WITHIN... FEMINISM (2)		
Liberal feminism	**VS**	**Radical feminism**
female emancipation	⬌	women's liberation
gender inequality	⬌	patriarchy
individualism	⬌	sisterhood
conventional politics	⬌	the personal is political
public/private divide	⬌	transform private realm
access to public realm	⬌	gender equality
equal rights/opportunities	⬌	sexual politics
reform/gradualism	⬌	revolutionary change
political activism	⬌	consciousness raising

KEY FIGURES IN... FEMINISM

Mary Wollstonecraft (1759–97) A British social theorist, Wollstonecraft was a pioneer feminist thinker, drawn into radical politics by the French Revolution. Her *A Vindication of the Rights of Woman* (1792) stressed the equal rights of women, especially in education, on the basis of the notion of 'personhood'. Wollstonecraft's work drew on an Enlightenment liberal belief in reason, but developed a more complex analysis of women as the objects and subjects of desire; it also presented the domestic sphere as a model of community and social order.

Simone de Beauvoir (1906–86) A French novelist, playwright and social critic, de Beauvoir's work reopened the issue of gender politics and foreshadowed the ideas of later radical feminists. In *The Second Sex* (1949), she developed a complex critique of patriarchal culture, in which the masculine is represented as the positive or the norm, while the feminine is portrayed as the 'other' – fundamentally limiting women's freedom and denying them their full humanity. De Beauvoir placed her faith in rationality and critical analysis as the means of exposing this process.

Betty Friedan (1921–2006) A US political activist, Friedan is sometimes seen as the 'mother' of women's liberation. In *The Feminine Mystique* (1963) (often credited with having stimulated the emergence of second-wave feminism), Friedan attacked the cultural myths that sustained domesticity, highlighting the sense of frustration and despair that afflicted suburban American women confined to the roles of house-wife and mother. In *The Second Stage* (1983), she nevertheless warned that the quest for 'personhood' should not encourage women to deny the importance of children, the home and the family.

Kate Millett (born 1934) A US feminist writer, political activist and artist, Millett developed a comprehensive critique of patriarchy in western society and culture that had a profound impact on radical feminism. In *Sexual Politics* (1970), Millett analysed the work of male writers, from D. H. Lawrence to Norman Mailer, highlighting their use of sex to degrade and undermine women. In her view, such literature reflects deeply patriarchal attitudes that pervade culture and society at large, providing evidence that patriarchy is a historical and social constant.

needing to be understood in their own terms. Liberal and socialist ideas had already been adapted to throw light on the position of women in society, but neither acknowledged that gender is the most fundamental of all social divisions. During the 1960s and 1970s, however, the feminist movement sought to uncover the influence of patriarchy not only in politics, public life and the economy, but in all aspects of social, personal and sexual existence. This trend

Germaine Greer (born 1939) An Australian writer, academic and journalist, Greer's *The Female Eunuch* (1970) helped to stimulate radical feminist theorizing. Its principal theme, the extent to which male domination is upheld by a systematic process of sexual repression, was accompanied by a call for women to re-engage with their libido, their faculty of desire and their sexuality. In *Sex and Destiny* (1985), Greer celebrated the importance of childbearing and motherhood, while *The Whole Woman* (1999) criticized 'lifestyle feminists' and the alleged right to 'have it all'.

Jean Bethke Elshtain (1941–2013) A US political philosopher and social critic, Elshtain has made a major contribution to feminist scholarship and wider political debates. In *Public Man, Private Woman* (1993), she examined the role of gender in forming the division between the public and private spheres in political theory. Her *Women and War* (1987) discussed the perceptual lenses that determine the roles of men and women in war, highlighting the myths that men are 'just warriors' and women are 'beautiful souls' to be saved.

Andrea Dworkin (1946–2005) A feminist writer and activist, Dworkin was a trenchant critic of patriarchal culture and an advocate of radical lesbianism. In *Woman Hating* (1976) and (with Catharine MacKinnon) *Pornography and Civil Rights* (1988), Dworkin argued that pornography is the tool by which men control, objectify and subjugate women. With MacKinnon, she drafted a Minnesota ordinance that proposed that victims of rape and other sex crimes should be able to sue pornographers for damage, based on the belief that pornography supports sexual violence against women.

bell hooks (born 1952) A cultural critic, feminist and writer, Gloria Jean Watkins (better known by her pen name bell hooks) has emphasized that feminism must be approached through the lenses of gender, race and class. In her classic *Ain't I a Woman* (1985), hooks examined the history of black women in the USA. Arguing that in the USA racism took (and takes) precedence over sexism, she advanced a powerful critique of the implicit racism of the white women's movement. Her other books include *Feminism is for Everyone* (2000) and *Outlaw Culture* (2006).

was evident in the pioneering work of Simone de Beauvoir, and was developed by early radical feminists such as Eva Figes, Germaine Greer (see p. 237) and Kate Millett (see p. 236).

Figes's *Patriarchal Attitudes* (1970) drew attention not to the more familiar legal or social disadvantages suffered by women, but to the fact that patriarchal values and beliefs pervade the culture, philosophy, morality and religion of society. In all walks of life and learning, women are portrayed as inferior and subordinate to men, a stereotype of 'femininity' being imposed on women by men. In *The Female Eunuch* (1970), Greer suggested that women are conditioned to a passive sexual role, which has repressed their true sexuality as well as the more active and adventurous side of their personalities. In effect, women have been 'castrated' and turned into sexless objects by the cultural stereotype of the 'eternal feminine'. In *Sexual Politics* (1970), Millett described patriarchy as a 'social constant' running through all political, social and economic structures and found in every historical and contemporary society, as well as in all major religions. The different roles of women and men have their origin in a process of 'conditioning': from a very early age boys and girls are encouraged to conform to very specific gender identities. This process takes place largely within the family – 'patriarchy's chief institution' – but it is also evident in literature, art, public life and the economy. Millett proposed that patriarchy should be challenged through a process of '**consciousness-raising**', an idea influenced by the Black Power movement of the 1960s and early 1970s.

The central feature of radical feminism is the belief that sexual oppression is the most fundamental feature of society and that other forms of injustice – class exploitation, racial hatred and so on – are merely secondary. Gender is thought to be the deepest social cleavage and the most politically significant; more important, for example, than social class, race or nation. Radical feminists have therefore insisted that society be understood as 'patriarchal' to highlight the central role of sex oppression. Patriarchy thus refers to a systematic, institutionalized and pervasive process of gender oppression.

For most radical feminists, patriarchy is a system of politico-cultural oppression, whose origins lie in the structure of family, domestic and personal life. Female liberation thus requires a sexual revolution in which these structures are overthrown and replaced. Such a goal is based on the assumption that human nature is essentially androgynous. However, radical feminism encompasses a number of divergent elements, some of which emphasize the fundamental and unalterable difference between women and men. An example of this is the 'pro-woman' position, particularly strong in France and the USA. This position extols the positive virtues of fertility and motherhood. Women should not try to be 'more like men'. Instead, they should recognize and embrace their sisterhood, the bonds that link them to all other women. The pro-woman position therefore accepts that women's attitudes and values are different from men's, but implies that in certain respects women are superior, possessing the qualities of creativity, sensitivity and caring, which men can never fully appreciate or develop. Such ideas have been associated in particular with ecofeminism, which is examined in Chapter 9.

CONSCIOUSNESS-RAISING
Strategies to remodel social identity and challenge cultural inferiority by an emphasis on pride, self-worth and self-assertion.

The acceptance of deep and possibly unalterable differences between women and men has led some feminists towards cultural feminism, a retreat from the corrupting and aggressive male world of political activism into an apolitical, woman-centred culture and life-style. Conversely, other feminists have become

	Liberal feminism	Radical feminism	Socialist feminism	Black feminism	Postmodern feminism
Key themes	• Individualism • Rights • Legal and political equality	• Patriarchy • Personal is political • Sisterhood	• Class oppression • Bourgeois family • Capitalism and patriarchy linked	• Racism • Multiple oppressions • Differences between women	• Anti-foundationalism • Discourse • Deconstruct gender identities
Core goal	Equal access for women and men to the public realm	Radical transformation of all spheres of life	Restructure economic life to achieve gender equality	Counter interconnected racial, gender and class structures	Embrace fluid, free-floating gender identities

Figure 8.3 Types of feminism

politically assertive and even revolutionary. If sex differences are natural, then the roots of patriarchy lie within the male sex itself. 'All men' are physically and psychologically disposed to oppress 'all women'; in other words, 'men are the enemy'. This clearly leads in the direction of feminist separatism. Men constitute an oppressive 'sex-class' dedicated to aggression, domination and destruction; so the female 'sex-class' is therefore the 'universal victim'. For example, Susan Brownmiller's *Against Our Will* (1975) emphasized that men dominate women through a process of physical and sexual abuse. Men have created an 'ideology of rape', which amounts to a 'conscious process of intimidation by which all men keep all women in a state of fear'. Brownmiller argued that men rape because they can, because they have the 'biological capacity to rape', and that even men who do not rape nevertheless benefit from the fear and anxiety that rape provokes among all women.

Feminists who have pursued this line of argument also believe that it has profound implications for women's personal and sexual conduct. Sexual equality and harmony is impossible because all relationships between women and men must involve oppression. Heterosexual women are therefore thought to be 'male identified', incapable of fully realizing their true nature and becoming 'female identified'. This has led to the development of political lesbianism, which holds that sexual preferences are an issue of crucial political importance for women. Only women who remain celibate or choose lesbianism can regard themselves as 'woman-identified women'. In the slogan attributed to Ti-Grace Atkinson: 'feminism is the theory; lesbianism is the practice' (Charvet, 1982). However, the issues of separatism and lesbianism have deeply divided the women's movement. The majority of feminists see such uncompromising positions as a distorted reflection of the misogyny, or woman-hating, that pervades traditional male society. Instead, they remain faithful to the goal of sexual equality and the belief that it is possible to establish harmony between women and men in a non-sexist society. Hence, they believe that sexual preferences are strictly a matter of personal choice and not a question of political commitment.

Developments in modern feminism

Since the 1970s, it has become increasingly difficult to analyse feminism simply in terms of the threefold division into liberal, socialist and radical traditions. Tensions within the 'core' traditions have sometimes deepened, and, on other occasions, boundaries between the traditions have been blurred. New forms of feminism have also emerged, including third-wave feminism, transfeminism and postfeminism.

Third-wave feminism

The term 'third-wave feminism' has been adopted increasingly since the 1990s by a younger generation of feminist theorists for whom the campaigns and demands of the 1960s and 1970s women's movement have seemed to be of limited relevance to their own lives. This was both because of the emergence of new issues in feminist politics and because of the political and social transformations that second-wave feminism has brought about (Heywood and Drake, 1997). If there is a unifying theme within third-wave feminism it is a more radical engagement with the politics of difference, especially going beyond those strands within radical feminism that emphasize that women are different *from* men by showing a greater concern with differences *between* women. In so doing, third-wave feminists have tried to rectify an over-emphasis within earlier forms of feminism on the aspirations and experiences of middle-class, white women in developed societies, thereby illustrating the extent to which the contemporary women's movement is characterized by diversity and hybridity.

This has allowed the voices of, among others, low-income women, women in the developing world and 'women of colour' to be heard more effectively. Black feminism has been particularly effective in this respect, challenging the tendency within conventional forms of feminism to ignore racial differences and to suggest that women endure a common oppression by virtue of their sex. Especially strong in the USA, black feminism portrays sexism and racism as linked systems of oppression, and highlights the particular and complex range of gender, racial and economic disadvantages that confront women of colour.

In being concerned about issues of 'identity', and the processes through which women's identities are constructed (and can be reconstructed), third-wave feminism also reflects the influence of **poststructuralism**. Influenced particularly by the ideas of the French philosopher, Michel Foucault (1926–84), poststructuralism has drawn attention to the link between power and systems of thought using the idea of **discourse**, or 'discourses of power'. In crude terms, this implies that knowledge is

POSTSTRUCTURALISM
An intellectual tradition, related to postmodernism (see p. 59), that emphasizes that all ideas and concepts are expressed in language that itself is enmeshed in complex relations of power.

DISCOURSE
Human interaction, especially communication: discourse may disclose or illustrate power relations.

power. Poststructuralist or postmodernist feminists question the idea of a fixed female identity, also rejecting the notion that insights can be drawn from a distinctive set of women's experiences. From the poststructural perspective, even the idea of 'woman' may be nothing more than a fiction, as supposedly indisputable biological differences between women and men are, in significant ways, shaped by gendered discourses (not all women are capable of bearing children, for example). However, it is questionable whether the consistent application of poststructural or postmodern analysis is compatible with the maintenance of a distinctively feminist political orientation.

Transfeminism

Transfeminism (also written as 'trans feminism') emerged out of feminism's encounters, from the early 1990s onwards, with the concerns of people who identify themselves as **transgender** or **transsexual**. Although what is called 'trans politics' is not associated with a single or simple theory of gender, its central theme is a rejection of the binary conception of gender, with a stress, instead, on gender and sexual ambiguity, sometimes based on the idea of a gender continuum. People are thus seen as neither women nor men (Beasley, 2005). From the trans perspective, gender is not something ascribed to individuals by society, or imposed on them by cultural stereotypes; instead it is a matter of self-definition based on inner feelings. In this vein, Butler (2006) proposed a concept of gender as a reiterated social performance, rather than the expression of a prior reality.

Such thinking has nevertheless been viewed as deeply problematic by traditional feminists, not least because of the importance they placed on culturally-defined gender in explaining the oppression of women. However, over time, there has been a greater willingness by feminists to take on board issues raised by the trans movement, while supporters of trans politics have increasingly recognized the extent to which its thinking may be applicable to all women (Scott-Dixon, 2006). Not only does this reflect widening support within feminism for a more personalized and nuanced approach to gender, but it also demonstrates a growing awareness of the parallels and overlaps that exist between sexism and **transphobia**.

TRANSGENDER
Denoting or relating to people who do not conform to prevailing expectations about gender, usually by crossing over or moving between gender identities.

TRANSSEXUAL
Denoting or relating to people who do not conform to the sex they were assigned at birth, and who may seek to realign their gender and their sex through medical intervention.

TRANSPHOBIA
Prejudice against or dislike of people who do not conform to prevailing expectations about gender identity.

Postfeminism

The process of deradicalization within feminism has nevertheless been most marked in relation to so-called 'postfeminism', which is defined by a rejection of second-wave feminist issues and themes, rather than by an attempt to update or remodel them. For instance, Camille Paglia (1990) attacked the tendency of feminism to portray women as 'victims', and insisted on the need for women to take greater responsibility for their own sexual and personal conduct. Similarly, in *Fire with Fire* (1994), Naomi Wolf called on women to use the 'new female power', based on the belief that the principal impediments to women's social advancement are psychological rather than political. Confronted by such tendencies, established feminists have sometimes protested against the rise of what they see as 'life-style feminism'. In *The Whole Woman* (1999), Germaine Greer attacked the notion that women are 'having it all', arguing that they have abandoned the goal of liberation and settled for a phoney equality that amounts to assimilation, aping male behaviour and male values. This, perhaps, highlights the capacity of patriarchy to reproduce itself generation after generation, in part by subordinating women through creating bogus forms of emancipation.

Feminism in a global age

The advance of globalizing tendencies in modern society raises two important issues for feminists and feminism. First, to what extent has feminism, or can feminism, become a truly global ideology? Second, how should feminists respond to the process of globalization: is globalization an agent of female emancipation or its enemy? In relation to the first question, feminism has always had a global orientation: the desire to foster sisterhood is, by its nature, transnational. This has certainly been reflected in the worldwide growth of women's groups and organizations, which can now be found across Africa, Asia and Latin America, far beyond feminism's western heartland. This was also underlined by the 1995 Beijing Fourth World Conference on Women, which involved 189 governments and more than 5,000 representatives from some 2,100 non-governmental organizations. However, does evidence of an apparently worldwide women's movement indicate a genuinely global willingness to engage with feminist thinking? The key issue here is: are feminist ideas universally applicable, or are they tainted by Eurocentrism and therefore bear an indelibly western imprint? Postcolonial theorists, in particular, argue that women's rights are essentially a western concept, and may thus not be applicable to the non-western world. From this perspective, sexual equality may be seen both to devalue women's traditional roles as homemakers and mothers, and to undermine traditional institutions and cultural practices. Feminists, for their part, have argued that the postcolonialist emphasis on cultural rights over women's rights amounts to a thinly veiled defence of patriarchy.

On the second issue, the impact of globalization on the role and status of women, contrasting positions have been adopted. Pro-globalization theorists have argued that globalization has opened up opportunities for women in the developing world, not least through the 'feminization of work'. Examples of this include the growth of the Asian electronics industry and the clothing assembly plants in Mexico. The developed world has also witnessed the growth of new 'feminized', or 'pink-collar' jobs, through the expansion of service industries such as retailing, cleaning and data processing. Such trends have, arguably, helped to advance a sexual revolution, not least by giving women higher status and greater financial independence. However, although the number of women in paid work has grown, such trends have also been associated with growing vulnerability and exploitation. Not only are women workers usually cheap (in part because of their seemingly abundant supply), but they also tend to be employed in economic sectors where there are fewer workers' rights and weak labour organizations. Women workers therefore suffer from the double burden of undertaking low-paid work while still being expected to shoulder the burden of domestic responsibilities. Thanks to the advance of neoliberal globalization, this also often happens in the context of reduced state support for health, education and basic food subsidies. Many feminists, particularly those whose feminist orientation is not grounded in liberal individualism, have therefore found a home within the wider anti-globalization or anti-capitalist movement.

(?) QUESTIONS FOR DISCUSSION

- Why and how have feminists challenged conventional notions of politics?
- Why has the distinction between sex and gender been so important to feminist analysis?
- What role does patriarchy play in feminist theory?
- Why do some feminists reject the goal of gender equality?
- To what extent is feminism compatible with liberalism?
- In what sense is radical feminism revolutionary?
- Is socialist feminism a contradiction in terms?
- Are the differences within feminism greater than the similarities?
- Have the core liberal, socialist and radical feminist traditions been exhausted?
- To what extent can feminism engage with the politics of difference?
- Is feminism compatible with trans theory?
- Have the objectives of feminism largely been achieved?

(📖) FURTHER READING

Bryson, V., *Feminist Political Theory: An Introduction*, 2nd edn (2003). A thorough and accessible introduction to the development and range of feminist theories.

Butler, J., *Gender Trouble* (2006). A stimulating book that challenges traditional feminism's 'essentialist' notion of the female, and proposes a concept of gender as reiterated social performance.

Schneir, M., *The Vintage Book of Feminism: The Essential Writings of the Contemporary Women's Movement* (1995). A useful and comprehensive collection of writings from major feminist theorists.

Walter, M., *Feminism: A Very Short Introduction* (2005). A historical account of feminism that explores its earliest roots as well as the issues that have concerned feminism at different points in its development.

CHAPTER

9   Green Ideology

Preview

The term 'green' was first used in connection with environmentally-orientated politics when it was employed to describe conservation and preservation movements which had sprung up in late nineteenth-century USA. The term nevertheless became more prominent from the 1970s onwards, first through its use by environmental organizations such as Greenpeace, established in 1971, but more significantly through the tendency of many emerging environmental parties to brand themselves as 'Green parties'. The most influential of these new parties, and the model on which many other such parties were based, was the German Greens (*Die Grünen*), founded in 1980. From this point onwards, the term was adopted more widely, being used to refer, amongst other things, to green philosophy, green politics and green ideology (sometimes called 'ecologism', 'political ecology' or 'greenism').

Green ideology is based on the belief that nature is an interconnected whole, embracing humans and non-humans, as well as the inanimate world. This has encouraged green thinkers to question (but not necessarily reject) the anthropocentric, or human-centred, assumptions of conventional political ideologies, allowing them to come up with new ideas about, among other things, economics, morality and social organization. Nevertheless, there are different strains and tendencies within green ideology. Some greens are committed to 'shallow' ecology (sometimes viewed as environmentalism, as opposed to ecologism), which attempts to harness the lessons of ecology to human ends and needs, and embraces a 'modernist' or reformist approach to environmental change. 'Deep' ecologists, on the other hand, completely reject any lingering belief that the human species is in some way superior to, or more important than, any other species. Moreover, green ideology has drawn from a variety of other ideologies, notably socialism, anarchism and feminism, thereby acknowledging that the relationship between humankind and nature has an important social dimension. Each of these approaches to the environment offers a different model of the ecologically viable society of the future.

Origins and development

Although modern environmental politics did not emerge until the 1960s and 1970s, ecological ideas can be traced back to much earlier times. Many have suggested that the principles of contemporary green ideology, or ecologism (see p. 247), owe much to ancient pagan religions, which stressed the concept of an Earth Mother, and to eastern religions such as Hinduism, Buddhism and Daoism. However, to a large extent, green ideology was, and remains, a reaction against the process of industrialization. This was evident in the nineteenth century, when the spread of urban and industrial life created a profound nostalgia for an idealized rural existence, as conveyed by novelists such as Thomas Hardy and political thinkers such as the UK libertarian socialist William Morris (1834–96) and Peter Kropotkin (see p. 153). This reaction was often strongest in those countries that had experienced the most rapid and dramatic process of industrialization. For example, Germany's rapid industrialization in the nineteenth century deeply scarred its political culture, creating powerful myths about the purity and dignity of peasant life, and giving rise to a strong 'back to nature' movement among German youth. Such romantic pastoralism was most likely to surface during the twentieth century in right-wing political doctrines, not least the 'Blood and Soil' ideas of the German Nazis.

The growth of green ideology since the 1960s has been provoked by the further and more intense advance of industrialization and urbanization, linked to the emergence of post-material sensibilities among young people in particular. Environmental concern has become more acute because of the fear that economic growth is endangering both the survival of the human race and the very planet it lives on. Such anxieties have been expressed in a growing body of literature. Rachel Carson's *The Silent Spring* (1962), a critique of the damage done to wildlife and the human world by the increased use of pesticides and other agricultural chemicals, is often considered to have been the first book to draw attention to a developing ecological crisis. Other important early works included Ehrlich and Harriman's *How to Be a Survivor* (1971), Goldsmith *et al.*'s *Blueprint for Survival* (1972), the unofficial UN report *Only One Earth* (1972) and the Club of Rome's *The Limits to Growth* (1972).

A new generation of activist pressure groups have also developed – ranging from Greenpeace and Friends of the Earth to animal liberation activists and so-called 'eco-warrior' groups – campaigning on issues such as the dangers of pollution, the dwindling reserves of fossil fuels, deforestation and animal experimentation. Together with established and much larger groups, such as the Worldwide Fund for Nature, this has led to the emergence of a high profile and increasingly influential green movement. From the 1980s onwards, environmental questions have been kept high on the political agenda by green parties, which now exist in most industrialized countries, often modelling themselves on the pioneering efforts of the

PASTORALISM
(German) Literally, a 'world-view'; a distinctive, even unique, set of presuppositions that structure how a people understands and engages emotionally with the world.

Key concept

Ecologism

Ecologism is, broadly, the belief in nature as an interconnected whole, embracing humans and non-humans as well as the inanimate world. A distinction is often drawn between ecologism and environmentalism. 'Environmentalism' refers to a moderate or reformist approach to the environment that responds to ecological crises but without fundamentally questioning conventional assumptions about the natural world. It thus includes the activities of most environmental pressure groups and is a stance that may be adopted by a range of political parties. Ecologism, in contrast, is an ideology in its own right (otherwise known as green ideology), in that it adopts an ecocentric or biocentric perspective that accords priority to nature or the planet, and thus differs from the anthropocentric, or human-centred, perspective of conventional ideological traditions.

German Greens. Environmental issues have also become an increasingly major focus of international concern and activity. Indeed, as discussed in the final section of the chapter, the environment could arguably be regarded as *the* global political issue. The UN Conference on the Human Environment, held in Stockholm in 1972, was the first attempt to establish an international framework to promote a coordinated approach to environmental problems. The idea of 'sustainable development' (see p. 256) was advanced in the 1987 Brundtland Report, a product of the work of the UN World Commission on Environment and Development, and by the Rio 'Earth Summit' in 1992 (see p. 262).

Core themes: return to nature

Thinking about the environment only acquired a fully ideological character through the rise of the green movement. By the end of the 1970s, green thinking was widely viewed as an ideology in its own right, having gone beyond a mere pressure-group-like concern for the environment, commonly called 'environmentalism'. However, green ideology takes ideological thinking in novel and challenging directions. Its starting point is largely or entirely ignored by other political ideologies: the idea of an intrinsic relationship between humankind and nature (or non-human nature, to avoid confusion with the notion of 'human nature'). Green theorists believe that conventional ideologies commit the sad, even comic, mistake of believing that humans are the centrepiece of existence. David Ehrenfeld (1978) called this the 'arrogance of humanism'. Instead of preserving and respecting the Earth and the diverse species that live on it, humans have sought to become, in the words of John Locke (see p. 52), 'the masters and possessors of nature'. Green ideology has therefore uncovered new ideological terrain. It differs from both the 'politics of material

ENVIRONMENTALISM
A concern about the natural environment and particularly about reducing environmental degradation: a policy orientation rather than an ideological stance.

HUMANISM
A philosophy that gives moral priority to the achievement of human needs and ends.

distribution', as practised by the classical ideologies (notably liberalism, conservatism and socialism) and 'identity politics' (see p. 282), as practised by most of the so-called 'new' ideologies that have emerged since the 1960s (such as second-wave feminism, ethnocultural nationalism, religious fundamentalism (see p. 188) and multiculturalism). What makes green ideology deeper and, in a sense, more radical than other political ideologies is that it practises the 'politics of sensibilities'. By attempting to re-orientate people's relationship with and appreciation of 'the non-human' – the world 'out there' – green ideology sets out to do nothing less than transform human consciousness and, in the process, radically reconfigure our moral responsibilities. In order to give expression to this vision of interconnectedness, green thinkers have been forced to search for new concepts and ideas in the realm of science, or rediscover ancient ones from the realms of religion and mythology. The central themes of green ideology are:

- ecology
- holism
- sustainability
- environmental ethics
- from having to being.

Ecology

The central principle of all forms of green thought is **ecology**, a term coined in 1866 by the German zoologist Ernst Haeckel. Ecology developed as a distinct branch of biology through a growing recognition that plants and animals are sustained by self-regulating natural systems – ecosystems – composed of both living and non-living elements. Simple examples of an ecosystem are a field, a forest or, as illustrated in Figure 9.1, a pond. All ecosystems tend towards a state of harmony or equilibrium through a system of self-regulation. Biologists refer to this as **homeostasis**. Food and other resources are recycled, and the population size of animals, insects and plants adjusts naturally to the available food supply. However, such ecosystems are not 'closed' or entirely self-sustaining: each interreacts with other ecosystems. A lake may constitute an ecosystem, but it also needs to be fed with fresh water from tributaries, and receive warmth and energy from the sun. In turn, the lake provides water and food for species living along its shores, including human communities. The natural world is therefore made up of a complex web of ecosystems, the largest of which is the global ecosystem, commonly called the 'ecosphere' or 'biosphere'.

ECOLOGY
The study of the relationship between living organisms and the environment; ecology stresses the network of relationships that sustains all forms of life.

HOMEOSTASIS
The tendency of a system, especially the physiological systems of higher animals, to maintain internal equilibrium.

The development of scientific ecology radically altered our understanding of the natural world and of the place of human beings within it. Ecology conflicts quite dramatically with the notion of humankind as 'the master' of nature, and instead suggests that a delicate

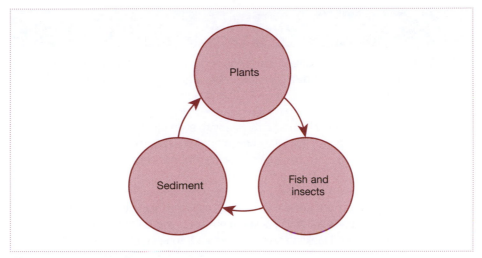

Figure 9.1   **A pond as an ecosystem**

network of interrelationships that had hitherto been ignored sustains each human community, indeed the entire human species. Green thinkers argue that humankind currently faces the prospect of environmental disaster precisely because, in its passionate but blinkered pursuit of material wealth, it has upset the 'balance of nature' and endangered the very ecosystems that make human life possible. This has happened in a broad variety of ways. These include the exponential growth in the world's human population; the depletion of finite and irreplaceable fuel resources such as coal, oil and natural gas; the eradication of tropical rain forests that help clean the air and regulate the Earth's climate; the pollution of rivers, lakes and forests and the air itself; the use of chemical, hormonal and other additives to foodstuffs; and the threat to biodiversity that has resulted from the thousandfold increase in species extinction that has coincided with the dominance of the human species.

Green ideology provides a radically different vision of nature and the place of human beings within it, one that favours **ecocentrism** and challenges **anthropocentrism**. However, green or environmental thinkers have applied ecological ideas in different ways, and sometimes drawn quite different conclusions. The most important distinction in the environmental movement is between what Arne Naess (see p. 265) termed '**shallow ecology**' and '**deep ecology**'. The 'shallow' or

ECOCENTRISM
A theoretical orientation that gives priority to the maintenance of ecological balance rather than the achievement of human ends.

ANTHROPOCENTRISM
A belief that human needs and interests are of overriding moral and philosophical importance; the opposite of ecocentrism.

SHALLOW ECOLOGY
A green ideological perspective that harnesses the lessons of ecology to human needs and ends, and is associated with values such as sustainability and conservation.

DEEP ECOLOGY
A green ideological perspective that rejects anthropocentrism and gives priority to the maintenance of nature, and is associated with values such as biocentric equality, diversity and decentralization.

PERSPECTIVES ON... NATURE

LIBERALS see nature as a resource to satisfy human needs, and thus rarely question human dominion over it. Lacking value in itself, nature is invested with value only when it is transformed by human labour, or when it is harnessed to human ends.

CONSERVATIVES often portray nature as threatening, even cruel, characterized by an amoral struggle and harshness that also shapes human existence. Humans may be seen as part of nature within a 'great chain of being', their superiority nevertheless being enshrined in their status as custodians of nature.

SOCIALISTS, like liberals, have viewed and treated nature as merely a resource. However, a romantic or pastoral tradition within socialism has also extolled the beauty, harmony and richness of nature, and looks to human fulfilment through a closeness to nature.

ANARCHISTS have often embraced a view of nature that stresses unregulated harmony and growth. Nature therefore offers a model of simplicity and balance, which humans would be wise to apply to social organization in the form of social ecology.

FASCISTS have often adopted a dark and mystical view of nature that stresses the power of instinct and primal life forces, nature being able to purge humans of their decadent intellectualism. Nature is characterized by brutal struggle and cyclical regeneration.

FEMINISTS generally hold nature to be creative and benign. By virtue of their fertility and disposition to nurture, women are often thought to be close to nature and in tune with natural forces, while men, creatures of culture, are out of step or in conflict with nature.

GREENS, particularly deep ecologists, regard nature as an interconnected whole, embracing humans and non-humans as well as the inanimate world. Nature is sometimes seen as a source of knowledge and 'right living', human fulfilment coming from a closeness to and respect for nature, not from the attempt to dominate it.

'humanist' perspective accepts the lessons of ecology but uses them essentially to further human needs and ends. In other words, it preaches that if we conserve and cherish the natural world, it will continue to sustain human life. This amounts to a form of 'light' or 'enlightened' anthropocentrism, and is reflected in a concern with issues such as cutting back on the use of finite, non-renewable resources and reducing pollution. While some regard such a stance as a form of 'weak' ecologism, others classify it as environmentalism to distinguish it more clearly from ecologism. The 'deep' perspective, however, advances a form of 'strong' ecologism that completely rejects any lingering belief that the human species is in some way superior to, or more important than, any other species, or indeed nature itself. It is based on the more

TENSIONS WITHIN... GREEN IDEOLOGY

'Shallow' ecology	VS	'Deep' ecology
environmentalism	⟷	ecologism
'light' anthropocentricism	⟷	ecocentrism
science	⟷	mysticism
humankind	⟷	nature
limited holism	⟷	radical holism
instrumental value	⟷	value-in-nature
modified humanism	⟷	biocentric equality
animal welfare	⟷	animal rights
sustainable growth	⟷	anti-growth
personal development	⟷	ecological consciousness

challenging idea that the purpose of human life is to help sustain nature, and not the other way around. (Deep ecology is discussed in greater detail on pp. 268–70.)

Holism

Traditional political ideologies have typically assumed that human beings are the masters of the natural world, and have therefore regarded nature as little more than an economic resource. In that sense, they have been part of the problem and not part of the solution. In *The Turning Point* (1982), Fritjof Capra traced the origin of such ideas to the scientists and philosophers, such as René Descartes (1596–1650) and Isaac Newton (1642–1727). The world had previously been seen as organic; however, these seventeenth-century philosophers portrayed it as a machine, whose parts could be analysed and understood through the newly discovered scientific method. Science enabled remarkable advances to be made in human knowledge and provided the basis for the development of modern industry and technology. So impressive were the fruits of science, that intellectual inquiry in the modern world has come to be dominated by scientism. However, Capra argued that orthodox science, what he referred to as the 'Cartesian–Newtonian paradigm', amounts to the philosophical basis of the contemporary environmental crisis. Science treats nature as a machine, implying that, like any other machine, it can be tinkered with, repaired, improved on or even replaced. If human beings are to learn that

SCIENTISM
The belief that scientific method is the only value-free and objective means of establishing truth, and is applicable to all fields of learning.

they are part of the natural world rather than its masters, Capra suggested that this fixation with the 'Newtonian world-machine' must be overthrown and replaced by a new paradigm.

In searching for this new paradigm, ecological thinkers have been attracted to a variety of ideas and theories, drawn from both modern science and ancient myths and religions. However, the unifying theme among these ideas is the notion of **holism**. The term 'holism' was coined in 1926 by Jan Smuts, a Boer general and twice prime minister of South Africa. He used it to describe the idea that the natural world could only be understood as a whole and not through its individual parts. Smuts believed that science commits the sin of reductionism: it reduces everything it studies to separate parts and tries to understand each part in itself. In contrast, holism suggests that each part only has meaning in relation to other parts, and ultimately in relation to the whole. For example, a holistic approach to medicine would consider not just physical ailments but would see these as a manifestation of imbalances within the patient as a whole, taking account of psychological, emotional, social and environmental factors.

Although many green thinkers criticize science, others have suggested that modern science may offer a new paradigm for human thought. Capra, for example, argued that the Cartesian–Newtonian world-view has now been abandoned by many scientists, particularly by physicists like himself. During the twentieth century, with the development of so-called 'new physics', physics moved a long way beyond the mechanistic and reductionist ideas of Newton. The breakthrough was achieved at the beginning of the twentieth century by the German-born US physicist Albert Einstein (1879–1955), whose theory of relativity fundamentally challenged the traditional concepts of time and space. Einstein's work was taken further by quantum theory, developed by physicists such as Niels Bohr (1885–1952) and Verner Heisenberg (1901–76). In quantum theory the physical world is understood not as a collection of individual molecules, atoms or even particles, but as a **system**, or, more accurately, a network of systems. A systems view of the world concentrates not on individual building blocks, but on the principles of organization within the system. It therefore stresses the relationships within the system and the integration of its various elements within the whole.

HOLISM
A belief that the whole is more important than its parts; holism implies that understanding is gained by studying relationships among the parts.

SYSTEM
A collection of parts that operate through a network of reciprocal interactions and thereby constitute a complex whole.

An alternative and particularly fertile source of new concepts and theories has been religion. In *The Tao of Physics* (1975), Capra drew attention to important parallels between the ideas of modern physics and those of eastern mysticism. He argued that religions such as Hinduism, Daoism and Buddhism, particularly Zen Buddhism, have long preached the unity or oneness of all things, a discovery that western science only made in the twentieth century. Many in the green movement have been attracted by eastern mysticism, seeing in it both a philosophy that gives expression to ecological wisdom and a way of life that encourages compassion for fellow human beings, other species and the natural world. Other writers believe that ecological principles are embodied in monotheistic religions such as Christianity, Judaism and Islam, which regard both humankind and nature as products of divine creation. In such circumstances, human beings are viewed as God's stewards on Earth, being invested thereby with a duty to cherish and preserve the planet.

However, perhaps the most influential concepts for modern greens have been developed by looking back to pre-Christian spiritual ideas. Primitive religions often drew no distinction between human and other forms of life, and, for that matter, little distinction between living and non-living objects. All things are alive: stones, rivers, mountains and even the Earth itself, often conceived of as 'Mother Earth'. The idea of an Earth Mother has been particularly important for green thinkers trying to articulate a new relationship between human beings and the natural world, especially so for those sympathetic to ecofeminism, examined later in the chapter.

In a similar vein, James Lovelock (see p. 265) developed the idea of the Gaia hypothesis (see p. 253). The idea of Gaia has developed into an 'ecological ideology' that conveys the powerful message that human beings must respect the health of the planet, and act to conserve its beauty and resources. It also contains a revolutionary vision of the relationship between the animate and inanimate world. However, Gaia philosophy does not always correspond to the concerns of the green movement. Humanist ecologists have typically wished to change policies and attitudes in order to ensure the continued survival of the human species. Gaia, on the other hand, is non-human, and Gaia theory suggests that the health of the planet matters more than that of any individual species living on it at present. Lovelock has suggested that those species that have prospered have been ones that have helped Gaia to regulate its own existence, while any species that poses a threat to the delicate balance of Gaia, as green thinkers argue that humans currently do, is likely to be extinguished. Lovelock has nevertheless been strongly committed to science, and, contrary to the views of many in the environmental movement, has stressed the importance of nuclear power in providing a solution to environmental problems.

Key concept

Gaia Hypothesis

The Gaia hypothesis advances the idea that the Earth is best understood as a living entity that acts to maintain its own existence (Gaia is the name of the Greek goddess of the Earth). The basis for the Gaia hypothesis is that the Earth's biosphere, atmosphere, oceans and soil exhibit precisely the same kind of self-regulating behaviour that characterizes other forms of life. Gaia has maintained 'homeostasis', a state of dynamic balance, despite the major changes that have taken place in the solar system. The most dramatic evidence of this is the fact that although the sun has warmed up by more than 25 per cent since life began, the temperature on Earth and the composition of its atmosphere have remained virtually unchanged.

Sustainability

Green thinkers argue that the ingrained assumption of conventional political creeds, articulated by virtually all mainstream political parties (so-called 'grey' parties), is that human life has unlimited possibilities for material growth and prosperity. Indeed, green thinkers commonly lump capitalism and socialism together, and portray them both as examples of 'industrialism'. A particularly influential metaphor for the environmental movement has been the idea of 'spaceship Earth', because this emphasizes the notion of limited and exhaustible wealth. The idea that Earth should be thought of as a spaceship was first suggested by Kenneth Boulding (1966). Boulding argued that human beings have traditionally acted as though they live in a 'cowboy economy', an economy with unlimited opportunities, like the American West during the frontier period. He suggested that this encourages, as it did in the American West, 'reckless, exploitative, and violent behaviour'. However, as a spaceship is a capsule, it is a 'closed' system. 'Open' systems receive energy or inputs from outside; for example, all ecosystems on Earth – ponds, forests, lakes and seas – are sustained by the sun. However, 'closed' systems, as the Earth itself becomes when it is thought of as a spaceship, show evidence of 'entropy'. All 'closed' systems tend to decay or disintegrate because they are not sustained by external inputs. Ultimately, however wisely and carefully human beings behave, the Earth, the sun, and indeed all planets and stars, will be exhausted and die. When the 'entropy law' is applied to social and economic issues it produces very radical conclusions.

ENTROPY
A tendency towards decay or disintegration, exhibited by all 'closed' systems.

FOSSIL FUELS
Fuels that are formed from the decomposition of buried dead organisms, making them rich in carbon; examples include oil, natural gas and coal.

No issue reflects the law of entropy more clearly than the 'energy crisis'. Industrialization and mass affluence have been made possible by the exploitation of coal, gas and oil reserves, providing fuel for power stations, factories, motor cars, aeroplanes and so on. These fuels are fossil fuels. They are also non-renewable: once used up they cannot be replaced. In *Small Is Beautiful* (1973), E. F. Schumacher (see p. 265) argued that human beings have made the mistake of regarding energy as an 'income' that is being constantly

Key concept

Industrialism

The term 'industrialism', as used by environmental theorists, relates to a 'super-ideology' that encompasses capitalism and socialism, left-wing and right-wing thought. As an economic system, industrialism is characterized by large-scale production, the accumulation of capital and relentless growth. As a philosophy, it is dedicated to materialism, utilitarian values, absolute faith in science and a worship of technology. Many green thinkers thus see industrialism as 'the problem'. Ecosocialists, however, blame capitalism rather than industrialism (which ignores important issues such as the role of ownership, profit and the market), while ecofeminists argue that industrialism has its origins in patriarchy.

topped-up each week or each month, rather than as 'natural capital' that they are forced to live off. This mistake has allowed energy demands to soar, especially in the industrialized West, at a time when finite fuel resources are, green thinkers warn, close to depletion and unlikely to last to the end of the twenty-first century. As the spaceship draws towards the close of the 'fossil-fuel age', it approaches disintegration because, as yet, there are insufficient alternative sources of energy to compensate for the loss of coal, oil and gas.

Not only have humans failed to recognize that they live within the constraints of a 'closed' ecosystem, but they have also been unwisely cavalier in plundering its resources. Garrett Hardin (1968) developed a particularly influential model to explain why over-exploitation of environmental resources has occurred, in the form of the 'tragedy of the commons'. The parable of the 'tragedy of the commons' sheds light on the behaviour of individuals within the community, the actions of groups within society, and the strategies adopted by states within the international system. However, the parable also highlights why it is often so difficult to tackle environmental problems at any level. Any viable solution to the environmental crisis must offer a means of dealing with the 'tragedy of the commons'.

Nevertheless, green economics is not only about warnings and threats; it is also about solutions. Entropy may be an inevitable process; however, its effects can be slowed down or delayed considerably if governments and private citizens respect ecological principles. Green thinkers argue that the human species will only survive and prosper if it recognizes that it is merely one element of a complex biosphere, and that only a healthy, balanced biosphere will sustain human life. Policies and actions must therefore be judged by the principle of '**sustainability**'. Sustainability sets clear limits on human ambitions and material dreams because it requires that production does as little damage as possible to the fragile global ecosystem. For example, a sustainable energy policy must be based on a dramatic reduction in the use of fossil fuels and a

> **SUSTAINABILITY**
> The capacity of a system to maintain its health and continue in existence over a period of time.

Key concept
Tragedy of the Commons

The idea of the 'tragedy of the commons' draws parallels between global environmental degradation and the fate of common land before the introduction of enclosures. Common land or common fisheries stocks encourage individuals to act in rationally self-interested ways, each exploiting the resources available to satisfy their needs and the needs of their families and communities. However, the collective impact of such behaviour may be devastating, as the vital resources on which all depend become depleted or despoiled. Thus, as Hardin (1968) put it, 'Freedom in a commons brings ruin to all.' The parable of the 'tragedy of the commons' is usually used to justify tackling environmental problems either by strengthening political authority or by restricting population growth.

search for alternative, renewable energy sources such as solar energy, wind power and wave power. These are by their very nature sustainable and can be treated as 'income' rather than 'natural capital'.

Sustainability, however, requires not merely the implementation of government controls or tax regimes to ensure a more enlightened use of natural resources, but, at a deeper level, the adoption of an alternative approach to economic activity. This is precisely what Schumacher (1973) sought to offer in his idea of 'Buddhist economics'. For Schumacher, Buddhist economics is based on the principle of 'right livelihood' and stands in stark contrast to conventional economic theories, which assume that individuals are nothing more than 'utility maximizers'. Buddhists believe that, in addition to generating goods and services, production facilitates personal growth by developing skills and talents, and helps to overcome egocentredness by forging social bonds and encouraging people to work together. Such a view moves economics a long way from its conventional obsession with wealth creation, creating what Schumacher called economics 'as if people mattered'.

There is nevertheless considerable debate about what sustainability implies in practice. Reformist or **modernist ecologists** support 'weak' sustainability, which tries to reconcile ecology with economic growth through getting richer but at a slower pace. One way in which this could be achieved would be through changes to the tax system, either to penalize and discourage pollution or to reduce the use of finite resources. However, radical ecologists, who include both **social ecologists** and deep ecologists, support (if to different degrees) 'strong' sustainability, which places far greater stress on preserving 'natural capital' and is more critical of economic growth. If, as some radical ecologists argue, the origin of the ecological crisis lies in materialism, consumerism and a fixation with economic growth, the solution lies in 'zero growth' and the construction of a 'post-industrial age' in which

MODERNIST ECOLOGY
A reformist tendency within green politics that seeks to reconcile ecology with the key features of capitalist modernity.

SOCIAL ECOLOGY
A broad tendency within green politics that links ecological sustainability to radical social change, or the eco-anarchist principle that human communities should be structured according to ecological principles.

Key concept

Sustainable Development

Sustainable development refers to 'development that meets the needs of the present without compromising the ability of future generations to meet their own needs' (Brundtland Report, 1987). It therefore embodies two concepts: (1) the concept of need, particularly the essential needs of the world's poor; and (2) the concept of limitations, especially related to the environment's ability to meet future as well as present needs. So-called *weak* sustainability takes economic growth to be desirable but simply insists that growth must be limited to ensure that ecological costs do not threaten its long-term sustainability, allowing 'human capital' to be substituted for 'natural capital'. *Strong* sustainability rejects the pro-growth implications of weak sustainability, and focuses just on the need to preserve and sustain 'natural capital'.

people live in small, rural communities and rely on craft skills. This could mean a fundamental and comprehensive rejection of industry and modern technology – literally a 'return to nature'.

Environmental ethics

Green politics, in all its forms, is concerned with extending moral thinking in a number of novel directions. This is because conventional ethical systems are clearly anthropocentric, orientated around the pleasure, needs and interests of human beings. In such philosophies, the non-human world is invested with value only to the extent that it satisfies human ends. One ethical issue that even humanist or 'shallow' ecologists grapple with extensively is the question of our moral obligations towards future generations (see p. 258). However, the notion of cross-generational justice has also been criticized. Conventional moral thinkers have sometimes argued that, as all rights depend on reciprocity, it is absurd to endow people who have yet to be born with rights that impose duties on people currently alive, since the unborn cannot discharge any duties towards the living. Moreover, in view of the potentially unlimited size of future generations, the burdens imposed by 'futurity' are, in practical terms, incalculable. The present generation may, therefore, either be making sacrifices for the benefit of future generations who may prove to be much better off than themselves, or their sacrifices may be entirely inadequate to meet future needs.

An alternative approach to environmental ethics involves applying moral standards and values developed in relation to human beings to other species and organisms. The most familiar attempt to do this is in the form of '**animal rights**'. Peter Singer's (1976) case for animal welfare had considerable impact on the growing animal liberation movement. Singer argued that an altruistic concern for the well-being of other species derives from the fact that, as sentient beings, they are capable of suffering. Drawing on utilitarianism, he pointed out that animals, like humans, have an interest in avoiding physical pain, and he therefore condemned any attempt to place the interests of humans above those of animals as '**speciesism**'. However, altruistic concern for other species does not imply equal treatment. Singer's argument does not apply to non-sentient life forms such as trees, rocks and rivers. Moreover, the moral imperative is the avoidance of suffering, with special consideration being given to more developed and self-aware animals, notably to the great apes. On the other hand, Singer's argument implies that a reduced moral consideration should be given to human foetuses and mentally impaired people who have no capacity for suffering (Singer, 1993).

Nevertheless, the moral stance of deep ecology goes much further, in particular by suggesting that nature has value in its own right; that is, intrinsic value. From this perspective, environmental ethics have nothing

ANIMAL RIGHTS
Moral entitlements that are based on the belief that as animals are non-human 'persons', they deserve the same consideration (at least in certain areas) as human beings.

SPECIESISM
A belief in the superiority of one species over other species, through the denial of their moral significance.

Key concept
Future Generations

The idea that the needs and interests of 'future generations', those yet to be born, should be taken into account in ethical reasoning is deeply rooted in green thought because the ecological impact of present actions may not be felt for decades or even centuries. What can be called cross-generational justice can be seen as a 'natural duty', an extension of a moral concern for our children and, by extension, their children, and so on. Concern for future generations has also been linked to the idea of 'ecological stewardship'. This is the notion that the present generation is merely the custodian of the wealth that has been generated by past generations and so is obliged to conserve it for the benefit of future generations.

to do with human instrumentality and cannot be articulated simply through the extension of human values to the non-human world. Goodin (1992), for instance, attempted to develop a 'green theory of value', which holds that resources should be valued precisely because they result from natural processes rather than human activity. However, since this value stems from the fact that the natural landscape helps people to see 'some sense and pattern in their lives' and to appreciate 'something larger' than themselves, it embodies a residual humanism that fails to satisfy some deep ecologists. The distinctive ethical stance of deep ecology is discussed at greater length later in the chapter.

From having to being

Green ideology seeks not only to revise conventional moral thinking, but also to reshape our understanding of happiness and human well-being. In particular, green thinkers have advanced a critique of **materialism** and consumerism. Consumerism is a psycho-cultural phenomenon whereby personal happiness is equated with the consumption of material possessions, giving rise to what the German psychoanalyst and social philosopher Erich Fromm (1979) called a 'having' attitude of mind. For green theorists, 'having' – the disposition to seek fulfilment in acquisition and control – is deficient in at least two respects. First, it tends to undermine, rather than enhance, psychological and emotional well-being. As modern advertising and marketing techniques tend to create ever-greater material desires, they leave consumers in a constant state of dissatisfaction because, however much they acquire and consume, they always want more. Consumerism thus works not through the satisfaction of desires, but through the generation of new desires, keeping people in an unending state of neediness, want and aspiration. Such thinking is sustained by the emerging discipline of 'happiness economics', which suggests that once citizens enjoy fairly comfortable living standards it is not absolute wealth but relative wealth that affects subjective well-being (Layard, 2011).

MATERIALISM
An emphasis on material needs and their satisfaction, usually implying a link between pleasure or happiness and the level of material consumption.

Key concept

Postmaterialism

Postmaterialism is a theory that explains the nature of political concerns and values in terms of levels of economic development. It is based loosely on Abraham Maslow's (1908–70) 'hierarchy of needs', which places self-esteem and self-actualization above material or economic needs. Postmaterialism assumes that conditions of material scarcity breed egoistical and acquisitive values, meaning that politics is dominated by economic issues (who gets what). However, in conditions of widespread prosperity, individuals tend to express more interest in 'postmaterial' or 'quality of life' issues. These are typically concerned with morality, political justice and personal fulfilment, and include gender equality, world peace, racial harmony, ecology and animal rights.

Second, materialism and consumerism provide the cultural basis for environmental degradation. This occurs as the 'consumer society' encourages people to place short-term economic considerations ahead of longer-term ecological concerns, in which case nature is nothing other than a commodity or resource. In this light, green ideology can be seen to be associated with the ideas of postmaterialism and anti-consumerism.

In line with green ideology's postmaterial orientation, green thinkers have tended to view human development as dangerously unbalanced: human beings are blessed with massive know-how and material wealth, but possess precious little 'know-why'. Humankind has acquired the ability to fulfil its material ambitions, but not the wisdom to question whether these ambitions are sensible, or even sane. As Schumacher (1973) warned, 'Man is now too clever to survive without wisdom.' However, some 'shallow' or humanistic ecologists have serious misgivings when this quest for wisdom draws green ideology into the realms of religious mysticism or New Age ideas. Many greens, particularly those who subscribe to deep ecology, have nevertheless embraced world-views that are quite different from those that have traditionally dominated political thought in the developed West. This, they argue, is the basis of the 'paradigm shift' that green ideology aims to bring about, and without which it is doomed to repeat the mistakes of the 'old' politics because it cannot move beyond its concepts and assumptions.

In their search for an alternative model of human well-being, green theorists have generally emphasized the importance of 'quality of life' issues and concerns, thereby divorcing happiness from a simple link to material acquisition. Such thinking is taken most seriously by eco-anarchists, ecofeminists and especially deep ecologists. In line with Fromm, they have been more willing to contrast 'having' with 'being', the latter representing satisfaction that is derived from experience and sharing, leading to personal growth, even spiritual awareness. The key feature of 'being' as an attitude of mind is that it seeks to transcend the self, or individual ego, and to recognize that each person is intrinsically linked to all other living things, and, indeed, to the universe itself. The Australian philosopher Warwick Fox (1990) claimed to go beyond deep ecology in embracing 'transpersonal ecology', the essence of which is the realization that 'things are', that human beings and all other entities are part of a single unfolding reality. For Naess, self-realization is attained through a broader and deeper 'identification with others'. Such ideas have often been shaped by Eastern religions, most profoundly by Buddhism, which has been portrayed as an ecological philosophy in its own right. One of the key doctrines of Buddhism is the idea of 'no self', the notion that the individual ego is a myth or delusion, and that awakening or enlightenment involves transcending the self and recognizing the oneness of life.

Types of green ideology

Deep ecologists typically dismiss conventional political creeds as merely different versions of anthropocentrism, each embodying an anti-nature bias. They claim to have developed an entirely new ideological paradigm (although many reject the term 'ideology' because of its association with human-centred thinking), developed through the radical application of ecological and holistic principles. Nevertheless, other ecological or environmental thinkers have drawn inspiration, to a greater or lesser extent, from established political traditions. Such a stance is based on the belief that these traditions contain values and doctrines that are capable of accommodating a positive view of non-human nature, and of shedding light on why the ecological crisis has come about and how it can be tackled. In this sense, green ideology, like nationalism and feminism, can be regarded as a cross-cutting ideology. At different times, conservatives, liberals, socialists, anarchists and feminists have claimed a special sympathy with the environment, associating green ideology with very different goals and themes (see Figure 9.2, p. 267). The most significant sub-traditions within green ideology are:

- modernist ecology
- social ecology
- deep ecology.

Modernist ecology

Modernist or reformist ecology refers to the form of green ideology that is practised by most environmental pressure groups and by a growing range of mainstream political parties. Modernist ecology is reformist in that it seeks to advance ecological principles and promote 'environmentally sound' practices, but without rejecting the central features of capitalist modernity – individual self-seeking, materialism, economic growth and so on. It is thus very clearly a form of 'shallow' or humanist ecology. The key feature of modernist ecology is the recognition that there are environmental 'limits to growth', in the sense that pollution, increased CO_2 emissions, the exhaustion of non-renewable energy sources and other forms of environmental degradation ultimately threaten prosperity and economic performance. The watchword of this form of green ideology is therefore sustainable development (in the sense of 'weak' sustainability) or, more specifically, environmentally-sustainable capitalism. As, in economic terms, this means 'getting richer more slowly', modernist ecology extends moral and philosophical sensibilities only in modest directions. Indeed, it is often condemned by more radical ecologists as hopelessly compromised: part of the problem rather than part of the solution.

The two main ideological influences on modernist ecology are liberalism and conservatism. Liberalism has, at best, an ambivalent relationship with green ideology. Radical ecologists criticize individualism (see p. 27) as a stark example of anthropocentrism, and condemn utilitarianism (see p. 46), the moral philosophy that underpins much of classical liberalism, on the grounds that it equates happiness with material consumption. On a larger scale, liberalism's atomistic view of society has been seen as the political expression of the 'Cartesian–Newtonian paradigm' (Capra, 1982). However, the stress found within modern liberalism on self-realization and developmental individualism can be said to sustain a form of 'enlightened' anthropocentrism, which encourages people to take into account long-term, and not merely short-term, interests, and to favour 'higher' pleasures (including an appreciation of the natural world) over 'lower' pleasures (such as material consumption). This can be seen, for example, in John Stuart Mill's (see p. 53) criticism of rampant industrialization and his defence of a stationary population and a steady-state economy, on the grounds that the contemplation of nature is an indispensable aspect of human fulfilment.

Conservatives, for their part, have evinced a sympathy for environmental issues, on two main grounds. First, ecoconservatism has drawn on a romantic and nostalgic attachment to a rural way of life threatened by the growth of towns and cities. It is clearly a reaction against industrialization and the idea of 'progress'. It does not envisage the construction of a post-industrial society, founded on the principles of cooperation and ecology, but rather a return to, or the maintenance of, a more familiar pre-industrial one. Such environmental sensibilities typically focus on the issue of conservation and on attempts to protect the natural heritage – woodlands, forests and so on – as well as the architectural and social heritage. The conservation of nature is therefore linked to a defence of traditional values and institutions.

Second, conservatives have advocated market-based solutions to environmental problems, even espousing the idea of '**green capitalism**'. Market-based environmental solutions include the adoption of tax structures that incentivize 'eco-friendly' individual and corporate behaviour, and emissions trading schemes

GREEN CAPITALISM
The idea that a reliance on the capitalist market mechanism will deliver ecologically sustainable outcomes, usually linked to assumptions about capitalism's consumer responsiveness.

such as that proposed by the 1997 Kyoto Protocol on climate change. The theory of green capitalism has two features. The first is the assumption that the market mechanism can and will respond to pressure from more ecologically aware consumers by forcing firms to produce 'environmentally sound' goods and adopt 'green' technologies. Such thinking relies on the idea of

POLITICAL IDEOLOGIES IN ACTION . . .
The Rio 'Earth Summit'

EVENTS: In June 1992, the UN Conference on Environment and Development (better known as the 'Earth Summit') took place in Rio de Janeiro, Brazil. With more than 150 states in attendance, together with 1,400 non-governmental organizations (NGOs) and 8,000 journalists, this was the largest international conference so far held. The conference approved a comprehensive plan to promote sustainable development, at the heart of which was the Framework Agreement on Climate Change. The Framework Agreement called for greenhouse gases to be stabilized at safe levels on the basis of equity and in accordance with states' 'common but differentiated responsibilities and respective capabilities'.

SIGNIFICANCE: The Rio 'Earth Summit' was a milestone conference in establishing the idea of environmental limits to growth, thereby challenging the then-dominant belief that markets effectively maintain a balance between population, resources and the environment. Moreover, it was the first international conference to give significant attention to the issue of climate change, helping to push climate change to the top of the international environmental agenda. In so doing, it was supported by both the burgeoning influence of environmental NGOs and a growing body of scientific evidence upholding the notion of anthropocentric climate change. The Framework Agreement on Climate Change was of particular importance, in that it provided the basis for all subsequent international agreements on the issue, including the Kyoto Protocol, negotiated in 1997, the only conference to date to set binding targets to reduce greenhouse gas emissions.

However, effective international action on environmental matters has been difficult to achieve, especially in relation to climate change, where greenhouse gas emissions have continued to increase. Even the Kyoto process had a limited impact, as binding emission targets only applied to developed states, and, even then, were rejected by major emitters such as the USA, Russia and Australia. The key problem is that, in the absence of a supranational global authority, states will only cooperate in areas where their national interests overlap, and, in the case of environmental issues, these are rare. This is because tackling climate change imposes significant costs on states in terms of investment in 'green' technologies, but especially through accepting lower levels of economic growth. Confronted by a trade-off between ecology and the economy, states are encouraged to be 'free riders', enjoying the benefits of a healthier atmosphere without having to pay for them.

consumer sovereignty and acknowledges the impact of the trend towards so-called 'responsible consumption'.

The second way in which capitalism is supposedly 'green' is linked to the idea that long-term corporate profitability can only be achieved in a context of sustainable development. Capitalism, in short, has no interest in destroying the planet.

> **CONSUMER SOVEREIGNTY**
> The notion, based on the theory of competitive capitalism, that consumer choice is the ultimately determining factor within a market economy.

However, there are important differences within modernist ecology over the proper balance between the state and capitalism. Although some supporters of green capitalism favour unregulated market competition, most modernist ecologists support a managed capitalist system in which environmental degradation is treated as an externality, or 'social cost', that can only be dealt with effectively by government.

Social ecology

Social ecology is a term coined by Murray Bookchin (see p. 265) to refer to the idea that ecological principles can and should be applied to social organization, in which case an anarchist commune can be thought of as an ecosystem. However, the term can also be used more broadly to refer to a range of ideas, each of which recognizes that environmental degradation is, in some way, linked to existing social structures. The advance of ecological principles therefore requires a process of radical social change. Social ecology, thus defined, encompasses three distinct traditions:

- ecosocialism
- eco-anarchism
- ecofeminism.

Ecosocialism

There is a distinct socialist strand within the green movement, which has been particularly pronounced among the German Greens, many of whose leaders have been former members of far-left groups. Ecosocialism has drawn from the pastoral socialism of thinkers such as William Morris, who extolled the virtues of small-scale craft communities living close to nature. However, it has more usually been associated with Marxism. For example, Rudolph Bahro (1982), argued that the root cause of the environmental crisis is capitalism. The natural world has been despoiled by industrialization, but this is merely a consequence of capitalism's relentless search for profit. In this view, capitalism's anti-ecological bias derives from a number of sources. These include that private property encourages the belief that humans are dominant over nature; that the market economy 'commodifies' nature, in the sense that it turns it into something that only has exchange-value and so can be bought and sold; and that the capitalist system breeds materialism and consumerism, and so leads to relentless growth. From this perspective, the idea of 'green capitalism' is a contradiction in terms. Any attempt to improve the environment must therefore involve a process of radical social change, some would say a social revolution.

The core theme of ecosocialism is the idea that capitalism is the enemy of the environment, while socialism is its friend. However, as with socialist feminism, such a formula embodies tension between two elements, this time between 'red' and 'green' priorities. If environmental catastrophe is nothing more than a by-product of capitalism, environmental problems are best tackled by abolishing capitalism, or at least taming it. Therefore, ecologists should not form separate green parties or set up narrow environmental organizations, but work within the larger socialist movement and address the real issue: the economic system. On the other hand, socialism has also been seen as another 'pro-production' political creed: it espouses exploiting the wealth of the planet, albeit for the good of humanity, rather than just the capitalist class. Socialist parties have been slow to adopt environmental policies because they, like other 'grey' parties, continue to base their electoral appeal on the promise of economic growth. As a result, ecologists have often been reluctant to subordinate the green to the red, hence the proclamation by the German Greens that they are 'neither left nor right'.

Ecosocialists argue that socialism is naturally ecological. If wealth is owned in common it will be used in the interests of all, which means in the long-term interests of humanity. However, it is unlikely that ecological problems can be solved simply by a change in the ownership of wealth. This was abundantly demonstrated by the experience of state socialism in the Soviet Union and eastern Europe, which produced some of the world's most intractable environmental problems. Examples include the Aral Sea in Central Asia, once the fourth biggest lake in the world, which has shrunk to 10 per cent of its original size as a result of the re-routing of two rivers; and the Chernobyl nuclear explosion in the Ukraine in 1986.

Eco-anarchism

Perhaps the ideology that has the best claim to being environmentally sensitive is anarchism. Some months before the publication of Rachel Carson's *The Silent Spring*, Murray Bookchin brought out *Our Synthetic Environment* ([1962] 1975). Many in the green movement also acknowledge a debt to nineteenth-century anarcho-communists, particularly Peter Kropotkin. Bookchin (1977) suggested that there is a clear correspondence between the ideas of anarchism and the principles of ecology, articulated in the idea of 'social ecology', based on the belief that ecological balance is the surest foundation for social stability. Anarchists believe in a stateless society, in which harmony develops out of mutual respect and social solidarity among human beings. The richness of such a society is founded on its variety and diversity. Green thinkers also believe that balance or harmony develops spontaneously within nature, in the form of ecosystems, and that these, like

KEY FIGURES IN... GREEN IDEOLOGY

Ernst Friedrich ('Fritz') Schumacher (1911–77) A German-born UK economist and environmental theorist, Schumacher championed the cause of human-scale production and advocated 'Buddhist economics', or 'economics as if people mattered'. In his seminal work *Small Is Beautiful* (1973), Schumacher attacked conventional economic thinking for its obsession with growth for growth's sake, and condemned the value system on which it is based, particularly the fact that it is divorced from nature. In contrast, he stressed the importance of morality and 'right livelihood'.

Arne Naess (1912–2008) A Norwegian philosopher, writer and mountaineer, Naess has been described as the 'father' of deep ecology. His philosophy, Ecosophy T (the 'T' is for the Tvergastein hut in which he lived in solitude high on a Norwegian mountain), which was influenced by the ideas of Spinoza, Gandhi's ethic of non-violence and Taoist thought, was based on the assertion that 'the Earth does not belong to human beings', as all creatures have an equal right to live and bloom.

James Lovelock (born 1919) A UK atmospheric chemist, inventor and environmental thinker, Lovelock is best known as the inventor of the 'Gaia hypothesis'. This proposes that the Earth is best understood as a complex, self-regulating, living 'being', implying that the prospects for humankind are closely linked to whether the species helps to sustain, or threaten, the planetary ecosystem. Lovelock was also the first person to alert the world to the global presence of CFCs in the atmosphere, and he is, controversially, a supporter of nuclear power.

Murray Bookchin (1921–2006) A US anarchist social philosopher and environmentalist, Bookchin was a leading proponent of the idea of 'social ecology'. As an anarchist, Bookchin emphasized the potential for non-hierarchic cooperation within conditions of post-scarcity and radical decentralization. Arguing that ecological principles should be applied to social organization, he linked the environmental crisis to the breakdown of the organic fabric of both society and nature. His major works in this field include *The Ecology of Freedom* (1982) and *Re-enchanting Humanity* (1995).

Caroline Merchant (born 1936) A US ecofeminist philosopher and historian of science, Merchant's work has highlighted links between gender oppression and the 'death of nature'. Merchant developed a feminist critique of a scientific revolution that explained environmental degradation ultimately in terms of the application by men of a mechanistic view of nature. On this basis, she argued that a global ecological revolution requires a radical restructuring of gender relations. Merchant's chief works include *The Death of Nature* (1983) and *Radical Ecology* (1992).

Rudolf Bahro (1936–98) A German writer and green activist, Bahro is best known for his attempts to reconcile socialism with ecological theories. In *Socialism and Survival* (1982), Bahro presented capitalism as the root cause of the environmental crisis, and socialism as its solution, thereby linking the issues of social justice and ecological sustainability. However, Bahro subsequently moved beyond conventional ecosocialism, arguing, in *From Red to Green* (1984), that the ecological crisis had become so pressing that it must take precedence over the class struggle.

anarchist communities, require no external authority or control. The anarchist rejection of government within human society thus parallels the green thinkers' warnings about human 'rule' within the natural world. Bookchin therefore likened an anarchist community to an ecosystem, and suggested that both are distinguished by respect for the principles of diversity, balance and harmony.

Anarchists have also advocated the construction of decentralized societies, organized as a collection of communes or villages, a social vision to which many deep ecologists are also attracted. Life in such communities would be lived close to nature, each community attempting to achieve a high degree of self-sufficiency. Such communities would be economically diverse; they would produce food and a wide range of goods and services, and therefore contain agriculture, craftwork and small-scale industry. Self-sufficiency would make each community dependent on its natural environment, spontaneously generating an understanding of organic relationships and ecology. In Bookchin's view, decentralization would lead to 'a more intelligent and more loving use of the environment'.

Without doubt, the conception that many green theorists have of a postindustrial society has been influenced by the writings of Kropotkin and William Morris. The green movement has also adopted ideas such as decentralization, participatory democracy and direct action from anarchist thought. However, even when anarchism is embraced as providing a vision of an ecologically sound future, it is seldom accepted as a means of getting there. Anarchists believe that progress will only be possible when government and all forms of political authority are overthrown. In contrast, many in the green movement see government as an agency through which collective action can be organized, and therefore as the most likely means through which the environmental crisis can be addressed, at least in the short term. They fear that dismantling or even weakening government may simply give free rein to those forces that generated industrialization and blighted the natural environment in the first place.

Ecofeminism

The idea that feminism offers a distinctive and valuable approach to green issues has grown to such a point that ecofeminism has developed into one of the major philosophical schools of environmentalist thought. Its basic theme is that ecological destruction has its origins in patriarchy: nature is under threat not from humankind but from men and the institutions of male power. Feminists who adopt an androgynous or sexless view of human nature argue that patriarchy has distorted the instincts and sensibilities of men by divorcing them from the 'private' world of nurturing, home-making and personal relationships. The sexual division of labour thus inclines men to subordinate both women and nature, seeing themselves as 'masters' of both. From this point of view, ecofeminism can be classified as a particular form of social ecology. However, many ecofeminists subscribe to essentialism, in that their theories are based on the belief that there are fundamental and ineradicable differences between women and men.

		Anthropocentrism ⟵			Ecocentrism ⟶

	Modernist ecology	**Social ecology**			**Deep ecology**
		Ecosocialism	**Eco-anarchism**	**Ecofeminism**	
Key themes	• Enlightened anthropo-centrism • Limits to growth • 'Weak' sustainability • Future generations	• End of commodifi-cation • Collectivize wealth • Production for use	• Decentraliz-ation • Self-management • Critique of consumerism	• Essential difference between women and men • Women linked to 'nature' • Men linked to 'culture'	• Radical holism • Value-in-nature • Biocentric equality • 'Strong' sustainability
Core goal	Balance between ecology and capitalist modernity	Social revolution: replace capitalism with socialism	Dismantle structures of political authority	Overthrow patriarchy and establish matriarchy	Paradigm shift: cast off mechanistic/atomistic world-view

Figure 9.2 **Types of green ideology**

Such a position is adopted, for instance, by Mary Daly in *Gyn/Ecology* (1979). Daly argued that women would liberate themselves from patriarchal culture if they aligned themselves with 'female nature'. The notion of an intrinsic link between women and nature is not a new one. Pre-Christian religions and 'primitive' cultures often portrayed the Earth or natural forces as a goddess, an idea resurrected in the Gaia hypothesis. Modern ecofeminists, however, highlight the biological basis for women's closeness to nature, in particular the fact that they bear children and suckle babies. The fact that women cannot live separate from natural rhythms and processes in turn structures their politico-cultural orientation. Traditional 'female' values therefore include reciprocity, cooperation and nurturing, values that have a 'soft' or ecological character. The idea that nature is a resource to be exploited or a force to be subdued is more abhorrent to women than men, because they recognize that nature operates in and through them, and intuitively sense that personal fulfilment stems from acting with nature rather than against it. The overthrow of patriarchy therefore promises to bring with it an entirely new relationship between human society and the natural world, meaning that ecofeminism shares with deep ecology a firm commitment to ecocentrism.

If there is an essential or 'natural' bond between women and nature, the relationship between men and nature is quite different. While women are creatures of nature, men are creatures of culture: their world is synthetic or (literally) man-made, a product of human ingenuity rather than natural creativity. In the male world, then, intellect is ranked above intuition, materialism is valued over spirituality, and mechanical relationships are emphasized over holistic ones. In politico-cultural terms, this is reflected in a belief in self-striving, competition and hierarchy. The implications of this for the natural world are clear. Patriarchy, in this view, establishes the supremacy of culture over nature, the latter being nothing more than a force to be subdued, exploited or risen above. Ecological destruction and gender inequality are therefore part of the same process in which 'cultured' men rule over 'natural' women.

Deep ecology

The term 'deep ecology' (sometimes called 'ecocentrism', 'ecosophy' or 'ecophilosophy') was coined in 1973 by Arne Naess. For Naess, deep ecology is 'deep' because it persists in asking deeper questions concerning 'why' and 'how', and is thus concerned with fundamental philosophical questions about the impact of the human species on the biosphere. The key belief of deep ecology is that ecology and anthropocentrism (in all its forms, including 'enlightened' anthropocentrism) are simply irreconcilable; indeed, anthropocentrism is an offence against the principle of ecology.

This rejection of anthropocentrism has had profound moral and political implications. Deep ecologists have viewed nature as the source of moral goodness. Nature thus has 'intrinsic' or inherent value, not just 'instrumental' value deriving from the benefits it brings to human beings. A classic statement of the ethical framework of deep ecology is articulated in Aldo Leopold's *Sand County Almanac* ([1948] 1968) in the form of the 'land ethic': 'A thing is right when it tends to preserve the integrity, stability and beauty of the biotic community. It is wrong when it tends otherwise'. Such a moral stance implies '**biocentric equality**'. Naess (1989) expressed this in the idea that all species have an 'equal right to live and bloom', reflecting the benefits of **biodiversity**. Such ecocentric ethical thinking has been accompanied by a deeper and more challenging philosophical approach that amounts to nothing less than a new **metaphysics**, a new way of thinking about and understanding the world. In addressing metaphysical issues, deep ecology is radical in a way and to a degree that does not apply elsewhere in ideological thought. Deep ecology calls for a change in consciousness, specifically the adoption of 'ecological consciousness', or 'cosmological consciousness'. At the heart of this is an 'inter-subjective' model of selfhood that allows for no distinction between the self and the 'other', thereby collapsing the distinction between humankind and nature.

BIOCENTRIC EQUALITY
The principle that all organisms and entities in the biosphere are of equal moral worth, each being an expression of the goodness of nature.

BIODIVERSITY
The range of species within a biotic community, often thought to be linked to its health and stability.

METAPHYSICS
The branch of philosophy that is concerned with explaining the fundamental nature of existence, or being.

Deep ecology is also associated with a distinctive analysis of environmental degradation and how it should be tackled. Instead of linking the environmental crisis to particular policies or a specific political, social or economic system (be it industrialization, capitalism, patriarchy or whatever), deep ecologists argue that it has more profound cultural and intellectual roots. The problem lies in the mechanistic world-view that has dominated the thinking of western societies since about the seventeenth century, and which subsequently came to affect most of the globe. Above all, this dominant paradigm is dualistic: it understands the world in terms of distinctions (self/other, humankind/nature, individual/society, mind/matter, reason/emotion and so on) and thus allows nature to be thought of as inert and valueless in itself, a mere resource for satisfying human ends. In this light, nothing less than a paradigm change – a change in how we approach and think about the world – will properly address the challenge of environmental degradation. Deep ecologists have looked to a wide range of ideas and theories to bring about this paradigm change, including, as discussed earlier, modern physics, Eastern mysticism and primitive religion. Each of these is attractive because it offers a vision of radical holism. In emphasizing that the whole is more important than its individual parts, they are clearly non-dualistic and provide a basis for an ecocentrism that prioritizes the maintenance of ecological balance over the achievement of narrowly human ends.

In addition to its moral and philosophical orientation, deep ecology has been associated with a wider set of goals and concerns. These include:

- *Wilderness preservation.* Deep ecologists seek to preserve nature 'wild and free', based on the belief that the natural world, unspoilt by human intervention, is a repository of wisdom and morality. **Preservationism** is nevertheless different from conservationism, in that the latter is usually taken to imply protecting nature in order to satisfy long-term human ends. The 'wilderness ethic' of deep ecology is often linked to the ideas of Henry David Thoreau (see p. 153), whose quest for spiritual truth and self-reliance led him to flee from civilized life and live for two years in virtual solitude, close to nature, an experience described in *Walden* ([1854] 1983).
- *Population control.* Although greens from many traditions have shown a concern about the exponential rise in the human population, deep ecologists have placed a particular emphasis on this issue, often arguing that a substantial decrease in the human population is the only way of ensuring the flourishing of non-human life. To this end, some deep ecologists have rejected aid to the developing world; called for a reduction in birth rates, especially in the developing world; or argued that immigration from the developing world to the developed world should be stopped.

> **PRESERVATIONISM**
> The disposition to protect natural systems, often implying keeping things 'just as they are' and restricting the impact of humans on the environment.

- *Simple living.* Deep ecologists believe that humans have no right to reduce the richness and diversity of nature except, as Naess put it, to satisfy vital needs. This is a philosophy of 'walking lighter on the Earth'. It certainly implies an emphasis on promoting the quality of life ('being') rather than the quantity of possessions ('having'), and is often linked to a postmaterial model of self-realization, commonly understood as self-actualization. This implies being 'inwardly rich but outwardly poor'.
- *Bioregionalism.* This is the idea that human society should be reconfigured in line with naturally-defined regions, each 'bioregion', in effect, being an ecosystem. Bioregionalism is clearly at odds with established territorial divisions, based on national or state borders. Although deep ecologists seldom look to prescribe how humans should organize themselves within such bioregions, there is general support for self-reliant, self-supporting, autonomous communities.

Nevertheless, the role and importance of deep ecology within larger green political thought has been a matter of considerable controversy. Not only has the significance of deep ecology, in terms of the philosophical and ethical debates it has stimulated, greatly outweighed its practical importance within the green movement, but it has also attracted sometimes passionate criticism from fellow green thinkers. Humanist ecologists roundly reject the idea that their views are merely a 'shallow' version of deep ecology, arguing instead that deep ecology is philosophically and morally flawed. The philosophical flaw of deep ecology is the belief that anthropocentrism and ecology are mutually exclusive. From this perspective, a concern with human well-being, or at least long-term and sustainable human well-being, requires respect for ecology rather than its betrayal. The moral flaws of deep ecology stem from the idea of the 'intrinsic' value of nature. In the humanist view, environmental ethics cannot be non-anthropocentric because morality is a human construct: 'good' and 'bad' are only meaningful when they are applied to human beings and their living conditions. Deep ecology has also come under attack from social ecologists, notably Murray Bookchin. For Bookchin, deep ecology is not only socially conservative (because it ignores the radical social change that needs to accompany any 'inner' revolution) but, in turning its back on rationalist thought and embracing mysticism, it is also guilty of succumbing to what Bookchin called 'vulgar Californian spiritualism' or 'Eco-la-la'.

SELF-ACTUALIZATION
An 'inner', even quasi-spiritual, fulfilment that is achieved by transcending egoism and materialism.

BIOREGIONALISM
The belief that the territorial organization of economic, social and political life should take into account the ecological integrity of bio-regions.

Green ideology in a global age

The environment is often viewed as the archetypal example of a 'global' issue. This is because environmental processes are no respecters of national borders; they have an intrinsically transnational character. As countries are peculiarly environmentally vulnerable to the activities that take place in other countries, meaningful progress on environmental issues can only be made at the international or even global level. This lesson has been particularly underlined by the issue of climate change, regarded by some as the most urgent and important challenge currently confronting the international community.

It is also clear that the modern green movement has a marked global orientation, reflected in strong concerns about globalization (see p. 20) and its tendency, as a result, to operate in alliance with the wider anti-globalization or anti-capitalist movement. Anti-capitalism (see p. 161) thus has a marked ecological dimension. This stems from the belief that industrialism and its underpinning values – competitive individualism, materialism, consumerism and so on – have become more deeply entrenched as a result of economic globalization. Globalization, in this sense, is a form of hyper-industrialism. While green activists have expressed general concerns about globalization, a key focus of their criticism has often been the policies of the institutions responsible for managing the modern global system. For example, the liberalization of global trade carried out under the auspices of the World Trade Organization has been held responsible for ever-higher levels of pollution, and the World Bank has been accused of engineering ecologically unsustainable 'development'.

However, major factors stand in the way of the worldwide spread of the green movement, making it difficult – and perhaps impossible – for green ideology to develop into a truly global ideology. One of these factors is that, although effective action over the environment has to be international or global in character, cooperation at this level has been very difficult to bring about. This occurs because what states accept would be generally beneficial to them may not be the same as what benefits each of them individually. The collective good therefore conflicts with the sum of states' national interests. On the issue of climate change, for instance, international cooperation is seriously hampered by the costs that reducing CO_2 emissions would impose on individual states, in terms of investment in sometimes expensive mitigation and adaptation strategies as well as, most important, accepting lower levels of economic growth. If each state has an interest in being a 'free rider', benefiting from the sacrifices that other states make without making similar sacrifices itself, international action over climate change – and perhaps over environmental issues generally – is doomed to be inadequate.

A further problem is that the environment may be destined to remain a concern only for the developed world. As far as the developing world is concerned, the strictures of green ideology appear to deny them the opportunity to catch up with the industrialized West. Western states developed through large-scale industrialization, the exploitation of finite resources and a willingness to pollute the natural world, practices they now seek to deny to the developing world. Such divisions can be illustrated clearly by the problem of burden-sharing over climate change. From the perspective of the global South, the developed world has a historical responsibility for the accumulated stock of carbon emitted since the beginning of the industrial age. In effect, developed countries have used up a large part of the safe, carbon-absorbing capacity of the atmosphere, and made substantial gains in terms of economic growth and prosperity as a result. The developing world, in contrast, is both disproportionately badly affected by climate change and has the fewest capabilities to tackle it. This implies either that emissions targets should not be imposed on developing countries (as in the Kyoto Protocol), or that such targets should take into account historical responsibilities and be structured accordingly, imposing significantly heavier burdens on the developed world than the developing world. The theory of postmaterialism, moreover, suggests that not until poverty levels in the developing world have reduced substantially will populations be prepared to prioritize quality of life issues, such as the environment, over their desire for prosperity and economic growth.

Finally, it is questionable whether the green movement, even supported by the larger anti-capitalist movement, has the capacity seriously to check the advance of economic globalization. Apart from the enormous, and perhaps irresistible, power of the corporate and other interests that are driving the globalization process, the anti-growth message with which green ideology is associated presents political difficulties. The politics of zero, or even sustainable, growth may be so electorally unattractive to populations (in both the developed and developing worlds) that it proves to be democratically impossible. If this is the case, green ideology may simply prove to be an urban fad, a form of post-industrial romanticism, which is likely to be restricted to the young and the materially affluent. A further challenge facing the green movement is the very scale of the changes it calls for. Green ideology – especially, but not only, in the guise of deep ecology – is associated with theories, values and sensibilities that are entirely at odds with those that have traditionally dominated industrialized societies. The problem confronting green ideology may therefore be that it is based on a philosophy that is deeply alien to the culture it must influence if it is to be successful. However, this may also be the source of its appeal.

? QUESTIONS FOR DISCUSSION

- How does an ecocentric perspective challenge conventional approaches to politics?
- Is 'enlightened' anthropocentrism a contradiction in terms?
- Why have green thinkers been ambivalent about science?
- Should all thinking strive to be holistic?
- What are the features of a sustainable economy?
- How has green ideology extended conventional moral thinking?
- Do we have obligations to future generations, and if so, how far do they extend?
- Why and how have green theorists rethought the nature of human fulfilment?
- Which political ideologies are most compatible with ecological thinking, and why?
- To what extent can the goals of green ideology only be achieved through radical social change?
- Does deep ecology constitute the philosophical core of green political thought?
- Can green ideology ever be electorally and politically viable?

📖 FURTHER READING

Baxter, B., *Ecologism: An Introduction* (1999). A clear and comprehensive survey of the main components of ecologism that considers its moral, political and economic implications.

Dobson, A., *Green Political Thought* (2007). An accessible and very useful account of the ideas behind green politics; sometimes seen as the classic text on the subject.

Eckersley, R., *Environmentalism and Political Theory: Towards an Ecocentric Approach* (1992). A detailed and comprehensive examination of the impact of environmentalist ideas on contemporary political thought.

Marshall, P., *Nature's Web: Rethinking Our Place on Earth* (1995). A history of ecological ideas that serves as a compendium of the various approaches to nature in different periods and from different cultures.

CHAPTER

10 Multiculturalism

Preview

Although multicultural societies have long existed – examples include the Ottoman empire, which reached its peak in the late sixteenth and early seventeenth centuries, and the USA from the early nineteenth century onwards – the term 'multiculturalism' is of relatively recent origin. It was first used in 1965 in Canada to describe a distinctive approach to tackling the issue of cultural diversity. In 1971, multiculturalism, or 'multiculturalism within a bilingual framework', was formally adopted as public policy in Canada, providing the basis for the introduction of the Multiculturalism Act in 1988. Australia also officially declared itself multicultural and committed itself to multiculturalism in the early 1970s. However, the term 'multiculturalism' has only been prominent in wider political debate since the 1990s.

Multiculturalism is more an arena for ideological debate than an ideology in its own right. As an arena for debate, it encompasses a range of views about the implications of growing cultural diversity and, in particular, about how cultural difference can be reconciled with civic unity. Its key theme is therefore diversity within unity. A multiculturalist stance implies a positive endorsement of communal diversity, based on the right of different cultural groups to recognition and respect. In this sense, it acknowledges the importance of beliefs, values and ways of life in establishing a sense of self-worth for individuals and groups alike. Distinctive cultures thus deserve to be protected and strengthened, particularly when they belong to minority or vulnerable groups. However, there are a number of competing models of a multicultural society, which draw on, variously, the ideas of liberalism, pluralism and cosmopolitanism. On the other hand, the multiculturalist stance has also been deeply controversial, and has given rise to a range of objections and criticisms.

Origins and development

Multiculturalism first emerged as a theoretical stance through the activities of the black consciousness movement of the 1960s, primarily in the USA. The origins of black nationalism date back to the early twentieth century and the emergence of a 'back to Africa' movement inspired by figures such as Marcus Garvey (see p. 185). Black politics, however, gained greater prominence in the 1960s with an upsurge in both the reformist and revolutionary wings of the movement. In its reformist guise, the movement took the form of a struggle for civil rights that reached national prominence in the USA under the leadership of Martin Luther King (1929–68). The strategy of non-violent civil disobedience was nevertheless rejected by the Black Power movement, which supported black separatism and, under the leadership of the Black Panther Party, founded in 1966, promoted the use of armed confrontation. Of more enduring significance, however, have been the Black Muslims (now the Nation of Islam), who advocate a separatist creed based on the idea that black Americans are descended from an ancient Muslim tribe.

The late 1960s and early 1970s witnessed growing political assertiveness among minority groups, sometimes expressed through ethnocultural nationalism, in many parts of western Europe and elsewhere in North America. This was most evident among the French-speaking people of Quebec in Canada, but it was also apparent in the rise of Scottish and Welsh nationalism in the UK, and the growth of separatist movements in Catalonia and the Basque area in Spain, Corsica in France, and Flanders in Belgium. A trend towards ethnic assertiveness was also found among the Native Americans in Canada and the USA, the aboriginal peoples in Australia, and the Maoris in New Zealand. In response to these pressures, a growing number of countries adopted official multiculturalism policies, the Canadian Multiculturalism Act (see p. 288) being perhaps the classic example.

The common theme among these emergent forms of ethnic politics was a desire to challenge economic and social marginalization, and sometimes racial oppression. In this sense, ethnic politics was a vehicle for political liberation, its enemy being structural disadvantage and ingrained inequality. For blacks in North America and western Europe, for example, the establishment of an ethnic identity provided a means of confronting a dominant white culture that had traditionally emphasized their inferiority and demanded subservience.

Apart from growing assertiveness among established minority groups, multicultural politics has also been strengthened by trends in international migration since 1945 that have significantly widened cultural diversity in many societies. Migration

ETHNOCULTURAL NATIONALISM
A form of nationalism that is fuelled primarily by a keen sense of ethnic and cultural distinctiveness and the desire to preserve it.

rates rose steeply in the early post-1945 period, as western states sought to recruit workers from abroad to help in the process of post-war reconstruction. In many cases, migration routes were shaped by links between European states and their former colonies. Thus, immigrants to the UK in the 1950s and 1960s came mainly from the West Indies and the Indian subcontinent, while immigration in France came largely from Algeria, Morocco and Tunisia. In the case of West Germany, immigrants were *Gastarbeiter* (guest workers), usually recruited from Turkey or Yugoslavia. Immigration into the USA since the 1970s has come mainly from Mexico and other Latin American countries. For instance, the Latino or Hispanic community in the USA has exceeded the number of African-Americans, and it is estimated that by 2050 about a quarter of the US population will be Latinos.

However, during the 1990s there was a marked intensification of cross-border migration across the globe, creating what some have seen as a 'hyper-mobile planet'. There are two main reasons for this. First, there has been a growing number of refugees, reaching a peak of about 18 million in 1993. This resulted from an upsurge in war, ethnic conflict and political upheaval in the post-Cold War era, in areas ranging from Algeria, Rwanda and Uganda to Bangladesh, Indochina and Afghanistan. The collapse of communism in eastern Europe in 1989–91 contributed to this by creating, almost overnight, a new group of migrants as well as by sparking a series of ethnic conflicts, especially in the former Yugoslavia. Second, economic globalization (see p. 20) intensified pressures for international migration in a variety of ways, as discussed in the final section of this chapter.

By the early 2000s, a growing number of western states, including virtually all the member states of the European Union, had responded to such developments by incorporating multiculturalism in some way into public policy. This was in recognition of the fact that multi-ethnic, multireligious and multicultural trends within modern societies have become irreversible. In short, despite the continuing and sometimes increasing prominence of issues such as immigration and asylum, a return to *mono*culturalism, based on a unifying national culture, is no longer feasible. Indeed, arguably the most pressing ideological issue such societies now confront is how to reconcile cultural diversity with the maintenance of civic and political cohesion. Nevertheless, the advent of global terrorism (see p. 314) and the launch of the so-called 'war on terror' pushed multicultural politics further up the political agenda. The spread of religious fundamentalism (see p. 305), and particularly Islamism, to western states encouraged some to speculate on whether Samuel Huntington's (see p. 329) famous 'clash of civilizations' (see p. 310) is happening not just between societies but also *within* them. Whereas supporters of multiculturalism have argued that cultural recognition and minority rights help to keep political extremism at bay, opponents warn that multicultural politics may provide a cloak for, or even legitimize, political extremism.

Core themes: diversity within unity

The term 'multiculturalism' has been used in a variety of ways, both descriptive and normative. As a descriptive term, it refers to cultural diversity that arises from the existence within a society of two or more groups whose beliefs and practices generate a distinctive sense of collective identity. Multiculturalism, in this sense, is invariably reserved for communal diversity that arises from racial, ethnic and language differences. The term can also be used to describe governmental responses to such communal diversity, either in the form of public policy or in the design of institutions. Multicultural public policies, whether applied in education, health care, housing or other aspects of social policy, are characterized by a formal recognition of the distinctive needs of particular cultural groups and a desire to ensure **equality of opportunity** between and among them. Multicultural institutional design goes further than this by attempting to fashion the apparatus of government around the ethnic, religious and other divisions in society. In the form of **consociationalism**, it has shaped political practice in states such as the Netherlands, Switzerland and Belgium; it has also been applied in the form of 'power sharing' in Northern Ireland and in multilevel governance in post-conflict Bosnia-Herzegovina.

As a normative term, multiculturalism implies a positive endorsement, even celebration, of communal diversity, typically based on either the right of different cultural groups to respect and recognition, or to the alleged benefits to the larger society of moral and cultural diversity. However, multiculturalism is more an ideological 'space' than a political ideology in its own right. Instead of advancing a comprehensive world-view which maps out an economic, social and political vision of the 'good society', multiculturalism is, rather, an arena within which increasingly important debates about the balance in modern societies between cultural diversity and civic unity are conducted. Nevertheless, a distinctive multiculturalist ideological stance can be identified. The most significant themes within multiculturalism are:

> **EQUALITY OF OPPORTUNITY**
> Equality defined in terms of life chances or the existence of a 'level playing-field'.
>
> **CONSOCIATIONALISM**
> A form of power sharing involving a close association among a number of parties or political formations, typically used in deeply divided societies.

- politics of recognition
- culture and identity
- minority rights
- diversity.

Politics of recognition

Multiculturalists argue that minority cultural groups are disadvantaged in relation to majority groups, and that remedying this involves significant changes in society's rules and institutions. As such, multiculturalism, in common with many other ideological traditions (not least socialism and feminism), is associated with the advancement of marginalized, disadvantaged or oppressed groups. However, multiculturalism draws from a novel approach to such matters, one that departs from conventional approaches to social advancement. Three contrasting approaches can be adopted, based, respectively, on the ideas of rights, redistribution and recognition (see Figure 10.1).

The notion of the 'politics of rights' is rooted in the ideas of republicanism (see p. 279), which are associated by many (but by no means all) with

Approach	Main obstacle to advancement	Key theme	Reforms and policies
Politics of rights (republicanism)	Legal and political exclusion	Universal citizenship	• Formal equality (legal and political rights) • Ban discrimination • Prohibit ethical/ cultural/racial profiling
Politics of redistribution (social reformism)	Social disadvantage	Equality of opportunity	• Social rights • Welfare and redistribution • Positive discrimination
Politics of recognition (multiculturalism)	Cultural-based marginalization	Group self-assertion	• Right to respect and recognition • Minority rights • Group self-determination

Figure 10.1   **Contrasting approaches to social advancement**

liberalism. Republicanism is concerned primarily with the problem of legal and political exclusion, the denial to certain groups of rights that are enjoyed by their fellow citizens. Republican thinking was, for example, reflected in first-wave feminism, in that its campaign for female emancipation focused on the struggle for votes for women and equal access for women and men to education, careers and public life in general. The republican stance can, in this sense, be said to be 'difference-blind': it views difference as 'the problem' (because it leads to discriminatory or unfair treatment) and proposes that difference be banished or transcended in the name of equality. Republicans therefore believe that social advancement can be brought about largely through the establishment of **formal equality**.

FORMAL EQUALITY
Equality based on people's status in society, especially their legal and political rights (legal and political equality).

CITIZENSHIP
Membership of a state: a relationship between the individual and the state based on reciprocal rights and responsibilities.

The contrasting idea of the 'politics of redistribution' is rooted in a social reformist stance that embraces, among other traditions, modern liberalism and social democracy. It arose out of the belief that universal **citizenship** and formal equality are not sufficient, in themselves, to tackle the problems of subordination and marginalization. People are held back not merely by legal and political exclusion, but also, and more importantly, by social disadvantage – poverty, unemployment, poor housing, lack of education and

Key concept

Republicanism

Republicanism refers, most simply, to a preference for a republic over a monarchy. However, the term 'republic' suggests not merely the absence of a monarch but, in the light of its Latin root, res *publica* (meaning common or collective affairs), it implies that the people should have a decisive say in the organization of the public realm. The central theme of republican political theory is a concern with a particular form of freedom, sometimes seen as 'freedom as non-domination' (Pettit, 1999). This combines liberty, in the sense of protection against arbitrary or tyrannical rule, with active participation in public and political life. The moral core of republicanism is expressed in a belief in civic virtue, understood to include public spiritedness, honour and patriotism (see p. 164).

so on. The key idea of social reformism is the principle of equal opportunities, the belief in a 'level playing-field' that allows people to rise or fall in society strictly on the basis of personal ability and their willingness to work. This implies a shift from legal egalitarianism to social egalitarianism, the latter involving a system of social engineering that redistributes wealth so as to alleviate poverty and overcome disadvantage. In such an approach, difference is acknowledged as it highlights the existence of social injustice. Nevertheless, this amounts to no more than a provisional or temporary acknowledgement of difference, in that different groups are identified only in order to expose unfair practices and structures, which can then be reformed or removed.

Multiculturalism, for its part, developed out of the belief that group marginalization often has even deeper origins. It is not merely a legal, political or social phenomenon but is, rather, a cultural phenomenon, one that operates through stereotypes and values that structure how people see themselves and are seen by others. In other words, universal citizenship and equality of opportunity do not go far enough. Egalitarianism has limited value, in both its legal and social forms, and may even be part of the problem (in that it conceals deeper structures of cultural marginalization). In this light, multiculturalists have been inclined to emphasize difference rather than equality. This is reflected in the 'politics of recognition', which involves a positive endorsement, even a celebration, of cultural difference, allowing marginalized groups to assert themselves by reclaiming an authentic sense of cultural identity.

The foundations for such a politics of recognition were laid by the postcolonial theories that developed out of the collapse of the European empires in the early post-World War II period. Black nationalism and multiculturalism can, indeed, both be viewed as offshoots of postcolonialism (see p. 280). The significance of postcolonialism was that it sought to challenge and overturn the cultural dimensions of imperial rule by establishing the legitimacy of non-western, and sometimes anti-western, political ideas and traditions. Edward Said's *Orientalism* ([1978] 2003) is sometimes seen as the most influential text of postcolonialism,

Key concept

Postcolonialism

Postcolonialism originated as a trend in literary and cultural studies that sought to address the cultural conditions characteristic of newly-independent societies. Its purpose has been primarily to expose and overturn the cultural and psychological dimensions of colonial rule, recognizing that 'inner' subjugation can persist long after the

political structures of colonialism have been removed. A major thrust of postcolonialism has thus been to establish the legitimacy of non-western, and sometimes anti-western, political ideas and traditions. Postcolonialism has thus sought to give the developing world a distinctive political voice separate from the universalist pretensions of liberalism and socialism. However, critics of postcolonialism have argued that, all too often, it has been used as a justification for traditional values and authority structures.

developing, as it does, a critique of **Eurocentrism**. Orientalism highlights the extent to which western cultural and political hegemony over the rest of the world, but over the Orient in particular, had been maintained through elaborate stereotypical fictions that belittled and demeaned non-western peoples and cultures. Examples of such stereotypes include ideas such as the 'mysterious East', 'inscrutable Chinese' and 'lustful Turks'.

> **EUROCENTRISM**
> The application of values and theories drawn from European culture to other groups and peoples, implying a biased or distorted world-view.

Culture and identity

Multiculturalism's politics of recognition is shaped by a larger body of thought which holds that **culture** is basic to political and social identity. Multiculturalism, in that sense, is an example of the politics of cultural self-assertion. In this view, a pride in one's culture, and especially a public acknowledgement of one's cultural identity, gives people a sense of social and historical rootedness. In contrast, a weak or fractured sense of cultural identity leaves people feeling isolated and confused. In its extreme form, this can result in what has been called 'culturalism' – as practised by writers such as the French political philosopher Montesquieu (1689–1775), and the pioneer of cultural nationalism, Herder (see p. 184) – which portrays human beings as culturally defined creatures. In its modern form, cultural politics has been shaped by two main forces: communitarianism and identity politics (see p. 282).

Communitarianism advances a *philosophical* critique of liberal universalism – the idea that, as individuals, people in all societies and all cultures have essentially the same 'inner' identity. In contrast, communitarians champion a shift away from universalism to particularism, reflecting an emphasis less on what people share or have in common and more on what is distinctive about the groups to which they belong. Identity, in this sense, links the personal to the social, and sees the individual as 'embedded' in a particular cultural, social, institutional or ideological

> **CULTURE**
> Beliefs, values and practices that are passed on from one generation to the next through learning; culture is distinct from nature.

PERSPECTIVES ON... CULTURE

LIBERALS have sometimes been critical of traditional or 'popular' culture, seeing it as a source of conformism and a violation of individuality. 'High' culture, however, especially in the arts and literature, may nevertheless be viewed as a manifestation of, and stimulus to, individual self-development. Culture is thus valued only when it promotes intellectual development.

CONSERVATIVES place a strong emphasis on culture, emphasizing its benefits in terms of strengthening social cohesion and political unity. Culture, from this perspective, is strongest when it overlaps with tradition and therefore binds one generation to the next. Conservatives support monocultural societies, believing that only a common culture can inculcate the shared values that bind society together.

SOCIALISTS, and particularly Marxists, have viewed culture as part of the ideological and political 'superstructure' that is conditioned by the economic 'base'. In this view, culture is a reflection of the interests of the ruling class, its role being primarily ideological. Culture thus helps to reconcile subordinate classes to their oppression within the capitalist class system.

FASCISTS draw a sharp distinction between rationalist culture, which is a product of the Enlightenment and is shaped by the intellect alone, and organic culture, which embodies the spirit or essence of a people, often grounded in blood. In the latter sense, culture is of profound importance in preserving a distinctive national or racial identity and in generating a unifying political will. Fascists believe in strict and untrammelled monoculturalism.

FEMINISTS have often been critical of culture, believing that, in the form of patriarchal culture, it reflects male interests and values and serves to demean women, reconciling them to a system of gender oppression. Nevertheless, cultural feminists have used culture as a tool of feminism, arguing that, in strengthening distinctive female values and ways of life, it can safeguard the interests of women.

MULTICULTURALISTS view culture as the core feature of personal and social identity, giving people an orientation in the world and strengthening their sense of cultural belonging. They believe that different cultural groups can live peacefully and harmoniously within the same society because the recognition of cultural difference underpins, rather than threatens, social cohesion. However, cultural diversity must in some way, and at some level, be balanced against the need for common civic allegiances.

context. Multiculturalists therefore accept an essentially communitarian view of human nature, which stresses that people cannot be understood 'outside' society but are intrinsically shaped by the social, cultural and other structures within which they live and develop. Communitarian philosophers such as Alasdair MacIntyre (1981) and Michael Sandel (1982) portrayed the idea of the abstract individual – the 'unencumbered self' – as a recipe for rootless atomism. Only groups and communities can give people a genuine sense of identity and moral purpose. During the 1980s and 1990s, a major debate raged in philosophy between liberals and communitarians. However, one of the consequences of this debate was a growing willingness among many liberal thinkers to acknowledge the importance of culture. This, in turn, made liberalism more open to the attractions of multiculturalism, helping to give rise to the tradition of liberal multiculturalism (see p. 286).

Identity politics is a broad term that encompasses a wide range of political trends and ideological developments, ranging from ethnocultural nationalism and religious fundamentalism to second-wave feminism and pluralist multiculturalism (see p. 289). What all forms of identity politics nevertheless have in common is that they advance a *political* critique of liberal universalism. Liberal universalism is a source of oppression, even a form of cultural imperialism, in that it tends to marginalize and demoralize subordinate groups and peoples. It does this because, behind a façade of universalism, the culture of liberal societies is constructed in line with the values and interests of its dominant groups: men, whites, the wealthy and so on. Subordinate groups and peoples are either consigned an inferior or demeaning stereotype, or they are encouraged to identify with the values and interests of dominant groups (that is, their oppressors). However, identity politics does not only view culture as a source of oppression; it is also a source of liberation and empowerment, particularly when it seeks to cultivate a 'pure' or 'authentic' sense of identity. Embracing such an identity is therefore a political act, a statement of intent, and a form of defiance. This is what gives identity politics its typically combative character and imbues it with psycho-emotional force. All forms of identity politics thus attempt to fuse the personal and the political.

Key concept
Identity Politics

Identity politics is an orientation towards social or political theorizing, rather than a coherent body of ideas with a settled political character. It seeks to challenge and overthrow oppression by reshaping a group's identity through what amounts to a process of politico-cultural self-assertion. This reflects two core beliefs.

(1) Group marginalization operates through stereotypes and values developed by dominant groups that structure how marginalized groups see themselves and are seen by others. These inculcate a sense of inferiority, even shame. (2) Subordination can be challenged by reshaping identity to give the group concerned a sense of pride and self-respect (e.g. 'black is beautiful' or 'gay pride'). Embracing or proclaiming a positive social identity is thus an act of defiance or liberation.

Minority rights

The advance of multiculturalism has gone hand in hand with a willingness to recognize minority rights, sometimes called 'multicultural' rights. The most systematic attempt to identify such rights was undertaken by Will Kymlicka (see p. 293). Kymlicka (2000) identified three kinds of minority rights:

- self-government rights
- polyethnic rights
- representation rights.

Self-government rights belong, Kymlicka argued, to what he called national minorities, indigenous peoples who are territorially concentrated, possess a shared language and are characterized by a 'meaningful way of life across the full range of human activities'. Examples include the Native Americans; the First Nations, Inuits and Metis peoples in Canada; the Maoris in New Zealand; the aboriginal peoples in Australia; and the Sami people in parts of northern Sweden, Norway and Finland. In these cases, the right to self-government involves the devolution of political power, usually through federalism, to political units that are substantially controlled by their members, although it may extend to the right of secession and, therefore, to sovereign independence. For example, the territory of Nunavut in Canada, formed in 1999, is largely self-governing and has its own territorial legislature.

Polyethnic rights are rights that help ethnic groups and religious minorities, which have developed through immigration, to express and maintain their cultural distinctiveness. This would, for instance, provide the basis for legal exemptions, such as the exemption of Jews and Muslims from animal slaughtering laws, and the exemption of Muslim girls from school dress codes. Special *representation* rights attempt to redress the under-representation of minority or disadvantaged groups in education and in senior positions in political and public life. Kymlicka justified 'reverse' or '**positive**' **discrimination** in such cases, on the grounds that it is the only way of ensuring the full and equal participation of all groups in the life of their society, thus ensuring that public policy reflects the interests of diverse groups and peoples, and not merely those of traditionally dominant groups.

Minority or multicultural rights are distinct from the traditional liberal conception of rights, in that they belong to groups rather than to individuals. This highlights the extent to which multiculturalists subscribe to collectivism (see p. 99) rather than individualism (see p. 27). Minority rights are also often thought of as 'special' rights. These are rights that are specific to the groups to which they belong, each cultural group having different needs for recognition based on the particular character of its religion, traditions and way of life. For instance, legal exemptions for Sikhs to ride motorcycles without

POSITIVE DISCRIMINATION
Preferential treatment towards a group designed to compensate its members for past disadvantage or structural inequality.

wearing crash helmets, or perhaps to wear ceremonial daggers, would be meaning-less to other groups.

Minority rights have nevertheless been justified in a variety of ways. First, minority rights have been viewed, particularly by liberal multiculturalists, as a guarantee of individual freedom and personal autonomy. In this view, culture is a vital tool that enables people to live autonomous lives. Charles Taylor (see p. 292) thus argues that individual self-respect is intrinsically bound up with cultural membership. As people derive an important sense of who they are from their cultures, individual rights cannot but be entangled with minority rights.

Second, in many cases minority rights are seen as a way of countering oppression. In this view, societies can 'harm' their citizens by trivializing or ignoring their cultural identities – harm, in this case, being viewed as a 'failure of recognition' (Taylor, 1994). Minority groups are always threatened or vulnerable because the state, despite its pretence of neutrality, is inevitably aligned with a dominant culture, whose language is used, whose history is taught, and whose cultural and religious practices are observed in public life. Of particular importance in this respect is the issue of '**offence**' and the idea of a right not to be offended. This in particular concerns religious groups which consider certain beliefs to be sacred, and are therefore especially deserving of protection. To criticize, insult or even ridicule such beliefs is thus seen as an attack on the group itself – as was evident, for instance, in protests in 1989 against the publication of Salman Rushdie's *The Satanic Verses*, and against allegedly anti-Islamic cartoons published in Denmark in 2006. States such as the UK have, as a result, introduced laws banning expressions of religious hatred.

Third, minority rights have been supported on the grounds that they redress social injustice. In this view, minority rights are a compensation for unfair disadvantages and for under-representation, usually addressed through a programme of 'positive' discrimination. This has been particularly evident in the USA, where the political advancement of African-Americans has, since the 1960s, been associated with so-called '**affirmative action**'. For example, in the case of *Regents of the University of California* v. *Bakke* (1978), the Supreme Court upheld the principle of 'reverse' discrimination in educational admissions, allowing black students to gain admission to US universities with lower qualifications than white students.

Finally, multiculturalists such as Kymlicka believe that indigenous peoples or national minorities are entitled to rights that go beyond those of groups that have formed as a result of immigration. In particular, the former are entitled to rights of self-government, on at least two grounds. First, indigenous peoples have been dispossessed and subordinated through a process of colonization. In no way did they choose to give up their culture or distinctive way of life; neither did they consent to the formation of a new state. In these circumstances, minority rights are, at least potentially, 'national' rights. In contrast, as migration involves some level of choice and voluntary action

OFFENCE
(In this sense) to feel hurt, even humiliated; an injury against one's deepest beliefs.

AFFIRMATIVE ACTION
Policies or programmes that are designed to benefit disadvantaged minority groups (or, potentially, women) by affording them special assistance.

(even allowing for the possible impact of factors such as poverty and persecution), immigrant groups can be said to be under an obligation to accept the core values and governmental arrangements of their country of settlement. Migration and settlement can therefore be seen as a form of implicit consent. Second, indigenous peoples tend to be territorially concentrated, making the devolution of political authority practicable, something that very rarely applies in the same way, or to the same degree, to groups that have formed through immigration.

The issue of minority rights has nevertheless been highly controversial. These controversies have included, first, that because minority rights address the distinctive needs of particular groups, they have sometimes been criticized for blocking integration into the larger society. The issue of the veil, as worn by some Muslim women, has attracted particular attention in this respect. While supporters of the right of Muslim women to wear the veil have argued that it is basic to their cultural identity, critics have objected to it either because it discriminates against women or because the veil is a symbol of separateness. Second, 'positive' discrimination has been criticized, both by members of majority groups, who believe that it amounts to unfair discrimination, and by some members of minority groups, who argue that it is demeaning and possibly counter-productive (because it implies that such groups cannot gain advancement through their own efforts).

Third, the idea that 'offence' amounts to evidence of oppression has implications for traditional liberal rights, notably the right to freedom of expression. If freedom of expression means anything, it surely means the right to express views that others find objectionable or offensive, a stance that suggests that 'harm' must involve a physical threat, and not just a 'failure of recognition'. Finally, there is inevitable tension between minority rights and individual rights, in that cultural belonging, particularly when it is based on ethnicity or religion, is usually a product of family and social background, rather than personal choice. As most people do not 'join' an ethnic or religious group it is difficult to see why they should be *obliged* to accept its beliefs or follow its practices. Tensions between the individual and the group highlight the sometimes difficult relationship between liberalism and multiculturalism, discussed later in the chapter.

Diversity

Multiculturalism has much in common with nationalism. Both emphasize the capacity of culture to generate social and political cohesion, and both seek to bring political arrangements into line with patterns of cultural differentiation. Nevertheless, whereas nationalists believe that stable and successful societies are ones in which nationality, in the sense of a shared cultural identity, coincides with citizenship, multiculturalists hold that cultural diversity is compatible with, and perhaps provides the best basis for, political cohesion. Multiculturalism is characterized by a steadfast refusal to link diversity to conflict or instability. All forms of multiculturalism are based on the assumption that diversity and unity can, and should, be blended with one another: they are not opposing forces (even though, as discussed in the next section, multiculturalists have different views about where the balance between them should be drawn).

In this sense, multiculturalists accept that people can have multiple identities and multiple loyalties; for instance, to their country of origin and their country of settlement. Indeed, multiculturalists argue that cultural recognition underpins political stability. People are willing and able to participate in society precisely because they have a firm and secure identity, rooted in their own culture. From this perspective, the denial of cultural recognition results in isolation and power-lessness, providing a breeding ground for extremism and the politics of hate. For instance, growing support for Islamism (discussed in Chapter 11), and other forms of religious fundamentalism, have been interpreted in this light.

Multiculturalists do not just believe that diversity is possible; they believe it is also desirable and should be celebrated. Apart from its benefits to the individual in terms of a stronger sense of cultural identity and belonging, multiculturalists believe that diversity is of value to society at large. This can be seen, in particular, in terms of the vigour and vibrancy of a society in which there are a variety of life-styles, cultural practices, traditions and beliefs. Multiculturalism, in this sense, par-allels ecologism, in drawing links between diversity and systemic health. Cultural diversity is seen to benefit society in the same way that biodiversity benefits an ecosystem. An additional advantage of diversity is that, by promoting cultural exchange between groups that live side by side with one another, it fosters cross-cultural toleration and understanding, and therefore a willingness to respect 'dif-ference'. Diversity, in this sense, is the antidote to social polarization and prejudice.

Nevertheless, this may highlight internal tension within multiculturalism itself. On the one hand, multiculturalists emphasize the distinctive and particular nature of cultural groups and the need for individual identity to be firmly embed-ded in a cultural context. On the other hand, by encouraging cultural exchange and mutual understanding, they risk blurring the contours of group identity and creating a kind of 'pick-and-mix', melting-pot society in which individuals have a 'shallower' sense of social and historical identity. As people learn more about other cultures, the contours of their 'own' culture are, arguably, weakened.

> **TOLERATION**
> Forbearance; a willingness to accept views or actions with which one is in disagreement.

Types of multiculturalism

All forms of multiculturalism advance a political vision that claims to reconcile cultural diversity with civic cohesion. However, multiculturalism is not a single doctrine in the sense that there is no settled or agreed view of how multicultural society should operate. Indeed, multiculturalism is another example of a cross-cutting ideology that draws on a range of other political traditions and encom-passes a variety of ideological stances. Multiculturalists disagree both about how far they should go in positively endorsing cultural diversity, and about how civic cohesion can best be brought about. In short, there are competing models of multiculturalism, each offering a different view of the proper balance between diversity and unity. The three main models of multiculturalism (see Figure 10.3, p. 294) are:

- liberal multiculturalism
- pluralist multiculturalism
- cosmopolitan multiculturalism.

Liberal multiculturalism

There is a complex and, in many ways, ambivalent relationship between liberalism and multiculturalism. As is discussed in greater detail later in the chapter, some view liberalism and multiculturalism as rival political traditions, arguing that multiculturalism threatens cherished liberal values. Since the 1970s, however, liberal thinkers have taken the issue of cultural diversity increasingly seriously, and have developed a form of liberal multiculturalism. Its cornerstone has been a commitment to toleration and a desire to uphold freedom of choice in the moral sphere, especially in relation to matters that are of central concern to particular cultural or religious traditions. This has contributed to the idea that liberalism is 'neutral' in relation to the moral, cultural and other choices that citizens make. John Rawls (see p. 53), for example, championed this belief in arguing that liberalism strives to establish conditions in which people can establish the good life as each defines it ('the right'), but it does not prescribe or try to promote any particular values or moral beliefs ('the good'). Liberalism, in this sense, is 'difference-blind': it treats factors such as culture, ethnicity, race, religion and gender as, in effect, irrelevant, because all people should be evaluated as morally autonomous individuals.

However, toleration is not morally neutral, and only provides a limited endorsement of cultural diversity. In particular, toleration extends only to views, values and social practices that are themselves tolerant; that is, ideas and actions that are compatible with personal freedom and autonomy. Liberals thus cannot accommodate '**deep' diversity**. For example, liberal multiculturalists may be unwilling to endorse practices such as female circumcision, forced (and possibly arranged) marriages and female dress codes, however much the groups concerned may argue that these are crucial to the maintenance of their cultural identity. The individual's rights, and particularly his or her freedom of choice, must therefore come before the rights of the cultural group in question.

The second feature of liberal multiculturalism is that it draws an important distinction between 'private' and 'public' life. It sees the former as a realm of freedom, in which people are, or should be, free to express their cultural, religious and language identity, whereas the latter must be characterized by at least a bedrock of shared civic allegiances. Citizenship is thus divorced from cultural identity, making the latter essentially a private matter. Such a stance implies that multiculturalism is compatible with

DEEP DIVERSITY
Diversity that rejects the idea of objective or 'absolute' standards and so is based on moral relativism.

POLITICAL IDEOLOGIES IN ACTION . . .
The Canadian Multiculturalism Act

EVENTS: In 1971, the Canadian government declared its intention to adopt a multiculturalism policy. The key element of this was the 1988 Multiculturalism Act. The Act declares that multiculturalism reflects the cultural and racial diversity of Canadian society, and acknowledges the freedom of all members of Canadian society to preserve, enhance and share their cultural heritage. It recognizes the existence of communities whose members share a common origin and their historic contribution to Canadian society, and seeks to promote their development. The Multiculturalism Act nevertheless operates within a matrix of legislation that includes, for example, the Canadian Charter of Rights and Freedoms and the Canadian Human Rights Act.

SIGNIFICANCE: The framework of official multiculturalism in Canada, of which the Multiculturalism Act is the centrepiece, is the most advanced and comprehensive anywhere in the world. It was constructed primarily in response to demands from the French-speaking majority in Quebec that they should be treated as a distinct society, and that Canada should define itself as a binational country committed to nurturing its dual identity. Quebec's other demands were more specific, and often sought to bolster the position of the French language. Over time, Canada's official multiculturalism has ensured that many of Quebec's demands have been met. Canada is thus a classic example of the use of multiculturalism to underpin political stability and civic unity through an emphasis on cultural recognition. In this view, people are likely to be more willing to participate in the wider society so long as they have a firm and secure sense of identity.

Canada's official multiculturalism has nevertheless been criticized from two main directions. Quebec nationalists argue that biases in the Canadian state in favour of the Anglophone majority run so deep that only the establishment of a sovereign state can guarantee Quebec's status as a distinct cultural community. Such thinking led to the holding of independence referendums in Quebec in 1980 and 1995, although neither succeeded. Reservations about multiculturalism have been expressed in other parts of Canada, and were reflected in the failure of the 1987 Meech Lake Accord, which proposed granting Quebec further autonomy. These reservations have been fuelled by, amongst other things, the fear that asymmetrical federalism fractures the Canadian state and weakens Canadian national identity, and the concern that biculturalism, or binationalism, may ignore other political voices, notably those of Canada's aboriginal peoples.

civic nationalism. This can be seen in the so-called 'hyphenated nationality' that operates in the USA, through which people view themselves as African-Americans, Polish-Americans, German-Americans and so on. In this tradition, integration, rather than diversity, is emphasized in the public sphere. The USA, for instance, stresses proficiency in English and a knowledge of US political history as preconditions for gaining citizenship. In the more radical 'republican' multiculturalism that is practised in France, an emphasis on *laïcité*, or secularism, in public life has led to bans on the wearing of the *hijab*, or Muslim headscarf, in schools, and since 2003 to a ban on all forms of overt religious affiliation in French schools. In 2010, France passed legislation banning the full face veil (the *niqab* and *burqa*) in public, with Belgium following suit in 2011. Some multiculturalists, however, view such trends as an attack on multiculturalism itself.

The third and final aspect of liberal multiculturalism is that it regards liberal democracy (see p. 39) as the sole legitimate political system. The virtue of liberal democracy is that it alone ensures that government is based on the consent of the people, and, in providing guarantees for personal freedom and toleration, it helps to uphold diversity. Liberal multiculturalists would therefore oppose calls, for instance, for the establishment of an Islamic state based on the adoption of *Shari'a* law, and may even be willing to prohibit groups or movements that campaign for such a political end. Groups are therefore only entitled to toleration and respect, if they, in turn, are prepared to tolerate and respect other groups.

Pluralist multiculturalism

Pluralism (see p. 290) provides firmer foundations for a politics of difference than does liberalism. For liberals, as has been seen, diversity is endorsed but only when it is constructed within a framework of toleration and personal autonomy, amounting to a form of '**shallow**' **diversity**. This is the sense in which liberals 'absolutize' liberalism (Parekh, 2005). Isaiah Berlin (see p. 292) nevertheless went beyond liberal toleration in endorsing the idea of **value pluralism**. This holds, in short, that people are bound to disagree about the ultimate ends of life, as it is not possible to demonstrate the superiority of one moral system over another. As values clash, the human predicament is inevitably characterized by moral conflict. In this view, liberal or western beliefs, such as support for personal freedom, toleration and democracy, have no greater moral authority than illiberal or non-western beliefs. Berlin's ([1958] 1969) stance implies a form of live-and-let-live multiculturalism, or what has been called the politics of *in*difference. However, as Berlin remained a liberal to the extent that he believed that only within a society that respects individual liberty can value pluralism be contained, he failed to demonstrate how liberal and illiberal cultural beliefs can co-exist harmoniously within the same society. Nevertheless,

SHALLOW DIVERSITY
Diversity that is confined by the acceptance of certain values and beliefs as 'absolute' and therefore non-negotiable.

VALUE PLURALISM
The theory that there is no single, overriding conception of the 'good life', but rather a number of competing and equally legitimate conceptions.

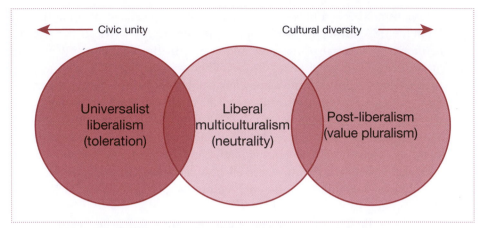

Figure 10.2 Liberalism and cultural diversity

once liberalism accepts moral pluralism, it is difficult to contain it within a liberal framework. John Gray (1995b), for instance, argued that pluralism implies a 'post-liberal' stance, in which liberal values, institutions and regimes are no longer seen to enjoy a monopoly of legitimacy (see Figure 10.2).

An alternative basis for pluralist multiculturalism has been advanced by Bhikhu Parekh (2005). In Parekh's (see p. 292) view, cultural diversity is, at heart, a reflection of the dialectic or interplay between human nature and culture. Although human beings are natural creatures, who possess a common species-derived physical and mental structure, they are also culturally constituted in the sense that their attitudes, behaviour and ways of life are shaped by the groups to which they belong. A recognition of the complexity of human nature, and the fact that any culture expresses only part of what it means to be truly human, therefore provides the basis for a politics of recognition and thus for a viable form of multiculturalism. Such a stance goes beyond liberal multiculturalism in

Key concept
Pluralism

Pluralism, in its broadest sense, is a belief in or commitment to diversity or multiplicity, the existence of many things. As a descriptive term, pluralism may denote the existence of party competition (*political* pluralism), a multiplicity of ethical values (*moral* or value pluralism), a variety of cultural beliefs (*cultural* pluralism) and so on. As a normative term it suggests that diversity is healthy and desirable, usually because it safeguards individual liberty and promotes debate, argument and understanding. More narrowly, pluralism is a theory of the distribution of political power. As such, it holds that power is widely and evenly dispersed in society, not concentrated in the hands of an elite or ruling class. In this form, pluralism is usually seen as a theory of 'group politics', implying that group access to government ensures broad democratic responsiveness.

that it stresses that western liberalism gives expression only to certain aspects of human nature.

Beyond pluralist multiculturalism, a form of 'particularist' multiculturalism can be identified. Particularist multiculturalists emphasize that cultural diversity takes place within a context of unequal power, in which certain groups have customarily enjoyed advantages and privileges that have been denied to other groups. Particularist multiculturalism is very clearly aligned to the needs and interests of marginalized or disadvantaged groups. The plight of such groups tends to be explained in terms of the corrupt and corrupting nature of western culture, values and lifestyles, which are either believed to be tainted by the inheritance of colonialism and racism (see p. 210) or associated with 'polluting' ideas such as materialism and permissiveness. In this context, an emphasis on cultural distinctiveness amounts to a form of political resistance, a refusal to succumb to repression or corruption. However, such an emphasis on cultural 'purity', which may extend to an unwillingness to engage in cultural exchange, raises concerns about the prospects for civic cohesion: diversity may be stressed at the expense of unity. Particularist multiculturalism may thus give rise to a form of 'plural monoculturalism' (Sen, 2006), in which each cultural group gravitates towards an undifferentiated communal ideal, which has less and less in common with the ideals of other groups.

Cosmopolitan multiculturalism

Cosmopolitanism (see p. 191) and multiculturalism can be seen as entirely distinct, even conflicting, ideological traditions. Whereas cosmopolitanism encourages people to adopt a global consciousness which emphasizes that ethical responsibility should not be confined by national borders, multiculturalism appears to particularize moral sensibilities, focusing on the specific needs and interests of a distinctive cultural group. However, for theorists such as Jeremy Waldron (1995), multiculturalism can effectively be equated with cosmopolitanism. Cosmopolitan multiculturalists endorse cultural diversity and identity politics, but they view them as essentially transitional states in a larger reconstruction of political sensibilities and priorities. This position celebrates diversity on the grounds of what each culture can learn from other cultures, and because of the prospects for personal self-development that are offered by a world of wider cultural opportunities and options. This results in what has been called a 'pick-and-mix' multiculturalism, in which cultural exchange and cultural mixing are positively encouraged. People, for instance, may eat Italian food, practise yoga, enjoy African music and develop an interest in world religions.

Culture, from this perspective, is fluid and responsive to changing social circumstances and personal needs; it is not fixed and historically embedded, as pluralist or particularist multiculturalists would argue. A multicultural society is

KEY FIGURES IN... MULTICULTURALISM

Isaiah Berlin (1909–97) A Riga-born UK historian of ideas and a philosopher, Berlin developed a form of liberal pluralism that was grounded in a lifelong commitment to empiricism. Basic to Berlin's philosophical stance was the idea that conflicts of values are intrinsic to human life, a position that has influenced 'postliberal' thinking about multiculturalism. A fierce critic of totalitarianism, Berlin's best-known political work is *Four Essays on Liberty* ([1958] 1969), in which he extolled the virtues of 'negative' freedom over 'positive' freedom.

Edward Said (1935–2003) A Jerusalem-born US academic and literary critic, Said was a prominent advocate of the Palestinian cause and a founding figure of postcolonial theory. He developed, from the 1970s onwards, a humanist critique of the western Enlightenment that uncovered its link to colonialism and highlighted 'narratives of oppression', cultural and ideological biases that disempower colonized peoples. He thereby condemned Eurocentrism's attempt to remake the world in its own image. Said's key works include *Orientalism* (1978) and *Culture and Imperialism* (1993).

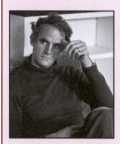

Charles Taylor (born 1931) A Canadian academic and political philosopher, Taylor drew on communitarian thinking to construct a theory of multiculturalism as 'the politics of recognition'. Emphasizing the twin ideas of equal dignity (rooted in an appeal to people's humanity) and equal respect (reflecting difference and the extent to which personal identity is culturally situated), Taylor's multiculturalism goes beyond classical liberalism, while also rejecting particularism and moral relativism. His most influential work in this area is *Multiculturalism and 'The Politics of Recognition'* (1994).

Bhikhu Parekh (born 1935) An Indian political theorist, Parekh has developed an influential defence of cultural diversity from a pluralist perspective. In *Rethinking Multiculturalism* (2005), he rejected universalist liberalism on the grounds that what is reasonable and moral is embedded in and mediated by culture, which, in turn, helps people to make sense of their lives and the world around them. 'Variegated' treatment, including affirmative action, is therefore required to put ethnic, cultural or religious minorities on an equal footing with the majority community.

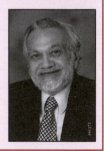

thus a 'melting pot' of different ideas, values and traditions, rather than a 'cultural mosaic' of separate ethnic and religious groups. In particular, the cosmopolitan stance positively embraces **hybridity**. This recognizes that, in the modern world, individual identity cannot be explained in terms of a single cultural structure, but rather exists, in Waldron's (1995) words, as a 'melange' of commitments, affiliations and roles. Indeed,

> **HYBRIDITY**
> A condition of social and cultural mixing in which people develop multiple identities.

James Tully (born 1946) A Canadian political theorist, Tully has championed a plural form of political society that accommodates the needs and interests of indigenous peoples. He portrayed modern constitutionalism, which stresses sovereignty and uniformity, as a form of imperialism that denies indigenous modes of self-government and land appropriation. In its place, he advocated 'ancient constitutionalism', which respects diversity and pluralism, and allows traditional values and practices to be accepted as legitimate. Tully's key work in this area is *Strange Multiplicity* (1995).

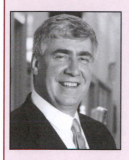

Jeremy Waldron (born 1953) A New Zealand legal and political theorist, Waldron has developed a 'cosmopolitan' understanding of multiculturalism that stresses the rise of 'hybridity'. Waldron's emphasis on the fluid, multifarious and often fractured nature of the human self provided the basis for the development of cosmopolitanism as a normative philosophy that challenges both liberalism and communitarianism. It rejects the 'rigid' liberal perception of what it means to lead an autonomous life, as well as the tendency within communitarianism to confine people within a single 'authentic' culture.

Will Kymlicka (born 1962) A Canadian political philosopher, Kymlicka is often seen as the leading theorist of liberal multiculturalism. In *Multicultural Citizenship* ([1995] 2000), he argued that certain 'collective rights' of minority cultures are consistent with liberal-democratic principles, but acknowledged that no single formula can be applied to all minority groups, particularly as the needs and aspirations of immigrants differ from those of indigenous peoples. For Kymlicka, cultural identity and minority rights are closely linked to personal autonomy. His other works in this area include *Multicultural Odysseys* (2007).

for Waldron, immersion in the traditions of a particular culture is like living in Disneyland and thinking that one's surroundings epitomize what it is for a culture to exist. If we are all now, to some degree, cultural 'mongrels', multiculturalism is as much an 'inner' condition as it is a feature of modern society. The benefit of this form of multiculturalism is that it broadens moral and political sensibilities, ultimately leading to the emergence of a 'one world' perspective. However, multiculturalists from rival traditions criticize the cosmopolitan stance for stressing unity at the expense of diversity. To treat cultural identity as a matter of self-definition, and to encourage hybridity and cultural mixing, is, arguably, to weaken any genuine sense of cultural belonging.

	Liberal multiculturalism	Pluralist multiculturalism	Cosmopolitan multiculturalism
Key themes	• Communitarianism • Minority rights • Diversity strengthens toleration and personal autonomy	• Identity politics • Cultural embeddedness • Diversity counters group oppression	• Cosmopolitanism • Cultural mixing • Hybridity
Core goal	Cultural diversity within a liberal-democratic framework	'Strong' diversity, recognizing legitimacy of non-liberal and liberal values	Fluid and multiple identities provide the basis for global citizenship

Figure 10.3 Types of multiculturalism

Critiques of multiculturalism

The advance of multicultural ideas and policies has stimulated considerable political controversy. Together with the conversion of liberal and other progressive thinkers to the cause of minority rights and cultural recognition, oppositional forces have also emerged. This has been expressed most clearly in the growing significance, since the 1980s, of anti-immigration parties and movements in many parts of the world. Examples of these include the *Front National* in France, the Freedom Party in Austria, *Vlaams Blok* in Belgium, Pim Fortuyn's List in the Netherlands and the One Nation party in Australia. Further evidence of a retreat from 'official' multiculturalism can be seen in bans on the wearing of veils by Muslim women in public places. Such bans have been introduced in France and Belgium, while at least four German states have banned the wearing of Muslim headscarves in schools. However, ideological opposition to multiculturalism has come from a variety of sources. The most significant of these have been:

- liberalism
- conservatism
- feminism
- social reformism.

While some liberals have sought to embrace wider cultural diversity, others have remained critical of the ideas and implications of multiculturalism. The key theme in liberal criticisms is the threat that multiculturalism poses to individualism, reflected in the core multiculturalist assumption that personal identity is embedded in group or social identity. Multiculturalism is therefore, like nationalism and even racism (see p. 210), just another form of collectivism, and, like all forms of collectivism, it subordinates the rights and needs of the individual to those of the social group. In this sense, it threatens individual freedom and personal self-development, and so implies that cultural belonging is a form of captivity. Amartya Sen (2006) developed a particularly sustained attack on what he called the 'solitaristic' theory that underpins multiculturalism (particularly in its pluralist and particularist forms), which suggests that human identities are formed by membership of a *single* social group. This, Sen argued, leads not only to the 'miniaturization' of humanity, but also makes violence more likely, as people identify only with their own monoculture and fail to recognize the rights and integrity of people from other cultural groups. Multiculturalism thus breeds a kind of 'ghettoization' that diminishes, rather than broadens, cross-cultural understanding. According to Sen, solitaristic thinking is also evident in ideas that emphasize the incompatibility of cultural traditions, such as the 'clash of civilizations' thesis (Huntington, 1996). Even when liberals are sympathetic to multiculturalism they condemn pluralist, and especially particularist, multiculturalism for endorsing as legitimate ideas which they view as anti-democratic and oppressive, such as the theories of militant Islam.

Conservatism is the political tradition that contrasts most starkly with multiculturalism. Indeed, most of the anti-immigration nationalist backlash against multiculturalism draws from essentially conservative assumptions. In other cases, it more closely resembles the racial nationalism of fascism, or even Nazi race theory. The chief conservative objection to multiculturalism is that shared values and a common culture are a necessary precondition for a stable and successful society. As discussed in Chapter 5, conservatives therefore favour nationalism over multiculturalism. The basis for such a view is the belief that human beings are drawn to others who are similar to themselves. A fear or distrust of strangers or foreigners is therefore 'natural' and unavoidable. From this perspective, multiculturalism is inherently flawed: multicultural societies are inevitably fractured and conflict-ridden societies, in which suspicion, hostility and even violence come to

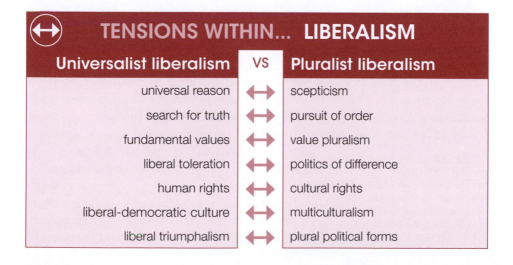

TENSIONS WITHIN... LIBERALISM		
Universalist liberalism	VS	**Pluralist liberalism**
universal reason	↔	scepticism
search for truth	↔	pursuit of order
fundamental values	↔	value pluralism
liberal toleration	↔	politics of difference
human rights	↔	cultural rights
liberal-democratic culture	↔	multiculturalism
liberal triumphalism	↔	plural political forms

be accepted as facts of life. The multiculturalist image of 'diversity within unity' is thus a myth, a sham exposed by the simple facts of social psychology.

The appropriate political responses to the threats embodied in multicultural-ism therefore include restrictions on immigration (particularly from parts of the world whose culture is different from the 'host' society) pressures for **assimilation** to ensure that minority ethnic communities are absorbed into the larger 'national' culture, and, in the view of the far right, the repatriation of immigrants to their country of origin. A further aspect of the conservative critique of multicultural-ism reflects concern about its implications for the majority or 'host' community. In this view, multiculturalism perpetrates a new, albeit 'reverse', set of injustices, by demeaning the culture of the majority group by associating it with colonialism and racism, while favouring the interests and culture of minority groups through 'positive' discrimination and the allocation of 'special' rights.

The relationship between feminism and multiculturalism has sometimes been a difficult one. Although forms of Islamic feminism (considered in Chapter 8) have sought to fuse the two traditions, feminists have more com-monly raised concerns about multiculturalism. This happens when minority rights and the politics of recognition serve to preserve and legitimize patri-archal and traditionalist beliefs that systematically disadvantage women, an argument that may equally be applied to gays and lesbians, and is sometimes seen as the 'minorities within minorities' problem. Cultural practices such as dress codes, family structures and access to elite positions have thus been seen to establish structural gender biases. Multiculturalism may therefore be little more than a concealed attempt to bolster male power, the politics of cultural recognition being used within minority communities to legitimize continued female subordination.

Social reformists have advanced a number of criticisms of multiculturalism, linked to its wider failure to address the interests of disadvantaged groups or sec-tions of society adequately. Concerns, for instance, have been raised about the extent to which multiculturalism encourages groups to seek advancement through cultural or ethnic assertiveness, rather than through a more explicit struggle for social jus-tice. In that sense, the flaw of multiculturalism is its failure to address issues of class inequality: the 'real' issue confronting minority groups is not their lack of cultural recognition but their lack of economic power and social status. Indeed, as Brian Barry (2002) argued, by virtue of its emphasis on cultural distinctiveness, mul-ticulturalism serves to divide, and therefore weaken, people who have a common economic interest in alleviating poverty and promoting social reform. Similarly, a more acute awareness of cultural difference may weaken support for welfarist and redistributive policies, as it may narrow people's sense of social responsibility (Goodhart, 2004). The existence of a unifying culture that transcends ethnic and cultural differences may therefore be a necessary precondition for the politics of social justice.

ASSIMILATION
The process through which immigrant communities lose their cultural distinctiveness by adjusting to the values, allegiances and lifestyles of the 'host' society.

Multiculturalism in a global age

In many ways, multiculturalism may turn out to be *the* ideology of the global age. This is because one of the chief features of globalization (see p. 20) has been a substantial increase in geographical, and particularly cross-border, mobility. More and more societies have, as a result, accepted multiculturalism as an irreversible fact of life. Not only is the relatively homogeneous nation-state a receding memory in many parts of the world, but attempts to reconstruct it – through, for example, strict immigration controls, enforced assimilation or pressure for repatriation – appear increasingly to be politically fanciful. If this is the case, just as nationalism was the major ideological force in world politics during the nineteenth and twentieth centuries, helping to reshape the nature of political community as well as the relationship between different societies, multiculturalism, its successor, may be the predominant ideological force of the twenty-first century. The major ideological issue for our time, and for succeeding generations, may therefore be the search for ways in which people with different moral values and from different cultural and religious traditions can find a way of living together without civil strife and violence. Multiculturalism is not only the ideology that addresses this question most squarely; it is also the one that offers solutions, albeit tentative ones.

On the other hand, multiculturalism may prove to be a once-fashionable idea whose limitations, even dangers, were quickly exposed. In this view, multicultural-ism is a particular response to an undeniable trend towards cultural and moral plu-ralism in modern, globalized societies. However, its long-term viability is more in question. Multicultural solutions may prove to be worse than the diseases they set out to tackle. The flaw of multiculturalism, from this perspective, is the belief that, by endorsing diversity, people will be drawn together as a collection of mutually respectful and tolerant cultural groups. Instead, diversity may endorse separation and lead to 'ghettoization', as groups become increasingly inward-looking and con-cerned to protect their 'own' traditions and cultural purity. Multiculturalism may thus encourage people to focus on what divides them rather than on what unites them. If this is the case, the twenty-first century is destined to witness a retreat from multiculturalism, seen as a non-viable means of addressing the undoubted challenge of cultural diversity. However, what will replace multiculturalism?

One possibility is that the failure of multiculturalism will lead to a return to nationalism, whose enduring potency derives from the recognition that, at some level and in some way, political unity always goes hand in hand with cultural cohesion. The strains generated by irreversible trends within globalization towards the construction of multi-ethnic, multireligious and multicultural societies can therefore only be contained by the establishment of a stronger and clearer sense of national identity. The other possibility is that multiculturalism will be superseded by a genuine form of cosmopolitanism (see p. 191). This would require (as some multiculturalists in any case hope) that differences of both culture and nationality are recognized gradually to be of secondary importance as people everywhere come to view themselves as global citizens, united by a common interest in addressing ecological, social and other challenges that are increasingly global in nature.

? QUESTIONS FOR DISCUSSION

- How and why is multiculturalism linked to the politics of recognition?

- Is multiculturalism a form of communitarianism?

- What is the justification for minority or multicultural rights?

- Is multiculturalism compatible with the idea of individual rights?

- Why do multiculturalists believe that diversity provides the basis for a politically stable society?

- Why have liberals supported diversity, and when do they believe that diversity is 'excessive'?

- How does pluralism go 'beyond' liberalism?

- Are western cultures tainted by the inheritance of colonialism and racism?

- Can multiculturalism be reconciled with any form of nationalism?

- To what extent is there tension between cultural rights and women's rights?

- What impact does multiculturalism have on the politics of redistribution?

- Could multiculturalism lead to cosmopolitanism?

📖 FURTHER READING

Kymlicka, W., *Multicultural Citizenship* (2000). A highly influential attempt to reconcile multiculturalism with liberalism by advancing a model of citizenship that is based on the recognition of minority or multicultural rights.

Modood, T., *Multiculturalism* (2013). A distinctive contribution to the debate about multiculturalism that highlights the urgent need to include Muslims in contemporary conceptions of democratic citizenship.

Parekh, B., *Rethinking Multiculturalism: Cultural Diversity and Political Theory*, 2nd edn (2005). A comprehensive defence of the pluralist perspective on cultural diversity that also discusses the practical problems confronting multicultural societies.

Taylor, C., *Multiculturalism: Examining the Politics of Recognition* (1995). A wide-ranging and authoritative set of essays on various aspects of multicultural politics.

CHAPTER

11 Islamism

Preview

Islam is not merely a religion. It is a total and complete way of life, providing guidance in every sphere of human existence – individual and social, material and moral, legal and cultural, economic and political, national and international. In Islam, then, politics and religion are two sides of the same coin. However, the notion of a fusion between Islam and politics has assumed a more radical and intense character due to the rise, since the early twentieth century, of 'Islamism' (also called 'political Islam', 'radical Islam' or 'activist Islam'). Although its ideas are embraced by only a small minority of Muslims worldwide, Islamism has had a dramatically disproportionate impact. Its central belief is in the construction of an 'Islamic state', usually viewed as a state based on divine Islamic law, the *sharia*. As such, Islamism extracts a political programme from the religious principles and ideals of Islam. A distinction is therefore usually drawn between the ideology of Islamism and the faith of Islam, although the relationship between Islamism and Islam is deeply contested.

Islamist ideology is characterized by, among other things, a revolt against the West and all it supposedly stands for. Some commentators, indeed, have gone as far as to suggest that Islamism is a manifestation of a 'civilizational' struggle between Islam and the West. The most controversial feature of Islamism is nevertheless its association with militancy and violence. While not all Islamists endorse violence, a doctrinal basis for militant Islam has been found in the notion of *jihad*, crudely translated as 'holy war', which has, since the 1980s, been taken by some to imply that all Muslims are obliged to support global jihadism. Islamism, however, has no single creed or political manifestation. Distinctive Sunni and Shia versions of Islamism have developed, the former associated with the related ideas of Wahhabism and Salafism, the latter with Iran's 'Islamic Revolution'. In addition, 'moderate' or 'conservative' trends can be identified within Islamism, characterized by the attempt to reconcile Islamism with pluralism and democracy.

Origins and development

In a process that can be traced back to the early twentieth century but has accelerated markedly since the 1970s, religion has become generally more important, not less important. Although its impact has been different in different parts of the world, this religious revivalism has had various manifestations. These include the emergence of new, and often more assertive, forms of **religiosity**, the growing influence of religious movements and, most importantly, a closer relationship between religion and politics, through what has been seen as either the politicization of religion or the religionization of politics. This trend has confounded advocates of the **secularization thesis**, even encouraging some to proclaim the 'de-secularization' of society. One of the earliest and most dramatic demonstrations of this was the 1979 'Islamic Revolution' in Iran (see p. 303), but it soon became clear that politicized religion was not an exclusively Islamic development. From the 1980s onwards, the 'new Christian Right' became increasingly prominent in the USA, while forms of sometimes militant religious nationalism emerged, in India, in relation to Hinduism and Sikhism, in Sri Lanka and Burma, in relation to Buddhism, and in Israel, in relation to Judaism. (Religious nationalism is discussed in greater detail in Chapter 6).

It is difficult to generalize about the causes of this upsurge in politicized religion, because it has taken different ideological and doctrinal forms in different parts of the world, but it has widely been interpreted as part of the larger phenomenon of identity politics (see p. 282). In this respect, religion has proved to be a particularly potent means of regenerating personal and social identity in modern circumstances. As modern societies are increasingly atomistic, diffuse and pluralized, there is, arguably, a greater thirst for the sense of meaning, purpose and certainty that religious consciousness appears to offer. This applies because religion provides believers with a world-view and moral vision that has

---

RELIGIOSITY
The quality of being religious; piety or devoutness.

SECULARIZATION THESIS
The theory that modernization is invariably accompanied by the victory of reason over religion and the displacement of religious values by secular ones.

Key concept

Religion

Religion, in its most general sense, is an organized community of people bound together by a shared body of beliefs concerning some kind of transcendent reality. However, 'transcendent' in this context may refer to anything from a belief in a distinctly 'other-worldly' supreme being or creator God, to a more 'this-worldly' experience of personal liberation, as in the Buddhist concept of nirvana. There are major differences between monotheistic religions (examples including Christianity, Islam and Judaism), which have a single, or limited number of, sacred texts and a clear authority system, and pantheistic, non-theistic and nature religions (Hinduism, Buddhism, Taoism, Jainism and so on), which tend to have looser, more decentralized and pluralized structures.

higher, and indeed supreme, authority, stemming as it does from a supposedly divine source. Religion thus defines the very grounds of people's being; it gives them an ultimate frame of reference as well as a moral orientation in a world increasingly marked by moral relativism. In addition, religion generates a powerful sense of social solidarity, connecting people to one another at a 'thick' or deeper level, as opposed to a 'thin' connectedness usually found in modern societies.

Although each of the major world religions has a capacity for politicization, since the 1970s the process has been particularly acute in relation to Islam, deriving from its capacity, among other things, to articulate the interests of the oppressed in less developed countries and to offer a non-western, and often anti-western, worldview. The potency of the link between Islam and politics in the contemporary period is evident in the emergence of 'political Islam', or 'Islamism', a political creed based on Islamic ideas and principles. At the heart of this creed is a commitment to the establishment of an Islamic state based on the *sharia* (see p. 312).

Early Islamist thinking emerged in the nineteenth century in response to European colonialism, as in the case of the Deobandi sect, a conservative and traditionally anti-British movement within Sunni Hanafi Islam that developed in British India and which later influenced the Taliban movement in Afghanistan and Pakistan. Islamism is nevertheless best understood as a reaction to twentieth-century social and political conditions, including rapid urbanization, the dislocation of traditional communities and crafts, and growing unemployment and anomie (Black, 2011). It gained a powerful impetus from the collapse and carve-up of the once-powerful Ottoman empire in the aftermath of World War I and its carve-up by the UK and France. In this context, the Middle East fell into stagnation, and interest in new ways of thinking about both Islam and politics spread. Building on the ideas of figures such as the Persian activist Jamal al-Din 'al-Afghani' (1838–97) and the Syrian Islamist reformer Rashid Rida (1865–1935), the Muslim Brotherhood was founded in 1928 in Ismailia, Egypt, by Hassan al-Banna (1906–49). The world's first and most influential Islamist movement, the Brotherhood pioneered a model of political, and sometimes militant, activism combined with Islamic charitable works that has subsequently been embraced across the Muslim world.

However, Islamism only emerged as a powerful political force during the post-World War II period, and especially from the 1980s onwards. A variety of developments contributed to the rise of Islamism, including the following:

MORAL RELATIVISM
The belief that there are no absolute values, or a condition in which there is a deep and widespread disagreement over moral issues.

NEO-IMPERIALISM
A form of imperialism that operates through economic and ideological domination rather than formal political control.

- The end of colonialism in the early post-1945 period brought little benefit to the Arab world, both because Middle Eastern regimes tended to be inefficient, corrupt and dictatorial, and because traditional imperialism (see p. 166) was succeeded by neo-imperialism, particularly as US influence expanded in the region.

PERSPECTIVES ON... RELIGION

LIBERALS see religion as a distinct 'private' matter linked to individual choice and personal development. Religious freedom is thus essential to civil liberty and can only be guaranteed by a strict division between religion and politics, and between church and state.

CONSERVATIVES regard religion as a valuable (perhaps essential) source of stability and social cohesion. As it provides society with a set of shared values and the bedrock of a common culture, overlaps between religion and politics, and church and state, are inevitable and desirable.

SOCIALISTS have usually portrayed religion in negative terms, as at best a diversion from the political struggle and at worst a form of ruling-class ideology (leading in some cases to the adoption of state atheism). In emphasizing love and compassion, religion may nevertheless provide socialism with an ethical basis.

ANARCHISTS generally regard religion as an institutionalized source of oppression. Church and state are invariably linked, with religion preaching obedience and submission to earthly rulers while also prescribing a set of authoritative values that rob the individual of moral autonomy.

FASCISTS have sometimes rejected religion on the grounds that it serves as a rival source of allegiance or belief, and that it preaches 'decadent' values such as compassion and human sympathy. Fascism nevertheless seeks to function as a 'political religion', embracing its terminology and internal structure – devotion, sacrifice, spirit, redemption and so on.

ISLAMISTS view religion as a body of 'essential' and unchallengeable principles, which dictate not only personal conduct but also the organization of social, economic and political life. Religion cannot and should not be confined to the 'private' sphere, but finds its highest and proper expression in the politics of popular mobilization and social regeneration.

- The protracted Arab–Israeli conflict, and especially the 1967 Six-Day War, which led to the seizure by Israel of the Occupied Territories and greatly increased the number of Palestinian refugees, sparked disillusionment with secular Arab nationalism and Arab socialism, and created opportunities for religiously-based forms of politics.

> **WAHHABISM**
> An ultra-conservative movement within Sunni Islam, sometimes portrayed as an orientation within Salafism.

- The 1973 oil crisis boosted the economic strength and ideological importance of Saudi Arabia and the Gulf states, allowing them to finance the spread of their distinctive brand of fundamentalist Islam, **Wahhabism**, across the Arab world.

POLITICAL IDEOLOGIES IN ACTION . . .
Iran's 'Islamic Revolution'

SIGNIFICANCE: Iran's 'Islamic Revolution' had profound implications. Khomeini's Shia Islamic regime focused on a jihadi approach to organizing and shaping Iran's domestic and foreign policy priorities. Stressing struggle against infidels and tyranny, this focus was reflected in antipathy to the 'Great Satan' (the USA) and the application of strict Islamic principles to social and political life. The wearing of headscarves and chador (a loose piece of cloth worn in addition to clothes) became obligatory for all women in Iran. Restrictions on polygamy were removed, contraception was banned, adultery was punished by public floggings or execution, and the death penalty was introduced for homosexuality. Both Iranian politics and society were thoroughly 'Islamized' and Friday prayers in Tehran became an expression of official government policy and a focal point of political life. More widely, in offering a specifically Islamic model of political and social development, the Iranian Revolution inspired and emboldened the forces of Islamism, despite the Iranian Shia regime being out of step with much of the mainly Sunni-dominated Muslim world.

Nevertheless, the survival and stability of the Khomeini regime cannot be explained solely in terms of the potency of its Islamist ideology. In addition to its religious focus, Iran tackled many of the failures of the Shah's period, bringing benefits especially to rural and underdeveloped parts of the country in the form of access to piped water, electricity and other facilities. A major expansion of the educational system also brought about near-universal literacy rates and greatly widened the social and career opportunities available to girls and women.

EVENTS: In February 1979, Ayatollah Khomeini (see p. 317) returned to Tehran from exile in Paris to be welcomed by a crowd of several million Iranians. This occurred after an escalating series of popular protests had forced the Shah, Mohammad Reza Pahlavi, to flee the country. Khomeini's huge popularity, based on his status as a symbol of resistance against the Shah, enabled him speedily to establish a system of personal rule and out-manoeuvre other opposition groups. In April 1979, following a rigged national referendum (98.8 per cent voted in favour), Iran was declared an 'Islamic Republic'. A theocratic constitution was adopted in December 1979, under which Khomeini was designated the Supreme Leader, presiding over a constitutional system consisting of an elected parliament and president, while substantive power remained in the hands of the Shia religious elite.

- The war in Afghanistan against the Soviet Union, during 1979–89, led to the growth of the Mujahideen, a loose collection of religiously-inspired resistance groups, out of which developed a collection of new **jihadi** groups, the most important of which was al-Qaeda, founded in 1988. A link can thus be made between the Soviet invasion of Afghanistan and the September 11, 2001, terrorist attacks on Washington and New York, and the outbreak of the 'war on terror'.

JIHAD
(Arabic) An Islamic term literally meaning 'strive' or 'struggle'; although the term is sometimes equated with 'holy war' (the lesser *jihad*), it can also be understood as an inner struggle for faith (the greater *jihad*).

- The 2003 US-led invasion of Iraq fomented bitter sectarian rivalry between Sunni and Shia (or Shi'ite) Muslims, which both spread across the region and contributed to the emergence of the Islamic State of Iraq and al-Sham or ISIS (also called Islamic State (IS) or Daesh), whose influence later expanded due to the seemingly intractable civil war in Syria.

Core themes: religion as ideology

As a child of the Enlightenment, political ideology has been closely associated with **secularism**, its advance from the French Revolution onwards contributing significantly to the larger process of secularization. In some cases, ideology has worn an explicitly anti-religious face. Karl Marx (see p. 124), for example, dismissed religion as the 'opium of the masses', treating it as an example of false consciousness. Ideologies may even be thought of as political or secular religions, in that their capacity to 'roll back' or displace religion derives, at least in part, from the fact they have absorbed some of religion's key functions and features. For instance, ideologies offer people the prospect of salvation, albeit a decidedly 'this-worldly' salvation (usually based on economic and social well-being), as opposed to the 'other-worldly' salvation of religion. In establishing a framework of morality, ideologies rival religions in their ability to invest personal existence with a sense of meaning and purpose. Similarly, ideologies have sometimes resembled religion in their use of ceremony and ritual to strengthen a sense of commitment and belief, examples including May Day demonstrations in communist states, and the Nuremberg Rallies in Nazi Germany.

And yet, the distinction between ideology and religion is often blurred. Political ideologies have not only absorbed some of the functions and features of religion, but have also sometimes incorporated religious beliefs and doctrines into their distinctive world-views. Religion has, for instance, commonly been a component of social conservatism, an emphasis on religious values being an important way of strengthening the moral fabric of society. Ethical socialism has been shaped, in a number of respects, by religious influences, including Christianity's stress on universal brotherhood and Islam's prohibition on usury and profiteering. The link

SECULARISM
The belief that religion should not intrude into secular (worldly) affairs, usually reflected in the desire to separate church from state.

between religion and ideology has been particularly prominent in the case of ethnic nationalism, where a stress has increasingly been placed on religion rather than the nation, on the grounds that religion provides a supposedly primordial and seemingly unchangeable basis for the establishment of group identity. Nevertheless, the above are examples of essentially secular political ideologies recruiting religious ideas and doctrines to their cause. By contrast, the present chapter considers a more radical and far-reaching phenomenon: the transformation of religion itself into ideology, a tendency that has been particularly evident in the case of Islamism. This is reflected in Ruhullah Khomeini's (see p. 317) assertion that 'Politics is religion'. The most significant themes in Islamism are the following:

- fundamentalism and modernity
- Islamism and Islam
- revolt against the West
- the Islamic state
- jihadism.

Fundamentalism and modernity

Islamism is often seen as part of the wider phenomenon of 'religious fundamentalism' (see p. 305). This implies that Islamism can be understood in terms of a fundamentalist impulse that can be found in most, if not all, religions, in which case Islamism amounts, at heart, to 'Islamic fundamentalism'. But what is fundamentalism, and how far can Islamism be seen as a form of fundamentalism? The term 'fundamentalism' was first used in a religious context in debates within American Protestantism in the early twentieth century. Between 1910 and 1915, evangelical Protestants published a series of pamphlets entitled *The Fundamentals*, upholding the inerrancy, or literal truth, of the Bible in the face of modern interpretations of Christianity. In its broadest sense, therefore, fundamentalism refers to a commitment to ideas and values that are seen as 'basic' or 'foundational'. Since fundamental ideas are regarded as the core of a belief system, as opposed to

Key concept

Fundamentalism

Fundamentalism is a style of thought in which certain principles are recognized as essential 'truths' that have unchallengeable and overriding authority, regardless of their content. Substantive fundamentalisms therefore have little or nothing in common, except that their supporters tend to evince an earnestness or fervour born out of doctrinal certainty. Although it is usually associated with religion and the literal truth of sacred texts, fundamentalism can also be found in political creeds. Even liberal scepticism can be said to incorporate the fundamental belief that all theories should be doubted (apart from its own). Although the term is often used pejoratively to imply inflexibility, dogmatism or authoritarianism, fundamentalism may also give expression to selflessness and a devotion to principle.

peripheral or more transitory ideas, they usually have an enduring and unchanging character, and are linked to the system's supposedly original or 'classical' form. However, the term religious fundamentalism is both controversial – being commonly taken to imply inflexibility, dogmatism and authoritarianism (see p. 78) – and contested. Many of those who are classified as fundamentalists reject the term as simplistic or demeaning, preferring instead to describe themselves as 'true believers', 'traditionalists', 'conservatives', 'evangelicals', 'revivalists' and so forth.

Religious fundamentalism is a complex phenomenon, with at least three dimensions. First, it is commonly linked to a belief in **scriptural literalism**. American Protestant fundamentalists thus reject Darwinian evolutionary theory and instead preach creationism, or 'creation science', on the grounds that humankind was created by God, as described in the Bible. A tendency towards scriptural literalism is found in all three 'religions of the book', Christianity, Islam and Judaism, but is particularly pronounced in the case of Islam because all Muslims accept the Koran as the revealed word of God, implying that all Muslims are fundamentalists, in this sense.

Second, as religious fundamentalism tends to be expressed through intense and all-consuming belief, it is often associated with a refusal to confine religion to the private sphere. Fundamentalist religion is therefore often expressed through the politics of popular mobilization and social regeneration. While some claim that such a tendency can be identified in all the world's major religions, others argue that it tends to be restricted to Islam, Protestant Christianity and possibly Catholicism, as only these religious traditions have the capacity to throw up comprehensive programmes of political renewal. In the case of Islam, the tendency may be particularly pronounced, as Islam has never been just a 'religion', as such; rather, it is a complete way of life, with instructions on moral, political and economic behaviour for individuals and nations alike. In this light, politics may be far more integral to Islam than it is to Christianity, which has traditionally relied on the God/Caesar distinction to separate the holy from the worldly (Hamid, 2016). Third, religious fundamentalism typically turns its back on a modern world that is associated with decline and decay, typified by the spread of godless secularism. Regeneration can thus be brought about only by a return to the spirit and traditions of some long-past 'golden age', often equated with the earliest, or 'classical', phase of a religion's history.

Although Islamism undoubtedly exhibits fundamentalist features – not least in its refusal to separate religion from politics – in other respects it departs from religious fundamentalism. Most importantly, and despite its rhetorical stress on 'return' and 'revival', Islamism embraces a modernist view of religion which relies on an 'activist' or 'dynamic' reading of sacred texts rather than faith in inherited structures and traditions. Islamism is therefore not an example of dyed-in-the-wool reaction, bound by the literal meaning of sacred texts, its back turned firmly against **modernity** and everything it represents. Rather, it is characterized as much by novelty and innovation as it is by tradition and established belief.

SCRIPTURAL LITERALISM
A belief in the literal truth of sacred texts, which, as the revealed word of God, have unquestionable authority.

MODERNITY
The condition of being 'modern', typically characterized by the questioning of established beliefs.

The hallmark of Islamism is that it sets out to remake the world by *re-imagining* the past, suggesting that the image of religious revivalism is largely a myth. Islamism may call for a return of Islamic history and glory, but the state to which it seeks to 'return' is, in Eric Hobsbawm's (1983) phrase, an 'invented tradition'. The Islamist utopia, an imagined system of divine governance named *hakimiyyat Allah* (God's rule), has thus never existed in Islamic history (Tibi, 2012). Similarly, the constitutional structure of Iran's Islamic republic (discussed later in the chapter) is not based on an Islamic historical model, but rather on theories and ideas developed by Rudhollah Khomeini while in exile in Paris during the 1970s (Adib-Moghaddam, 2014).

The adoption of an essentially modernist view of religion is, moreover, indicative of a wider compatibility between Islamism and modernity. For example, the willingness of Islamists to use the Internet and other new media, as well as the machinery of the modern state, suggests sympathy for the spirit of modernity, respect for 'this-worldly' rationalism rather than a descent into 'other-worldly' mysticism. In the same way, early interest in Iran in ideas such as 'Islamic science' and 'Islamic economics' quickly gave way to an acceptance of, respectively, conventional, and therefore western, science, and market principles derived from economic liberalism.

Islamism and Islam

Although Islamism is clearly based on Islamic ideas and principles, the relationship between Islamism and Islam is shrouded in controversy. In one view, Islam and Islamism are starkly different entities. As a faith and ethical framework, Islam implies certain political values but it does not presuppose a particular form of government. Islamism, by contrast, is centrally concerned with the issue of state order (Tibi, 2012). In this view, Islamism is an ideology with a political agenda that differentiates it from the religion of Islam. Some commentators go as far as to suggest that Islamism has 'hijacked' Islam for its political purposes, effectively redefining Islam as a project for the construction of a *sharia*-based state (Baran, 2011). The idea that Islamism can be firmly distinguished from Islam is not ideologically neutral, however. It implies, at the very least, that Islamism is 'inauthentic', a distortion of 'true' Islam. Indeed, those who take this stance invariably do so as part of a wider critique of Islamism, which is seen, among other things, as implicitly (and possibly explicitly) totalitarian, intrinsically linked to anti-Semitism (see p. 211), irreconcilable with democracy, and intolerant and prone to violence. Such a position suggests, furthermore, that any attempt to counter the spread of Islamism must involve a 'war of ideas', designed to weaken support for Islamist ideas and practices, in part by emphasizing that they do not represent the religion of Islam. A war against Islamism does not, therefore, imply a war against Islam.

At least two groups nevertheless dismiss the idea of a clear divide between Islam and Islamism. The first group consists of Islamists themselves, who argue not only that Islam and Islamism are linked, but also that the most basic concern of Islamism is to revive the 'true' religion of Islam. 'Islamism', indeed, is a term rejected out of hand by Islamists, who see it as demeaning or insulting, an example of **Orientalism**. In a message echoed by many later Islamists, Jamal ad-Din 'al-Afghani' thus called for a revival of Islam to reverse generations of decline and corruption, brought about by the influence of 'unIslamic' political leaders and foreign powers (Keddi, 1972). The second group that holds that the roots of Islamism lie within Islam itself are proponents of the 'clash of civilizations' thesis (see p. 310). This implies that there is a basic incompatibility between Islamic values and those of the liberal-democratic West. In this light, it is Islam, rather than Islamism, that is inherently totalitarian. The fact that Islam prescribes a complete way of life, embracing political and economic behaviour as well as moral conduct, implies both stark anti-pluralism and a rejection of the public–private divide. Such thinking was embraced in its most radical form by neoconservative US theorists, who, against a backdrop of the 'war on terror', attacked what they called 'Islamo-fascism', viewing it not as a perversion of Islam, but as a realization of certain of Islam's core beliefs.

An alternative approach to the relationship between Islamism and Islam is to identify contrasting tendencies within Islam, specifically between 'reformist' or 'moderate' Islam and 'radical' or 'extremist' Islam. This distinction underpins attempts to counter Islamism through a strategy of 'de-radicalization', which aims to undermine support for radical or militant forms of Islam by bolstering a form of Islam that is compatible with the standards of a liberal, secular society. In effect, this is to encourage Islam to go through a process of structural reform similar to the Protestant Reformation in the sixteenth and seventeenth centuries, which led to a growing acceptance that religion should operate primarily in the private sphere. However, the idea of a distinction between 'moderate' and 'extremist' strains within Islam is fraught with problems. For instance, supporters of radical Islam refuse to accept that their beliefs are 'extremist', both because the term 'extremism' is nakedly pejorative and because they see themselves as paragons of righteous behaviour. Moreover, some of those deemed to support 'moderate' Islam, possibly on the grounds that they condemn terrorism (see p. 314) and reject the use of violence, may nevertheless sympathize with views that may be seen as 'extremist'. These include a stark intolerance of other religions or rival forms of Islam and beliefs such as that **apostasy**, adultery and possibly homosexuality warrant the death penalty, that blasphemy and the depiction of images of the Prophet Mohammed should be severely punished, and that women and men should be segregated in public events.

In view of the difficulties involved in distinguishing between 'moderate' and 'radical' Islam, it is sometimes argued that the distinction can only be sustained when

ORIENTALISM
The theory that western cultural and political hegemony over the rest of the world, but over the Orient in particular, is maintained through elaborate stereotypical fictions that belittle non-western people and cultures.

APOSTASY
The abandonment of one's religious faith, sometimes applied to a cause, a set of principles or a political party.

it refers to the choice of political means, and specifically to the use of non-violent or violent strategies. Tibi (2012) thus distinguished between 'institutional' and 'jihadist' Islamism on this basis. However, as discussed later in relation to jihadism, the idea of a clear and consistent divide between Islamists over the use of violence may also be an illusion. A deeper problem nevertheless confronts the attempt to distinguish between 'moderate' and 'radical' forms of Islam, or, for that matter, between Islam and Islamism. This is that, like other manifestations of human culture, a religion is a porous and variable thing, forever mutating, a constantly evolving dialogue between the present and the past that is made up of multitudes of voices (Holland, 2015). Any attempt to reduce something as complex and multifarious as a religion to its 'essential' elements, or to outline an 'authentic' interpretation of a religion, is therefore to risk distortion and invite challenge.

Revolt against the West

Islamism is perhaps most of all characterized by a strident rejection of the West, rooted in the perception that 'the West' poses a threat to Islam that is new in both power and scope (Black, 2011). This applies because Islamism developed not through isolation from the West but through encounters with the West, and these encounters invariably had a bruising character. However, Islamist anti-westernism has been understood in a number of ways. For example, Paul Berman (2003) placed militant Islamism within the context of the totalitarian movements that emerged from the apparent failure of liberal society in the aftermath of World War I. The significance of World War I was that it exploded the optimistic belief in progress and the advance of reason, fuelling support for darker, anti-liberal movements. In this light, Islamism shares much in common with fascism and communism, in that each promises to rid society of corruption and immorality and to make society anew in a 'single block-like structure', solid and eternal (Buruma and Margalit, 2004). Islamism can therefore be portrayed as a form of occidentalism. From this perspective, western society is characterized by individualism, secularism and relativism; it is a mechanical civilization organized around greed and materialism. Occidentalism, in contrast, offers the prospect of organic unity, moral certainty and politico-spiritual renewal. Such ideas were first developed in the writings of counter-Enlightenment thinkers in Germany in the early nineteenth century, and helped to fuel the growth of European fascism and Japanese imperialism in the inter-war period. However, in the modern world they are most clearly articulated through political Islam.

OCCIDENTALISM
A rejection of the cultural and political inheritance of the West, particularly as shaped by the Reformation and the Enlightenment.

Islamism's revolt against the West was starkly expressed by figures such as Abul Ala Maududi (see p. 317) and Sayyid Qutb (see p. 317). Maududi's scathing criticism of the West focused on its supposed moral bankruptcy and preoccupation with sex. Qutb, who was radicalized during a two-year study visit

Key concept

Clash of civilizations

The 'clash of civilizations' thesis suggests that the twenty-first-century global order will be characterized by growing tension and conflict, but that this conflict will be cultural in character, rather than ideological, political or economic. According to Huntington (1996), the rise of culture as the key factor in world politics has occurred as ideology has faded in significance in the post-Cold War world and globalization has weakened the state's ability to generate a sense of civic belonging. Civilizations inevitably 'clash' because they are based on incommensurate values and meanings, with tension between China and the USA and between Islam and the West being particularly likely. The thesis may nevertheless underestimate both the complex and fluid nature of civilizations and their capacity for peaceful co-existence.

to the USA, expressed a profound distaste for the materialism, immorality and sexual licentiousness he claimed to have encountered there. Qutb's world-view, or 'Qutbism', as it is sometimes called, highlighted the barbarism and corruption that westernization had inflicted on the world, with a return to strict Islamic practice in all aspects of life offering the only possibility of salvation. In *Milestones* ([1962] 2007), Qutb portrayed a world divided into the *dar al-Islam* (home or territory of Islam) and *dar al-harb* (home or territory of war), with Islam being confronted with two possible relations with the rest of the world: 'peace with a contractual agreement, or war'. This Islamist conception of a global civilizational struggle between Islam and the non-Islamic world (not just the West) was later taken up by groups such as al-Qaeda and ISIS, especially once, during the 1990s, the object of Islamist hostility shifted beyond the 'near enemy' (corrupt or 'apostate' Muslim regimes) and came to encompass the 'far enemy' (the USA and the West in general). In due course, some western analysts were also converted to the idea of a civilizational struggle between Islam and the West, particularly as the 'clash of civilizations' thesis gained growing support in the aftermath of the September 11 attacks.

Radical or leftist theorists have nevertheless developed an account of Islamism that acknowledges tension between Islam and the West but without explaining it in civilizational terms. In this view, the rise of Islamism is best understood in the context of the USA's bid to establish and maintain global hegemony and the implications of this for the Muslim, and more specifically Arab, world. What has been called the 'American empire' is an empire of a new kind. For Hardt and Negri (2000), the empire is a 'de-centred' empire governed by a multiplicity of powerful agents, including the USA, the G8 and various transnational corporations. For Harvey (2003), it is an example of capitalist imperialism, linked to the spread of global neoliberalism (see p. 83). The impact of neo-imperialism on the Muslim world has been especially damaging because the desire to control the flow of oil has led to widespread western interference across the Middle East and beyond. This has taken various forms, including steadfast support for the state of Israel, the provision of political, diplomatic and military aid to bolster repressive, 'pro-western' regimes, and direct military intervention, in Afghanistan and Iraq in particular. In this light, Islamism can be seen as a counter-hegemonic force, a source of resistance to western, and, more narrowly, US, domination. Western interference has, moreover, been legitimized by the systematic use of '**Islamophobia**', fostering demeaning or hateful images of Muslim people and/or their religion.

> **ISLAMOPHOBIA**
> Negative or insulting representations of Islam or Muslim people in general, portraying them variously as inferior, violent, aggressive or threatening.

The Islamic state

Political Islam is 'political' largely in the sense that it is centrally concerned with the issue of political order and the construction of an 'Islamic state'. Although a clear and developed theory of the Islamic state only emerged during the second half of the twentieth century, the question of political authority and its location has been of vital importance within Islam since the death of Mohammed in 632. Thinking on this matter focused squarely on the **caliphate**, the term 'caliph' meaning substitute or stand-in. The first four caliphs acted as **imams** of the Muslim world, but in 680 the caliphate became hereditary when Mu'awiya passed it on to his son Yazid I, founding the Umayyad line which lasted until 750. The title caliph was revived by the Ottoman sultans, who ruled always as 'successors to the Prophet', but it was abolished by the Turkish National Assembly in 1924.

Although the Islamic state is often portrayed as the restoration of the caliphate, significant differences exist between traditional forms of Islamic administration and the Islamic state as conceived by modern Islamists (Feldman, 2012). As the caliphs possessed Mohammed's authority, but not his direct access to divine revelation, they were inclined to consult and consider the views of the scholars, a group of people who claimed legal expertise and came to be regarded as the guardians of the law. This created a constitutional balance of power, in which executive power, represented by the caliph, could be restrained by the scholars' ability to interpret and administer the *sharia*. The position of the scholars in this respect was bolstered by the influence they could exert over succession. This constitutional balance was nevertheless destroyed under Ottoman rule, resulting in unchecked executive dominance, the Ottoman caliphate effectively becoming a system of divinely-ordained personal rule.

> **CALIPHATE**
> A system of government by which, under the original custom of Islam, the faithful were ruled by a *khalifa* (caliph) who stood in the Prophet's stead.
>
> **IMAM**
> The prayer leader in a mosque or the leader of the Muslim community.

Islamist notions of the Islamic state emerged from the 1920s onwards, often through debates within the Muslim Brotherhood. Key figures in these disputes included Rashid Rida, in many ways the founding theoretician of the Islamic state in its modern sense, and Ali Abdel Raziq (1888–1966), who rejected the belief that in Islam, religion and politics form a unified whole, on the grounds that

Key concept

Sharia

The *sharia* (literally the 'way' or the 'path') is divine Islamic law. The *sharia* is based on the teachings of the Prophet Mohammed as revealed in the Koran, supplemented by the *sunnah*, or 'beaten path', the traditional customs observed by devout Muslims and said to be based on the Prophet's own life,

and the *hadith*, reports of the statements and actions of Mohammed. The *sharia* lays down a code for legal and righteous behaviour, including a system of punishment for most crimes, as well as rules of personal conduct for both women and men. Although it is widely believed to constitute broad principles and guidance from which responses to particular situations may be derived, Islamists attempt to transform the *sharia* into a set of fixed laws.

it associates politics primarily with the caliphate, and thus with despotic rule. Nevertheless, in Rida's conception, the Islamic state was far from being a system of regulation whose authority extended over every detail of social, political and cultural life (Enayat, 1982). Over time, however, the Islamic state has been defined increasingly by the predominance given to the enforcement of the *sharia*, so much so that the Islamic state has come, in effect, to be a *sharia* state. This development has effectively involved the reinvention of the *sharia* itself. Instead of being a system of interpretive law, mostly restricted to civil law and the penal code, and largely based on an accumulated body of individual judgements in particular cases, the *sharia* has come to be seen as the constitutional foundation of the Islamic state (Tibi, 2012). However, insofar as this implies that the purpose of the state is to uphold a single, authoritative set of values, it makes it difficult to reconcile the Islamic state with ideas such as party competition and ideological pluralism (see p. 290), conventionally seen as core features of democratic governance. This may be particularly the case because most calls for the restoration of *sharia* are not accompanied by calls for the restoration of the scholars to their former position of influence, thus implying that constitutional balances are absent from the Islamic state (Feldman, 2012).

However, the Islamic state is not merely a theory, it has also existed in practice. Although Saudi Arabia has been a fundamentalist Islamic state since the eighteenth century, and 'Islamic republics' have been set up in, for example, Pakistan in 1956, Mauritania in 1958, and Afghanistan, both during the Taliban period, 1996–2001, and since, the most systematic and elaborate attempt to establish an Islamist form of government has occurred in Iran since the 1979 revolution. The Iranian system of government is a complex mix of theocracy (see p. 313) and democracy. The Supreme Leader (currently Ali Khamenei) presides over a system of institutionalized clerical rule that operates through the Islamic Revolutionary Counsel, a body of 15 senior clerics. While a popularly elected president and parliament have been established, all legislation is ratified by the Council for the Protection of the Constitution, which ensures conformity to Islamic principles, with the *sharia*

Key concept

Theocracy

Theocracy (literally 'rule by God') is the principle that religious authority should prevail over political authority. A theocracy is therefore a regime in which government posts are filled on the basis of people's position in the religious hierarchy. Theocratic rule is illiberal in two senses. First, it violates the public/private divide, in that it takes religious rules and precepts to be the guiding principles of both personal life and political conduct. Second, it invests political authority with potentially unlimited power because, as temporal power derived from spiritual wisdom, it cannot be based on popular consent, or be properly constrained within a constitutional framework. Strict theocratic rule is therefore a form of autocracy, while limited theocratic rule may co-exist with democracy and constitutionalism (see p. 37).

being strictly enforced throughout Iran as both a legal and moral code. However, although the Iranian model of the Islamic state has clearly brought about the revival of the scholarly class, it has, arguably, created a new form of autocracy through the construction of an unfettered, supreme scholarly executive (Feldman, 2012).

Jihadism

The most controversial aspect of Islamism is its association with **militancy** and violence in general, and with terrorism (see p. 314) in particular. Groups such as Hezbollah, Hamas, Islamic Jihad, al-Qaeda (in its various manifestations), ISIS and Boko Haram have been viewed as exponents of 'Islamist terrorism', a distinctive form of terrorism characterized by both its religious motivation and the use of suicide tactics. Although the vast majority of Islamist parties are engaged in demo-cratic or at least electoral politics (in South and South East Asia in particular), and many of those who subscribe to Islamist beliefs, even in their radical guise, eschew the use of violence in principle, militant Islamism is a prominent tendency within the larger Islamist movement.

The chief doctrinal basis for Islamist militancy lies in the notion of *jihad*. *Jihad* lit-erally means to 'struggle' or 'strive'; it is used to refer to the religious duty of Muslims. However, the term has been used in at least two contrasting ways. In the form of the 'greater' *jihad*, struggle is understood as an inner spiritual quest to overcome one's sinful nature. In the form of the 'lesser' *jihad*, it is understood more as an outer or physical struggle against the enemies of Islam. This is the sense in which *jihad* is translated (often unhelpfully) as 'holy war'. Bernard Lewis (2004) argued that *jihad* has a military meaning in the large majority of cases, although other scholars stress the importance of non-violent ways of struggling against the enemies of Islam.

MILITANCY
Extreme commitment; that is the level of zeal and passion typically associated with struggle or war.

The notion of military *jihad*, or '*jihad* by the sword' (*jihad bis saif*), has gained particular prominence since the 1970s. Religiously inspired guerrillas fighting the Russian occupation of Afghanistan in the 1980s portrayed themselves as the Mujahideen (sometimes

Key concept

Terrorism

'Terrorism' is a controversial and contested term. Conventionally, it refers to the use of violence to further a political end by creating a climate of fear, anxiety and apprehension. Terrorism is therefore clandestine violence, its most common forms including assassinations, bombings, hostage seizures and plane hijacks.

However, as all forms of violence or warfare aim, at some level, to strike fear into the wider population, it may be difficult to distinguish between terrorism and other forms of political violence. Moreover, as the term is deeply pejorative, it may be used to de-legitimize a group and its cause, 'terrorists' being enemies of civilized society. Finally, although terrorism is usually associated only with non-state actors, the notion of 'state terrorism' is sometimes used.

translated as 'holy warriors'), denoting that they were engaged in a *jihad*. *Jihad* may nevertheless have either a defensive or an offensive character. 'Defensive *jihad*' refers to the individual obligation to defend the 'home of Islam' whenever it is threatened by aggression from the 'home of war'. As it focuses on the protection of Muslim communities and the expulsion of foreign invaders from Muslim lands, figures such as Yusuf al-Qaradawi (see p. 317), who oppose the wider use of violence, see defensive *jihad* as a legitimate basis for the use of force. Such a position may be bolstered by the claim that *jihad*, in its defensive sense, is compatible with modern international law and just war theory (Hashmi, 2012).

In contrast, 'offensive *jihad*' means a struggle, by fighting if necessary, to establish Islamic order over all unbelievers, a goal that Maududi upheld on the grounds that Islam constitutes a programme of 'well-being for all humanity'. As the number of jihadi groups started to proliferate during the 1990s, offensive *jihad* came to stand for a global struggle for supremacy. For militant Salafi Muslims in particular, jihadism (the waging of global *jihad*) became the core feature of their ideology, a development especially evident in relation to figures such as Abdallah Azzam (see p. 317) and the Saudi al-Qaeda leader Osama bin Laden (1957–2011). Some advocates of offensive *jihad* nevertheless cast it in non-violent terms, portraying it not as a justification for expansionism, terror campaigns and forcible conversion, but as 'waging war with tongues and pens'.

The doctrine of *jihad* may not be the only link between Islamism and violence, however. An alternative, or additional, explanation for Islamist militancy may be the unusual emphasis that Islam places on the afterlife. Not only does this perhaps suggest that 'bodily' life-and-death is a matter of lesser importance, but also the nature of the afterlife, in which, according to the *hadith* (reports of the statements and actions of Mohammed), 70 virgin maidens await each young man who has sacrificed himself for his religion, may encourage this view.

SALAFISM
A Sunni school of thought that is associated with a literalist, strict and puritanical approach to Islam.

However, Islamist terrorism may be better understood less in terms of the doctrine of *jihad* or expectations relating to the afterlife, and more as part of a broader tendency for terrorism to become entangled with religious motivations and justifications. This tendency can be found not just in Islam but, arguably, in all religions and religious cults. Examples of this include the 1994 assassination of the Indian prime minister Indira Gandhi by militant Sikhs, the 1995 Aum Shinrikyo attack on the Tokyo subway system, and the bombing of abortion centres in the USA by fundamentalist Christians. In this view, the inclination towards violence and terrorism may be a feature of fundamentalist religion generally. This applies because, as a form of identity politics, fundamentalist religion tends to be associated with the idea of a hostile and threatening 'other', which serves both to create a heightened sense of collective identity and to strengthen its oppositional or combative character. This demonized 'other' may take various guises, from secularism and permissiveness to rival religions, westernization, the USA and so forth. Fundamentalist religion therefore tends to be based on a Manichaean world-view, which emphasizes conflict between light and darkness, or good and evil. If 'we' are a chosen people acting according to the will of God, 'they' are not merely people with whom we disagree, but a body actively subverting God's purpose on earth. This not only makes violence against 'them' easier to justify; it may suggest that such violence amounts to a religious duty.

Islamist terrorism may, alternatively, be understood as an example of subaltern violence. The idea of subaltern violence (subalterns being the economically dispossessed) was developed in Frantz Fanon's *The Wretched of the Earth* (1965). For Fanon (see p. 185), decolonization pits two incompatible forces and two mutually exclusive world-views against one another. As successful decolonization requires that these forces and world-views should be reversed, so that 'the last shall be first and the first shall be last', it requires nothing less than the creation of 'new men'. Violence plays a crucial role in this process. Violence serves both a political and a strategic function, in that the violence that sustains colonial rule has to be turned against the settlers themselves, and, in ridding the native of his sense of powerlessness and inferiority, it plays an equally important psycho-therapeutic role. Such thinking may go some way to explaining the inclination within Islamist politics toward violence, its source being the desire, among at least sections of Muslim society, to rid themselves of their sense of injustice and humiliation.

Types of Islamism

Not all Islamists think alike, however. In particular, contrasting forms of Islamism have developed within Islam's two main sects, the Sunni and the Shia. This division in Islam developed within fifty years of Mohammed's death and stemmed from a disagreement over succession. Whereas Sunnis regarded the first four caliphs as 'The Rightly Guided Caliphs', Shias treated Mohammed's cousin and son-in-law, Ali ibn Abi Talib, as the rightful successor to Mohammed. The Sunni sect represents the large majority of Muslims, including 90 per cent or more of the populations of Egypt, Jordan and Saudi Arabia, while the Shia sect contains just over one tenth of Muslims, mainly living in Iran and Iraq. The Sunni–Shia divide within Islam has sharpened significantly in recent years. This occurred as the 2003–11 US-led occupation of Iraq left an inheritance of bitter sectarian rivalry, which then spread to Syria thanks to the civil war, in which pro-Assad forces, generally linked to Iran, have been pitted against anti-Assad fighters mainly supported by Saudi Arabia and other Gulf states. However, in addition to Sunni and Shia versions of Islamism, a third type can be identified, in the form of 'conservative' or 'moderate' Islamism.

Sunni Islamism

Sunni Islamism is rooted in the linked ideas of Wahhabism and Salafism (Wahhabis are Salafis, but not all Salafis are Wahhabis). Wahhabism (a term often considered to be derogatory by its adherents) is the official version of Islam in Saudi Arabia, the world's first fundamentalist Islamic state. The Wahhabi movement was started by Muhammad ibn Wahhad (1703–92), who championed a militant and puritanical form of Islam, which, unlike later forms of Islamism, was entirely a movement for internal reform and not in any sense a response to foreign intervention. In a pact agreed in 1744 between ibn Wahhad and Muhammad ibn Saud, then a minor tribal chief, an alliance was established between Wahhabism and the House of Saud, which has continued until the present day. Wahhabism advocates a return to the Islam of the first generation and opposes everything that has been added since. In that sense, there are parallels between Wahhabism and ultra-**orthodox** religious groups such as the Amish in the USA and the Haredim in Israel. Among other things, Wahhabis ban pictures, photographs, musical instruments, singing, videos and television, celebrations of Mohammed's birthday, and the cult of Mohammed as the perfect man. Any deviation from the *sharia* is treated by Wahhabis as an innovation, and therefore classified as 'unIslamic'. And any Muslim who disagrees with the Wahhabi interpretation of Islam is regarded as an unbelieving apostate who deserves severe punishment.

The origins of Salafism are different from those of Wahhabism. Salafism emerged as a school of Islamic thought in the second half of the nineteenth century, largely in reaction to the spread of European ideas and influences. Salafism advocates a return to the traditions of the devout ancestors (*salaf*), guided by the most literal, traditional interpretation of the sacred texts. In the process, it seeks to expose the roots of modernity within Muslim civilization, with a view to eradicating them. Initially, the Salafi mission of a return to primaeval Islam was entirely in harmony with the **puritanism** of the Wahhabi movement, both of them embracing a 'purification' creed that was consistent with a quietist political stance. However, these two faces of Sunni Islamism later drifted apart. Although 'reformist' trends could still be found in Salafism, associated with figures

ORTHODOXY
Strict adherence to an established or traditional view, usually enjoying 'official' sanction or support.

PURITANISM
Scrupulous moral vigour, especially reflected in the shunning of physical pleasures and luxury.

KEY FIGURES IN... ISLAMISM

Rudhollah Khomeini (1902–89) An Iranian cleric and political leader, Khomeini was the architect of the 'Iranian Revolution' and leader of Iran from 1979 to 1989. Khomeini's world-view was rooted in a clear division between the oppressed (understood largely as the poor and excluded of the developing world) and the oppressors (seen as the 'twin Satans': the USA and the Soviet Union, capitalism and communism). In Khomeini's Shia Islamism, Islam is a theo-political project aimed at regenerating the Islamic world by ridding it of occupation and corruption from outside.

Abul Ala Maududi (1903–79) An Indian-Pakistani scholar, philosopher, jurist and early exponent of Islamism, Maududi founded (in 1941) Jamaat-e Islami (the Islamic Party), which has developed into the most influential Islamist organization in modern Pakistan and Bangladesh. Committed to the spread of Islamic values in the subcontinent, Maududi viewed Islam as a 'revolutionary ideology and programme which seeks to alter the social order of the whole world and rebuild it in conformity with its own tenets and ideals'. Maududi rejected any identification of Islam with modern creeds, such as capitalism, communism and democracy.

Sayyid Qutb (1906–66) An Egyptian writer and religious leader, Qutb is sometimes seen as the 'father' of modern political Islam. A leading member of the Muslim Brotherhood, Qutb recoiled from what he saw as the moral and sexual corruption of the West, but, influenced by Maududi, highlighted the condition of *jihiliyyah* ('ignorance of divine guidance') into which the Muslim world had fallen. In the face of this, Qutb advocated Islam as a comprehensive political and social system that would both ensure social justice and sweep away corruption, oppression and luxury.

Yusuf al-Qaradawi (born 1926) An Egyptian Islamic theologian based in Doha, Qatar, Qaradawi is a leading exponent of 'new' or 'moderate' Islamism. While aiming to demonstrate Islamist support for such things as democracy, pluralism and human rights, Qaradawi has opposed the assimilation of 'western values' and insisted that Islam should be treated as a 'complete code of life'. Qaradawi supports military *jihad* in its defensive form, especially in relation to the Palestinian cause, but argues that offensive *jihad* is best pursued through the use of non-military means.

Abdallah Azzam (1941–89) A Palestinian Sunni theologian, scholar and founding member of al-Qaeda, Azzam played a leading role in developing, during the 1980s, a more radical ideological movement within Islamism dedicated to global *jihad*. Azzam implored Muslims to rally in defence of Muslim victims of aggression, to liberate Muslim lands from foreign domination, and to uphold the Muslim faith. Azzam was the mentor of Osama bin Laden (1957–2011), under whose leadership al-Qaeda extended Azzam's thinking by sanctioning struggle by 'all means' and in 'all places', justifying attacks against the USA and its allies.

Muhammad abd-al-Salam Faraj (1954–82) An Egyptian radical Islamist, Faraj was the leader of the Cairo branch of the Islamist group al-Jihad. Building on Qutb's belief that *jihad* is an individual duty incumbent on all Muslims, Faraj emphasized the role of armed combat and portrayed *jihad* as the sixth, 'forgotten' or 'neglected' pillar of Islam. Although for Faraj the primary target of the struggle was apostate Muslim rulers (the 'near enemy'), in The Neglected Duty, probably written in 1979, he maintained that *jihad* would enable Muslims to rule the world and to re-establish the caliphate.

such as the Egyptian jurist Muhammad Abduh (1849–1905), the more prominent tendency within Salafism was drawn in an increasingly activist and revolutionary direction. Wahhabism, in contrast, continued to represent staunch conservatism. The jihadi groups that emerged out of, or drew inspiration from, the Afghan war in the 1980s transformed Salafism into an ideology of global anti-western struggle, giving rise to 'jihadist-Salafism', or 'Salafi-jihadism' (Kepel, 2006). The most influential militant Salafi groups have been al-Qaeda and ISIS. However, only after the outbreak of the 'Arab Spring' in 2011 did openly Salafist parties and groups enter the political arena, usually offering a radical alternative to Muslim Brotherhood-linked groups in North Africa and elsewhere.

The Muslim Brotherhood has been the most enduringly important Sunni Islamist organization. Initially focused on building up a network of schools, hospitals and social services, the Brotherhood turned to politics during the 1930s, although its concern with social welfare continued to be important. The Brotherhood was at first committed to the use of peaceful and democratic means, but, when these failed, turned to violence, operating in and out of the shadows until it was banned in the 1950s by President Nasser. By this time, it had developed into a transnational organization, having spread from Egypt into Jordan, Syria, Palestine, Libya, Sudan and elsewhere. Although it remained outlawed in Egypt under President Mubarak, 1981–2011, the Brotherhood fielded 'independent' candidates in the 2005 parliamentary elections, winning 88 seats and becoming, in effect, the first legitimate opposition force in modern Egypt. Following the overthrow of Mubarak in 2011, the Brotherhood formally entered politics under the banner of the Freedom and Justice Party. When parliamentary elections were held in Tunisia, Egypt and Morocco in late 2011 and early 2012, in each case, parties set up, or inspired by, the Muslim Brotherhood were brought to power. Mohamed Morsi, the Brotherhood-backed candidate, became Egypt's president in 2012. However, Morsi was removed by the military in July 2013, after massed protests provoked by what many Egyptians saw as a power grab by Morsi. The Egyptian courts later outlawing the Muslim Brotherhood and any organization or activity associated with it. These events nevertheless raise questions about the extent to which the Brotherhood can adjust to a pluralist and constitutional political environment given its Islamist orientation.

Shia Islamism

While Sunnis tend to see Islamic history as a gradual movement away from the ideal community which existed during the life of Mohammed and his immediate

MAHDI
Literally, 'one rightly guided'; a prophesied spiritual and temporal leader who is destined to be the redeemer of Islam.

successors, Shias have believed that divine guidance is always available in the teachings of the infallible imam, or that divine wisdom is about to re-emerge into the world with the return of the 'hidden Imam', or the arrival of the Mahdi. Shias thus see history as a movement towards the goal of an ideal community, not away from it. Such ideas of revival and imminent salvation have given the Shia sect a messianic and emotional quality not enjoyed by the traditionally more sober Sunnis.

The religious temper of the Shia sect is also different from that of the Sunnis. Shias believe that it is possible for an individual to remove the stains of sin through the experience of suffering and by leading a devout and simple life. The prospect of spiritual salvation has given the Shia sect its characteristic intensity and emotional strength. When such religious zeal has been harnessed to a political goal it has generated fierce commitment and devotion. The Shia sect has, at least since the sixteenth century, sometimes been seen as more political than the Sunni sect. This has been because it is especially attractive to the poor and the downtrodden, for whom the re-emergence of divine wisdom in the world has represented the purification of society, the overthrow of injustice, and liberation from oppression. Nevertheless, there continues to be a tradition within Shia Islam that is reluctant to engage fully in politics, as represented, for instance, by Ali al-Sistani (born 1930), the spiritual leader of the Iraqi Shias.

However, the politico-religious propensities of Shia Islam were clearly illustrated by the popular demonstrations that in Iran precipitated the overthrow of the Shah and prepared the way for the creation of an Islamic Republic under Ayatollah Khomeini. The revolutionary enthusiasm generated by the Islamic Revolution reached new heights during the Iran–Iraq war, 1980–88, sustained as it also was by the continuing messianic influence of Khomeini himself. The end of the war and the death of Khomeini in 1989 nevertheless laid the foundations for more moderate forces to surface within Iran. The Iranian economy had been devastated by the massive cost of the eight-year war and a lack of foreign trade and investment. There was a growing recognition that economic revival would be impossible unless Iran's diplomatic isolation from the industrialized West was brought to an end. This was reflected in the emergence of Hashemi Rafsanjani, speaker of the Iranian parliament (the Islamic Consultative Assembly), and his election as president in 1989 marked a more pragmatic and less ideological turn in Iranian politics.

Nevertheless, the election of Mahmoud Ahmadinejad as president in 2005 signalled a return to conservative politics and the emergence of a form of explicit 'Khomeinism'. The brutal suppression of popular protests against Ahmadinejad's disputed re-election in 2009 intensified the polarized nature of Iranian politics and emphasized the extent to which the continued ascendancy of radical Islamism is dependent on the support of paramilitary forces. However, deepening concern about the economy, linked to the impact of the US-led sanctions regime, and a widening divide between Ahmadinejad and the clerical elite, and especially the Supreme Leader, Ali Khamenei, led in 2013 to the election as president of the pragmatic conservative, Hassan Rouhani. This laid the ground for the historic 2015 deal between Iran and the five permanent members of the UN Security Council plus Germany and the EU, under which economic sanctions were lifted in return for Iran accepting restrictions on its pursuit of nuclear technology. For some, this development underlined the fact that exclusive and militant Islamism is unworkable in an increasingly globalized world. It is notable, however, that greater pragmatism (see p. 9) in political and economic life in Iran has not so far been matched by a decline in religious observance or commitment, or by an end to Iran's links to, and support for, radical Islamist groups in Palestine and elsewhere.

'Moderate' or 'conservative' Islamism

Not all forms of Islamism are militant and revolutionary. Although, as discussed earlier, much confusion surrounds the idea of 'moderate' (as opposed to 'radical') Islamism, there is a school of Islamist thought that is distinguished by the attempt to reconcile political Islam with democratic elections and party pluralism. The issue of democracy has been particularly problematic in this respect, since it appears to place popular sovereignty ahead of the will of God. Rashid Rida nevertheless saw no threat to Islam in the principle of popular sovereignty. For Rida, democracy for Muslims is ensured by both the implementation of the principle of *shura*, or consultation, between the rulers and the ruled, and the predominance of the ulama, who he argued are ideally placed to act as the natural and genuine representatives of the people. Yusuf al-Qaradawi (1990), for his part, argued that democracy can be reconciled with the rule of God providing that democracy is put on an Islamic basis. This, he suggested, could be achieved through the introduction of a single constitutional provision stipulating that 'any legislation contradicting the incontestable provisions of Islam shall be null and void'. By rectifying what Islamists see as the normative shortcomings of secular democracy, this would create a system of 'true, not false democracy'. In line with such thinking, both the Afghan constitution of 2004 and the Iraqi constitution of 2005 contain what is sometimes called a 'repugnancy clause', under which the judiciary is authorized to overturn laws that are repugnant to Islam.

Political developments in modern Turkey provide a particularly telling example of the relationship between Islamism and democracy in the sphere of practical politics. This is because tensions have existed between the military, committed to the strict secular principles on which the state of Turkey was established, and a growing Islamist movement. The Justice and Development Party (AKP) has been in power since 2003, advancing a form of constitutional Islamism. The AKP has attempted to balance moderate conservative politics based on Islamic values with an acceptance of Turkey's secular democratic framework. Rather than choosing between East and West, it has tried to establish a Turkish identity that is confident in being part of both. A key aspect of this compromise is continuing attempts by Turkey to gain membership of the EU.

Critics have nevertheless warned that the AKP plans to overturn the secular nature of the Turkish

---

ULAMA
A body of Muslim scholars who are recognized as having specialist knowledge of Islamic sacred law and theology.

state, possibly establishing an Iranian-style Islamic republic through a process of 'Islamification'. The ban on the wearing of the Islamic headscarf in Turkish universities (which had been enforced only since the 1980s) was lifted in 2010, and restrictions on the sale of alcohol have been imposed in some parts of the country. Turkey has also increasingly looked to build ties with the Arab world and has become more critical of Israel. In July 2016, deepening tension between elements in the military, possibly supported by wider forces, and the AKP government headed by President Tayyip Erdoğan resulted in a failed coup. In the aftermath of the coup, over 4,000 institutions were shut down and tens of thousands of public servants, teachers, academics and others were sacked or suspended in a purge through which the Erdoğan government solidified its control over the police, the military, the judiciary, the media and the education system. These events sparked intensified concerns about the fate of political pluralism in Turkey. Turkey may thus be facing a predicament that is the opposite of Iran's. While in Turkey democracy may be under threat from invigorated Islamism, in Iran radical Islamism may be under threat from the pressures generated by democracy.

Islamism in a global age

Islam, like Christianity, has had a global orientation from its earliest days. This has been the case for two reasons. First, Islam often served as the cultural dimension of imperial expansion, reflecting, in broad terms, the fact that conquerors and colonists have frequently used religion as both a moral justification for expansionism and as a means of consolidating political rule. Islam thus spread across central and western Asia and into North Africa and parts of Europe through the activities of successive Mughal, Safavid and Ottoman empires, in the same way that Christianity was spread throughout Europe and into Asia Minor by the Roman Empire, and later arrived in the Americas thanks to the Spanish and Portuguese conquistadores. Second, Islam, once again in common with Christianity, has exhibited a strong global orientation by virtue of its doctrinal character, and especially its tendency towards evangelicalism. This reflects the tendency within both Islam and Christianity to claim to be the one, true religion, and to preach that salvation in the afterlife will be restricted to believers; non-believers, in effect, being damned. Converting others to Islamic or Christian beliefs can therefore be seen as nothing less than a religious duty, inspired by the need to counter 'false' religions and gods, as well as to save people's immortal souls.

Such globalizing tendencies have nevertheless become more pronounced due to the rise of Islamism. During the 1970s and 1980s, domestic *jihad* predominated over global *jihad*, as hostility to the USA and the idea that Islam was engaged in a larger struggle against the West provided merely a backdrop to attempts to achieve power at the national level. This nevertheless changed from the 1990s onwards, and did so, according to Kepel (2006), largely through the failure of

EVANGELICALISM
The theory and practice of spreading (in origin, Christian) religious beliefs, usually through missionary campaigns.

political Islam to achieve its domestic goals. 'Apostate' regimes often proved to be more stable and enduring than anticipated, and, in cases such as Egypt and Algeria, military repression was used successfully to quell Islamist insurgents. In this context, *jihad* went global, as growing elements within the Islamist movement realigned their strategies around the 'far enemy'. This process was significantly assisted by the war in Afghanistan against the Soviet invasion, which served to forge a 'corporate' sense of belonging among Islamist groups that often had different backgrounds and sometimes different doctrinal beliefs.

This shift to a global strategy was facilitated, in part, by the process of globalization (see p. 20). Global jihadism could, indeed, be portrayed as a by-product of globalization (Gray, 2003). This can be seen in at least two senses. In the first place, increased cross-border flows of people, goods, money, technology and ideas have generally benefited non-state actors, and there is no doubt that Islamist groups have been particularly adept at exploiting this hyper-mobility. For example, new media, and especially the Internet and mobile phones, have been widely used by jihadi groups, both for recruitment purposes and to increase their operational effectiveness. Similarly, increased international migration flows and the growth in the West of substantial Muslim communities have helped to sustain and extend Islamist terrorist campaigns, in part through the phenomenon of 'home-grown' terrorism. Second, globalization has generated pressures that have contributed to the growth in Islamist militancy generally. This has occurred either as a backlash against cultural globalization and the spread of western goods, ideas and values, portrayed by Barber (2003) as the clash between 'McWorld' and 'Jihad', or as a consequence of imbalances in the global capitalist system that have impoverished and destabilized much of the Middle East, and especially the Arab world.

The global character of the modern Islamist or jihadist movement should not be overstated, however. For example, the Islamist movement is by no means a single, cohesive entity; rather, it encompasses groups with often very different beliefs and goals, many of them being better classified as religious nationalists, or perhaps pan-Islamic nationalists, than as global revolutionaries. Thus to treat attacks such as September 11, the 2002 and 2005 Bali bombings, the 2002 Moscow theatre hostage crisis and the 2008 Mumbai bombings as manifestations of the single phenomenon of 'jihadist terrorism', implying that they had a common inspiration and purpose, may be seriously to misunderstand them.

? QUESTIONS FOR DISCUSSION

- To what extent is Islamism part of a larger phenomenon of religious revivalism?

- Is Islamism best understood as an example of religious fundamentalism?

- Can a meaningful distinction be drawn between Islamism and Islam?

- To what extent is Islamism a manifestation of a 'civilizational' struggle between Islam and the West?

- Is 'moderate Islamism' a contradiction in terms?

- Should the Islamic state be viewed as the restoration of the caliphate?

- Is Islamism necessarily linked to militancy and violence?

- Is there such a thing as 'Islamist terrorism'?

- How did Salafism come to be associated with the doctrine of global jihadism?

- In what ways does Shia Islamism differ from Sunni Islamism?

- Can Islamism ever co-exist with pluralism and democracy?

- How, and to what extent, can Islamism be seen as a by-product of globalization?

📖 FURTHER READING

Buck-Morss, S., *Thinking Past Terror: Islamism and Critical Theory on the Left* (2006). A study of Islamism that argues that we should look beyond the 'twin insanities' of terrorism and counter-terrorism, drawing, variously, on ideas from critical theory, feminism and postcolonialism.

Martin, R. C. and Barzegar, A. (eds), *Islamism: Contested Perspectives on Political Islam* (2009). A stimulating collection, written by Muslim and non-Muslim intellectuals, that examines contrasting approaches to Islamism and explores their implications.

Osman, T., *Islamism: What it Means for the Middle East and the World* (2016). A provocative exploration of the development of the largest and most influential Islamist groups in the Middle East over the past century, which also speculates on prospects for the future.

Tibi, B., *Islamism and Islam* (2012). A trenchant analysis of Islamism as a political ideology based on a reinvented version of Islamic law, which highlights the gulf between Islamism and its emphasis on political order, and the faith of Islam.

CHAPTER

12 Ideology Without End?

Preview

Political ideology has been an essential component of world history for over 200 years. Ideology sprang out of the upheavals – economic, social and political – through which the modern world took shape, and has been intimately involved in the continuing process of social transformation and political development. Although ideology emerged first in the industrializing West, it has subsequently appeared throughout the globe, creating a worldwide language of political discourse. However, opinion has been deeply divided about the role that ideology has played in human history. Has ideology served the cause of truth, progress and justice, or has it generated distorted and blinkered world-views, resulting in intolerance and oppression?

This debate has often been carried out in negative terms, highlighting criticisms of ideology, often by predicting its imminent demise. However, what is remarkable is how many and how varied the obituaries for political ideology have been. The various obituaries have been viewed as different forms of 'endism'. The idea of the 'end of ideology' became fashionable in the 1950s and early 1960s, and suggested that politics was no longer concerned with larger normative issues, as technical questions about how to deliver affluence had come to dominate political debate. In the aftermath of the collapse of communism, so-called 'end of history' theorists argued that ideological disagreement had ended in the final victory of western liberal democracy. Alternative forms of endism have highlighted the alleged redundancy of the left/right divide, on which the 'classical' ideological traditions depended, and held that the triumph of rationalism and modern technology has fatally undermined the ideological style of thought. Ideological politics, however, remains stubbornly resistant to being disinvented. Indeed, as the principal source of meaning and idealism in politics, ideology is destined to be a continuing and unending process.

Endism

End of ideology?

The idea of the 'end of ideology' became fashionable in the 1950s and 1960s. The most influential statement of this position was advanced by Daniel Bell (1960). Bell (see p. 329) was impressed by the fact that, after World War II politics in the West was characterized by broad agreement among major political parties and the absence of ideological division or debate. Fascism and communism had both lost their appeal, while the remaining parties disagreed only about which of them could best be relied on to deliver economic growth and material prosperity. In effect, economics had triumphed over politics. Politics had been reduced to technical questions about 'how' to deliver affluence, and had ceased to address moral or philosophical questions about the nature of the 'good society'. To all intents and purposes, ideology had become an irrelevance.

However, the process to which Bell drew attention was not the 'end of ideology' so much as the emergence of a broad ideological consensus among major parties, and therefore the suspension of ideological debate. In the immediate postwar period, representatives of the three major western ideologies – liberalism, socialism and conservatism – came to accept the common goal of managed capitalism. This goal, however, was itself ideological – for example, it reflected an enduring faith in market economics, private property and material incentives, tempered by a belief in social welfare and economic intervention. In effect, an ideology of 'welfare capitalism' or 'social democracy' had triumphed over its rivals, although this triumph proved to be only temporary. The 1960s witnessed the rise of more radical New Left ideas, reflected in a revival of interest in Marxist and anarchist thought and the growth of modern ideologies such as feminism and ecologism. The onset of economic recession in the 1970s provoked renewed interest in long-neglected, free-market doctrines and stimulated the development of New Right theories, which also challenged the post-war consensus. Finally, the 'end of ideology' thesis focused attention exclusively on developments in the industrialized West and ignored the fact that in the 1950s and 1960s communism remained firmly entrenched in the Soviet Union, eastern Europe, China and elsewhere, and that revolutionary political movements were operating in Asia, Africa and parts of Latin America.

End of history?

A broader perspective was adopted by Francis Fukuyama (see p. 329) in his essay 'The End of History' (1989), later developed into *The End of History and the Last Man* (1992). Unlike Bell, Fukuyama did not suggest that political ideas had become irrelevant, but that one particular set of ideas, western liberalism, had triumphed over all its rivals. Fascism had been defeated in 1945, and Fukuyama clearly believed that the collapse of communist rule in eastern Europe in 1989 marked the passing of Marxism-Leninism as an ideology of world significance. By the 'end of history',

PERSPECTIVES ON... HISTORY

LIBERALS see history as progress, brought about as each generation advances further than the last through the accumulation of knowledge and understanding. Liberals generally believe that this will happen through gradual or incremental reform, not through revolution.

CONSERVATIVES understand history in terms of tradition and continuity, allowing little scope for progress. The lessons of the past provide guidance for present and future conduct. Reactionary conservatives believe that history is marked by decline, and wish to return to an earlier and preferred time.

SOCIALISTS are committed to a progressive view of history, which places heavy emphasis on the scope for social and personal development. Marxists believe that class conflict is the motor of history and that a classless, communist society is history's determinant end-point.

FASCISTS generally view history as a process of degeneration and decay, a decline from a past 'golden age'. They nevertheless subscribe to a cyclical theory of history that holds out the possibility of national rebirth and regeneration, usually through violent struggle and war.

ISLAMISTS have an ambivalent attitude towards history. Although they are strongly inclined to see the present as morally and spiritually corrupt in comparison with an idealized past, they conceive of social regeneration in modernist terms, thus rejecting conservative traditionalism.

Fukuyama meant that the history of ideas had ended, and with it, fundamental ideological debate. Throughout the world there was, he argued, an emerging agreement about the desirability of liberal democracy (see p. 40), in the form of a market or capitalist economy and an open, competitive political system.

Without doubt, the eastern European revolutions of 1989–91 and the dramatic reform of surviving communist regimes such as China profoundly altered the worldwide balance of ideological debate. However, it is far less certain that this process amounted to the 'end of history'. One difficulty with the 'end of history' thesis is that no sooner had it been proclaimed than new ideological forces rose to the surface. While liberal democracy may have made impressive progress during the twentieth century, as the century drew to a close there was undoubted evidence of the revival of very different ideologies, notably Islamism, whose influence has come to extend from the Muslim countries of Asia and Africa into the former Soviet Union and the industrialized West. It is possible, for example, that the 'death of communism' in the Soviet Union and eastern Europe prepared the way for the revival of nationalism, racism (see p. 210) or religious fundamentalism (see p. 188), rather than led to the final victory of liberal democracy.

Underlying Fukuyama's thesis was the optimistic belief, inherited from classical liberalism, that industrial capitalism offers all members of society the prospect of social mobility and material security, encouraging every citizen to regard it as reasonable and attractive. In other words, it is possible for a broad, even universal, agreement to be achieved about the nature of the 'good society'. This can nevertheless only be achieved if a society can be constructed that is capable both of satisfying the interests of all major social groups and of fulfilling the aspirations of at least a substantial majority of individual citizens. Despite the undoubted vigour and efficiency that the capitalist market has demonstrated, it certainly cannot be said that capitalism has treated all social classes or all individuals alike. Ideological conflict and debate are thus unlikely to have ended in the late twentieth century with the ultimate worldwide triumph of liberalism, any more than they did with the 'inevitable' victory of socialism so widely predicted at the end of the nineteenth century.

Beyond left and right?

Yet another form of 'endism' is the belief that, as the established features of modern society have crumbled, the political creeds and doctrines it threw up have been rendered irrelevant. This notion is usually advanced through the idea of postmodernity. Not only have the major ideologies, both left-wing and right-wing, been adapted to the 'postmodern condition', giving rise to 'post-isms' such as postliberalism, post-Marxism and postfeminism, but, according to postmodern theorists, our way of understanding and interpreting the world has changed, or needs to change. This reflects a shift from modernism to postmodernism (see p. 59). Modernism stemmed largely from Enlightenment ideas and theories, and was expressed politically in ideological traditions that offer rival conceptions of the good life. The clearest examples are liberalism and Marxism. Modernist thought is characterized by foundationalism. In contrast, postmodernism is anti-foundationalist; the central theme of postmodernism was summed up by Jean-François Lyotard (1984) as 'incredulity towards meta-narratives', meta-narratives being universal theories of history that view society as a coherent totality.

However, such tendencies also provide evidence of the decline of the left/right divide (see pp. 15–17), which marks an important transition in ideological politics. The left/right divide helped to structure ideological debate in the nineteenth and twentieth centuries, in that, to a large extent, competing ideological positions and arguments offered different solutions to essentially the same problem. The problem was the destiny of industrial society, and the various solutions offered ranged from free-market capitalism, on the one hand, to central planning and state collectivization on the other. Ideological debate, then, tended to focus on the desirable balance between the market and the state. Since the 1960s, however, politics

FOUNDATIONALISM
The belief that it is possible to establish objective truths and universal values, usually associated with a strong faith in progress.

has certainly not become less ideological, but ideological developments have become increasingly fragmented. The 'new' ideologies – feminism, green ideology, religious fundamentalism and multiculturalism – have each, in their different ways, opened up new directions for ideological thinking. However, because each, in a sense, has thrown up its own ideological discourse (based on gender, nature, religion, culture and so on), they are not part of a larger discourse, as applied in the case of the clash between capitalism and socialism.

Nevertheless, various explanations have been offered for the declining salience of the left/right divide. Samuel Huntington's (see p. 329) vision of a 'clash of civilizations' (see p. 310) linked it to changes in global politics that have occurred because of the end of the Cold War. A world divided along ideological lines, with the USA and the Soviet Union respectively representing the forces of capitalism and communism, had faded and eventually disappeared, leaving politics to be structured by issues of identity and, in particular, culture. In this view, developments such as the growth of Islamism and the rise of China and India constitute 'civilizational', rather than an ideological, threats to the West.

Anthony Giddens (1994), in contrast, linked the exhaustion of both left-wing and right-wing ideological traditions to sociological developments associated with the emergence of so-called 'high modernity'. Giddens (see p. 329) placed a particular emphasis on the impact of globalization (see p. 20) and the tendency for peoples' lives to be shaped increasingly by developments that occur, and events that happen, at a great distance from them. This, together with the emergence of a 'post-traditional' social order and the expansion of social reflexivity, has created societies that are so fluid and complex that they have, effectively, outgrown the major ideological traditions. Politics, therefore, has gone beyond left and right, a development that has been particularly evident in the 'hollowing out' of parliamentary socialism since the 1990s. In an alternative analysis of the implications of an interconnected or interdependent world, Sil and Katzenstein (2010) have argued that it is necessary to go 'beyond' paradigms, including academic disciplines as well as theoretical or ideological systems, in order to understand political realities that are increasingly multifaceted and multidimensional. In this view, no paradigm, ideological or otherwise, is capable, on its own, of fully explaining the almost infinitely complex realities it purports to disclose.

SOCIAL REFLEXIVITY
Interaction between people who enjoy a high level of autonomy within a context of reciprocity and interdependence.

Triumph of reason?

The debate about the replacement of ideology by rationalism (see p. 31) goes back to the nineteenth century and the firm distinction that Marx (see p. 124) drew between 'ideology' and 'science'. For Marx, ideology was intrinsically false because it serves as a vehicle for advancing class interests. In contrast, he portrayed his own

KEY FIGURES IN... ENDISM

Daniel Bell (1919–2011) A US academic and essayist, Bell drew attention, in *The End of Ideology* (1960), to the exhaustion of rationalist approaches to social and political issues, also warning, in the afterword to the 1988 edition, against the tyranny of utopian end-states. He helped to popularize the idea of 'post-industrialism', highlighting the emergence of 'information societies' dominated by a new 'knowledge class'. In *The Cultural Contradictions of Capitalism* (1976), Bell analysed the tension between capitalism's productivist and consumerist values and tendencies.

Samuel P. Huntington (1927–2008) A US academic and political commentator, Huntington's most widely discussed work, *The Clash of Civilizations and the Remaking of World Order* (1996), advanced the controversial thesis that, in the twenty-first century, conflict between the world's major civilizations would lead to warfare and international disorder. In *Who Are We?* (2004), Huntington discussed the challenges posed to the USA's national identity by large-scale Latino immigration and the unwillingness of Latino communities to assimilate into the language and culture of majority societies.

Anthony Giddens (born 1938) A UK social theorist, Giddens was an adviser to Tony Blair in the early years of 'new' Labour. His theory of 'structuration' reinvigorated social theory by setting out to transcend the conventional dualism of structure and agency. In works including *Beyond Left and Right* (1994), *The Third Way* (1998) and *The Runaway World* (1999), Giddens sought to remodel social democracy in the light of the advent of late modernity, taking into account developments such as globalization, de-traditionalization and increased social reflexivity.

Francis Fukuyama (born 1952) A US social analyst and political commentator, Fukuyama's essay, 'The End of History?' (1989), argued that the eastern European revolutions indicated that the history of ideas had ended with the recognition of liberal democracy as the 'final form of human government'. In *Trust* (1996) and *The Great Disruption* (1999), he discussed the relationship between economic development and social cohesion, highlighting contrasting forms of capitalist development. In *After the Neocons* (2006), Fukuyama developed a post-9/11 critique of US foreign policy.

ideas as a form of 'scientific' socialism. Science, in this view, provides an objective and value-free method of advancing human knowledge, so releasing humanity from enslavement to irrational beliefs, which includes superstitions, prejudices and, in this case, political ideologies. This, indeed, has proved to be one of the enduring myths of modern times. It has recurred, for instance, in relation to the cultural and intellectual implications of globalization, one of the chief features of the emerging global age being an acceptance of a western model of rationality,

SCIENCE
A method of acquiring knowledge through a process of careful observation and the testing of hypotheses by reproducible experiments.

reflected, most obviously, in the value placed on technology and technological development. In this sense, ideology may be in the process of being displaced by scientism.

However, science is not the antithesis of ideology, but can perhaps be seen as an ideology in its own right. For example, science has been linked to powerful social forces, in particular those represented by industry and technology. Scientism could therefore be viewed as the ideology of the technocratic elite, its main beneficiary being the transnational corporations that are increasingly responsible for funding scientific and technological developments. Moreover, significant ideological controversy has surrounded the advance of science. This can be seen in the case of some ecologists, who view science and technology as the source of the environmental crisis. Multiculturalists and religious fundamentalists, for their part, have sometimes interpreted rationalism as a form of cultural imperialism, on the grounds that it undermines faith-based belief systems and helps to strengthen western and often materialist modes of understanding.

The resilience of ideology

However, each of these versions of endism has one thing in common: they are conducted within an ongoing framework of ideological thinking. In different ways, each of them heralds the demise of ideology by highlighting the triumph of a particular ideological tradition, be it welfare capitalism, liberal democracy, postmodernism or scientism. Rather than demonstrating the weakened grasp of ideology, endism in fact shows its remarkable resilience and robustness. Once invented, ideological politics has proved stubbornly resistant to being *dis*invented.

What, nevertheless, is the source of ideology's survival and success? The first answer to this question is undoubtedly its flexibility, the fact that ideological traditions and forms go through a seemingly endless process of redefinition and renewal, and, if necessary, new ideologies emerge as old ones fade or fail. The world of ideologies thus does not stand still, but changes in response to changing social and historical circumstances. The second and deeper explanation is that, as the principal source of meaning and idealism in politics, ideology touches those aspects of politics that other political form cannot reach. In effect, ideology gives people a reason to believe in something larger than themselves, because people's personal narratives only make sense when they are situated within a broader historical narrative. A post-ideological age would therefore be an age without hope, without vision. This is evident in modern, 'de-ideologized' party politics, in which, as parties of both left and right become detached from their ideological roots, they lose their sense of purpose and direction, failing to provide members and supporters alike with a basis for emotional attachment. As parties come to sell 'products' (leaders or policies) rather than hopes or dreams, party membership and voter turnout both fall, and politicians become increasingly desperate to re-engage with the 'vision thing'. By creating an appetite for the resurgence of ideology, post-ideological politics contains the seeds of its own undoing, a tendency that helps to explain, for instance, the rise of both right- and left-wing populism (see p. 85) in the period since the 2007–9 global financial crisis. For this, if for no other reason, political ideology is destined to be a continuing and unending process.

⑦ QUESTIONS FOR DISCUSSION

- What were the flaws of the 'end of ideology' thesis?
- Why have 'end of history' theorists viewed liberal democracy as the final solution to the problem of governance?
- Could history ever come to an end?
- Can intellectuals rise above ideology?
- Why have postmodernists proclaimed the death of 'metanarratives'?
- Is the left/right divide now redundant?
- Can science be thought of as an ideological tradition?
- To what extent has ideology created a worldwide language of political discourse?
- Is ideology a help or a hindrance to a political party?
- Can politics exist without ideology?
- Does ideology enlighten or delude?

📖 FURTHER READING

Freeden, M., *Reassessing Political Ideologies: The Durability of Dissent* (2001). A volume of essays that consider and reassess the major ideological traditions in a so-called 'post-ideological' age.

Gamble, A., *Politics and Fate* (2000). A defence of politics and the political that reflects the source of disenchantment with politics and the endless discourses on 'endism'.

Gray, J., *Endgames: Questions in Late Modern Political Thought* (1997). A fascinating and insightful discussion of the condition of the major ideological traditions as they confront the collapse of the 'Enlightenment project'.

Shtromas, A. (ed.), *The End of 'isms'? Reflections on the Fate of Ideological Politics after Communism's Collapse* (1994). A collection of considered and carefully argued essays on the state of and future prospects for the politics of ideology after the collapse of communism.

Bibliography

Acton, Lord (1956) *Essays on Freedom and Power*. London: Meridian.

Adams, I. (1989) *The Logic of Political Belief: A Philosophical Analysis*. London and New York: Harvester Wheatsheaf.

Adams, I. (2001) *Political Ideology Today*, 2nd edn. Manchester: Manchester University Press.

Adib-Moghaddam, A. (ed.) (2014) *Introduction to Khomeini*. New York: Cambridge University Press.

Adonis, A. and Hames, T. (1994) *A Conservative Revolution? The Thatcher–Reagan Decade in Perspective*. Manchester: Manchester University Press.

Adorno, T., Frenkel-Brunswik, E., Levinson, D. and Sandford, R. (1950) *The Authoritarian Personality*. New York: Harper.

Ahmed, A. and Donnan, H. (1994) *Islam, Globalization and Postmodernity*. London and New York: Routledge.

Ahmed, R. (2001) *Jihad: The Rise of Militant Islam in Central Asia*. New Haven, CT: Yale University Press.

Ali, T. (2003) *The Clash of Fundamentalism: Crusades, Jihads and Modernity*. London: Verso.

al-Qaradawi, Y. (1990) *Islamic Awakening between Rejection and Extremism*. Herndon, VA: International Institute of Islamic Thought.

Anderson, B. (1983) *Imagined Communities: Reflections on the Origins and Spread of Nationalism*. London: Verso.

Arblaster, A. (1984) *The Rise and Decline of Western Liberalism*. Oxford: Basil Blackwell.

Arendt, H. (1951) *The Origins of Totalitarianism*. London: Allen & Unwin.

Aristotle (1962) *The Politics*, trans. T. Sinclair. Harmondsworth: Penguin (Chicago, IL: University of Chicago Press, 1985).

Aughey, A., Jones, G. and Riches, W. T. M. (1992) *The Conservative Political Tradition in Britain and the United States*. London: Pinter.

Bahro, R. (1982) *Socialism and Survival*. London: Heretic Books.

Bahro, R. (1984) *From Red to Green*. London: Verso/New Left Books.

Bakunin, M. (1973) *Selected Writings*, ed. A. Lehning. London: Cape.

Bakunin, M. (1977) 'Church and State', in G. Woodcock (ed.), *The Anarchist Reader*. London: Fontana.

Ball, T., Dagger, R. and O'Neill, R. (2016) *Political Ideologies and the Democratic Ideal*. Abingdon and New York: Routledge.

Baradat, L. P. (2003) *Political Ideologies: Their Origins and Impact*, 8th edn. Upper Saddle River, NJ: Prentice Hall.

Baran, Z. with Touhy, E. (2011) *Citizen Islam: The Future of Muslim Integration in the West*. New York and London: Continuum Books.

Barber, B. (2003) *Jihad vs. the World: How Globalism and Tribalism Are Reshaping the World*. London: Corgi Books.

Barker, R. (1997) *Political Ideas in Modern Britain: In and After the 20th Century*, 2nd edn. London and New York: Routledge.

Barry, B. (2002) *Culture and Equality*. Cambridge and New York: Polity Press.

Barry, J. (1999) *Rethinking Green Politics*. London and Thousand Oaks, CA: Sage.

Barry, N. (1987) *The New Right*. London: Croom Helm.

Baumann, Z. (1999) *In Search of Politics*. Cambridge and Malden, MA: Polity Press.

Baumann, Z. (2000) *Liquid Modernity*. Cambridge and New York: Polity Press.

Baxter, B. (1999) *Ecologism: An Introduction*. Edinburgh: Edinburgh University Press.

Beard, C. ([1913] 1952) *An Economic Interpretation of the Constitution*. New York: Macmillan.

Beasley, C. (1999) *What Is Feminism?* London: Sage.

Beasley, C. (2005) *Gender and Sexuality: Critical Theories and Critical Thinkers*. London and Thousand Oaks, CA: Sage Publications.

Beauvoir, S. de (1968) *The Second Sex*, trans. H. M. Parshley. New York: Bantam.

Beck, U. (1992) *Risk Society: Towards a New Modernity*. London and New York: Sage.

Bell, D. (1960) *The End of Ideology*. Glencoe, IL: Free Press.

Bellamy, R. (1992) *Liberalism and Modern Society: An Historical Argument*. Cambridge: Polity Press.

Benn, T. (1980) *Arguments for Democracy*. Harmondsworth: Penguin.

Bentham, J. (1970) *Introduction to the Principles of Morals and Legislation*, ed. J. Burns and H. L. A. Hart. London: Athlone Press and Glencoe, IL: Free Press.

Berki, R. N. (1975) *Socialism*. London: Dent.

Berlin, I. ([1958] 1969) 'Two Concepts of Liberty', in *Four Essays on Liberty*. London: Oxford University Press.

Berman, P. (2003) *Terror and Liberalism*. New York: W. W. Norton.

Bernstein, E. ([1898] 1962) *Evolutionary Socialism*. New York: Schocken.

Black, A. (2011) *History of Islamic Political Thought: From the Prophet to the Present*. Edinburgh: Edinburgh University Press.

Blakeley, G. and Bryson, V. (eds) (2002) *Contemporary Political Concepts: A Critical Introduction*. London: Pluto Press.

Bobbio, N. (1996) *Left and Right: The Significance of a Political Distinction*. Oxford: Polity Press.

Bobbitt, P. (2002) *The Shield of Achilles*. New York: Knopf and London: Allen Lane.

Boff, L. (2006) *Fundamentalism, Terrorism and the Future of Humanity*. London: Society for Promoting Christian Knowledge.

Bookchin, M. ([1962] 1975) *Our Synthetic Environment*. London: Harper & Row.

Bookchin, M. (1977) 'Anarchism and Ecology', in G. Woodcock (ed.), *The Anarchist Reader*. London: Fontana.

Boulding, K. (1966) 'The Economics of the Coming Spaceship Earth', in H. Jarrett (ed.), *Environmental Quality in a Growing Economy*. Baltimore, MD: Johns Hopkins Press.

Bourne, R. (1977) 'War Is the Health of the State', in G. Woodcock (ed.), *The Anarchist Reader*. London: Fontana.

Bracher, K. D. (1985) *The Age of Ideologies: A History of Political Thought in the Twentieth Century*. London: Methuen.

Bramwell, A. (1989) *Ecology in the Twentieth Century: A History*. New Haven, CT and London: Yale University Press.

Bramwell, A. (1994) *The Fading of the Greens: The Decline of Environmental Politics in the West*. New Haven, CT and London: Yale University Press.

Browers, M. (2015) 'Islamic Political Ideologies', in M. Freeden, L. T. Sargent, and M. Stears (eds), *The Oxford Handbook of Political Ideologies*. Oxford and New York: Oxford University Press.

Brown, D. (2000) *Contemporary Nationalism: Civic, Ethnocultural and Multicultural Politics*. London: Routledge.

Brownmiller, S. (1975) *Against Our Will: Men, Women and Rape*. New York: Simon & Schuster.

Bruce, S. (1993) 'Fundamentalism, Ethnicity and Enclave', in M. Marty and R. S. Appleby (eds), *Fundamentalism and the State*. Chicago, IL and London: Chicago University Press.

Bruce, S. (2008) *Fundamentalism*. Cambridge: Polity Press.

Bryson, V. (2003) *Feminist Political Theory: An Introduction*, 2nd edn. Basingstoke and New York: Palgrave Macmillan.

Buck-Morss, S. (2006) *Thinking Past Terror: Islamism and Critical Theory on the Left*. London: Verso Books.

Burke, E. ([1790] 1968) *Reflections on the Revolution in France*. Harmondsworth: Penguin.

Burke, E. ([1790] 1975) *On Government, Politics and Society*, ed. B. W. Hill. London: Fontana.

Burnham, J. (1960) *The Managerial Revolution*. Harmondsworth: Penguin and Bloomington, IN: Indiana University Press.

Buruma, I. and Margalit, A. (2004) *Occidentalism: A Short History of Anti-Westernism*. London: Atlantic Books.

Butler, C. (2002) *Postmodernism: A Very Short Introduction*. Oxford and New York: Oxford University Press.

Butler, J. (2006) *Gender Trouble*. Abingdon and New York: Routledge.

Capra, F. (1975) *The Tao of Physics*. London: Fontana.

Capra, F. (1982) *The Turning Point*. London: Fontana (Boston, MA: Shambhala, 1983).

Capra, F. (1997) *The Web of Life: A New Synthesis of Mind and Matter*. London: Flamingo.

Carson, R. (1962) *The Silent Spring*. Boston, MA: Houghton Mifflin.

Carter, A. (1971) *The Political Theory of Anarchism*. London: Routledge & Kegan Paul.

Castells, M. (2000) *The Rise of the Network Society*. Oxford and Malden, MA: Blackwell.

Cecil, H. (1912) *Conservatism*. London and New York: Home University Library.

Chamberlain, H. S. ([1899] 1913) *Foundations of the Nineteenth Century*. New York: John Lane.

Charvet, J. (1982) *Feminism*. London: Dent.

Chesterton, G. K. (1908) *Orthodoxy*. London: John Lane, The Bodley Head.

Chomsky, N. (1999) *The New Military Humanism*. Monroe, ME: Common Courage Press.

Chomsky, N. (2003) *Hegemony and Survival: America's Quest for Global Domination*. New York: Henry Holt & Company.

Chomsky, N. (2013) *Anarchism*. New York: The New Press.

Christoyannopoulos, A. (2009) *Religious Anarchism: New Perspectives*. Newcastle upon Tyne: Cambridge Scholars Publishing.

Club of Rome. See Meadows *et al.* (1972).

Collins, P. (1993) *Ideology after the Fall of Communism*. London: Bowerdean.

Constant, B. (1988) *Political Writings*. Cambridge: Cambridge University Press.

Conway, D. (1995) *Classical Liberalism: The Unvanquished Ideal*. Basingstoke and New York: Palgrave Macmillan.

Coole, D. (1993) *Women in Political Theory: From Ancient Misogyny to Contemporary Feminism*, 2nd edn. Hemel Hempstead: Harvester Wheatsheaf.

Costa, M. D. and James, S. (1972) *The Power of Women and the Subordination of the Community*. Bristol: Falling Wall Press.

Crewe, I. (1989) 'Values: The Crusade that Failed', in D. Kavanagh and A. Seldon (eds), *The Thatcher Effect*. Oxford: Oxford University Press.

Crick, B. (1962) *A Defence of Politics*. Harmondsworth: Penguin.

Critchley, T. A. (1970) *The Conquest of Violence*. London: Constable.

Crosland, C. A. R. (1956) *The Future of Socialism*. London: Cape (Des Plaines, IL: Greenwood, 1977).

Curran, G. (ed.) (2007) *21st Century Dissent: Anarchism, Globalization and Environmentalism*. Basingstoke: Palgrave Macmillan.

Dahl, R. (1961) *Who Governs? Democracy and Power in an American City*. New Haven, CT: Yale University Press.

Dalai Lama (1996) *The Power of Buddhism*. London: Newleaf.

Daly, H. (1974) 'Steady-state Economics vs Growthmania: A Critique of Orthodox Conceptions of Growth, Wants, Scarcity and Efficiency', *Policy Sciences*, vol. 5, pp. 149–67.

Daly, M. (1979) *Gyn/Ecology: The Meta-Ethics of Radical Feminism*. Boston, MA: Beacon Press.

Darwin, C. ([1859] 1972) *On the Origin of Species*. London: Dent.

Dickinson, G. L. (1916) *The European Anarchy*. London: Allen & Unwin.

Dobson, A. (1991) *The Green Reader*. London: André Deutsch.

Dobson, A. (2007) *Green Political Thought*, 4th edn. London: Routledge.

Dolgoff, D. (1974) *The Anarchist Collective: Workers' Self-Management in the Spanish Revolution, 1936–1939*. Montreal, Quebec: Black Rose Books.

Downs, A. (1957) *An Economic Theory of Democracy*. New York: Harper & Row.

Dupuis-Deri, F. (2014) *Who's Afraid of the Black Blocs: Anarchy in Action*. Oakland, CA: PM Press.

Dworkin, A. (1976) *Woman Hating: A Radical Look at Sexuality*. Harmondsworth: Penguin.

Dworkin, A. and K. MacKinnon (1988) *Pornography and Civil Rights*. Minneapolis, MN: Organizing Against Pornography.

Dworkin, R. (2000) *Sovereign Virtue: The Theory and Practice of Equality*. Cambridge, MA: Harvard University Press.

Eagleton, T. (1991) *Ideology: An Introduction*. London and New York: Verso.

Eatwell, R. (2003) *Fascism: A History*. London: Vintage.

Eatwell, R. and O'Sullivan, N. (eds) (1989) *The Nature of the Right: European and American Politics and Political Thought since 1789*. London: Pinter.

Eatwell, R. and Wright, A. (eds) (1999) *Contemporary Political Ideologies*, 2nd edn. London: Pinter.

Eccleshall, R. *et al.* (2003) *Political Ideologies: An Introduction*, 3rd edn. London and New York: Routledge.

Eckersley, R. (1992) *Environmentalism and Political Theory: Towards an Ecocentric Approach*. London: UCL Press.

Edgar, D. (1988) 'The Free or the Good', in R. Levitas (ed.) *The Ideology of the New Right*. Oxford: Polity Press.

Egoumenides, M. (2014) *Philosophical Anarchism and Political Obligation*. London: Bloomsbury.

Ehrenfeld, D. (1978) *The Arrogance of Humanism*. Oxford: Oxford University Press.

Ehrlich, P. and Ehrlich, A. (1970) *Population, Resources and Environment: Issues in Human Ecology*. London: W. H. Freeman.

Ehrlich, P. and Harriman, R. (1971) *How to Be a Survivor*. London: Pan.

Elshtain, J. B. (1993) *Public Man, Private Woman: Women in Social and Political Thought*. Oxford: Martin Robertson and Princeton, NJ: Princeton University Press.

Enayat, H. (1982) *Modern Islamic Political Thought*. Basingstoke: Macmillan.

Engels, F. ([1884] 1976) *The Origins of the Family, Private Property and the State*. London: Lawrence & Wishart (New York: Pathfinder, 1972).

Epstein, B. (2001) 'Anarchism & Anti-Globalization', *Monthly Review*, vol. 53, no. 4.

Etzioni, A. (1995) *The Spirit of Community: Rights, Responsibilities and the Communitarian Agenda*. London: Fontana.

Eysenck, H. (1964) *Sense and Nonsense in Psychology*. Harmondsworth: Penguin.

Faludi, S. (1991) *Backlash: The Undeclared War Against American Women*. New York: Crown.

Fanon, F. (1965) *The Wretched of the Earth*. Harmondsworth: Penguin (New York: Grove-Weidenfeld, 1988).

Faure, S. ([1925] 1977) 'Anarchy–Anarchist', in G. Woodcock (ed.), *The Anarchist Reader*. London: Fontana.

Fawcett, E. (2015) *Liberalism: The Life of an Idea*. Princeton, NJ: Princeton University Press.

Feldman, N. (2012) *The Fall and Rise of the Islamic State*. Princeton, NJ: Princeton University Press.

Festenstein, M. and Kenny, M. (eds) (2005) *Political Ideologies: A Reader and Guide*. Oxford and New York: Oxford University Press.

Figes, E. (1970) *Patriarchal Attitudes*. Greenwich, CT: Fawcett.

Firestone, S. (1972) *The Dialectic of Sex*. New York: Basic Books.

Foley, M. (1994) (ed.) *Ideas that Shape Politics*. Manchester and New York: Manchester University Press.

Foucault, M. (1991) *Discipline and Punishment: The Birth of the Prison*. London: Penguin.

Fox, W. (1990) *Towards a Transpersonal Ecology: Developing the Foundations for Environmentalism*. Boston, MA: Shambhala.

Freeden, M. (1996) *Ideologies and Political Theory: A Conceptual Approach*. Oxford and New York: Oxford University Press.

Freeden, M. (2001) *Reassessing Political Ideologies: The Durability of Dissent*. London and New York: Routledge.

Freeden, M. (2004) *Ideology: A Very Short Introduction*. Oxford and New York: Oxford University Press.

Freeden, M., Sargent, L. T. and Stears, M. (eds) (2015) *The Oxford Handbook of Political Ideologies*. Oxford: Oxford University Press.

Freedman, J. (2001) *Feminism*. Buckingham and Philadelphia, PA: Open University Press.

Friedan, B. (1963) *The Feminine Mystique*. New York: Norton.

Friedan, B. (1983) *The Second Stage*. London: Abacus (New York: Summit, 1981).

Friedman, D. (1973) *The Machinery of Freedom: Guide to a Radical Capitalism*. New York: Harper & Row.

Friedman, M. (1962) *Capitalism and Freedom*. Chicago, IL: University of Chicago Press.

Friedman, M. and Friedman, R. (1980) *Free to Choose*. Harmondsworth: Penguin (New York: Bantam, 1983).

Friedrich, C. J. and Brzezinski, Z. (1963) *Totalitarian Dictatorships and Autocracy*. New York: Praeger.

Fromm, E. (1979) *To Have or To Be*. London: Abacus.

Fromm, E. (1984) *The Fear of Freedom*. London: Ark.

Fukuyama, F. (1989) 'The End of History?', *National Interest*, Summer.

Fukuyama, F. (1992) *The End of History and the Last Man*, Harmondsworth: Penguin.

Galbraith, J. K. (1992) *The Culture of Contentment*. London: Sinclair Stevenson.

Gallie, W. B. (1955–6) 'Essentially Contested Context', in *Proceedings of the Aristotelian Society*, vol. 56.

Gamble, A. (1994) *The Free Economy and the Strong State*, 2nd edn. Basingstoke: Palgrave Macmillan.

Gamble, A. (2000) *Politics and Fate*. Cambridge, UK and Maldon, MA: Polity Press.

Gandhi, M. (1971) *Selected Writings of Mahatma Gandhi*, ed. R. Duncan. London: Fontana.

Garvey, J. H. (1993) 'Fundamentalism and Politics', in Martin E. Marty and R. Scott Appleby (eds), *Fundamentalisms and the State*. Chicago, IL and London: University of Chicago Press.

Gasset, J. Ortega y ([1930] 1972) *The Revolt of the Masses*. London: Allen & Unwin.

Gellner, E. (1983) *Nations and Nationalism*. Oxford: Blackwell.

Geoghegan, V. and Wilford, R. (eds) (2014) *Political Ideologies: An Introduction*. Abingdon and New York: Routledge.

Giddens, A. (1984) *The Constitution of Society*. Cambridge: Polity Press.

Giddens, A. (1994) *Beyond Left and Right: The Future of Radical Politics*. Cambridge: Polity Press.

Giddens, A. (1998) *The Third Way: The Renewal of Social Democracy*. Cambridge: Polity Press.

Giddens, A. (2000) *The Third Way and Its Critics*. Cambridge: Polity Press.

Gillis, S., Howie, G. and Mumford, R. (eds) (2007) *Third Wave Feminism: Critical Exploration*. Basingstoke and New York: Palgrave Macmillan.

Gilmour, I. (1978) *Inside Right: A Study of Conservatism*. London: Quartet Books.

Gilmour, I. (1992) *Dancing with Dogma: Britain under Thatcherism*. London: Simon & Schuster.

Gobineau, J.-A. (1970) *Gobineau: Selected Political Writings*, ed. M. D. Biddiss. New York: Harper & Row.

Godwin, W. ([1793] 1971) *Enquiry Concerning Political Justice*, ed. K. C. Carter. Oxford: Oxford University Press.

Goldman, E. (1969) *Anarchism and Other Essays*. New York: Dover.

Goldsmith, E. (1988) *The Great U-Turn: De-industrialising Society*. Totnes: Green Books.

Goldsmith, E., Allen, R. and others (eds) (1972) *Blueprint for Survival*. Harmondsworth: Penguin.

Goodhart, D. (2004) 'The Discomfort of Strangers', *Prospect*, February.

Goodin, R. E. (1992) *Green Political Theory*. Oxford: Polity Press.

Goodman, P. (1964) *Compulsory Miseducation*. New York: Vintage Books.

Goodman, P. (1977) 'Normal Politics and the Psychology of Power', in G. Woodcock (ed.), *The Anarchist Reader*. London: Fontana.

Goodwin, B. (1997) *Using Political Ideas*, 4th edn. London: John Wiley & Sons.

Gorz, A. (1982) *Farewell to the Working Class*. London: Pluto Press (Boston, MA: South End Press, 1982).

Gould, B. (1985) *Socialism and Freedom*. Basingstoke: Palgrave Macmillan (Wakefield, NH: Longwood, 1986).

Gramsci, A. ([1935] 1971) *Selections from the Prison Notebooks*, ed. Q. Hoare and G. Nowell-Smith. London: Lawrence & Wishart.

Gray, J. (1995a) *Enlightenment's Wake: Politics and Culture at the Close of the Modern Age*. London: Routledge.

Gray, J. (1995b) *Liberalism*, 2nd edn. Milton Keynes: Open University Press.

Gray, J. (1996) *Post-liberalism: Studies in Political Thought*. London: Routledge.

Gray, J. (1997) *Endgames: Questions in Late Modern Political Thought*. Cambridge and Malden, MA: Blackwell.

Gray, J. (2000) *Two Faces of Liberalism*. Cambridge: Polity Press.

Gray, J. (2003) *Al Qaeda and What it Means to be Modern*. London: Faber & Faber.

Gray, J. and Willetts, D. (1997) *Is Conservatism Dead?* London: Profile Books.

Green, T. H. (1988) *Works*, ed. R. Nettleship. London: Oxford University Press (New York: AMS Press, 1984).

Greenleaf, W. H. (1983) *The British Political Tradition: The Ideological Heritage*, Vol. 2. London: Methuen.

Greer, G. (1970) *The Female Eunuch*. New York: McGraw-Hill.

Greer, G. (1985) *Sex and Destiny*. New York: Harper & Row.

Greer, G. (1999) *The Whole Woman*. London: Doubleday.

Gregor, A. J. (1969) *The Ideology of Fascism*. New York: Free Press.

Griffin, R. (1993) *The Nature of Fascism*. London: Routledge.

Griffin, R. (ed.) (1995) *Fascism*. Oxford and New York: Oxford University Press.

Griffin, R. (ed.) (1998) *International Fascism: Theories, Causes and the New Consensus*. London: Arnold and New York: Oxford University Press.

Hadden, J. K. and Shupe, A. (eds) (1986) *Prophetic Religions and Politics: Religion and Political Order*. New York: Paragon House.

Hall, J. A. (1988) *Liberalism: Politics, Ideology and the Market*. London: Paladin.

Hall, S. and Jacques, M. (eds) (1983) *The Politics of Thatcherism*. London: Lawrence & Wishart.

Hamid. S. (2016) *Islamic Exceptionalism*. New York: St. Martin's Press.

Hardin, G. (1968) 'The Tragedy of the Commons', *Science*, vol. 162, pp. 1243–8.

Hardt, M. and Negri, A. (2000) *Empire*. Cambridge, MA: Harvard University Press.

Harrington, M. (1993) *Socialism, Past and Future*. London: Pluto Press.

Harvey, D. (2003) *The New Imperialism*. Oxford: Oxford University Press.

Harvey, D. (2005) *A Brief History of Neoliberalism*. Oxford and New York: Oxford University Press.

Hashmi, S. (ed.) (2012) *Just Wars, Holy Wars and Jihads: Christian, Jewish and Muslim Encounters and Exchanges*. Oxford and New York: Oxford University Press.

Hattersley, R. (1987) *Choose Freedom*. Harmondsworth: Penguin.

Hayek, F. A. von (1944) *The Road to Serfdom*. London: Routledge & Kegan Paul (Chicago, IL: University of Chicago Press, 1956, new edn).

Hayek, F. A. von (1960) *The Constitution of Liberty*. London: Routledge & Kegan Paul.

Hayward, T. (1998) *Political Theory and Ecological Values*. Cambridge: Polity Press.

Hearn, J. (2006) *Rethinking Nationalism: A Critical Introduction*. Basingstoke and New York: Palgrave Macmillan.

Heath, A., Jowell, R. and Curtice, J. (1985) *How Britain Votes*. Oxford: Pergamon.

Heffernan, R. (2001) *New Labour and Thatcherism*. London: Palgrave.

Hegel, G. W. F. (1942) *The Philosophy of Right*, trans. T. M. Knox. Oxford: Clarendon Press.

Heywood, L. and J. Drake (eds) (1997) *Third Wave Agenda: Being Feminist, Doing Feminism*. Minneapolis, MN: University of Minnesota Press.

Hiro, D. (1988) *Islamic Fundamentalism*. London: Paladin.

Hitler, A. ([1925] 1969) *Mein Kampf*. London: Hutchinson (Boston, MA: Houghton Mifflin, 1973).

Hobbes, T. ([1651] 1968) *Leviathan*, ed. C. B. Macpherson. Harmondsworth: Penguin.

Hobhouse, L. T. (1911) *Liberalism*. London: Thornton Butterworth.

Hobsbawm, E. (1983) 'Inventing Tradition', in E. Hobsbawm and T. Ranger (eds), *The Invention of Tradition*. Cambridge: Cambridge University Press.

Hobsbawm, E. (1992) *Nations and Nationalism since 1780: Programme, Myth and Reality*, 2nd edn. Cambridge: Cambridge University Press.

Hobsbawm, E. (1994) *Age of Extremes: The Short Twentieth Century, 1914–1991*. London: Michael Joseph.

Hobsbawm, E. (2011) *How to Change the World: Tales of Marx and Marxism*. London: Little, Brown.

Hobson, J. A. (1902) *Imperialism: A Study*. London: Nisbet.

Hoffman, J. and P. Graham (2006) *Introduction to Political Ideologies*. London: Pearson Education.

Holden, B. (1993) *Understanding Liberal Democracy*, 2nd edn. Hemel Hempstead: Harvester Wheatsheaf.

Holland, T. (2015) 'In Search of the True Prophet', *The Sunday Times*, 31 May.

Honderich, T. (1991) *Conservatism*. Harmondsworth: Penguin.

Honderich, T. (2005) *Conservatism: Burke, Nozick, Bush, Blair?* London and Ann Arbor, MI: Pluto Press.

Huntington, S. (1993) 'The Clash of Civilizations', *Foreign Affairs*, vol. 72, no. 3.

Huntington, S. (1996) *The Clash of Civilizations and the Remaking of World Order*. New York: Simon & Schuster.

Hutchinson, J. and Smith, A. D. (eds) (1994) *Nationalism*. Oxford and New York: Oxford University Press.

Hutton, W. (1995) *The State We're In*. London: Jonathan Cape.

Illich, I. (1973) *Deschooling Society*. Harmondsworth: Penguin (New York: Harper & Row, 1983).

Inglehart, R. (1977) *The Silent Revolution: Changing Values and Political Styles Among Western Publics*. Princeton, NJ: Princeton University Press.

Jansen, G. H. (1979) *Militant Islam*. London: Pan Books.

Jefferson, T. (1972) *Notes on the State of Virginia*. New York: W. W. Norton.

Jefferson, T. (1979) 'The United States Declaration of Independence', in W. Laqueur and B. Rubin (eds), *The Human Rights Reader*. New York: Meridian.

Jost, J., Kruglanski, A. and Sulloway, F. (2003) 'Political Conservatism as Motivated Social Cognition', *Psychological Bulletin*, p. 129.

Journal of Political Ideologies. Abingdon, UK and Cambridge, MA: Carfax.

Kallis, A. A. (ed.) (2003) *The Fascist Reader*. London and New York: Routledge.

Kant, I. (1991) *Kant: Political Writings*, ed. Hans Reiss, trans. H. B. Nisbet. Cambridge: Cambridge University Press.

Kautsky, K. (1902) *The Social Revolution*. Chicago: Kerr.

Keddi, N. (1972) *Sayyid Jamal ad-Din 'Al-Afghani'*. Berkeley, CA: California University Press.

Kelly, P. (2005) *Liberalism*. Malden, MA and Cambridge: Polity Press.

Kepel, G. (2006) *Jihad: The Trail of Political Islam*. London: I. B. Tauris.

Keynes, J. M. ([1936] 1963) *The General Theory of Employment, Interest and Money*. London: Macmillan (San Diego: Harcourt Brace Jovanovich, 1965).

Kingdom, J. (1992) *No Such Thing as Society? Individualism and Community*. Buckingham, UK and Philadelphia, PA: Open University Press.

Kinna, R. (2009) *Anarchism: A Beginner's Guide*. Oxford: Oneworld Publications.

Klein, M. (2001) *No Logo*. London: Flamingo.

Kropotkin, P. ([1902] 1914) *Mutual Aid*. Boston, MA: Porter Sargent.

Kuhn, T. (1962) *The Structure of Scientific Revolutions*. Chicago, IL: Chicago University Press.

Kymlicka, W. (2000) *Multicultural Citizenship*. Oxford: Oxford University Press.

Laclau, E. and Mouffe, C. (2014) *Hegemony and Socialist Strategy*. London: Verso.

Lane, D. (1996) *The Rise and Fall of State Socialism*. Oxford: Polity Press.

Laqueur, W. (ed.) (1979) *Fascism: A Reader's Guide*. Harmondsworth: Penguin.

Larrain, J. (1983) *Marxism and Ideology*. Basingstoke: Macmillan.

Layard, R. (2011) *Happiness: Lessons from a New Science*. Harmondsworth and New York: Penguin Books.

Leach, R. (2002) *Political Ideology in Britain*. Basingstoke: Palgrave Macmillan.

Lenin, V. I. (1964) *The State and Revolution*. Peking: People's Publishing House.

Lenin, V. I. ([1916] 1970) *Imperialism, the Highest Stage of Capitalism*. Moscow: Progress Publishers.

Lenin, V. I. ([1902] 1988) *What Is to Be Done?* Harmondsworth and New York: Penguin.

Leopold, A. (1968) *Sand County Almanac*. Oxford: Oxford University Press.

Letwin, S. R. (1992) *The Anatomy of Thatcherism*. London: Fontana.

Lewis, B. (2004) *The Crisis of Islam: Holy War and Unholy Terror*. London and New York: Random House.

Lindblom, C. (1977) *Politics and Markets*. New York: Basic Books.

Lipset, S. M. (1983) *Political Man: The Social Bases of Behaviour*. London: Heinemann.

Locke, J. (1962) *Two Treatises of Government*. Cambridge: Cambridge University Press.

Locke, J. (1963) *A Letter Concerning Toleration*. The Hague: Martinus Nijhoff.

Lovelock, J. (1979) *Gaia: A New Look at Life on Earth*. Oxford and New York: Oxford University Press.

Lovelock, J. (1988) 'Man and Gaia', in E. Goldsmith and N. Hilyard (eds), *The Earth Report*. London: Mitchell Beazley.

Lyotard, J.-F. (1984) *The Postmodern Condition: The Power of Knowledge*. Minneapolis, MN: University of Minnesota Press.

MacIntyre, A. (1981) *After Virtue*. London: Duckworth.

Macmillan, H. ([1938] 1966) *The Middle Way*. London: Macmillan.

Macpherson, C. B. (1973) *Democratic Theory: Essays in Retrieval*. Oxford: Clarendon Press.

Maistre, J. de ([1817] 1971) *The Works of Joseph de Maistre*, trans. J. Lively. New York: Schocken.

Mannheim, K. ([1929] 1960) *Ideology and Utopia*. London: Routledge & Kegan Paul.

Manning, D. (1976) *Liberalism*. London: Dent.

Marcuse, H. (1964) *One Dimensional Man: Studies in the Ideology of Advanced Industrial Society*. Boston, MA: Beacon.

Maritain, J. ([1936] 1996) *Integral Humanism*. Notre Dame, IN: University of Notre Dame Press.

Marquand, D. (1988) *The Unprincipled Society*. London: Fontana.

Marquand, D. (1992) *The Progressive Dilemma*. London: Heinemann.

Marquand, D. and Seldon, A. (1996) *The Ideas that Shaped Post-War Britain*. London: Fontana.

Marshall, P. (1995) *Nature's Web: Rethinking Our Place on Earth*. London: Cassell.

Marshall, P. (2007) *Demanding the Impossible: A History of Anarchism*. London: Fontana.

Martell, L. (2001) *Social Democracy: Global and National Perspectives*. Basingstoke and New York: Palgrave Macmillan.

Martin, R. C. and Barzegar, A. (eds) (2009) *Islamism: Contested Perspectives on Political Islam*. Redwood City, CA: Stanford University Press.

Marty, M. E. (1988) 'Fundamentalism as a Social Phenomenon', *Bulletin of the American Academy of Arts and Sciences*, vol. 42, pp. 15–29.

Marty, M. E. and Appleby, R. S. (eds) (1993) *Fundamentalisms and the State: Remaking Polities, Economies, and Militance*. Chicago, IL and London: University of Chicago Press.

Marx, K. and Engels, F. (1968) *Selected Works*. London: Lawrence & Wishart.

Marx, K. and Engels, F. ([1846] 1970) *The German Ideology*. London: Lawrence & Wishart.

McLellan, D. (1980) *The Thought of Karl Marx*, 2nd edn. London: Macmillan.

McLellan, D. (1995) *Ideology*, 2nd edn. Milton Keynes: Open University Press.

McLellan, D. (2007) *Marxism after Marx*, 4th edn. Basingstoke: Palgrave Macmillan.

Mead, W. R. (2006) 'God's Country?', *Foreign Affairs*, vol. 85, no. 5.

Meadows, D. H., Meadows, D. L., Randers, D. and Williams, W. (1972) *The Limits to Growth*. London: Pan (New York: New American Library, 1972).

Michels, R. (1958) *Political Parties*. Glencoe, IL: Free Press.

Miliband, R. (1969) *The State in Capitalist Society*. London: Verso (New York: Basic Books, 1978).

Miliband, R. (1995) *Socialism for a Sceptical Age*. Oxford: Polity Press.

Mill, J. S. ([1869] 1970) *On the Subjection of Women*. London: Dent.

Mill, J. S. ([1859] 1972) *Utilitarianism, On Liberty and Consideration on Representative Government*. London: Dent.

Miller, D. (1984) *Anarchism*. London: Dent.

Millett, K. (1970) *Sexual Politics*. New York: Doubleday.

Mintz, F. (2012) *Workers' Self-Management in Revolutionary Spain*. Oakland, CA and Edinburgh: AK Press.

Mitchell, J. (1971) *Women's Estate*. Harmondsworth: Penguin.

Mitchell, J. (1975) *Psychoanalysis and Feminism*. Harmondsworth: Penguin.

Modood, T. (2013) *Multiculturalism*. Cambridge and Malden, MA: Polity Press.

Montesquieu, C. de ([1748] 1969) *The Spirit of Laws*. Glencoe, IL: Free Press.

More, T. ([1516] 1965) *Utopia*. Harmondsworth: Penguin (New York: Norton, 1976).

Morland, D. (1997) *Demanding the Impossible: Human Nature and Politics in Nineteenth-Century Social Anarchism*. London and Washington, DC: Cassell.

Mosca, G. (1939) *The Ruling Class*, trans. and ed. A. Livingstone. New York: McGraw-Hill.

Moschonas, G. (2002) *In the Name of Social Democracy – The Great Transformation: 1945 to the Present*. London and New York: Verso.

Murray, C. (1984) *Losing Ground: American Social Policy: 1950–1980*. New York: Basic Books.

Murray, C. and Herrnstein, R. (1995) *The Bell Curve: Intelligence and Class Structure in American Life*. New York: Free Press.

Naess, A. (1973) 'The Shallow and the Deep, Long-range Ecology Movement: A Summary', *Inquiry*, vol. 16.

Naess, A. (1989) *Community and Lifestyle: Outline of an Ecosophy*. Cambridge: Cambridge University Press.

Neocleous, M. (1997) *Fascism*. Milton Keynes: Open University Press.

Newman, M. (2005) *Socialism: A Very Short Introduction*. Oxford and New York: Oxford University Press.

Nietzsche, F. ([1884] 1961) *Thus Spoke Zarathustra*, trans. R. J. Hollingdale. Harmondsworth: Penguin (New York: Random, 1982).

Nolte, E. (1965) *Three Faces of Fascism: Action Française, Italian Fascism and National Socialism*. London: Weidenfeld & Nicolson.

Nozick, R. (1974) *Anarchy, State and Utopia*. Oxford: Blackwell (New York: Basic Books, 1974).

Oakeshott, M. (1962) *Rationalism in Politics and Other Essays*. London: Methuen (New York: Routledge Chapman & Hall, 1981).

O'Hara, K. (2011) *Conservatism*. London: Reaktion Books.

Ohmae, K. (1989) *Borderless World: Power and Strategy in the Interlinked Economy* (London: HarperCollins).

Osman, T. (2016) *Islamism: What it Means for the Middle East and the World*. New Haven, CT and London: Yale University Press.

O'Sullivan, N. (1976) *Conservatism*. London: Dent and New York: St Martin's Press.

O'Sullivan, N. (1983) *Fascism*. London: Dent.

Özkirimli, V. (2010) *Theories of Nationalism: A Critical Introduction*. Basingstoke and New York: Palgrave Macmillan.

Paglia, C. (1990) *Sex, Art and American Culture*. New Haven, CT: Yale University Press.

Paglia, C. (1992) *Sexual Personae: Art and Decadence from Nefertiti to Emily Dickinson*. Harmondsworth: Penguin.

Parekh, B. (1994) 'The Concept of Fundamentalism', in A. Shtromas (ed.), *The End of 'isms'? Reflections on the Fate of Ideological Politics after Communism's Collapse*. Oxford, UK and Cambridge, MA: Blackwell.

Parekh, B. (2005) *Rethinking Multiculturalism: Cultural Diversity and Political Theory*, 2nd edn. Basingstoke and New York: Palgrave Macmillan.

Pareto, V. (1935) *The Mind and Society*. London: Cape and New York: AMS Press.

Passmore, K. (2014) *Fascism: A Very Short Introduction*. Oxford and New York: Oxford University Press.

Pettit, P. (1999) *Republicanism: A Theory of Freedom and Government*. Oxford: Oxford University Press.

Pierson, C. (1995) *Socialism After Communism*. Cambridge: Polity Press.

Plato (1955) *The Republic*, trans. H. D. Lee. Harmondsworth: Penguin (New York: Random House, 1983).

Popper, K. (1945) *The Open Society and Its Enemies*. London: Routledge & Kegan Paul.

Popper, K. (1957) *The Poverty of Historicism*. London: Routledge.

Porritt, J. (2005) *Capitalism as if the World Matters*. London: Earthscan.

Poulantzas, N. (1968) *Political Power and Social Class*. London: New Left Books (New York: Routledge Chapman & Hall, 1987).

Proudhon, P.-J. ([1851] 1923) *General Idea of Revolution in the Nineteenth Century*, trans. J. B. Robinson. London: Freedom Press.

Proudhon, P.-J. ([1840] 1970) *What Is Property?*, trans. B. R. Tucker. New York: Dover.

Pugh, J. (ed.) (2009) *What Is Radical Politics Today?* Basingstoke: Palgrave Macmillan.

Purkis, J. and Bowen, J. (1997) *Twenty-First Century Anarchism: Unorthodox Ideas for a New Millennium*. London: Cassell.

Purkis, J. and Bowen, J. (eds) (2004) *Changing Anarchism: Anarchist Theory and Practice in a Global Age*. Manchester: Manchester University Press.

Qutb, S. ([1962] 2007) *Milestones*. New Delhi: Islamic Book Services.

Ramsay, M. (1997) *What's Wrong with Liberalism? A Radical Critique of Liberal Political Philosophy*. London: Leicester University Press.

Randall, V. (1987) *Women and Politics: An International Perspective*, 2nd edn. Basingstoke: Palgrave Macmillan.

Rawls, J. (1970) *A Theory of Justice*. Oxford: Oxford University Press (Cambridge, MA: Harvard University Press, 1971).

Rawls, J. (1993) *Political Liberalism*. New York: Colombia University Press.

Regan, T. (1983) *The Case for Animal Rights*. London: Routledge & Kegan Paul.

Robins, A. and Jones, A. (eds) (2009) *Genocide of the Oppressed*. Bloomington, IN: Indiana University Press.

Roemer, J. (ed.) (1986) *Analytical Marxism*. Cambridge: Cambridge University Press.

Rorty, R. (1989) *Contingency, Irony and Solidarity*. Cambridge: Cambridge University Press.

Rothbard, M. (1978) *For a New Liberty*. New York: Macmillan.

Rousseau, J.-J. ([1762] 1913) *The Social Contract and Discourse*, ed. G. D. H. Cole. London: Dent (Glencoe, IL: Free Press, 1969).

Roussopoulos, D. (ed.) (2002) *The Anarchist Papers*. New York and London: Black Rose Books.

Ruthven, M. (2007) *Fundamentalism: A Very Short Introduction*. Oxford and New York: Oxford University Press.

Said, E. ([1978] 2003) *Orientalism*. Harmondsworth: Penguin.

Sandel, M. (1982) *Liberalism and the Limits of Justice*. Cambridge: Cambridge University Press.

Sassoon, D. (2013) *One Hundred Years of Socialism*. London: Fontana.

Schneir, M. (1995) *The Vintage Book of Feminism: The Essential Writings of the Contemporary Women's Movement*. London: Vintage.

Scholte, J. A. (2005) *Globalization: An Introduction*, 2nd edn. Basingstoke and New York: Palgrave Macmillan.

Schumacher, E. F. (1973) *Small Is Beautiful: A Study of Economics as if People Mattered*. London: Blond & Briggs (New York: Harper & Row, 1989).

Schumpeter, J. (1976) *Capitalism, Socialism and Democracy*. London: Allen & Unwin (Magnolia, MA: Peter Smith, 1983).

Schwarzmantel, J. (1991) *Socialism and the Idea of the Nation*. Hemel Hempstead: Harvester Wheatsheaf.

Schwartzmantel, J. (1998) *The Age of Ideology: Political Ideologies from the American Revolution to Post-Modern Times*. Basingstoke: Palgrave Macmillan.

Scott-Dixon, K. (ed.) (2006) *Trans/Forming Feminism: Transfeminist Voices Speak Out*. Canadian Scholars' Press: Toronto.

Scruton, R. (2001) *The Meaning of Conservatism*, 3rd edn. Basingstoke: Macmillan.

Seabright, P. (2004) *The Company of Strangers*. Princeton, NJ: Princeton University Press.

Seliger, M. (1976) *Politics and Ideology*. London: Allen & Unwin (Glencoe, IL: Free Press, 1976).

Sen, A. (1999) *Development as Freedom*. Oxford: Oxford University Press.

Sen, A. (2006) *Identity and Violence*. London: Penguin.

Shtromas, A. (ed.) (1994) *The End of 'isms'? Reflections on the Fate of Ideological Politics after Communism's Collapse*. Oxford and Cambridge, MA: Blackwell.

Sil, R. and P. J. Katzenstein (2010) *Beyond Paradigms: Analytic Eclecticism in the Study of World Politics*. Basingstoke and New York: Palgrave Macmillan.

Singer, P. (1976) *Animal Liberation*. New York: Jonathan Cape.

Singer, P. (1993) *Practical Ethics*, 2nd edn. Cambridge: Cambridge University Press.

Smart, B. (1993) *Postmodernity*. London and New York: Routledge.

Smiles, S. ([1859] 1986) *Self-Help*. Harmondsworth: Penguin.

Smith, A. ([1776] 1976) *An Enquiry into the Nature and Causes of the Wealth of Nations*. Chicago, IL: University of Chicago Press.

Smith, A. D. (1986) *The Ethnic Origins of Nations*. Oxford: Blackwell.

Smith, A. D. (1991) *National Identity*. Harmondsworth: Penguin.

Smith, A. D. (2001) *Nationalism: Theory, Ideology, History*. Cambridge and Malden, MA: Polity Press.

Sorel, G. ([1908] 1950) *Reflections on Violence*, trans. T. E. Hulme and J. Roth. New York: Macmillan.

Spencer, H. ([1884] 1940) *The Man versus the State*. London: Watts & Co.

Spencer, H. (1967) *On Social Evolution: Selected Writings*. Chicago, IL: University of Chicago Press.

Spencer, P. and Wollman, H. (2002) *Nationalism: A Critical Introduction*. London and Thousand Oaks, CA: Sage.

Squires, J. (1999) *Gender in Political Theory*. Cambridge, UK and Malden, MA: Polity Press.

Stelzer, I. (ed.) (2004) *Neoconservatism*. London: Atlantic Books.

Stirner, M. ([1845] 1971) *The Ego and His Own*, ed. J. Carroll. London: Cape.

Sumner, W. (1959) *Folkways*. New York: Doubleday.

Sydie, R. A. (1987) *Natural Women, Cultured Men: A Feminist Perspective on Sociological Theory*. Milton Keynes: Open University Press.

Talmon, J. L. (1952) *The Origins of Totalitarian Democracy*. London: Secker & Warburg.

Tam, H. (1998) *Communitarianism: A New Agenda for Politics and Citizenship*. Basingstoke: Palgrave Macmillan.

Tawney, R. H. (1921) *The Acquisitive Society*. London: Bell (San Diego: Harcourt Brace Jovanovich, 1955).

Tawney, R. H. (1969) *Equality*. London: Allen & Unwin.

Taylor, C. (1994) *Multiculturalism and 'The Politics of Recognition'*. Princeton, NJ: Princeton University Press.

Taylor, C. (ed.) (1995) *Multiculturalism: Examining the Politics of Recognition*. Princeton, NJ: Princeton University Press.

Thoreau, H. D. ([1845] 1983) *Walden and 'Civil Disobedience'*. Harmondsworth: Penguin.

Tibi, B. (2012) *Islamism and Islam*. New Haven, CT and London: Yale University Press.

Tocqueville, A. de (1968) *Democracy in America*. London: Fontana (New York: McGraw, 1981).

Tolstoy, L. (1937) *Recollections and Essays*. Oxford: Oxford University Press.

United Nations (1972). See Ward and Dubois (1972).

United Nations (1980) *Compendium of Statistics: 1977*. New York: United Nations.

Vincent, A. (2009) *Modern Political Ideologies*, 2nd edn. Oxford: Blackwell.

Waldron, J. (1995) 'Minority Cultures and the Cosmopolitan Alternative', in W. Kymlicka (ed.), *The Rights of Minority Cultures*. London and New York: Open University Press.

Wallerstein, I. (1974) *The Modern World System*. New York: Academic Press.

Wallerstein, I. (1984) *The Politics of the World Economy: States, Movements and Civilizations*. Oxford: Polity Press.

Walter, N. (1999) *The New Feminism*. London: Virago.

Walter, N. (2010) *Living Dolls: The Return of Sexism*. London: Virago.

Walters, M. (2005) *Feminism: A Very Short Introduction*. Oxford and New York: Oxford University Press.

Ward, B. and Dubois, R. (1972) *Only One Earth*. Harmondsworth: Penguin.

Ward, C. (2004) *Anarchism: A Very Short Introduction*. Oxford and New York: Oxford University Press.

Weber, M. ([1904–5] 2011) *The Protestant Ethic and the Spirit of Capitalism*. Oxford and New York: Oxford University Press.

White, S. (ed.) (2001) *New Labour: The Progressive Future?* Basingstoke and New York: Palgrave Macmillan.

Willetts, D. (1992) *Modern Conservatism*. Harmondsworth: Penguin.

Wolf, N. (1994) *Fire with Fire: The New Female Power and How to Use It*. New York: Fawcett.

Wolff, R. P. (1998) *In Defence of Anarchism*, 2nd edn. Berkeley, CA: University of California Press.

Wollstonecraft, M. ([1792] 1967) *A Vindication of the Rights of Woman*, ed. C. W. Hagelman. New York: Norton.

Woodcock, G. (1992) *Anarchism: A History of Libertarian Ideas and Movements*. Harmondsworth and New York: Penguin.

Woolf, S. J. (1981) (ed.) *European Fascism*. London: Weidenfeld & Nicolson.

Wright, A. (1996) *Socialisms: Theories and Practices*. Oxford and New York: Oxford University Press.

Index

Note: page numbers that are in bold type refer to figures, tables and boxes; page numbers that are in italics refer to on-page definitions.